Secrets of Heaven

SECRETS OF HEAVEN

The Portable New Century Edition

EMANUEL SWEDENBORG

Volume 10

Translated from the Latin by Lisa Hyatt Cooper

SWEDENBORG FOUNDATION

Royersford, Pennsylvania

Originally published in Latin as *Arcana Coelestia,* London, 1749–1756. The volume contents of this and the original Latin edition, along with ISBNs of the annotated version, are as follows:

Volume number in this edition	Text treated	Volume number in the Latin first edition	Section numbers	ISBN (hardcover)
1	Genesis 1–8	1	§§1–946	978-0-87785-486-9
2	Genesis 9–15	1	§§947–1885	978-0-87785-487-6
3	Genesis 16–21	2 (in 6 fascicles)	§§1886–2759	978-0-87785-488-3
4	Genesis 22–26	3	§§2760–3485	978-0-87785-489-0
5	Genesis 27–30	3	§§3486–4055	978-0-87785-490-6
6	Genesis 31–35	4	§§4056–4634	978-0-87785-491-3
7	Genesis 36–40	4	§§4635–5190	978-0-87785-492-0
8	Genesis 41–44	5	§§5191–5866	978-0-87785-493-7
9	Genesis 45–50	5	§§5867–6626	978-0-87785-494-4
10	Exodus 1–8	6	§§6627–7487	978-0-87785-495-1
11	Exodus 9–15	6	§§7488–8386	978-0-87785-496-8
12	Exodus 16–21	7	§§8387–9111	978-0-87785-497-5
13	Exodus 22–24	7	§§9112–9442	978-0-87785-498-2
14	Exodus 25–29	8	§§9443–10166	978-0-87785-499-9
15	Exodus 30–40	8	§§10167–10837	978-0-87785-500-2

ISBN of e-book of library edition, vol. 10: 978-0-87785-741-9
ISBN of Portable Edition, vol. 10, containing translation only: 978-0-87785-437-1
ISBN of e-book of Portable Edition, vol. 10: 978-0-87785-740-2

(The ISBN in the Library of Congress data shown below is that of volume 1.)

Library of Congress Cataloging-in-Publication Data

Swedenborg, Emanuel, 1688–1772.
[Arcana coelestia. English]
Secrets of heaven / Emanuel Swedenborg ; translated from the Latin by Lisa Hyatt Cooper. — Portable New Century ed.
p. cm.
Includes bibliographical references and indexes.
ISBN 978-0-87785-408-1 (alk. paper)
1. New Jerusalem Church—Doctrines. 2. Bible. O.T. Genesis—Commentaries—Early works to 1800. 3. Bible. O.T. Exodus—Commentaries—Early works to 1800. I. Title.
BX8712.A8 2010
230'.94—dc22

2009054171

Ornaments from the first Latin edition, 1749–1756
Text designed by Joanna V. Hill
Senior copy editor, Alicia L. Dole
Typesetting by Mary M. Wachsmann and Sarah Dole
Cover design by Karen Connor
Cover photograph by Magda Indigo

Further information about the New Century Edition of the Works of Emanuel Swedenborg can be obtained directly from the Swedenborg Foundation, 70 Buckwalter Road, Suite 900 PMB 405, Royersford, PA 19468 U.S.A.
Telephone: (610) 430-3222 • Web: www.swedenborg.com • E-mail: info@swedenborg.com

Contents

Volume 10

Exodus Chapter 5

Exodus Chapter 6

Exodus Chapter 7

Exodus Chapter 8

Conventions Used in This Work

MOST of the following conventions apply generally to the translations in the New Century Edition Portable series. For introductory material on the content and history of *Secrets of Heaven,* and for annotations on the subject matter, including obscure or problematic content, and extensive indexes, the reader is referred to the Deluxe New Century Edition volumes.

Volume designation *Secrets of Heaven* was originally published in eight volumes; in this edition all but the second original volume have been divided into two. Thus Swedenborg's eight volumes now fill fifteen volumes, of which this is the tenth. It corresponds to approximately the first half of Swedenborg's volume 6.

Section numbers Following a practice common in his time, Swedenborg divided his published theological works into sections numbered in sequence from beginning to end. His original section numbers have been preserved in this edition; they appear in boxes in the outside margins. Traditionally, these sections have been referred to as "numbers" and designated by the abbreviation "n." In this edition, however, the more common section symbol (§) is used to designate the section numbers, and the sections are referred to as such.

Subsection numbers Because many sections throughout Swedenborg's works are too long for precise cross-referencing, Swedenborgian scholar John Faulkner Potts (1838–1923) further divided them into subsections; these have since become standard, though minor variations occur from one edition to another. These subsections are indicated by bracketed numbers that appear in the text itself: [2], [3], and so on. Because the beginning of the first *subsection* always coincides with the beginning of the *section* proper, it is not labeled in the text.

Citations of Swedenborg's text As is common in Swedenborgian studies, text citations of Swedenborg's works refer not to page numbers but to section numbers, which unlike page numbers are uniform in most editions.

In citations the section symbol (§) is generally omitted after the title of a work by Swedenborg. Thus "*Secrets of Heaven* 29" refers to section 29 (§29) of Swedenborg's *Secrets of Heaven,* not to page 29 of any edition. Subsection numbers are given after a colon; a reference such as "29:2" indicates subsection 2 of section 29. The reference "29:1" would indicate the first subsection of section 29, though that subsection is not in fact labeled in the text. Where section numbers stand alone without titles, their function is indicated by the prefixed section symbol; for example, "§29:2".

Citations of Swedenborg's unnumbered sections Some material in *Secrets of Heaven* was not given a section number. Swedenborg assigns no section numbers to his quoting of a biblical chapter before he takes up each verse in turn. He also gives no section numbers to occasional prefatory material, such as his author's table of contents in *Secrets of Heaven* (before §1), his prefaces to Genesis 16 and 18 (before §§1886 and 2135, respectively), and his preface to Genesis 22 (before §2760). The biblical material needs no section number, as it is referred to simply by chapter and verse. In this edition, references to the author's unnumbered prefaces follow these models: "(preface to Genesis 22)"; "see the preface to Genesis 18."

Citations of the Bible Biblical citations in this edition follow the accepted standard: a semicolon is used between book references and between chapter references, and a comma between verse references. Therefore "Matthew 5:11, 12; 6:1; 10:41, 42; Luke 6:23, 35" would refer to Matthew chapter 5, verses 11 and 12; Matthew chapter 6, verse 1; Matthew chapter 10, verses 41 and 42; and Luke chapter 6, verses 23 and 35. Swedenborg often incorporated the numbers of verses not actually represented in his text when listing verse numbers for a passage he quoted; these apparently constitute a kind of "see also" reference to other material he felt was relevant. This edition includes these extra verses and also follows Swedenborg where he cites contiguous verses individually (for example, John 14:8, 9, 10, 11), rather than as a range (John 14:8–11). Occasionally this edition supplies a full, conventional Bible reference where Swedenborg omits one after a quotation.

Discrepancies in verse numbering The divisions of the Bible into numbered chapters and verses—its versification, for short—were added centuries after the texts were written and are not uniform in all versions. In fact, the discrepancies among the various versions are many, and the dozen Bibles owned by Swedenborg are typical in this regard. These discrepancies complicate the structure of his exegesis because sometimes he chose the versification of one source and sometimes that of another. In representing Swedenborg's choice of versification, the current edition has found it necessary to distinguish between two categories. The first is the versification of Swedenborg's *exegetical structure;* that is, the verse numbering of the chapters in Genesis and Exodus that are the focus of his explanations in *Secrets of Heaven.* The second is the versification of his biblical *cross-references;* for example, when discussing Exodus 1:15 in §6674, he quotes twenty-two passages from elsewhere in the Bible, starting with Matthew 18:20, John 1:12, and John 20:31, and then adds, without quotation, citations of Isaiah 18:7, Jeremiah 7:12, Isaiah 26:8, and twenty-eight further passages. For this second category, the biblical cross-references, the current edition always uses the versification of the New Revised Standard Version (NRSV), which is identical virtually throughout to that of the King James Version and many other widely used translations. But this practice could not be adopted in the first category, the exegetical structure, in four places where the NRSV differs from Swedenborg's versification: Exodus 7, 8, 21, and 22. To have imposed the NRSV versification on the structure of Swedenborg's exegesis in those chapters would have done violence to that structure and put his section numbers out of order. Therefore the current edition's exegetical structure generally reflects the versification of the NRSV; but where the versification of Swedenborg's first edition differs from that of the NRSV in Exodus 7, 8, 21, and 22, this edition adds the verse numbers of the NRSV as alternates in brackets after an equals sign. At the first occurrence of one of these double citations in a chapter, the abbreviation "NRSV" is included; for example, "7:26 [= NRSV 8:1]." Citations of subsequent such verses within the same chapter omit reference to the NRSV for the sake of brevity; for example, "7:27 [= 8:2]." Thus the numbering in brackets in such references matches the verse numbers used as cross-references elsewhere in *Secrets of Heaven.*

Quotations in Swedenborg's works Some features of the original Latin text of *Secrets of Heaven* have been modernized in this edition. For example, Swedenborg's first edition generally relies on context or italics rather than on quotation marks to indicate passages taken from the Bible or from other works. The manner in which these conventions are used in the original suggests that Swedenborg did not belabor the distinction between direct quotation and paraphrase; but in this edition, directly quoted material is indicated by either block quotations or quotation marks, and paraphrased material is usually presented without such indicators. In passages of dialog as well, quotation marks have been introduced that were not present as such in the original. Furthermore, Swedenborg did not mark his omissions from or changes to material he quoted, a practice in which this edition generally follows him. One exception consists of those instances in which Swedenborg did not include a complete sentence at the beginning or end of a Bible quotation. The omission in such cases has been marked in this edition with added points of ellipsis.

Special use of singular verbs Swedenborg sometimes uses a singular verb with certain dual subjects such as love and wisdom, goodness and truth, and love and charity. The wider context of his works indicates that his reason for doing so is that he understands the two given subjects as forming a unity. This translation generally preserves such singular verbs.

Special use of singular nouns In the Bible we often find references to a plural number of persons to which is ascribed a single personal feature, such as a *heart, soul, mind, face, body, head,* or *life;* indeed, we might well term this usage the *biblical singular.* Swedenborg generally adopted this usage, and not only in his Bible translations. It has often been retained in this edition. For an example, see *Secrets of Heaven* 5573:2: "They engaged in commerce only for the sake of their job in the world, and beyond that they did not set their heart on [riches]."

Italicized terms Any words in indented scriptural extracts that are here set in italics reflect a similar emphasis in the first edition.

Special use of vertical rule The opening passages of the early chapters of *Secrets of Heaven,* as well as the ends of all chapters, contain material that derives in some way from Swedenborg's experiences in the spiritual world. Swedenborg specified that the text of these and similar passages be set in continuous italics to distinguish it from exegetical and other material. For this edition, the heavy use of italic text was felt to be antithetical to modern tastes, as well as difficult to read, and so such passages are instead marked by a vertical rule in the margin.

Changes to and insertions in the text This translation is based on the first Latin edition, published by Swedenborg himself (1749–1756); it also reflects emendations in the third Latin edition, edited by P. H. Johnson, John E. Elliott, and others, and published by the Swedenborg Society (1949–1973). It incorporates the silent correction of minor errors, not only in the text proper but in Bible verse references and in section references to this and other volumes of *Secrets of Heaven.* As previously noted, the text has usually been changed without notice where the verse numbering of the Latin Bible cited by Swedenborg differs from that of modern English Bibles. Throughout the translation, references or cross-references that were implied but not stated have been inserted in brackets; for example, [John 3:27]. In many cases, it is very difficult to determine what Swedenborg had in mind when he referred to other passages giving evidence for a statement or providing further discussion on a topic. Because of this difficulty, the missing references that are occasionally supplied in this edition should not be considered definitive or exhaustive. In contrast to such references in square brackets, references that occur in parentheses are those that appear in the first edition; for example, (1 Samuel 30:16), (see §42 above). Occasionally square brackets signal an insertion of other material that was not present in the first edition. These insertions fall into two classes: words likely to have been deleted through a copying or typesetting error, and words supplied by the translator as necessary for the understanding of the English text, though they have no direct parallel in the Latin. The latter device has been used sparingly, however, even at the risk of some inconsistency in its application. Unfortunately, no annotations concerning these insertions can be supplied in this Portable edition.

Biblical titles Swedenborg refers to the Hebrew Scriptures as the Old Testament and to the Greek Scriptures as the New Testament; his terminology has been adopted in this edition. As was the custom in his day, he refers to the Pentateuch (Genesis, Exodus, Leviticus, Numbers, and Deuteronomy) simply as "Moses"; for example, in §6752:4 he writes, "This can be seen in Moses," and then quotes a passage from Deuteronomy. Similarly, in sentences or phrases introducing quotations he sometimes refers to the Psalms as "David," to Lamentations as "Jeremiah," and to the Gospel of John, the Epistles of John, and the Book of Revelation as simply "John." Conventional references supplied in parentheses after such quotations specify their sources more precisely.

Problematic content Occasionally Swedenborg makes statements that, although mild by the standards of eighteenth-century theological discourse, now read as harsh, dismissive, or insensitive. The most problematic are assertions about or criticisms of various religious traditions and their adherents—including Judaism, ancient or contemporary; Roman Catholicism; Islam; and the Protestantism in which Swedenborg himself grew up. These statements are far outweighed in size and importance by other passages in Swedenborg's works earnestly maintaining the value of every individual and of all religions. This wider context is discussed in the introductions and annotations of the Deluxe edition mentioned above. In the present format, however, problematic statements must be retained without comment. The other option—to omit them—would obscure some aspects of Swedenborg's presentation and in any case compromise its historicity.

Allusive References in Expositional Material

Swedenborg's use of pronouns that refer back to vague or distant antecedents may cause confusion for readers. Such allusive references occur in two situations in his expositions:

In mentions of Jesus If the pronoun *he* without a nearby antecedent appears in a proposition, the reader can assume that it refers to Jesus, the main topic of the exegesis as a whole.

In preview material Swedenborg's preview sections (see the Deluxe edition of *Secrets of Heaven,* vol. 1, pages 30–35) feature a series of propositions, each of which consists of a phrase of biblical text followed by a brief assertion of its inner meaning. These glimpses of the inner meaning quite often use pronouns that point back to other inner meanings mentioned earlier in the preview section. For instance, in *Secrets of Heaven* volume 7, §4962, a preview section, we read this:

> *And Joseph* symbolizes spiritual heavenliness drawing on rationality. *Was taken down to Egypt* means to religious learning. *And Potiphar, Pharaoh's chamberlain, bought him* means that **it** had a place among items of inner knowledge. *The chief of the bodyguards* means **that** were of primary importance in interpretation. *An Egyptian man* symbolizes earthly truth.

The words "it" and "that" (shown here in boldface) are confusing: *What* had a place among items of inner knowledge? *What things* were of primary importance in interpretation? The answers lie in the fragments of inner meaning given in propositions earlier in the preview section: The "it" refers back to the "spiritual heavenliness" mentioned in the first proposition. The referent of "that" is the "items of inner knowledge" mentioned at the end of the immediately preceding proposition. Thus Swedenborg has laid the propositions out in such a way that if put together, the five statements might read as follows:

> *And Joseph was taken down to Egypt, and Potiphar, Pharaoh's chamberlain, the chief of the bodyguards, an Egyptian man, bought him* means that spiritual heavenliness drawing on rationality was brought to religious learning and given a place among items of inner knowledge and earthly truth that were of primary importance in interpretation.

Secrets of Heaven

Exodus 1

[Teachings on Neighborly Love]

THE Exodus chapters will be prefaced by doctrinal teachings—first, *teachings on neighborly love,* and later, teachings on faith. The purpose is to take some concepts that have been conveyed in a scattered way in the explanations and set them out systematically. This will reveal in its proper arrangement the kind of theology that belongs to the church and ought to belong, if this theology is to harmonize with the goodness and truth in heaven. 6627

In various places in preceding explanations I have shown that a theology of neighborly love was the theology of the ancient churches, that this theology united all the churches, and that it therefore created one religion out of many. The people of those religions, you see, acknowledged as members of the church everyone who lived a life of neighborly kindness. They called such people family, no matter how far they diverged otherwise on truth—the truth that people now identify with faith. 6628

As for religious truth, one individual would teach another, which they counted as an act of neighborly love. What is more, no offense was taken if one individual did not yield to another's point of view. They knew that the more intent we are on what is good, the more truth we accept.

6629 As this is what the ancient churches were like, the people in them had depth, and as they had depth, they were wise. People intent on doing good out of love and charity are in heaven, as far as their inner self is concerned, and in an angelic community there devoted to the same kind of goodness. This raises their minds inward and therefore yields them wisdom. Wisdom cannot come from anywhere but heaven, or rather from the Lord through heaven, and heaven holds wisdom because its inhabitants are dedicated to what is good.

6630 However, this ancient wisdom dwindled over time. The farther the human race moved from doing good out of love for the Lord and out of charity for one's neighbor, the farther it also moved from heaven and consequently from wisdom. That is why humankind changed from being internal to being more and more external.

6631 When humankind became external, it also became worldly and body-centered, and when people become worldly and body-centered, they lose all interest in heavenly matters. Heavenly realities seem too distant to believe in, because the pleasures of earthly kinds of love then take over completely, and along with them, all the evils rendered pleasant by those kinds of love. Then anything a person hears about life after death, heaven, or hell is like a straw in the wind: now seen, now gone.

6632 For the same reason, the theology of neighborly love that was so precious to the ancients is among today's lost knowledge. Who today knows what neighborly love really is, or what our neighbor really is? And yet that theology abounds with so many secrets of such tremendous importance that not a thousandth of it can be written down. The whole Sacred Scripture is nothing but teachings about love and charity. The Lord teaches this, too, saying, "*You shall love the Lord your God with all your heart and with all your soul and with all your mind. This is the first and great commandment. A second is similar to it: You shall love your neighbor as yourself. On these two commandments depend the Law and the Prophets*" (Matthew 22:37, 38, 39, 40; the Law and the Prophets being the Word in its entirety).

6633 Since the theology of neighborly love is among today's lost knowledge, the theology of faith is divorced from the truth; so with the Lord's divine mercy, let me convey that theology before every Exodus chapter and in this way restore it to the church.

Exodus 1

1. And these are the names of Israel's sons coming to Egypt with Jacob; a man and his household they came:

2. Reuben, Simeon, Levi, and Judah,

3. Issachar, Zebulun, and Benjamin,

4. Dan and Naphtali, Gad and Asher.

5. And every soul, those issuing from Jacob's thigh, was seventy souls. And Joseph was in Egypt.

6. And Joseph died, and all his brothers, and all that generation.

7. And Israel's sons became fruitful and productive, and multiplied and became very, very numerous, and the land was filled with them.

8. And there arose a new king over Egypt who did not know Joseph.

9. And he said to his people, "Look: the people of the children of Israel is greater in number and more numerous than we.

10. Come, let us deal prudently with them. Maybe they will multiply and it will happen that wars occur and they will go so far as to join with our enemies and fight against us and go up from the land."

11. And they placed over [that people] chiefs of tribute so as to afflict [that people] with burdens. And [that people] built storehouse cities for Pharaoh: Pithom and Rameses.

12. And as they afflicted [that people], so they multiplied and so they grew. And [the Egyptians] felt disgust because of the children of Israel.

13. And the Egyptians forced servitude on the children of Israel, with harshness.

14. And [the Egyptians] rendered their life bitter with heavy servitude in mortar and in bricks and in all servitude in the field, along with all the servitude that [the Egyptians] forced on them, with harshness.

15. And the king of Egypt said to the midwives of the Hebrews—of whom the name of one was Shiphrah and the name of the other was Puah—

16. and he said, "In your midwifing to the Hebrews, when you look on the [birthing] stools, if it is a son you shall kill him, and if it is a daughter let her live."

17. And the midwives feared God and did not do as the king of Egypt had spoken to them and kept the boys alive.

18. And the king of Egypt called the midwives and said to them, "On what account do you do this thing and keep the boys alive?"

19. And the midwives said to Pharaoh, "Because the Hebrew women are not like the Egyptian women, because they are full of life. Before the midwife comes to them they have given birth."

20. And God dealt well with the midwives, and the people multiplied and became very numerous.

21. And it happened, because the midwives feared God, that he made households for them.

22. And Pharaoh commanded all his people, saying, "Every son that is born you shall cast into the river, and every daughter you shall keep alive."

Summary

6634 THE inner meaning of this first chapter is about the state of the church, now established, when goodness plays the leading role and becomes fruitful through the multiplication of religious truth.

6635 The next subject is the way this truth is attacked by earthly-level falsity and evil. The persecution causes goodness to become even more fruitful through truth. The end of the chapter deals further with that persecution, the series of increments by which it grows, and its result, which is that truth-from-goodness takes root and receives confirmation.

Inner Meaning

6636 EXODUS 1:1, 2, 3, 4, 5. *And these are the names of Israel's sons coming to Egypt with Jacob; a man and his household they came: Reuben, Simeon, Levi, and Judah; Issachar, Zebulun, and Benjamin; Dan and Naphtali, Gad and Asher. And every soul, those issuing from Jacob's thigh, was seventy souls. And Joseph was in Egypt.*

These are the names of Israel's sons symbolizes the quality of the church. *Coming to Egypt with Jacob* means after truth had been introduced into knowledge. *A man and his household they came* symbolizes [its quality] in regard to truth and to goodness. *Reuben, Simeon, Levi, and Judah; Issachar, Zebulun, and Benjamin; Dan and Naphtali, Gad and Asher* symbolize the process from beginning to end. *And every soul, those issuing from Jacob's thigh,* symbolizes everything springing from general truth. *Was seventy souls* symbolizes completion. *And Joseph was in Egypt* means that inner heavenliness was present on the earthly level.

These are the names of Israel's sons symbolizes the quality of the church. **6637**
This can be seen from the symbolism of a *name* as the quality of something (discussed in §§144, 145, 1754, 1896, 2009, 2628, 2724, 3006, 3421), from the representation of *Israel's sons* as spiritual truths (discussed in §§5414, 5879, 5951), and from the representation of *Israel* as goodness-from-truth, or spiritual goodness (discussed in §§3654, 4598, 5803, 5807, 5812, 5817, 5819, 5826, 5833).

Since Israel represents goodness-from-truth, or spiritual goodness, and his sons represent spiritual truths on the earthly plane, the children of Israel represent the church, because spiritual goodness and the truth born of it make a church a church. No one who ignores spiritual goodness (good that is done out of neighborly love) and spiritual truth (truth that leads to faith) is part of the church, even if born within the church. After all, the Lord's entire heavenly kingdom is committed to goodness that is urged by love and faith. If the church lacks the same commitment, it cannot be a church because it is not united with heaven—the church being the Lord's kingdom on earth.

[2] It is called a church not because it has the Word and teachings drawn from the Word, or because it knows about the Lord and observes the sacraments. No, what makes it a church is that it lives by the Word, or by a theology drawn from the Word, and that its theology tells how to live. People who do not live this way are not part of the church but stand outside it. People who go so far as to live a life of evil and therefore a life opposed to what the church teaches stand further outside the church even than outsiders, who know nothing whatever about the Word, the Lord, or the sacraments. Since they know about the goodness and truth that properly characterize the church, they annihilate the church in themselves, which outsiders in their ignorance can never do.

It is also important to realize that everyone who lives a good life, as inspired by neighborly love and taught by faith, is a church and a kingdom of the Lord. Such a person is consequently called a temple, too, and a house of God. People who are individual churches go to make up the church as a whole, no matter how far apart they live.

This then is the church meant by the children of Israel here and in what follows.

6638 *Coming to Egypt with Jacob* means after truth had been introduced into knowledge, as the following shows: *Egypt* symbolizes knowledge, as addressed in §§1164, 1165, 1186, 1462, 4749, 4964, 4966, 5700, 5702, 6004, 6015, 6125. *Jacob* represents truth and also goodness on the earthly plane—that is, the earthly plane in regard to truth and goodness—as dealt with in §§3305, 3509, 3525, 3546, 3576, 3599, 3659, 3669, 3677, 3775, 3829, 4009, 4234, 4286, 4337, 4538, 5506, 5533, 5535, 6001, 6236. *Coming to Egypt* means being introduced into knowledge, as can be seen from explanations of subject matter in the chapters that tell about the travels to Egypt by Jacob's sons to buy grain and then about their arrival there with Jacob. To learn what it is to introduce the church's truth into knowledge, see §§6004, 6023, 6052, 6071, 6077.

This shows that Israel's sons coming to Egypt symbolize the truths introduced into knowledge.

6639 *A man and his household they came* symbolizes [its quality] in regard to truth and to goodness. This is evident from the symbolism of a *man* as truth (discussed in §§3134, 3459) and from that of a *household* as goodness (discussed in §§3720, 4982).

The Genesis chapters that dealt with the arrival of Jacob's sons and of Jacob himself in Egypt, where Joseph was, were about truth known to the church and its introduction into knowledge. The church cannot be established until this introduction has taken place. Continuing in the same vein, then, the inner meaning of the text here treats of the church as now established and of the way it is continuously harassed by knowledge and falsity. No matter how firmly truth has been introduced and the church has been established in us, knowledge and falsity still constantly rise up and attack what belongs to the church in us. That is what is represented by Pharaoh and the Egyptians' afflicting the children of Israel and wanting to kill their baby boys.

[2] You will never believe this is so if you do not know about the way knowledge and falsity in the other life attack religious truth in people belonging to the church. When people in the church go to the other world, they need to be purified of anything that attacks truth and goodness. Otherwise they cannot be taken up into heaven and be part of a community there that has been purified of such influences. If they were taken up there too soon, they would be like a thick fog in the clear blue, or like a darkening mass in white light. In order for these church people

just arriving from the world to be purified, then, they are kept in a state in which they are attacked by knowledge that clashes with truth and also by falsity, and they are kept in that state until such types of knowledge lose any value for them and disappear. This rarely happens while they are living in their body, but it does happen in the other life to people who are being lifted into heaven. Nonetheless, it happens in a large variety of ways.

Much experience has enabled me to see that this is true, but if I cited it all, it would fill too many pages.

[3] This is the process described in the inner meaning by the oppression of the children of Israel by the Egyptians, by their eventual liberation, by various stages they went through in the wilderness, and finally by their entrance into the land of Canaan.

Grasping that this is how matters stand is completely impossible for people who believe that salvation consists simply in being brought into heaven on the basis of mercy. They believe mercy is extended to everyone who has the apparent confidence (which is called faith) to think, "Because the Lord suffered for me, I am saved, no matter how I live." If salvation were mere admission to heaven on the basis of mercy, everyone on earth would be saved, because the Lord, who is mercy itself, desires the salvation of all and the death (or damnation) of no one.

Reuben, Simeon, Levi, and Judah; Issachar, Zebulun, and Benjamin; **6640**
Dan and Naphtali, Gad and Asher symbolize the process from beginning to end—the process of establishing the church, which is the subject of the next few phrases. Jacob's twelve sons and the tribes named for them symbolize everything good and true, that is, everything connected with love and faith, in its entirety (see §§3858, 3926, 3939, 4060, 6335). However, their symbolism varies with the order in which they are named (§§3862, 3939, 4603 and following sections). The attributes they symbolize are as far beyond counting as all the attributes in general and in particular that constitute the church and the Lord's kingdom (§6337). No one but the Lord knows what their specific symbolism is when they are listed in one order or another. Not even heaven's inhabitants know, unless they learn from the Lord—and in heaven the true ideas and good desires being symbolized are revealed by lights that carry perception with them.

[2] Because the twelve tribes represented the Lord's kingdom and everything in it, those lights needed to be represented too so that all truth and goodness in the church would be represented. On this account,

twelve precious stones in their proper order were set in gold, one stone for every tribe, and the whole was called the breastplate. It was placed on Aaron's ephod and from it [the priests] received answers, through various flashes of light connected with either an audible voice or an inner perception. This too shows that the twelve tribes of Israel symbolize all truth and goodness in the Lord's kingdom and the church, in its entirety, and that their symbolism varies with the order in which they are named.

Of course they are not named in their birth order here. Issachar and Zebulun are listed before Dan and Naphtali, even though the latter were born before them. Benjamin comes before Dan, Naphtali, Gad, and Asher even though he was born last. And Gad and Asher are listed after all the others. Likewise elsewhere in the Word, where they come in still other orders.

6641 *And every soul, those issuing from Jacob's thigh,* symbolizes everything springing from general truth, as the following shows: A *soul* in a general sense means a person, and here a person in a spiritual religion. In an inner sense, though, a soul symbolizes truth and goodness because they are what make a person human (§§6605, 6626). A *thigh* symbolizes marriage love, as discussed in §§3021, 4277, 4280, 5050–5062, and since it symbolizes marriage love, it symbolizes all love, both heavenly and spiritual (§§3021, 4277, 4280, 4575). *Issuing from* someone's thigh therefore symbolizes truth and goodness yielded by the heavenly marriage. As a consequence, it symbolizes truth and goodness in the church, because when these are genuine, they are born of the heavenly marriage, which is the marriage of goodness and truth. And *Jacob* represents truth and also goodness on the earthly plane, but truth and goodness in general, because his sons are distinct types of truth and goodness within that general category, as suggested in §6637.

The reason Jacob represents truths in general here is that the focus is on a spiritual religion. Such a religion starts with general truths, which introduce it to its proper goodness. People in a spiritual religion do not know what spiritual goodness is and so have no way of recognizing it except through truth. Goodness does not yield them any perception of truth as it does for people in a heavenly religion.

6642 *Was seventy souls* symbolizes completion. This is established by the symbolism of *seventy* as something complete, which is discussed at §6508.

6643 *And Joseph was in Egypt* means that inner heavenliness was present on the earthly level. This can be seen from the representation of *Joseph* as inner heavenliness (dealt with in §§5869, 5877, 6224) and from the symbolism of *Egypt* as the earthly plane (dealt with in §§6147, 6252).

Inner heavenliness was present on the earthly plane, where knowledge resides, and it oversaw everything there. This was represented by Joseph's being made lord over the whole land of Egypt and set in charge of Pharaoh's household. The reason for representing this was that the inner sense was dealing with the establishment of a spiritual religion, and the earthly level could be made into a church only if inner heavenliness was present there, doing everything. To learn about these matters, see earlier discussions in §§6275, 6284, 6299, 6451, 6587.

Exodus 1:6, 7. *And Joseph died, and all his brothers, and all that generation. And Israel's sons became fruitful and productive, and multiplied and became very, very numerous, and the land was filled with them.* **6644**

And Joseph died means that the situation with the inner part of the church now changed. *And all his brothers, and all that generation* means that so did the situation with the outer part of the church, in particular and in general. *And Israel's sons became fruitful and productive* means that the church's truth grew in goodness. *And multiplied and became very, very numerous* means that it grew most in truth-from-goodness. *And the land was filled with them* means until the church reached a state of fullness.

Joseph died means that the situation with the inner part of the church **6645** now changed, as the following shows: *Dying* means the end of the previous stage and the start of a new one, so it means that the state of the church now changed. For the meaning of dying as something's ceasing to be what it was, see §§494, 6587, 6593. For its meaning as the end of a previous representation, §§3253, 3259, 3276, 6302. And *Joseph* represents the inner dimension, as noted in §§6177, 6224.

The inner meaning of what follows tells what the state of the church's inner part was now like, and also what the state of its outer part was now like, as symbolized by "his brothers died, and all that generation."

[2] Regarding the church in a person, it undergoes new states, one after another. Once we have been strengthened in truth that leads to faith and good that is done out of neighborly love, we are introduced into other states. The earlier stage then serves as a foundation for the next one, and so on, constantly. So a person who is a church, or who is being reborn, is always being led farther within and therefore deeper into heaven.

The reason this happens is that the Lord in his love (which is infinite because it is divine) wants to draw us all the way to himself and in this way bless us with all glory and happiness. This is obvious from his words in John:

> *I pray that they may all be one; as you, Father, are in me, and I in you, so that they too may be one in us. I have given them the glory that you have given me so that they can be one as we are one—I in them and you in me. Father, those whom you have given me I want to have with me where I am so that they can see my glory, which you gave me. For I made your name known to them, and I will make it known, so that the love with which you loved me can exist in them, and I in them.* (John 17:20–26)

It is quite plain that these are words of divine love for everyone open to that love. [3] The same thing can be seen from the fact that the Lord appears as the sun in the other life and therefore fills all of heaven with warmth and light. The flames of that sun are pure divine love, and the light from it is the holy radiance of love, which is divine truth. That shows how immense the Lord's love is.

This then is why people in the church are led step by step to new stages, constantly farther into heaven, and therefore closer to the Lord.

6646 *And all his brothers, and all that generation* means that so did the situation with the outer part of the church, in particular and in general, as the following shows: Jacob's sons, the *brothers,* represent earthly-level truth known to the church, as noted in §§5403, 5419, 5427, 5458, 5512, and consequently the church's outer part. And *that generation* symbolizes the church's outer part in general, because the generation here means the same thing as Joseph's brothers, only in a broader sense.

6647 *And Israel's sons became fruitful and productive* means that the church's truth grew in goodness, as the following shows: *Israel's sons* represent spiritual truth (discussed in §§5414, 5879) and the church (§6637). *Becoming fruitful* means growing in goodness (discussed in §§43, 55, 913, 983, 2846, 2847, 3146). And *becoming productive* symbolizes further development. When the church has been established in us, goodness constantly grows and develops, not only on our inner plane but also from our inner to our outer plane and on our outer plane as well.

In people of a spiritual religion, truth causes goodness to grow, as I have shown many times before [§§2937, 2954, 2979, 5113, 6289, 6427]. People in a spiritual religion do not have perception, as people in a heavenly religion do, so it is only through truth that they learn to recognize the goodness belonging to the church, or spiritual goodness. While they are being reborn, then, the Lord uses the angels with them to stir up truth and in this way lead them to goodness. Once they have been reborn, though, he leads them by stirring up both truth and goodness. However, the quality of goodness in people of a spiritual religion depends on the quality of the truth they know, so truth also determines the quality of their conscience, which is their version of perception and their guide to life.

And multiplied and became very, very numerous means that it grew most in truth-from-goodness. This can be seen from the symbolism of *multiplying* as growing in truth (discussed in §§43, 55, 913, 983, 2846, 2847) and from that of *becoming numerous* as further development, and accordingly a constant increase in truth. It symbolizes an increase in truth-from-goodness because the focus now is on the church after it has been established. Here is the case with the church in us: While it is being established, we concentrate on truth, which causes goodness to grow. Once the church has been established in us, though, we possess goodness, and from goodness, truth, which then grows unceasingly. It does not grow much while we are living in the world, because concern for food, clothing, and other necessities hinders us there. In the other world, though, truth grows beyond measure, perpetually, to eternity. After all, there is no end to wisdom, which comes from the Divine. That is what allows for constant improvement in angels, and also in everyone else who becomes an angel upon arrival in the other life. Any wise perspective is capable of infinite extension, you see, and such perspectives are infinite in number. Clearly, then, wisdom can grow forever and still not reach much farther than the first step. That is because the Divine is infinite, and what comes from the Infinite is like this. 6648

And the land was filled with them means until the church reached a state of fullness. This can be seen from the symbolism of *being filled* as reaching a state of fullness and from that of the *land* as the church (discussed in §§82, 662, 1066, 1068, 1262, 1411, 1413, 1607, 1733, 1850, 2117, 2118 at the end, 2928, 3355, 4447, 4535, 5577). The land of Goshen, where the children of Israel were now situated, symbolizes the church. That is where the church existed in the time before the children of Israel arrived in the land of Canaan, as subsequent events show: the land of Goshen was free of plagues that afflicted other parts of Egypt [Exodus 8:22; 9:6, 26; 11:7] and it enjoyed light when darkness struck elsewhere (Exodus 10:21, 22, 23), which means that it was totally separate from the other lands in Egypt. Another point of evidence is the symbolism of the land of Goshen as the central, inmost part of the earthly level (§§5910, 6028, 6031, 6068) 6649 and therefore as the church, because the spiritual church exists at the core of the earthly level.

6650 Exodus 1:8–14. *And there arose a new king over Egypt who did not know Joseph. And he said to his people, "Look: the people of the children of Israel is greater in number and more numerous than we. Come, let us deal prudently with them. Maybe they will multiply and it will happen that wars occur and they will go so far as to join with our enemies and fight against us and go up from the land." And they placed over [that people] chiefs of tribute so as to afflict [that people] with burdens. And [that people] built storehouse cities for Pharaoh: Pithom and Rameses. And as they afflicted [that people], so they multiplied and so they grew. And [the Egyptians] felt disgust because of the children of Israel. And the Egyptians forced servitude on the children of Israel, with harshness. And [the Egyptians] rendered their life bitter with heavy servitude in mortar and in bricks and in all servitude in the field, along with all the servitude that [the Egyptians] forced on them, with harshness.*

And there arose a new king over Egypt symbolizes separate types of knowledge opposed to the church's truth. *Who did not know Joseph* means that they were completely alienated from the inner dimension. *And he said to his people* symbolizes subordinate items of information. *Look: the people of the children of Israel is greater in number and more numerous than we* means that the church's truth is stronger than alienated types of knowledge. *Come, let us deal prudently with them* symbolizes cunning. *Maybe they will multiply and it will happen that wars occur* means that if they increase they will prevail. *And they will go so far as to join with our enemies and fight against us* means that allies that intend them harm will then gain power. *And go up from the land* means that the church will then be established. *And they placed over [that people] chiefs of tribute* symbolizes falsities that enslaved them. *So as to afflict [that people] with burdens* means making matters worse by forced service. *And [that people] built storehouse cities for Pharaoh* symbolizes doctrines consisting of distorted truth, on the earthly plane, where alienated types of knowledge reside. *Pithom and Rameses* symbolizes their quality. *And as they afflicted [that people], so they multiplied* means that truth increased in proportion to the persecution. *And so they grew* means that it was confirmed. *And [the Egyptians] felt disgust because of the children of Israel* symbolizes even greater loathing. *And the Egyptians forced servitude on the children of Israel* symbolizes an intent to subdue them. *With harshness* symbolizes mercilessness. *And [the*

Egyptians] rendered their life bitter with heavy servitude means until the intent to subdue them became galling. *In mortar and in bricks* means on account of the evils they made up and the falsities they invented. *And in all servitude in the field* symbolizes an intent to subdue the church's strengths. *Along with all the servitude that [the Egyptians] forced on them, with harshness* symbolizes a merciless intent to subdue them in many different ways.

And there arose a new king over Egypt symbolizes separate types of 6651
knowledge opposed to the church's truth. This can be seen from the representation of Pharaoh, the *king* here, as knowledge in general, which is discussed at §6015. He is called a king because in a positive sense a king symbolizes truth (§§1672, 2015, 2069, 3670, 4581, 4966, 5044, 6148) and in a negative sense falsity. When the word *king* means Pharaoh, it symbolizes falsity in the form of knowledge, or types of knowledge that oppose the church's truth. That is why he is called a *new* king, because the king of Joseph's era represented types of knowledge that agreed with the church's truth. For the meaning of *Egypt* as knowledge, particularly in this context, see above at §6638.

Who did not know Joseph means that they were completely alienated 6652
from the inner dimension, as the following shows: *Not knowing* means being alienated. One who does not know the truth and does not want to know it is alienated from the church's truth. Later verses show that alienation is meant here, because [the king of Egypt] severely and harshly afflicted the children of Israel, who represent the church (§6637). And *Joseph* represents the inner dimension, as mentioned at §§6177, 6224. A type of knowledge alienated from the inner dimension is knowledge that is opposed to religion, because it is through the inner dimension that the goodness and truth composing a religion flow in, and if they are not accepted by the earthly plane, the inner dimension closes off. A person is then alienated from goodness and truth. At that point, the only earthly-level items of knowledge recognized as true are the ones that are actually false. The false knowledge multiplies, and real truth is banished.

And he said to his people symbolizes subordinate items of information. 6653
This can be seen from the symbolism of a *people* as truth, and in a negative sense as falsity (discussed in §§1259, 1260, 3295, 3581). This people symbolizes information separated from truth, because it is the people of Egypt. On the point that Egypt stands for knowledge, see §6638. This information is subordinate because it says *the king said to his people.*

The reason a people symbolizes truth is that a *people* is the term for those under a monarch, and a monarch symbolizes truth (§6651).

A people symbolizes truth, but by this I mean *those awake to* truth. I speak of it as truth in the abstract because that is how spirits and angels think and speak. Doing so enables them to comprehend the concept as a whole while also grasping its particulars without reflecting on any specific people in possession of truth. Such reflection would distract them from the universal concept and therefore from broad insight and accordingly from wisdom. Narrowing one's thoughts to a specific people or a specific individual limits and confines those thoughts, turning one aside from a perception of the matter in its full range.

Just as a people in an inner sense symbolizes something that is not restricted, so do other terms. Take a nation, which means goodness; a king, which means truth; a chieftain, which means a primary truth; a priest, which means goodness; or a son, daughter, son-in-law, daughter-in-law, brother, sister, father, mother, and many others.

6654 *Look: the people of the children of Israel is greater in number and more numerous than we* means that the church's truth is stronger than alienated types of knowledge, as the following shows: The *children of Israel* represent religious truth and goodness, as noted above in §6647. *Great in number and numerous* symbolizes being strong, and multiplication—growing in number and becoming numerous—is mentioned in connection with truth (again, see above, at §6648). And the king of Egypt and his people, referred to here by *more than we,* represent alienated types of knowledge, as above in §6652. This shows that *look: the people of Israel is greater in number and more numerous than we* means that truth is stronger than alienated types of knowledge.

6655 *Come, let us deal prudently with them* symbolizes cunning. This is evident from the symbolism of *prudence* as cunning when mentioned by the evil, who are alienated from truth and goodness. Anything they do with cunning or with deceit they call prudence.

Let me say a bit here about the cunning symbolized by prudence. Everyone in whom evil is active refers to cunning as prudence, and such people equate intelligence and wisdom with cunning alone. People who are like this in the world turn even worse in the other life, where they are always scheming against goodness and truth. The types recognized as smart and wise among them are those who seem to themselves to be able to undermine and destroy truth by the use of falsity, whatever malicious arts they employ. This shows what those people in the church are like who identify prudence with cunning: they are in touch with the hells.

True members of the church find cunning so foreign that they absolutely shrink from it. The angelic among them would like, if possible, to lay their minds bare and show everyone plainly what they are thinking. This is because they intend nothing but good to their neighbor, and if they see anything bad in anyone, they excuse it. Not so the evil-minded. They are afraid to let anything they think or wish leak out, because they intend nothing but evil to their neighbor—or if they intend good, it is for selfish reasons. If they actually do good, it is good only in outward appearance, for show, in pursuit of wealth and rank. After all, they realize that goodness and truth, justice and fairness, and honor possess a powerful hidden force to attract minds, even those of the wicked.

Maybe they will multiply and it will happen that wars occur means that 6656
if they increase they will prevail. This can be seen from the symbolism of *multiplying* as increasing in truth (discussed at §§43, 55, 913, 983, 2846, 2847) and from that of *wars* as struggles over truth and falsity, or spiritual struggles (discussed at §§1664, 2686). Since the next clause says, "They will go so far as to join with our enemies," it symbolizes prevailing in those struggles.

And they will go so far as to join with our enemies and fight against us 6657
means that allies that intend them harm will then gain power, as the following shows: *Joining* means gaining power, because one's foes gain power when joined by large numbers. *Enemies* symbolize military allies. And *fighting against us* means inflicting harm, because to the extent that one cannot resist an attacking force, it inflicts harm.

Here is the situation: Every person on earth and every good spirit is surrounded by a general environment of efforts from hell and a general environment of efforts from heaven. The environment created by hell involves efforts to hurt and destroy. The environment created by heaven involves efforts to help and save. See §6477. These are the general environments. There are also particular environments around every person on earth, because we each have spirits from hell and angels from heaven with us, as described in §§5846–5866, 5976–5993. This leaves us in equilibrium, with the freedom to think and will what is evil, and the freedom to think and will what is good.

[2] When people in the church encounter trials (which happens when they are let into their evil), then a fight between spirits from hell and

angels from heaven takes place around them (§§3927, 4249, 5036). The fight lasts as long as they are kept in their evil.

While the fight rages, it sometimes looks to the spirits from hell as though they will win, and at those times they surge forward. Sometimes it looks as though they will lose, and then they retreat. When they expect to lose, they worry that many from heaven will combine against them and that they will consequently be thrown down into hell. They fear they will never leave hell again, and that is indeed what happens when they have been conquered.

This is what is meant by the idea that if they increase they will prevail and that harmful allies will gain power.

[3] When fighting against angels, spirits from hell are situated in the world of spirits, where they enjoy a state of freedom (§5852).

All of this now shows what it means in an inner sense that the children of Israel were persecuted and oppressed by the Egyptians in this way; that the more they were persecuted, the more they multiplied; that Jehovah, the Lord, fought for them; and that he used plagues to restrain the Egyptians, finally drowning them all in the Suph Sea.

6658 *And go up from the land* means that the church will then be established, as the following shows: *Going up* means being lifted—lifted toward inner religious levels—as discussed in §§3084, 4539, 4969, 5406, 5817, 6007. And the *land,* here the land of Goshen, symbolizes the church, as discussed above at §6649.

Being lifted toward inner levels, as symbolized by going up from the land and arriving in Canaan, means that the church will be established. The church admittedly is established in us when we do good because we like to, but it is not fully established until after we have fought against evil and falsity—that is, until after we have endured times of trial. Then we truly become a church. At that point we are led into heaven, which is represented by the Israelites' being led into the land of Canaan.

6659 *And they placed over [that people] chiefs of tribute* symbolizes falsities that enslaved them. This can be seen from the symbolism of *chiefs* as the most important truths (dealt with in §§1482, 2089, 5044), and here, in a negative sense, as the most important falsities, and from the symbolism of *tribute*—the tribute to which they were forced by the chiefs set over them—as slavery (dealt with in §6394).

6660 *So as to afflict [that people] with burdens* means making matters worse by forced service. This can be seen from the symbolism of *afflicting* as worsening and from that of *burdens* as tribute, which is slavery.

And [that people] built storehouse cities for Pharaoh symbolizes doctrines consisting of distorted truth, on the earthly plane, where alienated types of knowledge reside. This is clear from the symbolism of *cities* as doctrines in both [positive and negative] senses (discussed in §§402, 2449, 2943, 3216, 4492, 4493), from that of *storehouses* as distorted truth (discussed below), and from the representation of *Pharaoh* as the earthly plane (mentioned in §§5160, 5799, 6015 at the end). For the fact that the earthly level held alienated types of knowledge, see above at §§6651, 6652. 6661

The storehouse cities that the people of Israel built for Pharaoh mean doctrines consisting of distorted truth because when people are focused on knowledge that is alienated from truth (symbolized here by Pharaoh and the Egyptians), they corrupt and distort all religious truth. From this corrupt, distorted truth they make doctrines for themselves.

The word used for storehouses in the original language also means armories and treasuries, which have almost the same symbolism on an inner level. Storehouses are places to gather grain provisions, and grain provisions symbolize truth (§§5276, 5280, 5292, 5402), and in a negative sense falsity. Armories, on the other hand, are places to stockpile weapons, which symbolize the tools that truth uses to fight falsity, and in a negative sense, the tools that falsity uses to fight truth (§§1788, 2686). Treasuries are places to hold wealth, and wealth and riches symbolize concepts of goodness and truth (§4508), and in a negative sense, concepts of evil and falsity. So storehouse cities, or armory cities, or treasury cities, symbolize overall doctrines consisting of distorted truth.

Pithom and Rameses symbolize their quality—the nature of doctrines consisting of distorted truth. This can be seen from names in the Word, which stand for the quality and state of whatever is being discussed. 6662

And as they afflicted [that people], so they multiplied means that truth increased in proportion to the persecution. This is indicated by the symbolism of *afflicting* as persecution and from that of *multiplying* as increasing in truth (noted above at §6656). 6663

I need to say how this works, because it cannot be known today without a background of experiences in the other life. Before they can be taken up to heaven and be attached to communities there, most spirits arriving from the world who have lived by the Lord's commandments find themselves attacked by the evil and falsity they possess. The purpose of the attack is for those evils and falsities to be removed. See §6639. There are impure qualities these individuals had taken on during bodily life that are anything but compatible with heaven. The way the new arrivals come under attack is to be immersed in their evils and falsities. When this happens, spirits with the same evils and falsities become present and strive in every possible way to lead them away from what is true and good. Still, they are not plunged to a place deeper in their evils and falsities than the Lord's inflow through angels can address. It is all measured precisely, down to the ounce, so to speak. The goal is for the spirits under attack to feel as though they are free and consequently to fight evil and falsity on their own. Later, though, if not at the time, they need to acknowledge that all the power to resist came from the Lord. See §§1937, 1947, 2881, 5660. [2] When all this happens, the truth and goodness already implanted in them are strengthened, and not only that, more is instilled. This is a feature of all spiritual battles won by the person struggling.

The fact that this happens is also evident from common experience. When you defend your opinion against others who criticize it, you reinforce your belief. You also discover new points in favor of your position—points you had not noticed before—and new arguments against the opposition. In this way you confirm yourself in your point of view and shed much new light on it.

The process is still more perfect when it comes to spiritual challenges. This is because the battle then takes place in spirit; because it concerns goodness and truth; and especially because the Lord is then present and gives guidance through his angels—since eternal life and salvation hang in the balance. In such struggles, the Lord usually turns all the evil intended by the hells into something good. As a result, he does not allow them to produce any more evil (or any other kind of evil) than he can turn to the particular benefit of the person fighting. The reason the Lord does this traces its origin to the fact that his kingdom is a kingdom of useful activity. Nothing can happen there that is not a source of goodness.

This evidence now shows how to understand the idea that truth increases in proportion to persecution—the symbolic meaning of *as they afflicted [that people], so they multiplied.*

6664 *And so they grew* means that it—the truth—was confirmed. This can be seen from the symbolism of *growing* as being confirmed, when it applies to truth that has multiplied through persecution by evil and falsity. No truth remains with us except truth that is confirmed, so the more truth is confirmed, the more it grows. For the idea that persecution confirms truth, see directly above at §6663.

6665 *And [the Egyptians] felt disgust because of the children of Israel* symbolizes even greater loathing. This is clear from the symbolism of *feeling* *disgust* as loathing. Here it symbolizes greater loathing because affliction caused [truth] to multiply and grow even more.

And the Egyptians forced servitude on the children of Israel symbolizes an intent to subdue them, as the following shows: *Forcing servitude on* means subduing, and here, an intent to subdue, because they are constantly trying to subdue others, though they never manage to subdue the good. The *Egyptians* symbolize separate types of knowledge opposed to the church's truth, as dealt with at §6651. And the *children of Israel* symbolize the church, as discussed at §6637. Plainly, then, *the Egyptians forced servitude on the children of Israel* symbolizes an intent to subdue on the part of people engrossed in types of knowledge disconnected from and opposed to the church's truth. **6666**

[2] In regard to this will for mastery, I have had the opportunity to learn what it is like among the evil in hell. Their effort and intent to subdue people who possess goodness and truth is too terrible to describe. They use all possible malice, all cunning and fraud, all deceit, and all cruelty. These devices are so extreme in intensity and nature that if I only partly described them, hardly anyone in the world could believe it. That is how cunning and skillful and also how unspeakable the devices are. In short, they are so extreme that they cannot possibly be resisted by any person on earth or even by any angel, but only by the Lord.

The reason for this kind of effort and intent on the part of people in hell is that all their pleasure in life and consequently their life itself consists in doing evil. Nothing else occupies their thoughts, so they have no other intent. Doing good is utterly impossible because it repels them. If they do help anyone it is for their own sake, to help themselves.

[3] People like this vastly augment the numbers in hell today. Surprisingly, it is especially people within the church who add to their number, on account of the wiles, frauds, hatred, vengefulness, and adulteries that flourish more in the church than elsewhere. Guile is taken for genius there, adultery is taken for honor, and anyone who disagrees is laughed at. That is the situation in the church today, which is a sign that its last days are at hand. For "if the end did not come, no flesh would be saved," as the Lord said in Matthew 24:22. All evil is contagious, of course; like bad yeast spreading through a lump of dough, it eventually infects everyone.

With harshness symbolizes mercilessness, as is self-evident. The kind of people described just above have no mercy because they have no love for their neighbor, only for themselves. What appears to be love for their neighbor is nothing but love for themselves. They love others so far as others **6667** cater to them, that is, so far as others belong to them. So far as others do not cater to them, or do not belong to them, they reject those others and hate any who had previously been friends. These qualities are inherent in self-love. Such qualities are revealed not in the world but in the other life, where they burst out into the open. The reason they come out in the open is that outer surfaces are stripped away there. It then becomes obvious what a person had been like inside.

6668 *And [the Egyptians] rendered their life bitter with heavy servitude* means until the intent to subdue them became galling. This can be seen from the meaning of the statement that *life was rendered bitter,* which is that it became galling, and from the symbolism of *servitude* as subjection, and here, the intent to subdue, as above at §6666.

6669 *In mortar and in bricks* means on account of the evils they made up and the falsities they invented. This can be seen from the symbolism of *mortar* as goodness, and in a negative sense as the evil [that people make up] (discussed below), and from that of *bricks* as the falsities people invent (discussed at §1296). About the evils and falsities that the hellish make up and invent, see just above at §6666.

The meaning of mortar, [or clay,] as evil that gives rise to falsity is clear from the following Scripture passages. In Isaiah:

> The ungodly are like the wind-battered sea when it cannot lie quiet; *its waters spew mud and clay.* (Isaiah 57:20)

The mud stands for falsity that gives rise to evil, and the clay for evil that gives rise to falsity. [2] In Jeremiah:

> *Your feet have sunk into the clay;* [men at peace with you] have backed away. (Jeremiah 38:22)

Feet sunk in clay stand for an earthly level sunk in evil. In Nahum:

> Draw water for the siege for yourselves; shore up your strongholds; *go into the clay* and *tread mortar;* repair the brick kiln. There fire will consume you and the sword will cut you off. (Nahum 3:14, 15)

Treading mortar stands for thinking up falsity out of evil. In Habakkuk:

> They will say, "Doom to those multiplying what is not theirs, for how long? And *to those loading clay on themselves."* Will not those nipping at you suddenly rise up? (Habakkuk 2:6, 7)

Loading clay on themselves stands for loading evil on. [3] In David:

> Jehovah brought me up out of the pit of devastation, *out of the muddy clay,* and set my feet on a rock. (Psalms 40:2)

In the same author:

> *I have sunk in deep clay* and cannot stand; I have come into the depths of the waters, and a wave has overwhelmed me. *Rescue me from the clay so that I do not sink,* and from the depths of the waters, and may the deep not swallow me! (Psalms 69:2, 14, 15)

The clay stands for evil that leads to falsity. In Isaiah:

> Priestly rulers will come *like mortar* and as a potter *treads clay.* (Isaiah 41:25)

[4] In the following passages, though, clay stands for something good. In Isaiah:

> Now Jehovah, you are our Father; *we are clay,* and you are our *potter,* and we are all the work of your hand. (Isaiah 64:8)

The clay stands for someone who is being formed into a member of the church and consequently for the faith-born goodness that shapes, or "re-forms," a person. [5] Likewise in Jeremiah:

> Jehovah said to Jeremiah, "Rise and go down *to the potter's house* and there I will let you hear my words." So I went down *to the potter's house,* when, look: He made a work on a slab, but the pot that he was making was ruined *like clay in the potter's hand,* and he went back and made it into another pot, as felt right in the *potter's* hand to make. Then the word of Jehovah came to me, saying, "'As this potter has done can I not do to you, house of Israel?' says Jehovah. 'Look: *like clay in a potter's hand*—that is how you are in my hand, house of Israel.'" (Jeremiah 18:1–6)

The house of Israel stands for a religion yet to be formed. What forms a religion is neighborly kindness and religious truth, which are symbolized by the clay and the potter's pot. That is why the prophet was ordered to go to the potter's house. He would not have been sent there if clay and a potter's pot did not have this symbolism. [6] There are also other passages where Jehovah (the Lord) is called a *potter* and a person being reformed is called *clay:* Isaiah 29:15, 16; 45:9; Job 10:9; 33:6.

The Lord once *made clay from his spit,* smeared it on the eyes of a person born blind, and ordered the person to wash in the pool of Siloam, which gave the blind person sight (John 9:6, 7, 11). The reason for this event was that it represented the reformation of a human being, who is born without knowledge of the truth. It also represented the fact that what reforms us is the goodness promoted by faith, meant by the clay.

6670 *And in all servitude in the field* symbolizes an intent to subdue the church's strengths. This is established by the symbolism of *servitude* as an intent to subdue (discussed above at §6666) and by that of a *field* as the church (discussed in §§2971, 3766).

6671 *Along with all the servitude that [the Egyptians] forced on them, with harshness* symbolizes a merciless intent to subdue them in many different ways, as the following shows: *Servitude* symbolizes an intent to subdue, as above in §§6666, 6668, 6670, and since the text says *all* the servitude, it means in many different ways. And *harshness* symbolizes mercilessness, as discussed at §6667.

6672 Exodus 1:15–21. *And the king of Egypt said to the midwives of the Hebrews—of whom the name of one was Shiphrah and the name of the other was Puah—and he said, "In your midwifing to the Hebrews, when you look on the [birthing] stools, if it is a son you shall kill him, and if it is a daughter let her live." And the midwives feared God and did not do as the king of Egypt had spoken to them and kept the boys alive. And the king of Egypt called the midwives and said to them, "On what account do you do this thing and keep the boys alive?" And the midwives said to Pharaoh, "Because the Hebrew women are not like the Egyptian women, because they are full of life. Before the midwife comes to them they have given birth." And God dealt well with the midwives, and the people multiplied and became very numerous. And it happened, because the midwives feared God, that he made households for them.*

And the king of Egypt said to the midwives of the Hebrews symbolizes an inflow coming from knowledge on the earthly plane, where the church's truth resides in the form of knowledge. *Of whom the name of one was Shiphrah and the name of the other was Puah* symbolizes the quality and state of the earthly level, where knowledge resides. *And he said, "In your midwifing to the Hebrews, when you look on the [birthing] stools,"* symbolizes a perception of truth and goodness flowing from the inner dimension into [the church's] knowledge. *If it is a son you shall kill him* means that if it was truth, they were to destroy it any way they could. *And if it is a daughter let her live* means that they were not to if it was goodness. *And the midwives feared God* means that truth in the form of knowledge was kept inviolate because it came from the Divine. *And did not do as the king of Egypt had spoken to them* means that what was intended by people devoted to falsity did not happen. *And kept the boys alive* means that truth was preserved because it was marked by goodness. *And the king of Egypt called the midwives* means that people subscribing to falsity plotted against people subscribing to truth in the form of knowledge on the earthly level. *And said to them, "On what account do you do this thing and keep the boys alive?"* symbolizes exasperation that truth had not been destroyed. *And the midwives said to Pharaoh* symbolizes a perception about this truth in the form of knowledge on the earthly plane. *Because the Hebrew women are not like the Egyptian women* means that the church's knowledge is unlike the knowledge that contradicts it. *Because they are full of life* means that it contains spiritual life. *Before the midwife comes to them they have given birth* means that the earthly plane is unaware until that truth comes to life. *And God dealt well with the midwives* means that the Divine blessed the earthly plane. *And the people multiplied and became very numerous* means that truth was constantly produced on that plane and therefore grew. *And it happened, because the midwives feared God* means because the Divine protected truth in the form of knowledge. *That he made households for them* means that it was arranged in a heavenly pattern.

And the king of Egypt said to the midwives of the Hebrews symbolizes an inflow coming from the separate types of knowledge on the earthly plane, where the church's truth resides in the form of knowledge. This can be seen from the symbolism of *saying* as an inflow (mentioned at §§5743, 6291), from that of the *king of Egypt* as separate types of knowledge opposed to the church's truth (mentioned at §6651), from that of *midwives* as the earthly plane (discussed at §§4588, 4921), and from that of *Hebrews* as attributes of the church (discussed at §§5136, 5236), including the church's truth in the form of knowledge. **6673**

The reason *midwives* mean the earthly plane is that the earthly level catches what flows in from the inner dimension and therefore acts as a kind of midwife.

Of whom the name of one was Shiphrah and the name of the other was Puah symbolizes the quality and state of the earthly level, where knowledge resides. This can be seen from the symbolism of a *name* as the quality of a thing (discussed in §§144, 145, 1896, 2009) and also as its state (§§1946, 2643, 3422, 4298). All names in the Word have a symbolic meaning that sums up everything involved in the topic under discussion and **6674** consequently its quality and state. The names Shiphrah and Puah here, then, symbolically summarize the quality and state of the earthly plane, where truth resides in the form of knowledge, because that is the focus of discussion, as is plain from the remarks directly above at §6673.

People who do not know that a name means the quality and state of the subject under discussion might believe that when a name is mentioned, it simply means a name. So when the Lord talks about his name, they might think it is only a name, when in reality it means the quality of worship. Specifically, it means all the faith and neighborly love with which the Lord is to be worshiped. [2] In Matthew, for example:

> Where two or three are *gathered in my name,* there I am in their midst. (Matthew 18:20)

This does not mean a name but worship rooted in faith and neighborly love. In John:

> As many as did accept him, to them he gave the power to be God's children, *to those believing in his name.* (John 1:12)

Again the name means the faith and neighborly love with which the Lord is worshiped. In the same author:

> These things have been written so that you can believe that Jesus is Christ, the Son of God, *so that as believers you can have life in his name.* (John 20:31)

Likewise. [3] In the same author:

> If you *ask anything in my name,* that I will do. (John 14:13, 14)

And in another place:

> *Whatever you ask the Father in my name,* he will give it to you. (John 15:16, 17; 16:23, 24)

This does not mean that they would ask the Father in the Lord's name but that they would ask the Lord himself. Divine goodness, which is the Father (§3704), is unapproachable except through the Lord's divine humanity, as the churches know. Making one's petition to the Lord himself is therefore in keeping with the faith and its truth. If we ask in accordance with that truth, what we ask is given. The Lord says the same thing in the previous quotation from John: "If you ask anything in my name, that I will do." As further evidence, consider that the Lord is Jehovah's name. Moses says this about it:

> I am sending an angel before you to guard you on the way. Be careful before him and listen to his voice and do not vex him, *because my name is within him.* (Exodus 23:20, 21)

[4] In John:

> "Father, *glorify your name.*" A voice went out from heaven: "I both have glorified it and will glorify it again." (John 12:28)

In the same author:

> *I have revealed your name* to the people whom you gave to me out of the world. *I made your name known to them,* and I will make it known, so that the love with which you loved me can exist in them, and I in them. (John 17:6, 26)

This shows that the Lord in his divine humanity is the name, or the whole nature, of Jehovah. Divine humanity is therefore the source of all divine worship and is what ought to be worshiped, because in worshiping divine humanity we worship divinity itself. Otherwise divinity itself is beyond the reach of thought, and if we cannot even think about it, we cannot be united with it.

[5] The following passages also make it clear that the Lord's name is all the faith and love with which we ought to worship him. In Matthew:

> You will be hated by everyone *because of my name.* (Matthew 10:22)

In the same author:

> Whoever welcomes one such little child *in my name* welcomes me. (Matthew 18:5)

In the same author:

> Everyone who leaves behind houses or brothers or sisters or father or mother or wife or children or fields *for my name* will receive a hundredfold. (Matthew 19:29)

In the same author:

> They shouted, "Hosanna to the Son of David! *A blessing on the one who comes in the Lord's name!*" (Matthew 21:9)

In Luke:

> Truly, I say to you that you will not see me till [the time] comes for you to say, "*A blessing on the one who comes in the Lord's name!*" (Luke 13:35)

In Mark:

> Any who give you a cup of water to drink *in my name* because you are Christ's—truly, I say to you, they will not lose their reward. (Mark 9:41)

In Luke:

> The seventy returned with joy, saying, "Lord, even the demons obey us *in your name!*" Jesus said to them, "Don't rejoice in this, that spirits obey you, but rejoice rather *that your names have been written in heaven.*" (Luke 10:17, 20)

[6] The names written in heaven are not names but the quality of these people's faith and their love for their neighbor. The same is true of the names written in the book of life in Revelation:

> *You have a few names* also in Sardis that have not defiled their clothes. Those who conquer will be dressed in white clothes, *and I will not delete their name from the book of life;* and I will *proclaim their name* before my Father and before his angels. (Revelation 3:4, 5)

Likewise in John:

> The one entering through the door is the shepherd of the sheep; *this one calls his own sheep by name.* (John 10:2, 3)

In Exodus:

> Jehovah to Moses: "*I know you by name.*" (Exodus 33:12, 17)

In John:

> *Many believed in his name,* seeing his signs that he performed. (John 2:23)

In the same author:

> Those who believe in him are not judged, but those who do not believe have already been judged, *because they have not believed in the name of the Only-Born of God.* (John 3:18)

In Isaiah:

> They will *fear Jehovah's name* from the west. (Isaiah 59:19)

In Micah:

> All peoples *walk in the name of their god,* and we will *walk in the name of Jehovah our God.* (Micah 4:5)

[7] In Moses:

> They were to *worship Jehovah God* in the place which he would choose and in which he would *put his name.* (Deuteronomy 12:5, 11, 14)

The same is true in Isaiah 18:7 and Jeremiah 7:12. Not to mention many other passages, such as Isaiah 26:8, 13; 41:25; 43:7; 49:1; 50:10; 52:5; 62:2; Jeremiah 23:27; 26:16; Ezekiel 20:14, 44; 36:21, 22, 23; Micah 5:4; Malachi 1:11; Deuteronomy 10:8; Revelation 2:17; 3:12; 13:8; 17:8; 14:11; 15:2; 19:12, 13, 16; 22:3, 4.

[8] The fact that Jehovah's name means every quality with which Jehovah is worshiped—in the highest sense, then, everything that comes from the Lord—can be seen from the benediction:

> Jehovah bless you and guard you; Jehovah light up his face over you and have mercy on you. Jehovah raise his face toward you and give you peace. *So will they put my name on the children of Israel.* (Numbers 6:23–27)

This discussion now shows what is meant by the following commandment in the Decalogue:

> *You shall not lift up the name of your God for an evil purpose,* because Jehovah will not hold innocent the person *who has lifted up his name for an evil purpose.* (Exodus 20:7)

It also shows what is meant by "*may your name be held sacred*" in the Lord's Prayer (Matthew 6:9).

And he said, "In your midwifing to the Hebrews, when you look on the 6675
[birthing] stools," symbolizes a perception of truth and goodness flowing from the inner dimension into the church's knowledge, as the following shows: *Midwifing* symbolizes the act of receiving goodness and truth that flow into the earthly level from the inner dimension, because a midwife stands for the earthly level in the role it plays as receiver of that inflow; see §§4588, 6673. The *Hebrews* symbolize attributes of the church, as discussed in §§5136, 5236. *Looking,* [or seeing,] symbolizes a perception, as noted in §§2150, 3764, 4567, 4723, 5400. And *stools* symbolize the entity on the earthly level that catches goodness and truth flowing from an inner level. So they symbolize truth in the form of knowledge, since this is what receives the inflow.

This shows that *in your midwifing to the Hebrews, when you look on the [birthing] stools,* symbolizes a perception of truth and goodness flowing from the inner dimension into the church's knowledge, which resides on the earthly level.

6676 *If it is a son you shall kill him* means that if it was truth, they were to destroy it any way they could. This can be seen from the symbolism of a *son* as truth (discussed in §§489, 491, 533, 1147, 2623, 3373) and from that of *killing* as destroying, since it applies to truth. They were to destroy it "any way they could," though, because the evil cannot actually destroy truth in the good.

6677 *If it is a daughter let her live* means that they were not to if it was goodness. This can be seen from the symbolism of a *daughter* as goodness (discussed in §§489, 490, 491, 2362) and from that of *living,* which means that it must not be destroyed.

The reason the king of Egypt said to kill a son but not a daughter is plain from the inner meaning, which is that they were to strive to destroy truth but not goodness. When hellish spirits persecute others, they are allowed to attack truth but not goodness because it is truth rather than goodness that is vulnerable. The Lord safeguards what is good. When hellish spirits try to assault goodness, they are thrown deep down into hell; they cannot hold their ground in the face of goodness, since in all goodness the Lord is present. That is why angels with their devotion to goodness exert so much power over hellish spirits that one of them can tame thousands of such spirits.

[2] Bear in mind that goodness contains life, because goodness has to do with love, and love is human life. Evil is marked by love for oneself and one's material advantages and seems good to people who live for that kind of love. If evil attacks the goodness that goes with a heavenly kind of love, then, life on one side is pitted against life on the other. The Divine is the source of the life that grows out of the goodness connected with heavenly love, so if this type of life clashes with the type that grows out of self-love and materialism, the latter type of life starts to be extinguished because it suffocates. The people in whom it exists accordingly suffer as if they were in the throes of death, so they hurl themselves into hell, where they regain their life. See §§3938, 4225, 4226, 5057, 5058.

That is another reason evil demons and spirits cannot assault goodness and therefore do not dare destroy it. The situation with truth is different. It has no life in itself but only receives life from goodness, or rather from the Lord through goodness.

And the midwives feared God means that truth in the form of knowledge was kept inviolate because it came from the Divine, as the following shows: *Fearing God* means keeping the commandments of the Divine, because that is what people who fear God do. All holy fear (and therefore obedience and the keeping of the commandments) comes from the Divine, though; none of it comes from us. *They feared God,* then, means that it was kept inviolate by the Divine. And *midwives* symbolize the earthly plane, where truth in the form of knowledge resides, as discussed in §§4588, 6673, 6675. 6678

And did not do as the king of Egypt had spoken to them means that what was intended by people devoted to falsity did not happen, as the following shows: *Not doing as he had spoken* means that what they intended did not happen. That is, they could not destroy the truth symbolized by the sons, although they had intended to destroy it every way they possibly could (§6676). And the *king of Egypt* symbolizes knowledge separated from and opposed to the church's truth, as dealt with at §6651. He therefore symbolizes falsity, because such knowledge is false. 6679

And kept the boys alive means that truth was preserved because it was marked by goodness. This is established by the symbolism of *keeping alive* as preserving and from that of sons, here called *boys,* as truth (mentioned above at §6676). 6680

The sons are called boys here because children symbolize innocent goodness (§§430, 2782, 5236). Here, then, they symbolize truth marked by goodness.

And the king of Egypt called the midwives means that people subscribing to falsity plotted against people subscribing to truth in the form of knowledge on the earthly level, as the following shows: In this case, *calling* means plotting, because the reason for calling the midwives was to destroy truth. However, the plot was undone because the Divine was keeping truth inviolate, as symbolized by the midwives' fear of God (§6678). In the other life, the evil who trouble the good really do plot together, as I have been granted to learn from experience. The *king of Egypt* symbolizes people who subscribe to falsity, as noted just above at §6679. And *midwives* symbolize the earthly plane, where truth in the form of knowledge resides, as discussed in §§4588, 6673, 6675, 6678. 6681

From this it is evident that *the king of Egypt called the midwives* means that people subscribing to falsity plotted against people subscribing to truth in the form of knowledge on the earthly level.

6682 *And said to them, "On what account do you do this thing and keep the boys alive?"* symbolizes exasperation that truth had not been destroyed. This can be seen from the symbolism of *on what account do you do this thing* as words of reproach and therefore of exasperation. And *keeping alive* means not destroying, as above at §§6677, 6680. And *boys* symbolize truth marked by goodness, as discussed at §6680.

6683 *And the midwives said to Pharaoh* symbolizes a perception about this truth in the form of knowledge on the earthly plane. This can be seen from the symbolism of *saying* in the Word's narrative parts as a perception (discussed many times), from that of *midwives* as truth in the form of knowledge on the earthly plane (mentioned just above at §6681), and from the representation of *Pharaoh* as false knowledge in general (also mentioned above, at §§6679, 6681).

6684 *Because the Hebrew women are not like the Egyptian women* means that the church's knowledge is unlike the knowledge that contradicts it, as the following shows: *Hebrew women* symbolize attributes of the church, as discussed in §§5136, 5236, 6673, 6675. And *Egyptian women* symbolize whatever knowledge opposes these attributes of the church, as is plain from what precedes and from the symbolism of Egypt as knowledge (§6638). Here Egypt symbolizes types of knowledge that contradict the church's truth in the form of knowledge. For the meaning of *women* as attributes of the church, see §§252, 253.

6685 *Because they are full of life* means that it contains spiritual life. This can be seen from the symbolism of *having life* as spiritual life, which is dealt with at §5890. Here it symbolizes spiritual life in the attributes of the church symbolized by the Hebrew women.

I have defined spiritual life a number of times before, but since few today know what the spiritual dimension is, let me explain a little further. Spirituality in its first origin is divine truth issuing from the Lord's divine humanity. This truth contains divine goodness, because divine truth comes from the Lord's divine humanity, which consists in divine goodness. This divine truth, containing divine goodness, is the actual spiritual dimension at its point of origin. It is also the actual life that fills heaven and even fills the universe. Where a recipient form exists, there it flows in. It varies in its recipients, though, depending on their form. In recipients compatible with goodness, it creates spiritual life. In recipients incompatible with goodness, it will create an energy opposed to spiritual life, which the Word calls death.

This then demonstrates what spiritual life is. It is a commitment to truth-from-goodness, which originates in the Lord.

Before the midwife comes to them they have given birth means that the earthly plane is unaware until that truth—the church's truth in the form of knowledge—comes to life. This is evident from the symbolism of a *midwife* as the earthly plane, where the church's truth in the form of knowledge resides (noted above at §6681), and from that of *giving birth* as a process involving faith and neighborly love (discussed in §§3860, 3868, 3905, 3915) and therefore involving spiritual life. The fact that the earthly plane *is unaware* is symbolized by *before the midwife comes to them.* 6686

How is it that the earthly plane is unaware until truth in the form of knowledge comes to life? All the life in truth that takes the form of knowledge on the earthly plane comes from an inflow of goodness that arrives by way of the inner plane. When goodness flows in, the earthly dimension is completely unaware of it, because that dimension is comparatively in the dark. It is in the dark because it is awash in worldly light and therefore in worldly concerns as well. When the light of heaven falls on what is worldly, it generates a dim awareness. Another reason for dimness on the earthly level is that the components of that level are generalized, and generalizations are not perceptive of detail. The more general something is, the less detail it perceives and consequently the less it perceives what is happening to itself. Besides, the earthly plane does not hold actual goodness and truth but representations of them. This explains, then, why the earthly dimension is unaware when truth in the form of knowledge comes to life. As a result, when being reborn it has no idea that this is happening or how. As the Lord says in John: "The spirit blows where it wishes, and you hear its voice but do not know where it is coming from and where it is going. This is the way with everyone who is reborn from the spirit" (John 3:8).

The earthly plane means the outer self, which is also called the earthly self.

And God dealt well with the midwives means that the Divine blessed the earthly plane. This can be seen from the symbolism of *dealing well with,* when said of God, as blessing, and from that of *midwives* as the earthly plane, where truth in the form of knowledge resides (treated of above at §§4588, 6673, 6675, 6678). 6687

And the people multiplied and became very numerous means that truth on that plane was constantly produced and therefore grew. This can be seen from the discussion above at §6648, where similar words occur. For the association of a *people* with truth, see §§1259, 1260, 3295, 3581. 6688

6689 *And it happened, because the midwives feared God* means because the Divine protected truth in the form of knowledge. This can be seen from the discussion above at §6678, where similar words occur.

6690 *That he made households for them* means that truth in the form of knowledge on the earthly level was arranged in a heavenly pattern. This can be seen from the symbolism of a *household* as the earthly mind, which is discussed in §§4973, 5023, and therefore as the contents of that mind. In this case, since it is talking about midwives, the contents are truth in the form of knowledge on the earthly level (§6687). *Making households for them,* then, means arranging that truth in order, and it is arranged in order when it is arranged in a heavenly pattern.

It is not easy to see that this is the symbolism of making households for them unless one knows how matters stand with truth in the form of knowledge in the earthly mind, so I should explain briefly. Items of knowledge on the earthly plane are arranged in endless series. All the series connect seamlessly, one after the other, depending on the relationships they share and their nearness to each other. The situation is not too different from that of families and their succeeding generations: one element gives birth to another, and soon their numbers are increasing. That is why the ancients referred to the contents of the mind—that is, to goodness and truth—as a household. They called the dominant form of goodness there the father, and the truth attached to it, the mother. What developed out of these they named sons, daughters, sons-in-law, daughters-in-law, and so on.

However, the way truth in the form of knowledge is organized on the earthly level varies with every individual, because it has a pattern imposed on it by whatever we love the most. This dominant love stands at the center and arranges everything else around it, placing next to itself what conforms best with it, and the rest in order of compatibility. That is how items of knowledge come to take the pattern they do.

If a heavenly love is dominant, the Lord arranges everything on the earthly level in a heavenly pattern, which is the type of pattern heaven takes and is therefore the pattern of love and goodness itself. Truth is arranged in the same pattern, and when it has been arranged that way it acts in unison with goodness. From then on, when the Lord stimulates the one, he stimulates the other; when he stirs up our conceptions of faith, he stirs our feelings of neighborly love, and the reverse.

This is the patterning symbolized by *God made households for the midwives.*

Exodus 1:22. *And Pharaoh commanded all his people, saying, "Every son that is born you shall cast into the river, and every daughter you shall keep alive."* 6691

And Pharaoh commanded all his people symbolizes a general inflow into items of knowledge contrary to the church's truth. *Saying, "Every son that is born you shall cast into the river,"* means that they would take all the truth that appears and immerse it in falsity. *And every daughter you shall keep alive* means that they would not assault goodness.

And Pharaoh commanded all [his] people symbolizes a general inflow into items of knowledge contrary to the church's truth, as the following shows: *Commanding* symbolizes an inflow, as discussed in §§5486, 5732. Here it symbolizes a general inflow because it comes from *Pharaoh,* who represents knowledge in general (§6015). And *his people* symbolize items of knowledge contrary to the church's truth. The meaning of Egyptians (the people meant here) as items of knowledge has been demonstrated many times; see §6638. 6692

The reason Egyptians symbolize items of knowledge contrary to the church's truth is that Egyptians turned the representation and symbolism used in the ancient church (and the ancient church had indeed existed among them) into magic. In those days the church's representative and symbolic practices were a means of communicating with heaven. People who lived lives of neighborly kindness took part in such communication, and for many of them the communication was open. On the other hand, people who did not live lives of neighborly kindness but just the opposite were sometimes granted open communication with evil spirits, who corrupted all the church's truth and used it to destroy what was good. That was the origin of magic. This can be seen from Egyptian hieroglyphics, which the Egyptians applied to sacred purposes, using them to symbolize spiritual qualities and to pervert the divine design.

[2] Magic is actually a perversion of order, and above all, a misuse of correspondence. The proper pattern is for us to accept goodness and truth as they issue from the Lord. When we do, everything we intend and think is orderly. Suppose, though, that we do not accept goodness and truth according to the code set by the Lord; suppose we believe instead that everything is a blind ebb and flow and that if anything intentional happens, it is the result of our own prudence. In that case we pervert the proper order. We take what has been ordained and we appropriate it to ourselves, seeking only our own welfare, not our neighbor's, unless our neighbor curries our favor. Surprisingly, then, all who have firmly stamped

on their mind the idea that everything is due to their own prudence, and nothing to divine providence, are strongly drawn to magic in the other world and absorb all they can of it. This is especially true of self-reliant people who have credited everything to their own prudence and have therefore dreamed up many tricks and stratagems for getting ahead of others. After they have been judged in the other world, they are propelled toward the hells of magic-workers. These hells lie on a plane below the feet, to the right and slightly out in front, stretching a great distance, and their greatest depths are the home of the Egyptians.

This then is why Pharaoh, the Egyptians, and Egypt symbolize knowledge contrary to the church's truth.

[3] The Israelite people was chosen, then, to stop the representation and symbolism used in the church from being turned into magic anymore. Among them the church's representative and symbolic practices could be restored. By nature they were incapable of making magic out of those practices, because they were intent only on what is external and did not believe in anything internal, let alone anything spiritual. The kind of magic that existed among the Egyptians cannot exist among people like this.

6693 *Saying, "Every son that is born you shall cast into the river,"* means that they would take all the truth that appears and immerse it in falsity. This is established by the symbolism of a *son* as truth (discussed in §§489, 491, 533, 1147, 2623, 3373) and by that of a *river* as facets of understanding (discussed in §§108, 109, 2702, 3051). Here, in a negative sense, the river means the opposite, or falsity. *Casting in,* obviously, means immersing.

[2] The meaning of Egypt's river as the opposite of understanding and therefore as falsity is also plain in Isaiah:

> The *rivers* will recede; the *streams of Egypt* will shrink and *drain away.* Papyrus plants *by the river, by the mouth of the river,* and any *seed of the river, will dry up,* will be buffeted. And therefore the fishers will mourn, and all who cast a hook *into the river* will grieve, and those spreading a net *on the face of the water* will languish. (Isaiah 19:6, 7, 8)

The river of Egypt here does not mean a river, nor do the fishers mean fishers. They mean something else instead, and this something is invisible to one who does not know the meaning of Egypt, its river, and the fishers. To one who does know these meanings, the sense is plain. Every word of the passage shows that Egypt's river symbolizes falsity. [3] In Jeremiah:

> Who is this who rises *like a river,* whose *waters churn like rivers?* Egypt rises *like a river,* and *like rivers its waters churn,* for it has said, "I will go

> up; I will blanket the land; I will destroy the city and those living in it." (Jeremiah 46:7, 8)

Again Egypt's river stands for falsity. Going up and blanketing the land stands for doing so to the church. Destroying the city stands for destroying the church's theology, and destroying those living in it stands for destroying the goodness that comes from it. For the meaning of the land as the church, see §6649. For that of a city as the church's theology, §§402, 2449, 3216, 4492, 4493. For that of its residents as the goodness there, §§2268, 2451, 2712. [4] In Ezekiel:

> Here, now, I am against you, Pharaoh, king of Egypt, you great whale, *who lies in the middle of his rivers,* who has said, "*The river is mine,* and I have made myself." Therefore I will put hooks into your jaws and make the *fish of your rivers* stick to your scales and bring you up *out of the middle of your rivers,* and every *fish of your rivers* will stick to your scales. I will leave you *and every fish of your rivers* in the wilderness. (Ezekiel 29:3, 4, 5, 9, 10)

Here too no one can know the meaning without the inner sense. Clearly it does not mean Egypt. So one needs to know what Pharaoh, the river, the whale, the fish, and the scales are. Pharaoh is the earthly plane, where knowledge resides (see §§5160, 5799, 6015). Whales are general categories of knowledge on the earthly plane (§42). Fish are items of knowledge within a general category (§§40, 991). Scales are what is wholly superficial and are therefore sense impressions, to which items of knowledge that are false cling. When these meanings are known, it becomes clear that the river of Egypt means falsity. [5] In the same author:

> On the day when Pharaoh goes down into hell, I will cause him to mourn; I will make the abyss cover him and *hold back its rivers,* and great waters will be shut in. (Ezekiel 31:15)

In Amos:

> On this account will not the earth shake and everyone living in it mourn? So that all [the land] rises like the torrent and is spewed out and sinks *as if in the river of Egypt.* In that day I will make the sun set at noon and overshadow the earth on a day of light. (Amos 8:8, 9; 9:5)

The earth that will shake stands for the church (§6649). Sinking as if in the river of Egypt stands for perishing in falsity. Since falsity is being symbolized, the passage says that the sun will set at noon and the earth will be overshadowed on a day of light. The sun's setting at noon means that heavenly love and its goodness will withdraw, and the earth's being overshadowed on a day of light means that falsity will take over the church. (For the meaning of the sun as heavenly love and its goodness, see §§1529, 1530, 2441, 2495, 3636, 3643, 4060, 4696. For that of shadow, [or darkness,] as falsity, §§1839, 1860, 4418, 4531. And for that of the earth as the church, §§82, 662, 1066, 1068, 1262, 1411, 1413, 1607, 1733, 1850, 2117, 2118 at the end, 2928, 3355, 4447, 4535, 5577.) Anyone can see that something other is meant here than what appears in the literal text—that the earth will shake and everyone living in it will mourn, that the sun will set at noon and the earth be overshadowed on a day of light. Unless the earth means the church, the river means falsity, and the sun means heavenly love, there is no intelligible meaning to be found there.

[6] Because the river of Egypt symbolizes falsity, Moses was ordered to strike with his staff *on the waters of that river,* which turned them to blood, and every fish *in the river* died, and the *river* stank (Exodus 7:17, 18, 20, 21). For the same reason, he was also ordered to have Aaron stretch his hand with the staff *over the streams, over the rivers,* and *over the pools,* and frogs came up from there over the land of Egypt (Exodus 8:5, 6). For the negative symbolism of water as falsity, see §790. Since water goes in a river, a river in that case means general falsity.

6694 *And every daughter you shall keep alive* means that they would not assault goodness, as shown by the discussion above at §6677, where similar words occur.

Inhabitants of Other Planets

6695 BY the Lord's divine mercy the inner levels of my spirit have opened up to me, which has enabled me to talk with the inhabitants of the other world, and not only those from this planet but also those from other planets. As a result, because it was my desire to learn about this, and because what I learned is worth mentioning, let me tell about it at the end of the chapters that follow.

I did not speak with actual inhabitants of the planets but with spirits and angels who had once been inhabitants there. I spoke with them not for a day or a week but for many months and was taught openly from heaven where it was that they came from.

The fact that there are many other inhabited planets and that spirits and angels come from them is perfectly familiar in the other life, because anyone who wants to talk with those spirits and angels is given the opportunity.

There are spirits in the universal human who relate to the memory, 6696
and they are from Mercury. They are allowed to wander around picking up information about what is in the universe and even to pass outside our own solar system into others. They have said that there are planets with people on them not only in this solar system but also out in the universe, in immense numbers.

I have discussed this subject with spirits a number of times. People 6697
with a good intellect, I have said, can tell from many clues that there are other planets with people living on them. Reason can lead them to conclude that such large bodies as the planets—some of them bigger than ours—are not empty masses, created just to parade around the Sun and shine for one earth. They ought to have a nobler function than that.

The human race is the breeding ground for heaven, and if you believe (as everyone should) that the sole purpose for which the Divine created the universe was the emergence of a human race, and from it, heaven, you must believe there are people wherever there is a planet.

[2] The planets that are visible to our eyes because they are within the limits of our solar system are obviously inhabited. After all, they are bodies made of earthly stuff, since they reflect [rather than generate] sunlight. They circle the Sun just as our own planet does and consequently create years for themselves, and the seasons of spring, summer, fall, and winter (with differences, depending on climate). They also rotate on their axes as our planet does and consequently create days for themselves, and the times of day: morning, afternoon, evening, and night. Some of them have moons, which are called satellites and which travel their regular orbits just as our moon travels its. And since Saturn is farthest from the Sun, it has in addition a big lunar ring that sheds a great deal of light on its planet, even if the light is reflected. Can anyone who knows all this and thinks rationally possibly say they are empty bodies?

In my conversations with spirits I have also given another reason for 6698
believing there is more than one inhabited planet in the universe. The visible universe, alight with countless numbers of stars, is huge, yet it is merely a means to the ultimate purpose of creation: a heavenly kingdom

in which the Divine can dwell. The visible universe exists to bring planets into being, with people on them, from whom a heavenly kingdom can arise. Who can presume to think that so immense a means was created for so tiny and narrow a purpose as to populate a single planet and produce heaven from that one planet alone? How fitting would that be for the Divine, who is infinite and for whom thousands or even millions of planets, all full of inhabitants, would be so little a thing as to be almost nothing?

What is more, heaven with its angels is so vast that it corresponds to everything in us, and many thousands [of angels] correspond to each of our limbs, organs, and viscera. I was allowed to see that heaven with all its correspondences could not exist if it were not made up of the inhabitants of many, many planets.

6699 A number of times I have seen a kind of large, steady river off to the right and fairly far away, at foot level, and angels have told me this is the route by which people come from the worlds. They look like a river because of their large numbers, the angels have said. By the volume and speed of the river I was able to determine that tens of thousands of people arrive every day. This too told me there were lots of inhabited planets.

6700 Regarding worship of God by inhabitants of other planets: The people there are not idolaters; they all acknowledge the Lord as the only God. Of course none but a very few of them know that the Lord took on a human nature on this planet and made it divine. Still, they venerate the Divine not as a divinity that is totally unknowable but as one that can be known through its human form. This is because when the Divine appears to them it appears in human form, as it also appeared long ago to Abraham and others on this planet. Since they worship the Divine in a human form, then, they worship the Lord.

They also realize that no one can be united with the Divine in faith and love unless the Divine has a form they can comprehend under some mental image. If it did not have a form, their idea of it would dissolve, like a line of sight vanishing into the universe.

Told by spirits from our planet that the Lord took on a human form here, they pondered a bit, then said this had been done for the salvation of the human race. They also said that with utmost reverence they worship the Divine that shines as the sun in heaven, which appears in human form when it presents itself to view. The Lord appears as the sun in the other life and radiates all the light in heaven; see §§1053, 1521, 1529, 1530, 1531, 3636, 3643, 4060, 4321 at the end, 5097.

I will give more details on this later, though [§§7173, 9594, 10809].

The spirits and angels from other planets are all separate from each 6701
other, divided up by planet; they do not appear together in one place. The reason is that the inhabitants of one planet have an entirely different character from the inhabitants of another. They do not associate with each other in the heavens, except in the third and inmost one. Spirits who go there gather from every planet and unite very closely to form that heaven.

Spirits from Mercury will be discussed at the end of the next chapter 6702
[§§6807–6817].

Exodus 2

Teachings on Neighborly Love

6703 HAVING established a plan [§6627] to convey teachings about neighborly love before the Exodus chapters, I should start by defining the neighbor toward whom we are to practice that love. Those who do not know which people are their neighbor are liable to exercise charity indiscriminately, in the same way toward the evil as toward the good. Charity then ceases to be charity, because the evil use the kindnesses done to them to hurt their neighbor, but the good use them to help.

6704 The general opinion today is that every human being is equally our neighbor and that we ought to help everyone who needs it. Christian prudence, though, requires that we closely examine a person's way of life and exercise neighborly love accordingly. When people on an inner level of the church do so, they make distinctions and therefore use intelligence. People on an outer level of the church are not very good at sorting things out, so they fail to make such distinctions.

6705 The ancients divided the neighbor into categories and named the categories after those people in the world who seem more in need of aid than others. They also taught each other how to exercise neighborly love to the members of one category and to the members of another. That is how they organized the teachings and brought their lives in line with the teachings. This meant that the teachings of their religion contained rules on how to live. The teachings also showed them the character of this or that other person in the church, whom they called sister or brother—though with differences in the inner meaning. The differences depended on the way people exercised neighborly love, either under the inspiration of the church's genuine teachings, or else under teachings they themselves had altered. (We all want to look blameless and defend the way we live, so we turn theological rules to our favor either by the way we interpret them or by changing them.)

In order to know what kind of charity [to exercise], people in the church definitely need to know about the differences in types of neighbor. These differences depend on the individual kind of goodness in each neighbor. Furthermore, since everything good comes from the Lord, the Lord in the highest sense and in a surpassing degree is the ultimate neighbor, the origin of what it means to be a neighbor. From this it follows that the more of the Lord each person has in him- or herself, the more he or she is our neighbor. In addition, since no one receives the Lord the same way—that is, receives the goodness that radiates from him the same way—no one is our neighbor in the same way as another either. Absolutely everyone in the heavens and on earth has a different sort of goodness. One and the same kind of goodness can never exist in two people; it has to vary in order for each kind to remain in existence separately. 6706

However, no one, not even an angel, can know all these variations and therefore all the differences in types of neighbor, as determined by acceptance of the Lord—in other words, acceptance of the goodness radiating from him. We can know only in general, which means that we can know only the overall categories and several subcategories. Besides, the Lord asks no more of people in the church than for them to live by what they know.

This discussion now clarifies that the kind of Christian goodness a person has determines how far that person is a neighbor. The Lord is present in goodness because goodness is his, and the extent of his presence depends on the quality of the goodness. Moreover, since the origin of the neighbor is to be traced to the Lord, distinctions among different kinds of neighbor depend on the Lord's presence within goodness and therefore on the quality of the goodness. 6707

The fact that we are a neighbor according to the quality of our goodness is evident from the Lord's parable about the man who fell among robbers (Luke 10:29–37). Though he was half dead, a priest passed him by, as did a Levite; but a Samaritan bandaged his wounds, poured on oil and wine, then lifted the man onto his (the Samaritan's) own beast of burden, brought him to an inn, and took care of him. The Samaritan is the one called neighbor, because he exercised neighborly kindness. This shows that a neighbor means people with goodness. It is true that people with evil are our neighbor, but in an entirely different respect, and that being so, they are to be helped in quite another way. But this 6708 needs to be discussed later, with the Lord's divine mercy [§§8120, 8121, 8223].

6709 Since it is the nature of goodness that determines in what way an individual is our neighbor, it is love that does so. No goodness can exist that does not belong to love. Love is the source of all goodness and therefore of the quality of a given kind of goodness.

6710 The fact that love is what makes a person a neighbor and that the quality of the love determines what kind of neighbor a person is can be plainly seen from people who love themselves. The individuals they acknowledge as their neighbor are those who love them the most. That is, so far as another belongs to them and is therefore subsumed by them, they hug and kiss that other, help that other, and call that other family. In fact, because they are evil they even call that other their neighbor to a greater degree than all others. Anyone else they regard as a neighbor only so far as the person loves them. So how they define their neighbor depends on the type and amount of love they have. People like this see the neighbor in relation to themselves, because the type of love one has determines who is considered one's neighbor.

6711 On the other hand, people who do not love themselves more than others (and this is true of everyone in the Lord's kingdom) will trace the origin of the neighbor to the one they ought to love above all: the Lord. They will consider everyone their neighbor according to the nature of that other's love for the Lord.

People who love others as they love themselves, then—and especially people who love others more than themselves, as angels do—all view the Lord as the origin of the neighbor. They see it this way because the Lord himself is present in what is good, since goodness issues from him.

This too shows that the nature of the love determines who is one's neighbor.

In Matthew (25:34–40) the Lord himself teaches that he is present in what is good. After all, addressing people governed by goodness, he says that they gave him something to eat, gave him a drink, gathered him in, dressed him, visited him, and came to him in prison. Then he says that so far as they did it for one of his least consequential brothers and sisters, they did it for him.

6712 This discussion now shows where religious people ought to look to determine how much someone is their neighbor; that the closer another is to the Lord, the more that person is our neighbor; and that since the

Lord is present in charitable goodness, others are our neighbor according to the quality of their goodness and consequently according to the quality of their neighborly love.

Exodus 2

1. And a man from the house of Levi went and took a daughter of Levi.

2. And the woman conceived and bore a son and saw him, that he was good, and hid him three months.

3. And she could no longer hide him, and she took herself a wicker chest and tarred it with tar and pitch and put the child in it and put [him] in the seaweed on the bank of the river.

4. And his sister stood far off to know what would happen to him.

5. And Pharaoh's daughter went down to wash at the river. And her girls were going to the riverside, and she saw the chest in the middle of the seaweed and sent her slave and took it.

6. And she opened it and saw him, the child, and here, the boy was crying, and she took pity on him and said, "This one is from the children of the Hebrews."

7. And his sister said to Pharaoh's daughter, "Shall I go and call a wet nurse from the Hebrews for you, and she will nurse the child for you?"

8. And Pharaoh's daughter said to her, "Go," and the girl went and called the child's mother.

9. And Pharaoh's daughter said to her, "Take along this child and nurse him for me, and I myself will give you your wage," and the woman took the child and nursed him.

10. And the child grew, and she brought him to Pharaoh's daughter, and he was like a son to her, and she called his name Moses and said, "Because from the waters I drew him."

11. And it happened in those days that Moses grew and went out to his brothers and saw their burdens, and he saw an Egyptian man striking a Hebrew man, one of his brothers.

12. And he looked out here and there and saw that there was no man, and he struck the Egyptian and hid him in the sand.

13. And he went out the second day, and look: two Hebrew men feuding, and he said to the one in the wrong, "Why do you strike your companion?"

14. And he said, "Who set you as chief man and judge over us? Are you talking about killing me as you killed the Egyptian?" And Moses was afraid and said, "Surely the matter is known!"

15. And Pharaoh heard of this matter and sought to kill Moses. And Moses fled from Pharaoh's presence and settled in the land of Midian and settled by a well.

16. And a priest of Midian had seven daughters, and they came and drew water and filled the channels to water their father's flock.

17. And the shepherds came and drove them off. And Moses got up and helped them. And he watered their flock.

18. And they came to Reuel their father. And he said, "Why are you hurrying to come [home] today?"

19. And they said, "An Egyptian man rescued us from the hand of the shepherds and even went so far as to draw water for us and watered the flock."

20. And he said to his daughters, "And where is he? Why did you leave the man behind like this? Call him and have him eat bread."

21. And Moses was willing to reside with the man, and he gave Zipporah, his daughter, to Moses.

22. And she bore a son, and he called his name Gershom, because he said, "I was an immigrant in a foreign land."

23. And it happened during those many days that the king of Egypt died. And the children of Israel sighed over their servitude and cried out, and their cry over their servitude rose to God.

24. And God heard their groan, and God remembered his pact with Abraham, with Isaac, and with Jacob.

25. And God saw the children of Israel, and God knew.

Summary

6713 THE inner meaning of this chapter has to do with divine truth and with its rudiments and developing states in a person of the church.

6714 In its highest sense it tells about the Lord and the way his human side became divine law. Moses represents the Lord as the divine law, that is, as the Word. In a secondary sense he represents divine truth in a person of the church.

Inner Meaning

EXODUS 2:1, 2, 3, 4. *And a man from the house of Levi went and took a daughter of Levi. And the woman conceived and bore a son and saw him, that he was good, and hid him three months. And she could no longer hide him, and she took herself a wicker chest and tarred it with tar and pitch and put the child in it and put [him] in the seaweed on the bank of the river. And his sister stood far off to know what would happen to him.* 6715

A man from the house of Levi went symbolizes truth's origin in goodness. *And took a daughter of Levi* symbolizes its union with goodness. *And the woman conceived* symbolizes a first appearance. *And bore a son* symbolizes divine law in its origin. *She saw him, that he was good,* symbolizes a perception that it came through heaven. *And hid him three months* symbolizes the whole of the period during which it was not visible. *And she could no longer hide him* symbolizes the point at which it had to become visible. *And she took herself a wicker chest* symbolizes its setting, which was lowly but was at least based on truth. *And tarred it with tar and pitch* symbolizes goodness mixed with evil and falsity. *And put the child in it* means that deep within lay divine law in its origin. *And put him in the seaweed on the bank of the river* means that at first it lay among false information. *And his sister stood far off to know what would happen to him* symbolizes religious truth distant from that information, and attentiveness.

A man from the house of Levi went symbolizes truth's origin in goodness. This is established by the symbolism of a *man* as truth (discussed at §3134), by that of being *from the house of* as its origin, and by the representation of *Levi* as goodness. In the highest sense Levi represents divine love (discussed at §3875), and in an inward sense spiritual love (§§3875, 4497, 4502, 4503). As he represents love, he represents goodness, because all goodness has to do with love. 6716

Regarding the origin of truth in goodness, as symbolized here by a man from the house of Levi: Be aware that in the highest sense the verses that follow treat of the Lord and the way his human side became the divine law, or truth itself.

People know that the Lord was born like any other person, that he learned to talk as a child like any other child, and that he then grew in knowledge, understanding, and wisdom. This shows that his human side was not divine from birth but that he made it divine by his own power.

[2] He did it by his own power because he was conceived from Jehovah, and the inmost core of his life was therefore Jehovah himself. The inmost core of anyone's life, called the soul, comes from the father. The layer that clothes the core, called the body, comes from the mother. The core of life from the father constantly flows in and affects the outer covering from the mother, working even in the womb to bring that covering into resemblance with itself. This can be seen from the fact that children are born with their father's character, and that grandchildren and great-grandchildren are sometimes born with the character of their grandfather and great-grandfather. The reason this happens is that the soul from the father always tries to make the covering from the mother into a likeness and image of itself.

[3] This being the case with us, it stands to reason that it was especially the case with the Lord. His inmost core was divinity itself because it was Jehovah himself, as he was Jehovah's only-born Son. Since his inmost core was divinity itself, would it not have more ability than the core of any mere human to turn the outer covering from the mother into its image? That is, to bring the outer covering into resemblance with itself? And therefore to make his human side, which was on the outside and came from his mother, divine? Moreover, he must have done this by his own power, because the divinity at his core, from which he actuated his human part, was his, just as our soul, at our core, is ours.

While the Lord was in the world, developing according to the divine plan, he turned his human side into divine truth. Later, after he had been fully glorified, he turned it into divine goodness and in this way made it one with Jehovah.

[4] The current chapter in its highest sense depicts the way the Lord did this. However, because the contents of the highest meaning, which are all about the Lord, lie beyond human understanding, let me switch now to explaining what the chapter contains in its inward sense. This level has to do with the rudiments and developing states of divine truth in people of the church, or in people who are being reborn (§§6713, 6714). That is what the inner meaning contains because human rebirth is an image of

the glorification of the Lord's human nature; see §§3138, 3212, 3296, 3490, 4402, 5688.

And took a daughter of Levi symbolizes its union with goodness. This can be seen from the symbolism of *taking someone's daughter* (in marriage) as union and from the representation of *Levi* as goodness (mentioned just above at §6716). 6717

I should explain how to understand the idea that truth originating in goodness united with goodness.

The truth the Lord instills in us when we are being reborn has its origin in goodness. At first the goodness does not make itself visible because it lives in our inner self, but the truth does make itself visible because it lives in our outer self. Since the inner plane acts on the outer, rather than the reverse (§6322), it is goodness that acts on truth and makes truth its own. Nothing acknowledges and accepts truth but goodness. You can see this from the desire for truth that people have when they are being reborn. Their desire itself comes from goodness; because it belongs to love, it cannot come from anywhere else.

However, this truth, accepted at this first stage, before rebirth, is not genuine truth-from-goodness but rather theological truth. At that stage we do not spend time figuring out whether it is true but rather acknowledge it because our religion teaches it. As long as we are not pondering whether it is true and acknowledging it on that account, it is not ours and is therefore not credited to us. This stage is the first stage for a person being reborn.

[2] Once we have been reborn, though, goodness reveals itself, mainly in the fact that we love to live by the truth that we acknowledge for ourselves to be true. At that point, since we intend and act on the truth we acknowledge, it is given to us as our own. After all, it no longer lives only in our intellect, as it had, but also in our will; and what we have in our will is assigned to us for our own. Our intellect now becomes one with our will, since our intellect acknowledges and our will acts; so these two, goodness and truth, unite.

When they have been united, the union, like a marriage, constantly gives birth to offspring, which are true ideas and good desires, along with their blessings and pleasures.

These two stages are what is meant by truth's origin in goodness and by their union.

[3] Nonetheless, the truth uniting with goodness symbolized here by "a man from the house of Levi went and took a daughter of Levi" is not

the kind we accept at the first stage, which is the theological truth taught by the religion we were born into. Instead it is real truth, because in the highest sense the passage is about the Lord and the way his human side became the divine law. The truth embedded in this law is what is meant.

Its source is goodness because the Lord's divinity, which was his core and the essence of his life, brought this truth out into the open in his humanity, which united it with goodness, since divinity is nothing but goodness.

6718 *And the woman conceived* symbolizes a first appearance—the first appearance of divine law in the Lord's human part. This can be seen from the symbolism of *conceiving* as a first appearance. The *woman* here has the same symbolism as the daughter of Levi taken by a man from the house of Levi, just above: truth united with goodness.

6719 *And bore a son* symbolizes divine law in its origin, as the following shows: *Bearing* symbolizes emerging (discussed in §§2621, 2629) and therefore an origin. And a *son* symbolizes truth (discussed in §§489, 491, 533, 1147, 2623, 3373), and in this case divine law, because by this son is meant Moses. What follows will demonstrate that Moses represented the Lord as divine law, or as the Word.

6720 *She saw him, that he was good,* symbolizes a perception that it came through heaven, as the following shows: *Seeing* symbolizes a perception, as mentioned in §§2150, 3764, 4567, 4723, 5400. And in this case, since *good* applies to divine law in the Lord, it means through heaven.

The idea that "good" here means "through heaven" is a secret that cannot be known unless it is revealed. When the Lord made his human side divine, he did so from his divine side by means of its passage through heaven. Heaven did not contribute anything of its own, but divinity itself flowed through heaven in order to flow into the Lord's humanity. What passed through was divine humanity as it existed before the Lord's Coming; it was Jehovah himself in the heavens, or the Lord. The divinity that passed through heaven was divine truth, or divine law, which Moses represented, and the divinity that now passes through heaven is goodness. This shows why *she saw him* (her son), *that he was good,* symbolizes a perception that it came through heaven.

6721 *And hid him three months* symbolizes the whole of the period during which it was not visible. This can be seen from the symbolism of being *hidden* as not being visible and from that of *three months* as a whole period and whole state. For the meaning of *three* as completion, or a whole time span from beginning to end, see §§2788, 4495; and for that of a *month,* like a day or a year, as a time span and a state, see §2788. "Three months," then, means a new state.

And she could no longer hide him symbolizes the point at which it had to become visible. This can be seen from the symbolism of being *hidden,* which means not being visible, as noted directly above at §6721, so that *no longer being hidden* means becoming visible. The reason it means the point at which it had to become visible is that the three months during which the child was hidden symbolized a whole period from beginning to end (see directly above at §6721). 6722

And she took a wicker chest symbolizes its setting, which was lowly but was at least based on truth, as the following shows: A *chest,* or little ark, symbolizes a setting or enclosure for something, as discussed below. And *wicker* symbolizes something that is lowly but is still based on truth. The fact that wicker means something humble is plain. It means something based on truth because that is what wicker, [or rattan,] symbolizes, as is clear in Isaiah: 6723

> Doom to a land casting shadow with its wings, a land across the rivers of Cush, which sends ambassadors onto the sea and [puts them] *in rattan vessels* on the face of the water. (Isaiah 18:1, 2)

A land casting shadow with its wings stands for a religion that robs itself of light through misguided reasoning based on accepted knowledge. "Across the rivers of Cush" stands for resorting to religious knowledge to confirm false assumptions (§1164). Sending ambassadors onto the sea stands for consulting accepted knowledge (§28). "In rattan vessels on the face of the water" stands for the humblest possible containers for truth. [2] Rattan is mentioned in a negative sense in the same author:

> Dry land will turn into a pool, and the thirsty place into wellsprings of water; *grass in place of reed and rattan.* (Isaiah 35:7)

Grass in place of reed and rattan means that truth in the form of knowledge will replace the kinds of ideas that are incapable of harboring any truth. The meaning of grass as truth in the form of knowledge is evident in Scripture passages that mention it.

[3] It had been provided that Moses would represent the Lord as divine law, or as the Word, and specifically as the narrative part of the Word, which was the reason for two events. One was that as a baby Moses was

put in a chest, or a little ark, but in a humble one because the divine law was only now appearing and because he merely *represented* its presence there. The other, though, was that the actual divine law, after shining out from Mount Sinai, was placed in an ark called the ark of the testimony. (For the divine law being put inside the ark, see Exodus 40:20; 1 Kings 8:9. For the books of Moses being put there, see Deuteronomy 31:24, 25, 26.) [4] The ark was consequently very sacred because it represented the Lord's divine humanity in the role of divine law. After all, the Lord's divine humanity is the source of divine law, or divine truth, which is the same as the Word, as John says:

> In the beginning there was the Word, and the Word was with God, and the Word was God. And the Word became flesh and resided with us, and we saw his glory: glory like that of the Only-Born of the Father. (John 1:1, 14)

Because the ark represented something this holy, an appeasement cover with guardian beings was placed on it. Next to its veil stood the lampstand with its lamps and the golden table with the loaves, both of which symbolized divine love.

This then is the reason the baby Moses was put in a little ark, because he was to represent divine law.

6724 *And tarred it with tar and pitch* symbolizes goodness mixed with evil and falsity. This is clear from the symbolism of *tar* as goodness mixed with evil and of *pitch* as goodness mixed with falsity. Tar and pitch have this symbolism because they are flammable, and in the Word, fiery material symbolizes goodness and, in a negative sense, evil. Since tar and pitch are sulfurous and also black, they symbolize evil and falsity. In Isaiah, for example:

> A day of vengeance for Jehovah! *[Zion's] watercourses will turn into pitch,* and its dirt *into sulfur,* and its land will become *burning pitch.* (Isaiah 34:8, 9)

The pitch and sulfur stand for falsity and evil. This, then, is why *she tarred it with tar and pitch* symbolizes goodness mixed with evil and falsity.

[2] As for the subject matter itself—that the setting for divine truth consisted of goodness mixed with evil and falsity—no one can understand it without knowing about human reformation.

When we are being reformed, the Lord anchors us internally in goodness and truth. Externally, though, he releases us to our evil ways and false thoughts and consequently to the companionship of hellish spirits immersed in the same kind of evil and falsity. They hover around us and make every effort to destroy us, but an internal inflow of goodness and truth protects us so well that the hellish spirits cannot inflict the slightest damage. Any force that acts inside us is immensely more powerful than a force that acts from the outside. What is within, being more refined, acts on every single part of the surface and in this way bends the outer level to its will. However, for this to happen the outer level must contain something good and true for the inflow from within to attach to. That is how goodness can exist among evil and falsity and yet remain safe.

Everyone being reformed is brought into this state. That is the way the evil and falsity to which we are prey are removed and the way goodness and truth are introduced in their place.

[3] People who do not know this secret cannot possibly see why the divine truth in us is surrounded by goodness mixed with evil and falsity, as symbolized by the tar and pitch that tarred the little ark in which the baby was placed.

It is also important to realize that just because goodness can mix with evil and falsity does not mean they can join together. The one flees the other, and a law of order leads both sides to put distance between them. Goodness belongs to heaven, and evil and falsity belongs to hell, so just as heaven and hell are separate, everything that comes out of them separates too.

And put the child in it means that deep within lay divine law in its origin. This can be seen from the symbolism of *putting [the child] in it* as deep within, since it was in a little ark, and from the representation of Moses as divine law, discussed below. Here he represents divine law in its origin, since he was a baby. 6725

And put him in the seaweed on the bank of the river means that at first it lay among false information. This can be seen from the symbolism of *seaweed* as information (discussed below) and from that of Egypt's *river* as falsity (discussed at §6693). 6726

For an explanation of the idea that people who are being introduced into divine truth are placed among falsities at first, see just above at §6724.

Seaweed stands for information because every plant in the Word symbolizes some variety of knowledge. The seaweed on the bank of a river symbolizes a lowly type of knowledge, as also in Isaiah:

> The streams will recede, and the rivers of Egypt will drain away; *reed and seaweed will wilt.* (Isaiah 19:6)

The streams stand for thoughts that display understanding (§§2702, 3051). "The rivers of Egypt will drain away" stands for items of knowledge. Reed and seaweed stand for the very lowliest forms of information, which are sense impressions. In Jonah seaweed stands for false information:

> Water surrounded me right to my soul; the abyss encircled me; *seaweed was bound to* my *head.* (Jonah 2:5)

This prophetic utterance depicts a state of trial. The water that surrounded the prophet right to his soul stands for falsity. For the meaning of flooding water as times of trial and desolation, see §§705, 739, 790, 5725. The abyss that encircled the prophet stands for evil that comes of falsity. The seaweed bound to his head means that false information was besieging truth and goodness. That is what a state of desolation is like.

6727 *And his sister stood far off to know what would happen to him* symbolizes religious truth distant from that information, and attentiveness, as the following shows: A *sister* symbolizes truth on the rational plane, as discussed in §§1495, 2508, 2524, 2556, 3160, 3386, and therefore religious truth, because this type of truth resides on the rational plane. And *to know what would happen* symbolizes attentiveness.

6728 Exodus 2:5, 6, 7, 8, 9. *And Pharaoh's daughter went down to wash at the river. And her girls were going to the riverside, and she saw the chest in the middle of the seaweed and sent her slave and took it. And she opened it and saw him, the child, and here, the boy was crying, and she took pity on him and said, "This one is from the children of the Hebrews." And his sister said to Pharaoh's daughter, "Shall I go and call a wet nurse from the Hebrews for you, and she will nurse the child for you?" And Pharaoh's daughter said to her, "Go," and the girl went and called the child's mother. And Pharaoh's daughter said to her, "Take along this child and nurse him for me, and I myself will give you your wage," and the woman took the child and nursed him.*

And Pharaoh's daughter went down symbolizes the religious persuasion there. *To wash at the river* symbolizes worship based on falsity. *And her girls were going to the riverside* means that the ministry of that religious persuasion relied on falsity. *And she saw the chest in the middle of the seaweed* symbolizes a perception of truth, lowly truth, set amid false information. *And sent her slave* symbolizes a service rendered. *And took it* symbolizes curiosity. *And she opened it and saw him, the child,* symbolizes examination into its nature and a perception that it was truth imparted by the Divine. *And here, the boy was crying* symbolizes sadness. *And she took pity on him* symbolizes being alerted by the Divine. *And said, "This one is from the children of the Hebrews,"* means that it came from true religion. *And his sister said to Pharaoh's daughter* symbolizes religious truth alongside the religious persuasion there. *Shall I go and call a wet nurse from the Hebrews for you?* symbolizes a perception that truth needed to have the goodness offered by true religion incorporated into it. *And Pharaoh's daughter said to her, "Go,"* symbolizes consent on the part of the religious persuasion there. *And the girl went and called the child's mother* means that truth-from-goodness in the church added other religious elements. *And Pharaoh's daughter said to her* symbolizes consent on the part of the religious persuasion there. *Take along this child* means to attach him to herself. *And nurse him for me* means that she would instill in truth a goodness compatible with that religious persuasion. *And I myself will give you your wage* symbolizes repayment. *And the woman took the child and nursed him* means that she instilled into truth the goodness offered by the church.

And Pharaoh's daughter went down symbolizes the religious persuasion **6729**
there. This can be seen from the symbolism of a *daughter* as a desire for truth and goodness and therefore as a religion, as discussed in §§2362, 3963. In a negative sense it symbolizes a desire for falsity and evil and therefore a religious persuasion based on falsity and evil (§3024). Here it represents a persuasion based on false information because it is *Pharaoh's* daughter, and Pharaoh currently represents false knowledge (§§6651, 6679, 6683, 6692).

The scriptural symbolism of daughters as religions is clear from the many passages in which the church is called *daughter of Zion* or *daughter of Jerusalem*. By the same token, the symbolism of daughters as the false religions of many nations is plain from the passages in which these are called daughters, such as *daughter of Tyre* (Psalms 45:12), *daughter of Edom* (Lamentations 4:22), *daughter of the Chaldeans and Babylon* (Isaiah 47:1, 5; Jeremiah 50:41, 42; 51:33; Zechariah 2:7; Psalms 137:8), *daughter of the Philistines* (Ezekiel 16:27, 57), *daughter of Tarshish* (Isaiah 23:10). "Daughter of Egypt" appears in Jeremiah:

> Go up to Gilead and take balsam, *virgin daughter of Egypt!* Pack baggage for deportation for yourself, inhabitant *daughter of Egypt!* The *daughter of Egypt* has been shamed, has been delivered into the hand of the people of the north. (Jeremiah 46:11, 19, 24)

The daughter of Egypt stands for the desire to debate the validity of religious truth on the basis of secular knowledge, under the sway of a negative attitude. So it stands for the belief system rising out of that desire, which by its nature accepts nothing but falsity.

6730 *To wash at the river* symbolizes worship based on falsity, as the following shows: *Washing* symbolizes being purified of filth, spiritually understood, as discussed in §3147, so it symbolizes worship because worship exists to purify us. And the *river* here—Egypt's river—symbolizes falsity, as discussed in §6693.

6731 *And the girls were going to the riverside* means that the ministry of that religious persuasion relied on falsity, as the following shows: *Girls* symbolize ministers, because when Pharaoh's daughter symbolizes a religious persuasion, her girls symbolize the ministry of that religion. And the *river* symbolizes falsity, as directly above at §6730. It is therefore a reliance on falsity by the ministry of that religious persuasion that is symbolized by *girls going to the riverside.*

6732 *And she saw the chest in the middle of the seaweed* symbolizes a perception of truth, lowly truth, set amid false information, as the following shows: *Seeing* symbolizes a perception, as noted in §§2150, 3764, 4567, 4723, 5400. A wicker *chest* symbolizes something that is lowly but is still based on truth, as discussed at §6723, so it symbolizes truth that is lowly. And *seaweed* symbolizes false information, as discussed at §6726. *In the middle* of the seaweed consequently means amid false information. What this is talking about was explained above [§6724].

6733 *And sent her slave* symbolizes a service rendered, as is self-evident.

6734 *And took it* symbolizes curiosity. This can be seen from the symbolism of *taking it,* namely, the chest. Since she sensed there was some truth amid the information, even if it was lowly (§6732), *taking it* means curiosity, specifically to learn what that truth was like.

6735 *And she opened it and saw him, the child,* symbolizes examination into its nature and a perception that it was truth imparted by the Divine, as the following shows: *Opening it* means examining its nature, because anyone who opens something to see what it is and what its characteristics are is examining it. *Seeing* symbolizes a perception, as mentioned just above at §6732. And Moses, the *child,* represents divine law, or divine truth, as discussed below, so he represents truth imparted by the Divine.

6736 *And here, the boy was crying* symbolizes sadness, as is self-evident.

6737 *And she took pity on him* symbolizes being alerted by the Divine. This is evident from the symbolism of taking pity as a rush of love for one's neighbor, received from the Lord. When we look with loving eyes on someone in misery—as Pharaoh's daughter here looked on the child in the wicker chest, crying—compassion rises in us, and because it comes from the Lord, it is an alert. What is more, when people with perception feel compassion, they know they are being advised by the Lord to help.

And said, "This one is from the children of the Hebrews," means that it came from true religion. This can be seen from the symbolism of *Hebrews,* who stand for religious attributes, as mentioned in §§6675, 6684. The *children* of the Hebrews, then, are people in a true religion. 6738

The reason Hebrews symbolize religious attributes is that when the ancient church came to an end, the Hebrew church, which was the second ancient church, had its start. This church kept much of the representation and symbolism from the ancient church and even acknowledged Jehovah. That is why Hebrews symbolize the church. For information on the Hebrew church, see §§1238, 1241, 1343, 4516, 4517, 4874, 5136.

And his sister said to Pharaoh's daughter symbolizes religious truth alongside the religious persuasion there. This is established by the symbolism of a *sister* as truth known to the church (noted above at §6727) and by that of *Pharaoh's daughter* as a religious persuasion (also noted above, at §6729). "Alongside" is symbolized by the fact that Moses' sister was at hand when Pharaoh's daughter opened the chest. 6739

Shall I go and call a wet nurse from the Hebrews for you? symbolizes a perception that [truth] needed to have the goodness offered by true religion incorporated into it, as the following shows: A *wet nurse* symbolizes the instilling of goodness, as noted at §4563, because the milk she gives symbolizes goodness that comes of truth, or to put it another way, a heavenly-spiritual attribute (§2184). And *Hebrews* symbolize religious attributes, as mentioned at §§6675, 6684. The fact that it means a *perception* that religious goodness needed to be instilled is symbolized by "she said, 'Shall I go and call?'" In an inner sense this means truth-from-goodness, which has perception, but in a literal sense it means the girl, who did not have perception. 6740

The meaning of a nurse as the incorporation of goodness is plain in Isaiah too:

> They will bring your sons in their embrace, and your daughters will be carried here on their shoulder. And *kings* will be *your nourishers,* and their ladies, *your nurses.* (Isaiah 49:22, 23)

Kings who nourish stand for the incorporation of truth, which comes with understanding. Ladies who are nurses stand for the incorporation of goodness, which comes with wisdom. In the same author:

> Raise your eyes all around and see: all are gathering; they come to you. Your sons come from far away, and *your daughters* are carried here *to your side by nurses.* (Isaiah 60:4)

The sons who come from far away stand for truth as it is known among people outside the church. Since this truth is distant from the church's truth, it is said to come from far away. The daughters that are carried to the people's side by nurses stand for goodness that is constantly being instilled, because daughters mean goodness, and nurses mean something that instills it.

6741 *And Pharaoh's daughter said to her, "Go,"* symbolizes consent on the part of that religious persuasion. This is established by the representation of *Pharaoh's daughter* as a religious persuasion, which is discussed above at §6729. The fact that consent is meant needs no explanation.

6742 *And the girl went and called the child's mother* means that truth-from-goodness in the church added other religious elements, as the following shows: A *girl* symbolizes truth-from-goodness in the church, as discussed below. *Calling* means adding, because the reason the girl called [her mother] was to include her. And a *mother* symbolizes the church, as discussed in §§289, 2691, 2717, 5581, so she symbolizes religious elements.

The Word speaks of virgins and of girls but it rarely refers to girls by the term used here in the original language. A virgin symbolizes the goodness in a heavenly religion, while a girl symbolizes the truth-from-goodness in a spiritual religion. In David, for instance:

> They had seen your strides, God, the strides of my God, my King, in the sanctuary; the singers went in front, the strummers came after, *in the middle of the girls playing tambourines.* (Psalms 68:24, 25)

All the words in this passage relate to truth-from-goodness, which characterizes a spiritual religion. The name *God* is used when the subject is truth (see §§2769, 2807, 2822, 4402). A king means truth (1672, 2015, 2069, 3009, 4575, 4581, 4966, 5044, 5068, 6148). Singers are mentioned in connection with the truth found in a spiritual religion (418, 419, 420). Tambourine players are mentioned in connection with spiritual goodness (4138). From this you can see that girls mean the truth-from-goodness in a spiritual religion.

And Pharaoh's daughter said to her obviously symbolizes consent on the part of the religious persuasion there, because she gave the child to his mother to nurse him. Therefore consent by that religious persuasion is meant here, as it was above at §6741, where similar words occur. 6743

Take along this child means to attach him to herself, as the following shows: *Taking along* means attaching. The mother—the person being addressed—symbolizes the church, as noted just above at §6742. Moses, the *child,* represents divine law in its origin. In the highest sense, he represents divine law in the Lord as it existed when he turned his human side into the divine law. In a secondary sense, Moses represents divine law in people being reborn as it exists when they are introduced to divine truth; see above at §6716. 6744

And nurse him for me means that she would instill in [truth] a goodness compatible with that religious persuasion. This can be seen from the symbolism of *nursing* as instilling goodness (discussed below) and from the representation of "Pharaoh's daughter" as a religious persuasion (mentioned at §6729). Because she says that the woman is to nurse the child for her, the symbolism is that she would instill a goodness compatible with that religious persuasion. 6745

The meaning of *nursing* as instilling goodness is evident from the symbolism of a wet nurse as the instilling of goodness, which is discussed above at §6740. It is also evident from the Scripture passages quoted there and from the following passages. [2] In Moses:

> They will call peoples onto the mountain; there they will offer sacrifices of righteousness, because *they will suck on the stream of riches from the sea* and what is covered and hidden in the sand. (Deuteronomy 33:19)

This is Moses' prophetical saying about Zebulun and Issachar. Calling peoples onto the mountain and offering sacrifices of righteousness there symbolizes worship inspired by love. Sucking on the stream of riches from the sea means that they will then drink up—be instilled with—quantities of truth in the form of knowledge. Here and in the following passages, "suck" is the same word as "be nursed." [3] In Isaiah:

> I will make you into an eternal excellence, a joy for generation after generation. And *you will suck the milk of the nations,* in fact *you will suck the breasts of kings.* (Isaiah 60:15, 16)

This is about Zion and Jerusalem, which are the heavenly church. Zion is its inner level and Jerusalem its outer. Sucking the milk of the nations stands for being instilled with heavenly goodness. Sucking the breasts of kings stands for being instilled with heavenly truth.

Anyone can see that these words contain a hidden meaning that does not show in the literal meaning, and that what lies hidden there is sacred, because it is God's Word. Otherwise, what would it mean to suck the milk of the nations and the breasts of kings? It is impossible for this hidden, holy meaning to come out in the open unless one knows the symbolism of sucking, of milk, of nations, of breasts, and of kings. Milk is something spiritual from something heavenly, or truth from goodness (see §2184). Nations are the goodness in a way of worshiping (1259, 1260, 1416, 1849, 6005). Breasts are desires for goodness and truth (6432). Kings are truth (1672, 2015, 2069, 3009, 4575, 4581, 4966, 5044, 5068, 6148). And sucking is having goodness instilled. [4] From these details the meaning of the words can now be seen as they apply to the heavenly church meant by Zion and Jerusalem. (As noted above, Zion and Jerusalem symbolize the heavenly church—Zion its inner level and Jerusalem its outer—when they are mentioned jointly. When Jerusalem is mentioned without Zion, it usually symbolizes the spiritual church.) [5] In the same author:

> May you *suck* and be filled from Jerusalem's comforting breast, and may you *milk* and enjoy her radiant glory. Watch: I myself am spreading peace over her like a river, and the glory of the nations like a flooding torrent, *so that you may suck on it.* You will be lifted onto her side and played with on her knees. (Isaiah 66:11, 12)

Here too sucking stands for having goodness instilled. [6] In Jeremiah:

> Even whales offer the breast; *they nurse their offspring.* The daughter of my people is cruel; the *tongue of the nursing baby* has stuck to the roof of its mouth from thirst. (Lamentations 4:3, 4)

"The daughter of my people" stands for a spiritual church, and here, for a spiritual church that has been devastated. Not nursing her offspring (even though whales do) means that truth is not being instilled. "The tongue of the nursing baby has stuck to the roof of its mouth from thirst" means truth is so lacking that all innocence dies. A nursing baby means innocence, and thirst means a lack of truth.

6746 *And I myself will give you your wage* symbolizes repayment, as can be seen without explanation.

And the woman took the child and nursed him means that she instilled 6747
into [truth] the goodness offered by the church. This can be seen from the symbolism of a *woman* as the church (discussed in §§252, 253) and from that of *nursing* as instilling goodness (discussed just above at §6745).

What is being depicted here is a second stage. The first stage was one of being set down among evils and falsities (§6724). This second stage is one of being instilled with the goodness offered by the church.

Exodus 2:10. *And the child grew, and she brought him to Pharaoh's daugh-* 6748
ter, and he was like a son to her, and she called his name Moses and said, "Because from the waters I drew him."

And the child grew means being increased by goodness. *And she brought him to Pharaoh's daughter* symbolizes a desire for knowledge. *And he was like a son to her* means that it was accordingly supplied with its first truths. *And she called his name Moses* symbolizes the quality of the state then. *And said, "Because from the waters I drew him,"* symbolizes being delivered from falsity.

And the child grew means being increased by goodness. This can be seen 6749
from the symbolism of *growing* as increase. The increase came from goodness because the child grew by nursing, and being nursed by a Hebrew woman means being instilled with the goodness the church has to offer (§6745).

And she brought him to Pharaoh's daughter symbolizes a desire for knowl- 6750
edge. This can be seen from the representation of *Pharaoh's daughter* as a religious persuasion (dealt with at §6729). Here, though, she represents a desire for knowledge, because the verse is depicting a third stage. At that stage a daughter symbolizes a desire (2362, 3963), and Pharaoh symbolizes knowledge in general (6015), so Pharaoh's daughter symbolizes a desire for knowledge. The meaning is also evident from the series of ideas in the inner sense, because Moses, representing the Lord as divine law, could not be brought to Pharaoh's daughter and be like a son to her if she still symbolized a religious persuasion, as before. Besides, knowledge is what people being reborn need to learn first. Knowledge forms a foundation for matters of the intellect, and the intellect is a container for the truth that leads to faith (6125). The truth that leads to faith, in turn, is a container for neighborly love and its goodness. From this you can see that knowledge forms the first supporting layer when a person is being reborn.

[2] Knowledge was also the first support for the Lord when he made his human side into divine truth, or divine law. This is symbolized by

his being taken to Egypt as a little child (Matthew 2:13, 14) and therefore by the prophecy in Hosea: "Out of Egypt I called my child" (Hosea 11:1; Matthew 2:15). The symbolism of Egypt as knowledge has been demonstrated many times. By knowledge, though, I do not mean scientific knowledge but religious knowledge. About this type of knowledge, see §§4749, 4964, 4965, 4966, 6004. Furthermore, this type of knowledge is what Egypt symbolizes in a positive sense.

For the idea that knowledge provides an initial foundation, see §5901.

6751 *And he was like a son to her* means that it was accordingly supplied with its first truths, as the following shows: Pharaoh's daughter—the *her* of *to her*—represents a desire for knowledge, as discussed directly above at §6750. And a *son* symbolizes truth, as discussed in §§489, 491, 533, 2623, 3373. In this case a son symbolizes first truth. *Being like a son to her* means arriving at truth for the first time through knowledge, because truth is initially born through knowledge and is therefore like a son to the desire for knowledge, its mother. For the idea that knowledge forms a foundation for truth genuinely understood, the truth that composes faith, see above at §6750.

The progress we make in matters of faith when we are being reborn is almost the same as the progress we make in secular truths when we are growing up. When we are growing up, sense impressions form the first supporting layer, then knowledge. Later these foundations support the growth of judgment—more in some of us, less in others.

When we are being reborn, the general tenets of faith or the rudiments of the church's theology form the first supporting layer, followed by particular tenets or teachings. Later they deepen more and more. These foundations are what heaven's light illuminates, bringing us genuine understanding and the perceptive ability that comes with faith and neighborly kindness.

6752 *And she called his name Moses* symbolizes the quality of the state then. This is established by the symbolism of a name and *calling a name* as the quality of something, which is discussed in §§144, 145, 1754, 1896, 2009, 2724, 3006, 3421, 6674. In this case it symbolizes the quality of a state because when someone is given a name, the very name symbolizes the conditions at that time (§§1946, 2643, 3422, 4298). The state whose quality is being symbolized here is the state of divine law as it first existed in the Lord, and the state of divine truth as it first exists in a person being reborn.

The Lord as the Word is primarily represented by two people: Moses and Elijah. Moses represents the Lord in regard to the narrative books;

Elijah, in regard to the Prophets. In addition there is Elisha and, last of all, John the Baptist—which is why John is meant by "the Elijah who was to come" (Matthew 17:10, 11, 12, 13; Luke 1:17). However, before I can show that Moses represents the divine law, I need to define it. In a broad sense divine law means the whole Word. In a less broad sense it means the narrative part. In a narrow sense it means the part written through Moses. And in the narrowest sense it means the ten commandments written on the stone tablets on Mount Sinai. Moses represents the Law in its less broad, narrow, and narrowest senses.

[2] *In a broad sense the law is the whole Word,* both the narrative and prophetic parts. This can be seen in John:

> We have *heard from the law* that Christ [the Messiah] remains forever. (John 12:34)

In this verse the law obviously means the prophetic part of the Word as well, because the saying was written in Isaiah (9:6, 7), David (Psalms 110:4), and Daniel (7:13, 14). In the same author:

> [This happened] *so that there would be a fulfillment of the word written in the law,* "they hated me without a reason." (John 15:25)

The same is true here, because this saying was written in David (Psalms 35:19). In Matthew:

> Truly, I say to you: until heaven and earth pass away, one jot or one serif *will not pass away from the law* till everything comes to pass. (Matthew 5:18)

"The law" is used in a broad sense here, for the whole Word.

[3] *In a less broad sense the Law is the narrative part of the Word.* This can be seen in Matthew:

> Everything whatever that you want people to do to you, also do to them yourselves; *because this is the Law and the Prophets.* (Matthew 7:12)

This verse distinguishes the Word into the Law and the Prophets, and since the Word has been divided into narrative and prophetic parts, it follows that the Law means the narrative part and the Prophets the prophetic part. Likewise in the same author:

> On these two commandments depend the *Law and the Prophets.* (Matthew 22:40)

In Luke:

> The *Law and the Prophets* lasted till John; from then on the good news of God's kingdom is being spread. (Luke 16:16; Matthew 11:13)

[4] *In a narrow sense the Law is the part of the Word written through Moses.* This can be seen in Moses:

> When Moses finished *writing the words of this law on a book until he came to the end of them,* Moses commanded the Levites carrying Jehovah's ark, saying, "Taking the *book of this law,* put it on the side of the ark of the covenant of Jehovah your God." (Deuteronomy 31:24, 25, 26)

The "book of [this] law" stands for the books of Moses. In the same author:

> If you do not watch *to do all the words of this law written in this book,* then every disease and every plague that is not written in the *book of this law* Jehovah will bring upon you until you are destroyed. (Deuteronomy 28:58, 61)

The same is true here. In David:

> *In Jehovah's law* is their good pleasure, and on *his law* they meditate day and night. (Psalms 1:2)

"Jehovah's law" stands for the books of Moses, because the prophetical books had not been written yet [by David's time], nor had the [other] narrative books, except for Joshua and Judges.

There are also passages dealt with below that mention the Law of Moses.

[5] *In the narrowest sense the law is the ten commandments written on the stone tablets on Mount Sinai,* as people know; see Joshua 8:32. This law is also called the testimony (Exodus 25:16, 21).

[6] *Moses represents the Law in its less broad sense (as the narrative part of the Word) and in its narrow and narrowest senses.* This can be seen from passages that use "Moses" instead of "the Law," and from passages that refer to the Law as the Law of Moses. In Luke, for instance:

> Abraham said to him, "They have *Moses and the Prophets;* let them listen to them. *If* they do not listen to *Moses and the Prophets,* neither will they be persuaded if someone rises from the dead." (Luke 16:29, 31)

"Moses and the Prophets" here means the same thing as the Law and the Prophets, namely, the narrative and prophetic parts of the Word. "Moses," then, is plainly the Law, or the narrative part of the Word. In the same author:

> And Jesus, starting *with Moses and with all the Prophets,* interpreted what pertained to him in all the Scriptures. (Luke 24:27)

In the same author:

> Everything that has been written in the *Law of Moses and the Prophets* and the Psalms about me must be fulfilled. (Luke 24:44)

In John:

> Philip said, "[The one about] whom *Moses* wrote *in the Law* we have found: Jesus." (John 1:45)

In the same author:

> *In the Law, Moses* commanded us. (John 8:5)

In Daniel:

> The curse and the oath *that was written in the Law of Moses, servant of God,* has poured down upon us because we have sinned against [God]. *As was written in the Law of Moses,* all the evil has come upon us. (Daniel 9:11, 13)

In Joshua:

> Joshua wrote on the altar stone a *copy of the Law of Moses.* (Joshua 8:32)

[7] It is called the Law of Moses because Moses represents the Lord as the law, that is, as the Word, and in a [relatively] broad sense as the narrative part of the Word. That is why something that belongs to the Lord is attributed to Moses. The same thing happens in John:

> *Moses has given you the Law. Moses has given you circumcision.* If a person receives circumcision on a Sabbath so that the *Law of Moses* will not be broken, . . . (John 7:19, 22, 23)

In Mark:

> *Moses said,* "Honor your father and your mother." (Mark 7:10)

In the same author:

> Jesus, answering, said to them, "*What did Moses command you?*" They said, "*Moses* allowed the writing of a divorce document and dismissal." (Mark 10:3, 4)

Since what belongs to the Lord is attributed to Moses on account of his representation, the Law is referred to as both the Law of Moses and the Law of the Lord in Luke:

> When the days of their purification were fulfilled *according to the Law of Moses,* they brought him into Jerusalem in order to present him to the Lord, as it has been written *in the Law of the Lord,* that every male opening the womb was to be called sacred to the Lord, and in order to offer a sacrifice according to what has been said *in the Law of the Lord:* a pair of turtledoves and two pigeon chicks. (Luke 2:22, 23, 24, 39)

[8] Because Moses represented the law, he was allowed to approach the Lord on Mount Sinai and not only receive the tablets of the law there but also listen to the statutes and judgments of the law and give them as commands to the people. The text also says *that the people would therefore believe in Moses forever:*

> Jehovah said to Moses, "Look: I come to you in a mass of cloud so that the people may listen *when I speak to you* and also *believe in you forever.*" (Exodus 19:9)

This says "in a mass of cloud" because cloud stands for the Word in its literal meaning. So when Moses approached the Lord on Mount Sinai, the text again says he entered a *cloud* (Exodus 20:21; 24:2, 18; 34:2, 3, 4, 5). For the meaning of cloud as the literal sense of the Word, see the preface to Genesis 18 and §§4060, 4391, 5922, 6343 at the end.

[9] It was also because Moses represented the law, or the Word, that when he came down from Mount Sinai *the skin of his face shone* when he spoke, and he put a veil over his face (Exodus 34:28–end). His shining face symbolized the inner law, because the inner level has heaven's light shining on it and is therefore called [the Word's] glory (§5922). The veil symbolized the outer law. Moses veiled his face when he talked with that people because the inner level was hidden from their eyes, and because they were so deeply in the dark about it that they could not bear any of the radiating light. For the meaning of a face as inner depths, see §§1999, 2434, 3527, 3573, 4066, 4796–4805, 5102, 5695.

To repeat, the Lord in regard to the narrative part of the Word was represented by Moses and in regard to the prophetical part by Elijah. That is why when the Lord was transfigured, "*Moses and Elijah* were seen conversing with him" (Matthew 17:3). Neither could any but those who represented the Word have conversed with the Lord when his divinity became visible in the world, because the way we converse with the Lord is through the Word. (For the idea that Elijah represented the Lord as the Word, see §§2762, 5247 at the end.)

[10] Since the two together, Moses and Elijah, represented the entire Word, both are mentioned in the passage in Malachi that says Elijah would be sent before the Lord:

> *Remember the Law of Moses, my servant,* which I commanded him in Horeb for the whole of Israel—the statutes and judgments. *Here, I am sending you Elijah the prophet* before the day of Jehovah comes, great and fearsome. (Malachi 4:4, 5, 6)

The meaning of this passage is that someone would arrive beforehand to announce the Coming in scriptural terms.

And said, "Because from the waters I drew him," symbolizes being delivered from falsity. This can be seen from the symbolism of *waters*—in this case the waters of Egypt's river—as falsity (discussed at §6693) and from that of *drawing out* as deliverance. 6753

Present in this clause is the quality of the state, as symbolized by the name Moses. In the highest sense this quality involves the steps the Lord took in order to become divine law in regard to his human side. What he did was to free his human side of any falsity clinging to it that he had received from his mother, to the point where he became divine law—in other words, divine truth itself. Later, when he had been glorified, he also became divine goodness, or the living essence of divine truth, which is Jehovah.

Exodus 2:11, 12, 13, 14. *And it happened in those days that Moses grew and went out to his brothers and saw their burdens, and he saw an Egyptian man striking a Hebrew man, one of his brothers. And he looked out here and there and saw that there was no man, and he struck the Egyptian and hid him in the sand. And he went out the second day, and look: two Hebrew men feuding, and he said to the one in the wrong, "Why do you strike your companion?" And he said, "Who set you as chief man and judge over us? Are you talking about killing me as you killed the Egyptian?" And Moses was afraid and said, "Surely the matter is known!"* 6754

And it happened in those days that Moses grew means that while those states lasted there was an increase in truth in the form of knowledge. *And went out to his brothers* symbolizes union with the church's truth. *And saw their burdens* symbolizes a perception that they were overrun with falsity. *And he saw an Egyptian man striking a Hebrew man* symbolizes alienated knowledge trying to destroy religious truth. *One of his brothers* means with which he had a bond. *And he looked out here and there and saw that there was no man* symbolizes prudence in determining whether he was safe. *And he struck the Egyptian* means that he destroyed alienated knowledge. *And hid him in the sand* means that he banished it to the abode of falsity. *And he went out the second day* symbolizes a renewed bond with the church. *And look: two Hebrew men feuding* symbolizes an awareness that people within the church were fighting with each other. *And he said to the one in the wrong, "Why do you strike your companion?"* means scolding them for wanting to destroy one another's beliefs. *And he said, "Who set you as chief man and judge over us?"* symbolizes a perception that he had not yet advanced far enough in the church's truth to settle disputes within the church. *Are you talking about killing me?* means, do you want to destroy my faith? *As you killed the Egyptian* means as you destroyed falsity. *And Moses was afraid and said, "Surely the matter is known!"* means that he was surrounded by alienated knowledge and did not yet know enough truth to be safe.

6755 *And it happened in those days that Moses grew* means that while those states lasted there was an increase in truth in the form of knowledge, as the following shows: *Days* symbolize states, as discussed at §§23, 487, 488, 493, 893, 2788, 3462, 3785, 4850, so *it happened in those days* means while those states lasted. And *growing* symbolizes an increase, as above at §6749. The explanation just above at §6751 shows that the increase was in truth in the form of knowledge.

6756 *And went out to his brothers* symbolizes union with the church's truth. This can be seen from the symbolism of *brothers* as the church's truth (discussed below) and from that of *going out to them* as uniting with them.

About *brothers:* At one point they symbolize the goodness found in the church and at another the truth found there. Where a heavenly religion is being treated of, they symbolize goodness, and when a spiritual religion is being treated of, truth. This is because a heavenly church is devoted to goodness but a spiritual church to truth. In ancient times everyone in the church called each other brothers and sisters. Admittedly, people in the spiritual church used these terms on the basis of goodness (§3803). But people in the inner part of the church did so in different ways, depending on the quality of the goodness and therefore on truth (since goodness takes its quality from truth).

Later, when the church turned away from goodness and consequently from truth too, people no longer called each other family on the basis of spiritual blood ties and family connections, which are determined by neighborly love and faith. Instead they did so only on the basis of physical ties and connections, and of loyalty. They also started to consider it degrading to call someone of lower social status a sister or brother. The reason for this behavior was that they counted the closeness resulting from spiritual considerations a small, worthless thing, and the closeness resulting from earthly and political considerations more important than anything else.

Clearly the church's true ideas are called brothers, since Jacob's sons represented that truth in its entirety (§§5403, 5419, 5427, 5458, 5512).

[2] In ancient times people were called sisters and brothers on account of spiritual kinship because rebirth, or regeneration, created higher-level relationships and connections than physical birth did. It was also [because all goodness is interrelated, as is all truth,] since it traces its origin to one Father: the Lord. That is why people arriving in heaven after death no longer acknowledge a sibling or even a mother and father on any other basis than goodness and truth; it is goodness and truth that determine their new siblings there. This then explains why people who belonged to the church called each other brother and sister.

[3] The children of Israel called everyone born of Jacob their brother, and the rest they called companions, as the following passages show. In Isaiah:

> I will mix Egypt up with Egypt so that they fight, a *man against his brother* and a man *against his companion.* (Isaiah 19:2)

In the same author:

> A man helps *his companion* and says to *his brother,* "Strengthen yourself." (Isaiah 41:6)

In Jeremiah:

> Be careful, a man *of his companion,* and put your trust *in no brother;* for *every brother* ruthlessly supplants [his brother], and every *companion* speaks slander. (Jeremiah 9:4)

[4] Regarding the mutual use of the name "brother" by everyone born of Jacob, see in Isaiah:

> Then they will bring *all your brothers* from all the nations, an offering to Jehovah, on horses, in a chariot, and in coaches. (Isaiah 66:20)

In Moses:

> You shall without fail put over them a monarch whom Jehovah your God chooses. *From the midst of your brothers* you shall put over them a monarch; you cannot set over them a foreign man who is *not their brother.* (Deuteronomy 17:15)

They also called the children of Esau brothers, since these too were relatives of Jacob. In Moses:

> We crossed over [from] *beside our brothers, the children of Esau* living in Seir. (Deuteronomy 2:8)

[5] The reason people in the church called each other siblings in ancient times was, as mentioned above, that they acknowledged the Lord as their only father and that from him they received a new soul and new life. That is why the Lord says:

> Do not use the name Rabbi; one person is your teacher: Christ. *You, though, are all siblings.* (Matthew 23:8)

Because being a spiritual sibling comes of love, that is, it comes of the fact that people belong to each other, and because people with goodness are in the Lord and the Lord is in them (John 14:20), therefore the Lord calls such people brothers and sisters in Matthew:

> Stretching out his hand over his disciples Jesus said, "Look: my mother *and my siblings.* For whoever does the will of my Father, who is in the heavens, that one is *my brother* and sister and mother." (Matthew 12:49, 50)

In the same author:

> So far as you did it for one *of my least consequential brothers,* you did it for me. (Matthew 25:40)

He also calls the disciples his brothers in Matthew 28:10; John 20:17. In a representative sense, disciples mean everyone dedicated to the truth that leads to faith and the goodness urged by neighborly love.

6757 *And saw their burdens* symbolizes a perception that they were overrun with falsity. This is established by the symbolism of *seeing* as a perception (noted above at §6732) and by that of *burdens* as times of being overrun with falsity. That is exactly what the burdens Pharaoh imposed on the children of Israel are in a spiritual sense. Pharaoh means false knowledge (§§6651, 6679, 6683), and to people focused on truth, onslaughts of falsity are nothing but burdens.

As long as people are living in the world, they cannot know much about the invasions of falsity that are burdens to people intent on truth. While they are in the world they are not badly attacked, because their mind then either clings to falsity or dispels it without being aware of harassment. When people intent on truth are overrun with falsity in the other life, though, evil spirits virtually chain them down in the falsity. The Lord, however, keeps the inner reaches of their mind trained on truth that dispels the falsity.

A state of being overrun with falsity, as that state is experienced in the other life, is meant in the inner sense here, as are many other subjects, because the Word was written not only for people on earth but also for spirits and angels.

And he saw an Egyptian man striking a Hebrew man symbolizes alien- 6758
ated knowledge trying to destroy religious truth. This is clear from the symbolism of an *Egyptian man* as knowledge alienated from truth (discussed at §6692), from that of *striking* as destroying (here, trying to destroy, since falsity cannot actually destroy truth), and from that of a *Hebrew man* as religious truth. A *man* symbolizes truth (§3134), and a *Hebrew* symbolizes the church (§§6675, 6684).

One of his brothers means with which he had a bond. This can be 6759
seen from the symbolism of *brothers* as religious truth, which is treated of above at §6756. [The Lord] possessed this truth, and the religious truth symbolized by the brothers was what he had a bond with, so a bond is meant here on account of the connections drawn in the inner meaning.

And he looked out here and there and saw that there was no man sym- 6760
bolizes prudence in determining whether he was safe, as can be seen without explanation.

And he struck the Egyptian means that he destroyed alienated knowl- 6761
edge. This is evident from the symbolism of *striking* as destroying (as above at §6758) and from that of an *Egyptian* as knowledge alienated from truth (discussed at §6692).

And hid him in the sand means that he banished it to the abode of 6762
falsity. This can be seen from the symbolism of *hiding* as banishing and

from that of *sand* as knowledge that is true and in a negative sense as knowledge that is false. The reason sand means this is that stone, which sand is made out of, symbolizes both (§§1298, 3720, 3769, 3771, 3773, 3789, 3798, 6426). Truth is also symbolized by sand in Moses:

> Zebulun and Issachar will call peoples onto the mountain and offer sacrifices of righteousness, because they will suck on the stream of riches from the sea and *what is covered and hidden in the sand.* (Deuteronomy 33:18, 19)

Calling peoples onto the mountain stands for turning truth into goodness, or faith into neighborly love, because peoples are the truth that leads to faith, and a mountain is the goodness that comes of neighborly love. Offering sacrifices of righteousness stands for worship inspired by neighborly love. Sucking on a stream of riches from the sea stands for abounding in knowledge that is true. What is covered and hidden in the sand stands for knowledge that is true but unknown. Because sand symbolizes truth in the form of knowledge, in a negative sense it symbolizes falsity in the form of knowledge. Most images in the Word also have a negative meaning, and the nature of that meaning can be told from the positive meaning.

About being banished to a place among falsities, as symbolized by "he hid him in the sand": Sometimes hellish spirits who are attached to falsity go to the world of spirits and work there at destroying truth in people undergoing trials. Afterward they are dispatched to hell, which they can no longer leave. This I was privileged to learn through a multitude of experiences, and it is what is meant by being relegated to a place among falsities.

6763 *And he went out the second day* symbolizes a renewed bond with the church. This can be seen from the comments above at §6756, where similar words occur.

6764 *And look: two Hebrew men feuding* symbolizes an awareness that people within the church were fighting with each other, as the following shows: *Look,* or seeing, symbolizes an awareness, as noted in §§2150, 3764, 4567, 4723, 5400. *Hebrew men* symbolize people in the church, as mentioned above at the end of §6758. And *feuding* symbolizes fighting.

6765 *And he said to the one in the wrong, "Why do you strike your companion?"* means scolding them for wanting to destroy one another's beliefs, as the following shows: The *one in the wrong* symbolizes people who do not accept religious truth but are nonetheless in the church. In the church there are people who accept the truth belonging to faith and people who do not, as is plain from various heresies. People with heretical views—people without religious truth—are meant here by the one in the wrong. *Striking* symbolizes destroying, as above at §6758. And the *companion* symbolizes someone who does accept religious truth. When a person without religious truth is symbolized by one who is in the wrong, a companion symbolizes a person who does possess that truth. Such a person is being called a companion rather than a brother (even though both are Hebrews) because they are foes. The scolding nature of the words is obvious.

[2] Here is the situation: When we are being reborn, we are compelled to battle falsity, and all the while the Lord keeps us in the truth, but in such truth as we had persuaded ourselves was true. From a stance on this truth we fight falsity. Fighting from a standpoint of nongenuine truth is also possible as long as that truth is capable of bonding with goodness in some way, and it bonds through innocence, because innocence is the means of union. That is why people of every theology in the church can be reborn, but above all those who have genuine truth.

And he said, "Who set you as chief man and judge over us?" symbolizes 6766
a perception that he had not yet advanced far enough in faith's truth to settle disputes within the church, as the following shows: *He said* symbolizes a perception, as noted many times. A *chief man* symbolizes someone acquainted with the most important truth and therefore someone more enlightened than others in true theology. Such a person was meant by a chieftain in the representative church, and that is why *who set you as chief man?* means that he had not yet advanced far enough in the church's truth. For the meaning of a chieftain as someone acquainted with the most important truth, see §5044. And a *judge* symbolizes someone who settles controversies, or disputes—in this case, disputes within the church because the dispute was between two Hebrew men, and they symbolize people who are part of the church.

[2] So far the highest meaning has dealt with the rudiments of divine law in the Lord's human side. Now it is dealing with progress in that law, although on an inward level it is dealing with the progress of divine truth in people being reborn. During the course of this progress, we first learn to distinguish between falsity and truth; from the truth that we know we can see falsity, because it contradicts truth. But at such an early stage we cannot settle disputes among true concepts of faith within the church. To do so, we need to make further progress, because a person's

enlightenment is gradual, as is quite plain from young adults. They believe the teachings of their religion to be truth itself and use them as a standard for telling what is false but cannot yet settle quarrels among different views of faith within the church. That comes over time. We need to be older, then, and to have our intellect more deeply enlightened in order to be given the ability.

6767 *Are you talking about killing me?* means, do you want to destroy my faith? This can be seen from the symbolism of *killing* as destroying (discussed below) and from that of a Hebrew man—*me*—as people in the church and therefore as faith too. Faith is the church, and they are so nearly one that anyone who destroys a person's faith destroys the church in that person. This is the same as killing the person, because to rob another of faith is to rob that other of spiritual life. What life remains is the kind of life called death. Clearly, then, *are you talking about killing me?* means, do you want to destroy my faith?

[2] Many passages in the Word clarify that killing means robbing of spiritual life. In Jeremiah, for instance:

> Drag them off like a lamb to the slaughter, and doom them *to the day of killing.* How long will the land mourn and the grass of every field wither? Because of the wickedness of those living in it, the animals and the bird will be consumed. (Jeremiah 12:3, 4)

The day of killing stands for a period of devastation for the church, when there is no longer any faith because there is no neighborly love. The land that will mourn stands for the church. The grass of all the fields stands for all truth in the form of knowledge in the church. "The animals and the bird will be consumed" means that goodness and truth will be consumed. For the meaning of the land as the church, see §§566, 662, 1066, 1262, 1413, 1607, 1733, 1850, 2117, 2118 at the end, 2928, 3355, 4447, 4535, 5577. The meaning of grass as truth in the form of knowledge is plain from Scripture passages that mention it. For the meaning of a field as something belonging to the church, see §§2971, 3310, 3766. For the meaning of animals as desires for what is good and therefore as goodness, 45, 46, 142, 143, 246, 714, 715, 719, 1823, 2179, 2180, 3218, 3519, 5198. For the meaning of birds as desires for what is true, 5149. This demonstrates the meaning of the words and shows that every word there contains a spiritual meaning. Anyone can see that one needs the inner meaning in order to understand what a day of killing is, and what it means to say that the land will mourn and the grass of all the fields wither because of the wickedness of those living in it, and that the animals and the bird will be consumed. [3] In Zechariah:

> This is what Jehovah my God has said: "*Pasture the sheep to be killed,* which their owners *kill.*" (Zechariah 11:4, 5)

The sheep to be killed obviously stand for people whose faith the "owners" destroy. In Ezekiel:

> You profaned me among my people for handfuls of barleycorns and for crumbs of bread, *to kill souls that should not die* and to keep souls alive that should not live. (Ezekiel 13:19)

Here too killing plainly stands for destroying spiritual life, or faith and neighborly love. In Isaiah:

> What will you do on the day of visitation and devastation? They will fall under prisoners and *under the slain.* (Isaiah 10:3, 4)

The slain in this passage stand for people in hell and therefore people who live for evil and falsity. [4] In the same author:

> You were thrown out of your grave like a despicable offshoot, [like] the *garment of the slain, [who were] stabbed with a sword;* you will not reunite with them in the grave, because you destroyed your land, *you killed your people.* (Isaiah 14:19, 20)

The slain stand for people deprived of spiritual life. "You killed [your] people" means that a person has destroyed faith's truth and goodness. In John:

> The thief will not come except to steal, *kill,* and *destroy.* Myself, I came so that they could have life. (John 10:10)

Killing stands for destroying the living energy of faith. So the text says, "Myself, I come so that they could have life." In Mark:

> Brother will hand brother over *to death,* and a father his children, and children will rise up against their parents and *kill them.* (Mark 13:12)

This is about the last days of the church, when there is no longer any neighborly love and therefore no faith either. The brother, children, and parents in an inner sense mean the church's good desires and true ideas, and killing them means destroying them.

[5] Because the slain symbolized people stripped of spiritual life, and a field symbolized the church, the representative church had a decree that if someone [went] on the *open field* [and] touched anyone *stabbed by a sword* or *slain,* that person would be unclean seven days (Numbers 19:16). A person stabbed by a sword means truth eradicated by falsity (see §4503), because a sword means falsity that eradicates truth (§§2799, 4499, 6353).

It was also decreed that if someone was found *killed* in the land of the people's inheritance, lying *in a field,* and it was not known who had *killed* the person, the elders and judges were to measure from there to the cities all around, and having found the nearest city, they were to take a heifer and break its neck at a swift river, and so on (Deuteronomy 21:1–9).

6768 *As you killed the Egyptian* means as you destroyed falsity. This is evident from the symbolism of *killing* as destroying (discussed directly above at §6767) and from that of an *Egyptian* as knowledge alienated from truth and therefore as falsity (discussed in §§6692, 6758, 6761).

6769 *And Moses was afraid and said, "Surely the matter is known!"* means that he was surrounded by alienated knowledge and did not yet know enough truth to be safe. This can be seen from the symbolism of *being afraid* as not being safe, because when there is no safety, there is fear. The reason he was not safe is that he lacked truth. People with truth are safe wherever they go, even if they are in the middle of the hells. They lack safety when they do not yet know the truth, because nontruth communicates with evil spirits. That is what is symbolized by the words *Moses was afraid and said, "Surely the matter is known!"*—known to the Egyptians he lived among, that is, as is plain from the next sentence: "Pharaoh heard of this matter and sought to kill Moses."

6770 Exodus 2:15, 16, 17, 18, 19. *And Pharaoh heard of this matter and sought to kill Moses. And Moses fled from Pharaoh's presence and settled in the land of Midian and settled by a well. And a priest of Midian had seven daughters, and they came and drew water and filled the channels to water their father's flock. And the shepherds came and drove them off. And Moses got up and helped them. And he watered their flock. And they came to Reuel their father. And he said, "Why are you hurrying to come [home] today?" And they said, "An Egyptian man rescued us from the hand of the shepherds and even went so far as to draw water for us and watered the flock."*

And Pharaoh heard of this matter and sought to kill Moses means that once false knowledge became aware of the situation, it wanted to destroy the truth in the law imparted by the Divine. *And Moses fled from Pharaoh's presence* means that it separated from falsity. *And settled in the land of*

Midian symbolizes a life lived within a religion found among people of simple goodness. *And settled by a well* symbolizes studying the Word there. *And a priest of Midian had seven daughters* symbolizes holy qualities in that religion. *And they came and drew water* means that they were taught truth from the Word. *And filled the channels* means that they used it to enrich teachings about neighborly love. *To water their [father's] flock* means so that the teachings could be used to instruct people intent on goodness. *And the shepherds came and drove them off* means that teachers of doctrine who were intent on evil opposed them. *And Moses got up and helped them* symbolizes aid given by truth belonging to the law imparted by the Divine. *And he watered their flock* means that people with goodness received instruction from it. *And they came to Reuel their father* symbolizes union with the core goodness in that religion. *And he said, "Why are you hurrying to come [home] today?"* symbolizes a perception that union was now assured. *And they said, "An Egyptian man rescued us from the hand of the shepherds,"* means because true knowledge, connected with the church, overcame the power of false teachings based on evil. *And even went so far as to draw water for us* means that he taught from the Word. *And watered the flock* symbolizes people belonging to the religion there.

And Pharaoh heard of this matter and sought to kill Moses means that **6771**
once false knowledge became aware of the situation, it wanted to destroy the truth in the law imparted by the Divine, as the following shows: *Hearing* symbolizes perceiving, as discussed in §5017. *Pharaoh* represents knowledge opposed to the church's truth, and therefore falsity, as dealt with in §§6651, 6679, 6683. *Killing* symbolizes destroying, as discussed at §6767, so *seeking to kill* means wanting to destroy. And *Moses* represents divine law and divine truth, as discussed at §6752, and therefore the truth in divine law.

I speak of the truth in divine law rather than of divine law itself because the text is still talking about the development of divine law in the Lord's human side.

From this you can see that *Pharaoh heard of this matter and sought to kill Moses* means that once false knowledge became aware of the situation, it wanted to destroy the truth in divine law.

And Moses fled from Pharaoh's presence means that it separated from **6772**
falsity. This can be seen from the symbolism of *fleeing* as separating, from the representation of *Moses* as truth in the law imparted by the Divine (discussed directly above at §6771), and from the representation of *Pharaoh* as falsity (mentioned at §§6651, 6679, 6683, 6771).

This is now the start of a fifth state in the development of divine law in the Lord's human part; and in relation to us, the start of a fifth state in the development of divine truth in a person being reborn. It is a state of separation from falsity and of connection with the truth that accompanies simple goodness. Afterward comes the sixth state, which is one of connection with goodness itself.

6773 *And settled in the land of Midian* symbolizes a life lived among people of simple goodness. This is established by the symbolism of *settling* as life (discussed in §§1293, 3384, 3613, 4451, 6051) and by the symbolism of *Midian* as people in possession of the truth that goes with simple goodness (discussed in §§3242, 4756, 4788). The *land* is mentioned because it symbolizes the religion in the place where those people lived. For the meaning of the land as a religion, see the middle of §6767.

6774 *And settled by a well* symbolizes studying the Word there. This is established by the symbolism of *settling* as life (mentioned directly above at §6773), and here as studying how to live, and by the symbolism of a *well* as the Word (discussed in §§2702, 3424).

The Word is sometimes called a well, sometimes a spring. When it is called a well it symbolizes the Word's literal meaning, and when it is called a spring it symbolizes the Word's inner meaning (§3765). Moses is here said to reside by a well because it symbolizes the Word's literal meaning, since the literal meaning is the first for people who are being reborn and are advancing toward divine truth—this being the current theme of the inner meaning. What is more, people who have the truth that goes with simple goodness (meant here by Midian) care about no meaning but the literal one.

6775 *And a priest of Midian had seven daughters* symbolizes holy qualities in that religion, as the following shows: *Daughters of a priest* symbolize religious qualities. A daughter symbolizes a religion (see §§2362, 3963, 6729), and a priest symbolizes a loving goodness (§§1728, 3670, 6148), so a priest's daughters symbolize the goodness in a religion. *Midian* symbolizes people with the truth that comes of simple goodness, as mentioned just above at §6773. And *seven* symbolizes something holy, as discussed in §§395, 433, 716, 881, 5265, 5268. So *a priest of Midian had seven daughters* symbolizes holy qualities in a religion for people who have the truth that comes of simple goodness.

"People of simple goodness" describes those who focus on the superficial aspects of religion, who believe the Word's literal meaning in all simplicity, each according to his or her understanding of it, and who live by what they believe. So they live a good life—a life as good as their truth renders it. An inner type of religion flows into them through this goodness, but since they do not know inner truth, the goodness that flows into them is vague and therefore dim. They have no detailed ideas for spiritual light to shine on in order to clear matters up. People of this type in the other life receive heaven as a gift in keeping with their goodness, as qualified by their truth.

Those are the people meant here by Midian, but, strictly speaking, Midian means people outside the church who live good lives as defined by their religious persuasion.

And they came and drew water means that they were taught truth 6776
from the Word. This can be seen from the symbolism of *drawing water* as being taught religious truth and being enlightened, which is dealt with in §§3058, 3071. Their being taught from the Word is symbolized by the well from which they drew. For the meaning of a well as the Word, see above at §6774.

And filled the channels means that they used it to enrich teachings 6777
about neighborly love. This is clear from the symbolism of *filling* something from a well as using it (the Word) to enrich something, and from the symbolism of a *channel* as teachings about neighborly love.

A channel or watering place means teachings about neighborly love because it is a wooden conduit into which water is drawn from a well for the purpose of watering flocks. On an inner plane a wooden object symbolizes charitable goodness (§3720), drawing water symbolizes being taught (3058, 3071), the water drawn symbolizes religious truth (2702, 3058, 4976, 5668), the well from which it is drawn symbolizes the Word (2702, 3424, 6774), and watering flocks symbolizes using the Word to teach about goodness (3772). This shows that a channel means teachings about neighborly love.

To water their father's flock means so that the teachings could be used 6778
to instruct people about goodness, as the following shows: *Watering* symbolizes instructing, as noted in §3772. A *flock* symbolizes people who learn about and are led to the goodness urged by neighborly love, as discussed in §§343, 3772, 5913, 6048. And Reuel, the *father,* a priest, represents goodness in the religion that existed where people had the truth that goes with simple goodness, as discussed above at §§6773, 6775.

And the shepherds came and drove them off means that teachers of doc- 6779
trine who were intent on evil opposed them, as the following shows: *Shepherds* symbolize people who teach doctrine and lead others to do good out

of neighborly love, as discussed in §§343, 3795, 6044. Here it symbolizes people who teach doctrine but, being intent on evil, do not lead anyone to neighborly goodness. This symbolism is discussed below. *Driving off* means opposing. And the daughters—the people they drove off—symbolize religious qualities, as mentioned above at §6775.

The shepherds here symbolize people who teach doctrine, yes, but who do not lead anyone to neighborly kindness because the teachers themselves are enmeshed in evil. People who take to evil never acknowledge that neighborly love or deeds of neighborly love contribute to salvation. They cannot acknowledge anything that goes against their life, because to do so would be to go against themselves. Since they are intent on evil, they cannot even see what neighborly love is, so they also cannot see what deeds of neighborly love are. They teach faith, they assign righteousness through faith, and they promise heaven as a reward for faith. These are the people who oppose scriptural teachings about neighborly love. As a consequence, they oppose anyone with the truth that comes of simple goodness—a person symbolized by the daughters of a Midianite priest, who after drawing water and filling the channels to water the flock were driven off from the well by the shepherds.

6780 *And Moses got up and helped them* symbolizes aid given by truth belonging to the law imparted by the Divine. This can be seen from the representation of *Moses* as the truth in the law imparted by the Divine (noted above at §6771) and from the symbolism of *helping* as bringing aid.

6781 *And he watered their flock* means that people with goodness received instruction from it. This can be seen from the symbolism of *watering,* or giving a drink, as teaching (discussed in §§3069, 3092, 3772) and from that of a *flock* as people who learn about and are led to neighborly kindness (discussed in §§343, 3772, 5913, 6048) and who therefore are people with goodness.

6782 *And they came to Reuel their father* symbolizes union with the core goodness in that religion. This is evident from the symbolism of *coming to someone* as uniting and from the representation of *Reuel,* since he was a priest, as goodness. For the meaning of a priest as a loving goodness, see §§1728, 3670, 6148.

The union symbolized here is the union of a religion's truth with its goodness.

6783 *And he said, "Why are you hurrying to come [home] today?"* symbolizes a perception that union was now assured. This is evident from the symbolism of *he said* in the Word's narratives as a perception (discussed many times) and from that of *hurrying to come [home]* as union that was assured. For the symbolism of hurrying as certainty, see §5284, and for that of coming [home] as union, see directly above at §6782. In this case the union that was assured is not that of the daughters hurrying to their father but that of the truth in the law imparted by the Divine, as represented by Moses. That is what was perceived.

And they said, "An Egyptian man rescued us from the hand of the 6784
shepherds," means because true knowledge, connected with the church, overcame the power of false teachings based on evil, as the following demonstrates: An *Egyptian man* symbolizes true knowledge. A man symbolizes truth (§3134), and an Egyptian symbolizes knowledge (1164, 1165, 1186, 1462, 4749, 4964, 4966, 4967, 5700, 6004, 6692). Moses is called an Egyptian man here because he is representing truth as understood by people whose truth is born of simple goodness, symbolized by the daughters of a Midianite priest. Truth in the form of knowledge is the kind of truth such people possess, because they belong to the outer part of the church (6775). That is why I describe it further as true knowledge connected with the church. And *rescuing someone from the hand of the shepherds* means that he overcame the power of falsity based on evil. Rescuing means overcoming because an individual who rescues one set of people from the hand of another overcomes those others. A hand means power (878, 3387, 4931–4937, 5327, 5328, 5544), and shepherds mean people who teach doctrine—in this instance, people who teach falsity based on evil (6779). As they mean teachers, they also mean teachings of this kind.

[2] The reason true knowledge overcomes the power of false teachings derived from evil is that all truth-from-goodness contains something divine, whereas falsity-from-evil contains the opposite. What is opposite to the Divine has no strength at all. Consequently in the other world a thousand people devoted to falsity-from-evil have not a shred of power against a solitary person devoted to truth-from-goodness. At the presence of that one person, the thousand run. If they do not run, they suffer torture and torment.

I am talking about falsity based on evil because such falsity is truly false; falsity resulting from ignorance of the truth rather than from evil is not. Evil, not falsity born of ignorance, is what opposes heaven. In fact, if the ignorance holds any innocence, the Lord accepts the falsity as true, because people with this kind of falsity accept truth.

And even drew water for us means that he taught from the Word. 6785
This is clear from the symbolism of *drawing water* as teaching about

religious truth and being enlightened, which is discussed in §§3058, 3071. The fact that the teaching came from the Word is symbolized by the well they drew water from. For the meaning of a well as the Word, see §6774.

6786 *And watered the flock* symbolizes people belonging to the religion there. This can be seen from the symbolism of a *flock* as people with goodness who allow themselves to be taught, as discussed in §§343, 3772, 5913, 6048. In this case it symbolizes people belonging to the religion there. These are people with the truth that comes of simple goodness, people symbolized by Midian, as shown above [§6773].

A flock symbolizes both goodness and the church—that is, people who have goodness and are part of the church, because the two qualities are so closely connected that neither can be separated from the other. A person dedicated to the goodness urged by faith is a church, and a person who is a church is dedicated to the goodness urged by faith.

6787 Exodus 2:20, 21, 22. *And he said to his daughters, "And where is he? Why did you leave the man behind like this? Call him and have him eat bread." And Moses was willing to reside with the man, and he gave Zipporah, his daughter, to Moses. And she bore a son, and he called his name Gershom, because he said, "I was an immigrant in a foreign land."*

And he said to his daughters symbolizes thought about the holy qualities of religion. *And where is he? Why did you leave the man behind like this?* means, without that truth, how could they unite with what was good in religion? *Call him* means that it was to be united. *And have him eat bread* symbolizes being strengthened in goodness. *And Moses was willing to reside with the man* means that they were in harmony. *And he gave Zipporah, his daughter, to Moses* means that he added on to it the goodness of his own religion. *And she bore a son* symbolizes the truth resulting. *And he called his name Gershom* symbolizes the quality of it. *Because he said, "I was an immigrant in a foreign land,"* means that he was taught truth in a religion that was not his own.

6788 *And he said to his daughters* symbolizes thought about the holy qualities of religion. This is established by the symbolism of *saying* as thought (touched on in §3395) and from that of *daughters* as the holy qualities of religion (discussed above at §6775).

The holy qualities symbolized by these daughters are true ideas. The Word applies the term *holy* to truth because for one thing, the truth that becomes part of our faith rises out of goodness, and for another, what radiates from the Lord's divine humanity is divine truth rising out of divine goodness. That is why the *Holy* Spirit is the *holy influence* that emanates from the Lord. The Spirit itself does not emanate, only the holy thing the Spirit speaks, as anyone who takes the time to think about it can understand.

The Lord's words in John show that the Holy Spirit, also called the Paraclete, is divine truth radiating from the Lord's divine humanity, and that the word *holy* applies to divine truth:

> I will ask the Father to give you another *Paraclete* to stay with you forever, the *Spirit of Truth,* whom the world cannot welcome, because it does not see him or know him. The Paraclete, the *Holy Spirit,* whom the Father will send in my name—*he will teach you everything* and remind you of all that I said to you. (John 14:16, 17, 26)

In the same author:

> When the *Paraclete* comes, whom *I am about to send* to you from the Father—the *Spirit of Truth* that comes from the Father—he will testify of me. (John 15:26)

Again in the same author:

> When *he—the Spirit of Truth*—comes, he will lead you *into all truth.* He will not speak from himself but will speak whatever he hears. He will give me glory, *because he will take from what is mine and proclaim it to you.* Everything whatever that the Father has is mine; that is why I said *that he will take of what is mine* and proclaim it to you. (John 16:13, 14, 15)

Put these passages together with many others and you can see that the Holy Spirit is the holy influence emanating from the Lord's divine humanity. After all, the Lord says, "whom the Father is about to send in my name," "whom I am about to send to you from the Father," and "he will take from what is mine and proclaim it to you; everything whatever that the Father has is mine; that is why I said that he will take of what is mine and proclaim it to you." It is also clear that this holy influence is an attribute of truth, since the Paraclete is called the Spirit of Truth.

And where is he? Why did you leave the man behind like this? means, 6789
without that truth, how could they unite with what was good in religion? This can be seen from the following: An Egyptian *man*—the man they left behind—symbolizes truth in the form of knowledge, as discussed above at §6784. And *Why did you leave the man behind like this?* means,

without that truth, how could they unite with what was good? Leaving the man behind means being unable to unite.

[2] I need to explain. The truth in the form of knowledge represented here by Moses is truth for the outward part of the church. This truth is born of the truth in the law imparted by the Divine, which is also Moses (§§6771, 6780), and the truth in the law imparted by the Divine is truth for the inner part of the church. Unless outward truth is a product of inward truth, it cannot unite with goodness. Take the Word, for example. Unless the Word's inner dimension flows into readers who are focused on its literal meaning, the truth it contains does not unite with goodness. The inner dimension flows in and unites with goodness when the reader holds the Word sacred, and the reader holds it sacred when committed to goodness.

[3] As a further example take the Holy Supper. Hardly anyone knows that the bread of the Holy Supper symbolizes the Lord's love for the whole human race and our love in return, or that the wine symbolizes neighborly love. Yet for people who take them in a reverent frame of mind the bread and wine provide a bond with heaven and with the Lord. The good things that love and charity bring with them flow in through angels, who are not thinking about the bread and wine but about love and charity (§§3464, 3735, 5915). Plainly, then, outer truth unites with inner truth when we are devoted to what is good, although we are unaware of the union.

6790 *Call him* means that it was to be united. This is established by the symbolism of *calling* as uniting, which is dealt with at §6047.

6791 *And have him eat bread* symbolizes being strengthened in goodness. This is established by the symbolism of *bread* as a loving goodness, which is discussed in §§2165, 2177, 3478, 3735, 3813, 4211, 4217, 4735.

Eating bread means being strengthened in goodness because eating here implies a meal together, which the Word calls a banquet. The ancients who were part of the church held group meals, or banquets, for the sake of forming bonds and being strengthened in goodness; see §§3596, 3832, 5161.

6792 *And Moses was willing to reside with the man* means that they were in harmony, as the following shows: *Moses* currently represents true knowledge, as explained above at §6784. *Residing* means living, as discussed in §§1293, 3384, 3613, and residing *with someone* means living together (§4451), so it means being in harmony. And the *man* symbolizes truth associated with the goodness in that religion. For the meaning of a man as truth, see §3134.

And he gave Zipporah, his daughter, to Moses means that he added on to it the goodness of his own religion, as the following shows: *Giving*—giving in marriage—symbolizes adding something on. A *daughter* symbolizes goodness, as discussed in §§489, 490, 491, and also a religion (§§2362, 3963, 6729). *Zipporah* symbolizes the nature of the goodness in that religion. And *Moses* represents true knowledge, as discussed in §6784. 6793

And she bore a son symbolizes the truth resulting. This can be seen from the symbolism of *bearing,* which applies to religious attributes, or to faith and neighborly love. These two are born of the heavenly marriage, a marriage of goodness and truth, which is represented by earthly marriages. And a *son* symbolizes truth, as discussed in §§489, 491, 533, 2623, 3373. 6794

And he called his name Gershom symbolizes the quality of it—of the truth. This can be seen from the symbolism of a name and *calling a name* as the quality of something, as treated of in §§144, 145, 1754, 2009, 2724, 3006, 3421, 6674. *Gershom* implies the quality of that truth—specifically, that it was truth he was taught in a religion not his own, as the next section explains. 6795

Because he said, "I was an immigrant in a foreign land," means that he was taught truth in a religion that was not his own. This can be seen from the symbolism of *being an immigrant* as being taught the beliefs of a religion and from that of the *land* as a religion, as discussed in §§662, 1066, 1262, 1733, 1850, 2117, 2118 at the end, 2928, 3355, 4447, 4535, 5577. A *foreign* land, then, is a religion that is not one's own. 6796

Exodus 2:23, 24, 25. *And it happened during those many days that the king of Egypt died. And the children of Israel sighed over their servitude and cried out, and their cry over their servitude rose to God. And God heard their groan, and God remembered his pact with Abraham, with Isaac, and with Jacob. And God saw the children of Israel, and God knew.* 6797

And it happened during those many days means after more changes of state. *That the king of Egypt died* symbolizes an end to the previous false idea. *And the children of Israel sighed over their servitude* symbolizes grief over the effort to subdue religious truth. *And cried out* symbolizes entreaty. *And their cry over their servitude rose to God* means that they were heard. *And God heard their groan* symbolizes help. *And God remembered his pact with Abraham, with Isaac, and with Jacob* means for the sake of union with the church through the Lord's divine humanity. *And God saw the children of Israel* means that he gave the church the gift of faith. *And knew them* means and of neighborly love.

6798 *And it happened during those many days* means after more changes of state. This is established by the symbolism of *days* as states, which is discussed in §§23, 487, 488, 493, 893, 2788, 3462, 3785, 4850. *It happened during those many days,* then, means after more states, or after more changes of state.

6799 *That the king of Egypt died* symbolizes an end to the previous false idea. This can be seen from the symbolism of *dying* as ceasing to be (discussed in §§494, 6587, 6593) and therefore as an end, and from the representation of Pharaoh, the *king of Egypt,* as falsity in the form of knowledge (discussed in §§6651, 6679, 6683, 6692).

6800 *And the children of Israel sighed over their servitude* symbolizes grief over the effort to subdue religious truth. This can be seen from the symbolism of *sighing* as grief, from the representation of the *children of Israel* as religious truth (discussed in §§5414, 5879, 5951), and from the symbolism of *servitude* as an effort to subdue (discussed in §§6666, 6670, 6671).

6801 *And cried out* symbolizes entreaty, as is self-evident.

6802 *And their cry over their servitude rose to God* means that they were heard, as is also self-evident, because the text goes on to say that God heard their groan and remembered his pact with Abraham, with Isaac, and with Jacob.

6803 *And God heard their groan* symbolizes help, as the following shows: *Hearing* means obeying, as discussed in §§2542, 3869, 4652–4660, 5017. When *God* is said to hear, though, it means providing and helping, because anyone the Lord hears he helps. And a *groan* symbolizes grief and pain over falsity's effort to subdue [truth].

6804 *And God remembered his pact with Abraham, with Isaac, and with Jacob* means for the sake of union with the church through the Lord's divine humanity. This is clear from the symbolism of a *pact,* [or covenant,] as union (discussed below) and from the representation of *Abraham, Isaac,* and *Jacob,* parties to the pact, as the Lord's divine humanity. Abraham represents the Lord's divinity itself, Isaac his divine rationality, and Jacob his earthly divinity; see §§1893, 2010, 2066, 2072, 2083, 2630, 3194, 3210, 3245, 3251, 3305 at the end, 3439, 3576, 3599, 3704, 4180, 4286, 4538, 4570, 4615, 6098, 6185, 6276, 6425.

Where the Word mentions Abraham, Isaac, and Jacob, it is of course not they themselves who are meant in the spiritual sense. After all, names never make it all the way to heaven, only the symbolic meaning of the people named. So what reaches heaven is the actual subject matter and the nature and state of the matter under discussion. These subjects have to do with the church, the Lord's kingdom, and the Lord himself.

[2] Besides, angels in heaven never restrict their thoughts to individuals. To do so would be to limit their thinking and abandon the universal view of matters that is the basis of angelic language. That is why the things angels in heaven say are ineffable and far transcend human thought, which does not expand to universal patterns but contracts to particular instances. When we read, then, that many will come from the east and the west and *recline at [the table] with Abraham and Isaac and Jacob* in the kingdom of the heavens (Matthew 8:11), what angels understand is the Lord's presence, and adoption of the truth and goodness radiating from his divine humanity. When we read that Lazarus was taken into Abraham's embrace (Luke 16:22), angels understand that he was taken to heaven, where the Lord is present. From this you can see that in an inner sense the pact with Abraham, Isaac, and Jacob means union through the Lord's divine humanity.

[3] The idea that divine humanity is a pact—is union itself—is clear from many passages in the Word. In Isaiah, for example:

> *I will give you as a pact for the people,* as a light for the nations. (Isaiah 42:6)

In the same author:

> *I gave you as a pact with the people,* to restore the earth, to distribute devastated inheritances. (Isaiah 49:8)

In the same author:

> Bend your ear and come to me; listen and let your soul live; so *I will strike with you an eternal pact*—the reliable mercies [that I showed] to David. Here, now, I have made him a witness to the peoples, a chieftain and lawgiver for the nations. (Isaiah 55:3, 4)

In Malachi:

> Suddenly to his Temple comes the Lord, whom you seek, and the *Angel of the Covenant,* whom you desire. Watch: He is coming! (Malachi 3:1)

In 2 Samuel:

> *He set up an eternal pact for me,* to be applied to everyone and kept. (2 Samuel 23:5)

[4] These passages are obviously about the Lord and the union of the human race with his divinity itself through his divine humanity. The church knows

that the Lord in his divine humanity is the Mediator and that no one can come to divinity itself, which is in the Lord and is called the Father, except through the Son—in other words, through his divine humanity [John 14:6]. It is therefore the Lord in his divine humanity who is the embodiment of the union.

How can we possibly grasp divinity itself in our thoughts? And if not, how can we form a loving bond with it? But we can all grasp divine humanity in our thoughts and form a loving bond with it.

[5] The idea that a pact means union can be seen from treaties between countries. A treaty unites the parties, and each side makes promises that have to be kept in order for the treaty to remain intact. These promises, or terms, are in fact referred to as the treaty.

In regard to the promises or terms that the Word designates as the pact, [or covenant]: The promises or terms laid out for us are in a narrow sense the Ten Commandments, or the Decalogue. In a wider sense they are all the statutes, requirements, laws, testimonies, and commandments the Lord imposed from Mount Sinai through Moses. In a still wider sense they are the books of Moses. The promises or terms laid out for the children of Israel in those books were rites they had to observe, but for the Lord they were mercy and the choosing of the chosen.

[6] *The Ten Commandments, or the Decalogue, are the pact,* as the following passages show. In Moses:

> Jehovah declared *his covenant* to you, which he commanded you to do: the *ten words* that he wrote onto two stone tablets. (Deuteronomy 4:13, 23)

The two stone tablets on which the Ten Commandments were written were laid away in the ark (Exodus 25:16, 21, 22; 31:18; 32:15, 16, 19; 40:20), so the ark was called the *ark of the covenant* (Deuteronomy 31:9, 24, 25, 26; Joshua 3:3, 6, 14; 4:7; Judges 20:27; 2 Samuel 15:24; 1 Kings 8:21). Here is what Solomon says in the last of these passages:

> *I set there a place for the ark, where lies the covenant of Jehovah,* which he struck with our ancestors. (1 Kings 8:21)

And in John:

> The temple of God was opened in heaven, and *the ark of his covenant was seen* in his temple. (Revelation 11:19)

[7] *All the judgments and statutes that the Lord commanded the Israelite people through Moses are called a pact, as are the books of Moses themselves.* In Moses:

> On the mouth of these words I have *struck a pact with you* and with Israel. (Exodus 34:27)

What is called a pact here consisted of many rules for sacrifices, feasts, and unleavened bread. In the same author:

> Moses took the *book of the covenant* and read it in the ears of the people, who said, "Everything that Jehovah has spoken we will do and hear." (Exodus 24:7, 8)

In 2 Kings:

> Josiah, king of Judah, in the house of Jehovah read before everyone the words of the *book of the covenant found in Jehovah's house.* And he *struck a covenant* before Jehovah to secure the *words of the covenant written in that book.* And all the people stood by the *covenant.* The king commanded all the people to perform the Passover offering to Jehovah God according to what was written in the *book of the covenant.* (2 Kings 23:2, 3, 21)

In David:

> If your children keep *my pact* and my testimony that I have taught them, their children too will sit forever on the throne for you. (Psalms 132:12)

[8] *The pact is the bond created by love and faith.* In Jeremiah:

> "Look! The days are coming," says Jehovah, "on which I will *strike a new pact* with the house of Israel and with the house of Judah unlike the *pact that I struck* with their ancestors, because they rendered *my pact* void. But *this is the pact that I will strike* with the house of Israel after these days: I will put my law in the midst of them, and upon their heart I will write it, and I will become their God, and they will become my people." (Jeremiah 31:31, 32, 33)

Putting his law in the midst of them and writing it on their heart means giving them the gift of faith and neighborly love. Faith and neighborly love lead to union, and this is depicted in the words "I will become their God, and they will become my people." In the same author:

> *I will strike an eternal pact with them,* [pledging] that I will never again turn away from them and will do good to them. *Fear of me, though, I will put into their heart so that they will not withdraw from me.* (Jeremiah 32:40)

The bond of love that is the pact is symbolized by "fear of me I will put into their heart so that they will not withdraw from me." [9] In Ezekiel:

> *I will strike a pact of peace with them;* it will be an *eternal pact* with them. And I will place them and multiply them and put a sanctuary in their midst, and my dwelling place will be among them, and I will become their God, and they will become my people. (Ezekiel 37:26, 27)

In this case the bond of love and faith that is the pact is depicted by the sanctuary in their midst, by the dwelling place among them, and by "I will become their God, and they will become my people." In the same author:

> When I passed right by you and saw you, that here, it was your time, a time for love, *then I entered into a pact with you, that you should be mine.* (Ezekiel 16:8)

This is about Jerusalem, which symbolizes the ancient church. "Entering a pact, that you should be mine," is plainly a marriage, or spiritual union.

Since a pact symbolizes union, a wife is also called a *contracted wife* (Malachi 2:14), and union among brothers is called a *brothers' pact* (Amos 1:9).

A pact again symbolizes union in David:

> *I struck a pact* with my chosen one; I swore to David my servant. (Psalms 89:3)

[10] *On the Lord's part the pact calls for mercy and for choosing the chosen.* This can be seen in David:

> All the ways of Jehovah are *mercy* and truth, *for those who keep his pact* and his testimonies. (Psalms 25:10)

In Isaiah:

> "The mountains will withdraw and the hills recede, but *my mercy* will not withdraw, and *my compact of peace* will not recede," says Jehovah, *who shows you compassion.* (Isaiah 54:10)

In Moses:

> Jehovah your God, he is God, a faithful God, *keeping his pact and his mercy with those who love him* and keep his commandments, to the thousandth generation. (Deuteronomy 7:9, 12)

In the same author:

> *If you keep my pact,* you will become a personal possession to me, out of all the peoples. (Exodus 19:5)

In the same author:

> I will turn to face you and make you fruitful and make you multiply and strengthen *my pact* with you. (Leviticus 26:9)

Turning to face them comes of mercy. Making them fruitful and making them multiply means giving them the gift of neighborly love and faith, and people receiving those gifts are called the chosen. So these words have to do with choosing, as does the statement that they would become a personal possession.

[11] *The representative church also had signs of the pact,* which reminded the people of the union. *Circumcision* was one such sign (Genesis 17:11), because it symbolized purification from unclean kinds of love. Once these kinds of love have been removed, we are instilled with heavenly love, which brings union. The *Sabbath* was called an *eternal pact* (Exodus 31:16). The *loaves of showbread* are said to have been for the children of Israel *by an eternal pact* (Leviticus 24:8). And *blood* especially was such a sign, as is plain in Moses:

> Moses took the *book of the covenant* and read it in the ears of the people, who said, "Everything that Jehovah has spoken we will do and hear." Then Moses took the *blood of the peace-offering sacrifice* and spattered it on the people and said, "Look: the *blood of the covenant* that Jehovah struck with you over all these words." (Exodus 24:7, 8)

In Zechariah:

> By the *blood of your pact* I will let the prisoners out of a pit in which there is no water. (Zechariah 9:11)

Blood was the pact, or a sign of the pact, because it symbolized union through spiritual love, that is, through charity for one's neighbor. Consequently, when the Lord established the Holy Supper, he called his blood the blood of the new covenant (Matthew 26:28).

This then shows what a pact means in the inner sense of the Word.

6805 *And God saw the children of Israel* means that he gave the church the gift of faith, as the following shows: *Seeing* is a symbol for believing, as discussed in §§897, 2325, 2807, 3863, 3869, 4403–4421, 5400. *God saw,* then, means giving the gift of faith, since faith comes from God. And the *children of Israel* symbolize the church, as treated of at §6637.

6806 *And knew them* means and (that he gave the gift) of neighborly love. This can be seen from the symbolism of *knowing* when ascribed to God—the Lord—as giving the gift of neighborly love. Neighborly love is what unites the Lord with us, enables him to be present with us, and therefore allows him to know us. It is true that the Lord knows everyone in the universe, but the only people he recognizes the way a father recognizes his children are those characterized by a loving, charitable goodness. [2] That is why he says the following about people characterized by goodness, whom he calls his sheep:

> I am the good shepherd, and *I know my own* and *am known by my own.* My sheep hear my voice, and *I know them,* and they follow me. (John 10:14, 27)

Concerning people characterized by evil, though, the Lord says *that he does not know them.* In Matthew:

> Many will say to me on that day, "Lord! Lord! Haven't we prophesied in your name and cast out demons in your name and exercised many powers in your name?" But then I will proclaim to them, "*I do not know you.* Leave me, you evildoers!" (Matthew 7:22, 23)

In the same author:

> At last the other young women also came, saying, "Lord! Lord! Open up to us!" But he, answering, said, "Truly, I say to you: *I do not know you.*" (Matthew 25:11, 12)

In Luke:

> From the time the householder has risen and shut the door, then you will start to stand outside and knock on the door, saying, "Lord! Lord! Open up to us!" But answering, he will say to you, "*I do not know you, where you are from.*" Then you will start to say, "We ate in front of you, and drank, and in our streets you taught." But he will say, "I tell you *I do not know you, where you are from.* Leave me, all you evildoers!" (Luke 13:25, 26, 27)

This shows that being known, when one is said to be known by the Lord, means being characterized by charitable goodness—that is, receiving the gift of such goodness—because all charitable goodness comes from the Lord. It also shows that not being known means being characterized by evil. [3] Recognition involves union, and the more closely we unite with the Lord, the more we are said to be known by him.

The Lord also knows people who have no bond with him—in fact, he knows every smallest detail about everyone (John 2:24, 25)—but they are engrossed in evil, so they experience a different kind of presence that seems to be absence. The Lord is not absent, though. It is the person or spirit engrossed in evil who is absent. This situation is described as being unknown to the Lord.

This relationship is mirrored in angels and spirits. Those living in a similar state appear near each other and recognize each other, but those living in dissimilar states appear far from each other and do not recognize each other as easily.

In short, similarity of state in the other world results in apparent presence and in recognizability, while dissimilarity of state results in apparent absence and in unrecognizability.

The Spirits of Mercury

AT the end of many chapters it has been demonstrated that heaven as a whole resembles a human being, which is called the universal human, and that each and every part of the body inside and out corresponds to that human, or to heaven. However, there are not enough people going to the other world from this planet to make up that universal human. They are relatively few. There have to be people from many other planets as well. In addition, the Lord provides that as soon as correspondence [with the body] is lacking anywhere in either type or amount, individuals are immediately summoned from some planet to make up the lack. This preserves the balance and therefore keeps heaven stable. 6807

Something else revealed to me from heaven was the role spirits from Mercury play in the universal human. They play the role of memory, but the memory of concepts abstracted from earthly objects and mere matter. 6808

Having been allowed to talk with those spirits for many weeks, to hear what they are like, and to find out how matters stand with the inhabitants of their planet, I would like to recount my experiences.

6809 One time they came to me and investigated the contents of my memory. Spirits are very good at this, because when they come to us they can see in our memory everything we know. When the spirits of Mercury looked into various memories of mine, then, including those of cities and other places I had been to, I noticed they had no interest in the churches, palaces, houses, or streets. All they wanted to know was what I had heard about events in those locations, about the way the places were governed, about the character and customs of the citizens, and so on. In our memory, such information attaches to the places, so that when we are reminded of the places, details like those come up too.

I was surprised to find they were like this, so I kept asking why they were skipping over the grand sights of those areas and examining only the culture and events there. They would answer that they took no pleasure in observing material, physical, or earthly things, only the state of affairs. This for the first time showed me that in the universal human the spirits of that planet correlate with the memory of concepts abstracted from what is matter-based and earthly.

6810 I learned that this attitude also shapes how the inhabitants of that planet live. That is to say, they care nothing for earthly or physical matters, only for the statutes, laws, and forms of government among the nations there, and for information on heaven, which is abundant. I was told further that people on that planet often talk with spirits, which means that they learn about spiritual realities and about the conditions of life after death. This gives them a disregard for anything physical or earthly. People who know for certain there is life after death and believe in it take heavenly concerns to heart, because what is heavenly is eternal and happy. They pay no more attention to worldly concerns than life and its necessities demand.

6811 I had an experience illustrating how eagerly they seek out and soak up knowledge about the kinds of concepts stored in the part of the memory that transcends the physical senses. Whenever they examined my knowledge of heavenly matters, they would run through all of it and repeatedly say, "That's right. That's right." You see, when spirits come to us, they penetrate every corner of our memory and stir up the information useful to them. In fact, they can read our memory like a book, as I have often observed. The spirits of Mercury would do this quite skillfully and quickly, because they ignored the kinds of things that take too long or that restrict inner vision and therefore slow it down. Everything earthly and physical bogs one down if it is one's goal—in other words, if it is the only thing one loves. Instead they focused on the ideas themselves. Concepts free of any earthly dregs bear the mind upward, into a broad vista, while mere matter drags the mind down, into a narrow field of vision.

Another illustration of their eagerness to acquire knowledge: Once, while I was writing about events in the future, the spirits were far away, in a place from which they could not explore my memory. I was unwilling to read the material to them, which upset them greatly, and in a departure from their usual manner they chose to rail against me, saying I was a terrible person, and so on. To show how angry they were, they put a painful kind of squeeze on the right side of my head that reached to my ear. Such efforts could not harm me at all, but because they had done wrong, they moved still farther away. Yet they stopped, still wanting to know what I had written about the future. That is how strong their craving for knowledge is.

The spirits of Mercury know more than any other spirits about the phe- 6812
nomena both of our own solar system and of the starry universe beyond. Moreover, once they have acquired information, they retain it, and they recall it to mind whenever something similar comes up. From this you can see plainly that spirits have a much more perfect memory than we do, and that they retain what they hear and see and sense. They hold on especially tight to information that gives them pleasure, like the knowledge of higher realities that gives pleasure to these particular spirits. What we delight in and love flows in of its own accord (so to speak) and stays. The rest does not penetrate but only glances off the surface and disappears.

When the spirits of Mercury go to other communities, they probe to 6813
find out what the inhabitants there know, departing once they have finished their investigation. It is also possible for the spirits to communicate together in such a way that, if they are welcomed and loved by a community, they share everything they know while they are there. This they do by an inflow rather than by any spoken word.

The spirits of Mercury take more pride in their knowledge than others do. "You may know a lot," I told them, "but what you don't know is still infinite. And if your store of knowledge grew forever, you could not achieve full command of even the most general knowledge. You are proud and conceited," I said, "which is unbecoming."

"It is not pride," they retorted. "We just revel in our power of memory." That is their way of excusing their faults.

6814 They shun audible speech, since it is a physical thing, so I could talk with them only through a kind of active thinking.

Since their memory retains concepts rather than purely physical images, it more directly supplies their minds with things to think about. The process of thought, which takes place on a higher level than the process of forming mental images, requires concepts abstracted from matter for its objects.

Nevertheless, the spirits of Mercury do not have a very well-developed capacity for judgment. They do not like exercising judgment or forming conclusions on the basis of knowledge; it is bare knowledge that pleases them.

6815 I was allowed to suggest that maybe they would like to put their knowledge to some use, because enjoying knowledge is not enough. Knowledge looks toward usefulness, and usefulness has to be its goal. Knowledge alone is of no use to them, only to others with whom they might want to share it. I added that halting at mere knowledge is completely inappropriate for a person seeking wisdom. Knowledge is simply an instrumental cause, designed to help us identify useful purposes, which must involve real life.

Their answer, though, was that they enjoy knowledge, and that for them, knowledge itself is a useful purpose.

6816 The spirits of Mercury differ radically from the spirits of our own planet, because the spirits of our planet do not care as much about abstract entities, only about material, worldly, physical, and earthly things. As a result, the spirits of Mercury cannot coexist with the spirits of our planet. Whenever the former run into the latter, they flee. The spiritual atmospheres wafting from the two parties are almost opposite.

The spirits of Mercury have a saying that they love the *offspring* of the material realm, and that they want to contemplate not the husk but things stripped of their husk and therefore the inner depths.

6817 I will continue with the spirits of Mercury at the end of the next chapter [§§6921–6932].

Exodus 3

Teachings on Neighborly Love

I need to say more about the neighbor, because without a concept of the neighbor it is impossible to understand how to exercise neighborly love. 6818

In remarks preceding the last chapter [§§6703–6712] I said that everyone is our neighbor but that one person is not our neighbor in the same way as another. I also said that a person with goodness is more our neighbor than others are and that it is therefore the goodness in another that we should love. When we love what is good, we love the Lord, because the Lord is the source of goodness, is the presence within goodness, and is goodness itself.

However, it is humankind not only in the singular but also in the plural that is our neighbor, because it is the community small or large, the country, the church, the Lord's kingdom, and above all the Lord. These are the neighbor to whom we ought to do good from selfless motives. 6819

Moreover, these are the ascending levels of neighbor. A community of many is our neighbor on a higher level than an individual, the country on a higher level than a community, the church on a still higher level, and the Lord's kingdom on a higher level yet. On the highest level our neighbor is the Lord. These ascending levels are like the steps of a ladder that has the Lord at the top.

A community is more our neighbor than an individual is because it consists of more people. Toward the community we ought to exercise neighborly love the same way as toward an individual—that is, with due regard for the kind of goodness it has. This means exercising love in a totally different way toward a group of upright people than toward a group of people who are not upright. 6820

Our country is more our neighbor than a community is because it is like a parent: we were born there, it nourishes us, and it protects us from harm. We have an obligation to benefit our country from love, according to its needs, which have mainly to do with its nourishment, 6821 its civic life, and its spiritual life. People who love their country and benefit it on account of wishing it well love the Lord's kingdom when they go to the other world because the Lord's kingdom is then their country. Furthermore, anyone who loves the Lord's kingdom loves the Lord, because he is the all-in-all of his kingdom. What is properly called the Lord's kingdom is the goodness and truth its inhabitants receive from him.

6822 The church is more our neighbor than our country is because to tend to the church is to tend to the souls and eternal life of one's fellow citizens. People care for the interests of the church when they lead someone in a good direction, and those who do so in a selfless way love their neighbor. After all, what they are seeking and desiring for the other person is heaven and the happiness of life everlasting.

Goodness can be instilled in others by any fellow citizen, but truth can be instilled in others only by ministers who teach. When others attempt it, heresies arise and the church undergoes turmoil and rifts.

We exercise neighborly love when we use religious truth to lead our neighbor in a good direction. If an idea that leads away from goodness is described by the church as true, we should not mention that idea, because it is not true.

We must all start by acquiring truth for ourselves from the teachings of our religion. Later we acquire it from the Lord's Word. This is the truth of which our faith must be composed.

6823 The Lord's kingdom is our neighbor on a higher level than the church we were born into, because it is made up of everyone both on earth and in the heavens who possesses goodness. So the Lord's kingdom is every kind of goodness taken together. When we love this goodness, we love everyone who displays it.

The whole, then—everything good taken together—is the neighbor at the highest level. It is also the universal human described at the end of many previous chapters. This human is an image representing the Lord himself. We love the universal human, or the Lord's kingdom, when our deepest feelings move us to help people who receive their humanity from the Lord through the universal human—in other words, people who have the Lord's kingdom in them.

6824 These are the different levels of the neighbor, and the excellence of neighborly love accords with them. The levels are arranged in order, meaning that a higher, superior level always surpasses a lower, inferior one. The Lord is at the very top, and he must be the focus at all levels, the goal to which they look; so he is to be loved above all people and above all things.

Exodus 3

1. And Moses was pasturing the flock of Jethro, his father-in-law, priest of Midian, and he led the flock to the back of the wilderness and came to the mountain of God, Horeb.

2. And the angel of Jehovah appeared to him in a fiery flame from the middle of the bramble, and he looked, and here, the bramble was burning with fire, and the bramble was not being consumed at all.

3. And Moses said, "I will turn aside, then, and see this great sight, why the bramble does not burn up."

4. And Jehovah saw that he turned aside to see, and God called to him from the middle of the bramble and said, "Moses! Moses!" and he said, "Here I am."

5. And he said, "You are not to come near here; slip your shoes off your feet, because the place that you are standing on is holy ground."

6. And he said, "I am the God of your father: the God of Abraham, the God of Isaac, and the God of Jacob." And Moses covered his face, because he was afraid of looking at God.

7. And Jehovah said, "I have seen clearly the affliction of my people, who are in Egypt, and have heard their cry over their taskmasters, because I know their pain.

8. And I have come down to deliver them from the hand of the Egyptians and to bring them up from that land to a land good and broad, to a land flowing with milk and honey, to the place of the Canaanite and the Hittite and the Amorite and the Perizzite and the Hivite and the Jebusite.

9. And now, look: the cry of the children of Israel has come to me, and I have also seen the oppression with which the Egyptians oppress them.

10. And now go, and I will send you to Pharaoh. And bring my people, the children of Israel, out of Egypt."

11. And Moses said to God, "Who am I, that I should go to Pharaoh and that I should bring the children of Israel out of Egypt?"

12. And he said, "Because I will be with you. And this will be the sign to you that I myself have sent you: In your bringing the people out of Egypt, you will worship God next to this mountain."

13. And Moses said to God, "Consider: I come to the children of Israel and tell them, 'The God of your fathers has sent me to you,' and suppose they say to me, 'What is his name?' What should I tell them?"

14. And God said to Moses, "I Am Who I Am," and he said, "This is what you shall say to the children of Israel: 'I Am has sent me to you.'"

15. And God said further to Moses, "This is what you are to say to the children of Israel: 'Jehovah, the God of your fathers—the God of Abraham, the God of Isaac, and the God of Jacob—has sent me to you.' This is my name forever, and this is my memorial to generation after generation.

16. Go, and you are to gather the elders of Israel and say to them, 'Jehovah, the God of your fathers, has appeared to me—the God of Abraham, Isaac, and Jacob—saying, "I have faithfully visited you and what has been done to you in Egypt.

17. And I say I will bring you up from the affliction of Egypt to the land of the Canaanite and the Hittite and the Amorite and the Perizzite and the Hivite and the Jebusite, to a land flowing with milk and honey."'

18. And should they hear your voice, you are to go in—you and the elders of Israel—to the king of Egypt and say to him, 'Jehovah, God of the Hebrews, has met us. And now please let us go a journey of three days into the wilderness and let us sacrifice to Jehovah our God.'

19. And I myself know that the king of Egypt will not grant you [your request] to go, not even under a strong hand.

20. And I will send out my hand and strike Egypt with all my wonders that I will do in the middle of it, and afterward he will send you away.

21. And I will give favor to this people in the eyes of the Egyptians, and it will happen when you go that you will not go empty-handed.

22. And have a woman ask her neighbor and her houseguest for vessels of silver and vessels of gold and for clothes, and you must put them on your sons and on your daughters and plunder the Egyptians."

Summary

6825 IN the first chapter the inner meaning described the way falsity and evil troubled people in the church. In the second it dealt with the rudiments and developing stages of divine truth in these people. The inner meaning of the current chapter is about their deliverance, which is when they first learn who the God is who has delivered them. They are taught that he is the Lord and that he will lead them to heaven once they have been endowed with abundant truth and goodness.

Inner Meaning

EXODUS 3:1, 2, 3. *And Moses was pasturing the flock of Jethro, his father-in-law, priest of Midian, and he led the flock to the back of the wilderness and came to the mountain of God, Horeb. And the angel of Jehovah appeared to him in a fiery flame from the middle of the bramble, and he looked, and here, the bramble was burning with fire, and the bramble was not being consumed at all. And Moses said, "I will turn aside, then, and see this great sight, why the bramble does not burn up."* 6826

And Moses was pasturing the flock of Jethro, his father-in-law, priest of Midian, means that the law imparted by the Divine instructed people who possessed truth born of simple goodness; the *priest of Midian* is goodness in the religion that existed among those people. *And he led the flock to the back of the wilderness* means after they underwent times of trial. *And came to the mountain of God* means that divine love and its goodness appeared to him. *Horeb* symbolizes its quality. *And the angel of Jehovah appeared to him* symbolizes the Lord in his divine humanity. *In a fiery flame from the middle of the bramble* symbolizes divine love present in truth in the form of knowledge. *And he looked, and here, the bramble was burning with fire* symbolizes a perception that truth in the form of knowledge was full of a goodness that comes from divine love. *And the bramble was not being consumed at all* symbolizes divine truth united with divine goodness on the earthly plane. *And Moses said,* symbolizes something perceived from the law imparted by the Divine. *I will turn aside, then, and see this great sight* means reflecting on this revelation. *Why the bramble does not burn up* means that such is the nature of the union.

And Moses was pasturing the flock of Jethro, his father-in-law, priest of Midian, means that the law imparted by the Divine instructed people who possessed truth born of simple goodness, and the *priest of Midian* 6827 is goodness in the religion that existed among those people. This can be seen from the following: *Moses* represents the Lord as the divine law, as discussed in §6752. At first he represented the Lord in his role as the *truth* in the law imparted by the Divine (§6771), but now he represents the Lord in his role as the law itself imparted by the Divine—it is allowable to use these terms for the steps of progress the Lord took on the way to making his human side the divine law itself.

Throughout the Word the inmost, or highest, meaning is about the Lord alone and about the glorification of his human nature. The inmost or highest meaning surpasses human understanding, though, so let me explain the Word on an inward level of meaning. This level has to do with the Lord's kingdom, the church and its establishment, and the way the Lord regenerates people in the church. The reason the inward level deals with these subjects is that human rebirth is an image representing the Lord's glorification; see §§3138, 3212, 3296, 3490, 4402, 5688.

[2] *Pasturing* means teaching, as discussed in §§3795, 5201. A *flock* symbolizes someone who learns truth and is led by it to charitable goodness, as discussed at §343, so in a broad sense it means the church (3767, 3768). Here it means the religion that existed where there were people with the truth that comes of simple goodness—people symbolized by Midian (3242, 4756). And a *father-in-law* symbolizes goodness that fathers such goodness as unites with truth (here, with truth in the law imparted by the Divine, as represented by Moses); see §6793. The quality of that [originating] goodness is *Jethro.* And *priest of Midian* symbolizes goodness in the religion that existed where there were people who possessed the truth that goes with simple goodness, as discussed at §6775. This shows that *Moses was pasturing the flock of Jethro, his father-in-law, priest of Midian,* means that the law imparted by the Divine instructed people who possessed truth that was born of simple goodness, and that a *priest of Midian* is goodness in the religion that existed among those people.

6828 *And he led the flock to the back of the wilderness* means after they (people in possession of the truth associated with simple goodness) underwent times of trial. This can be seen from the symbolism of the *flock* as the religion in the place inhabited by people with the truth belonging to simple goodness (noted directly above at §6827) and from that of a *wilderness* as a state of trial.

"Wilderness" means a place sparsely inhabited and underdeveloped, and also a place completely uninhabited and undeveloped. In a spiritual sense, then, it symbolizes a person devastated by a loss of goodness and desolate over a loss of truth, and therefore a person undergoing trial. When we are being tested, we feel devastated and desolate, because the falsity and evil in us emerge, hiding the Lord's inflowing truth and goodness from us and almost robbing us of it. The truth that does flow in appears too feeble to drive away the falsity and evil, and evil spirits are at hand to inflict pain and inspire despair over our salvation.

Many passages in the Word show that a wilderness symbolizes this kind of state; see §2708. Because a wilderness symbolizes a state of trial, and the number forty symbolizes the length of time it lasts, however long that is (§§730, 862, 2272, 2273), the children of Israel were *in the wilderness forty years* [Numbers 32:13]. For the same reason, the Lord was *in the wilderness forty days* when he was being tested (Matthew 4:2; Mark 1:13).

And came to the mountain of God means that divine love and its goodness then appeared. This is evident from the symbolism of the *mountain of God* as divine love and its goodness. For the symbolism of a mountain as a loving goodness, see §§795, 796, 2722, 4210, 6435. This goodness appeared after they underwent times of trial, as symbolized by the fact that Moses came to the mountain at the back of the wilderness. 6829

Here is the situation: When we undergo trial, we are besieged on all sides by falsity and evil, which block the inflow of light from the Divine—in other words, of truth and goodness. We are then in the dark. In the other life, darkness is nothing but a siege by falsity, because falsity kills the light and therefore any sense of comfort afforded by truth to the person being tested.

When we emerge from our trials, however, light accompanied by its spiritual warmth—or truth with its accompanying goodness—then appears, giving us gladness after all our cares. This is the morning that takes over from night in the other world.

The reason goodness then makes itself felt and truth then makes itself seen is that after the crisis truth and goodness penetrate deep within and take root. While we are being tested, we are essentially starving for goodness and dying of thirst for truth, so when we come out the other side, we absorb goodness like a person starved for food and take in truth like a person parched for drink. What is more, when the law imparted by the Divine appears, falsity and evil are removed, and once they are gone, truth and goodness have an opportunity to penetrate more deeply.

These are the reasons a loving goodness from the Lord, along with its light, appears after times of trial.

Everyone in the other world knows that brightness and good cheer emerge after the murk and anxiety of trials, because the experience is common there.

6830 *Horeb* symbolizes its quality—the quality of divine love and its goodness when it appeared. This can be seen from the fact that when the text adds names, they contain the quality of the attribute under discussion. The quality of attribute implied by *Horeb* is evident from the vision seen there, of a fiery flame from the middle of the bramble. The meaning is therefore God's loving goodness as it shines out through the truth in the divine law.

6831 *And the angel of Jehovah appeared to him* symbolizes the Lord in his divine humanity. This can be seen from the symbolism of the *angel of Jehovah* as the Lord's divine humanity, which is treated of at §6280.

The reason the divine humanity is called the angel of Jehovah is that until the Lord's Coming, Jehovah appeared in human form, as an angel, when he passed through heaven. The whole angelic heaven presents the image of a single human being, called the universal human, which is discussed at the end of many chapters. When divinity itself passed through heaven [to earth], then, it appeared in human form, as an angel, to the eyes of the people with whom it spoke. This was Jehovah's divine humanity as it existed before the Lord's Coming. Now that the Lord's humanity has become divine, it is identical with Jehovah's, since the Lord is Jehovah himself in his divine humanity.

For the idea that the Lord in his divine humanity is called an angel, see §6280. The same thing can be seen from numerous New Testament passages in which the Lord describes himself as one *sent* by the Father. To be sent means to issue forth, and the Hebrew word for an angel means one who has been sent. For the Lord referring to himself as having been sent, see Matthew 10:40; 15:24; Mark 9:37; Luke 4:43; 9:48; 10:16; John 3:17, 34; 4:34; 5:23, 24, 36, 37, 38; 6:29, 39, 40, 44, 57; 7:16, 18, 28, 29; 8:16, 18, 29, 42; 9:4; 10:36; 11:41, 42; 12:44, 45, 49; 13:20; 14:24; 16:5, 7; 17:3, 8, 18, 21, 23, 25.

6832 *In a fiery flame from the middle of the bramble* symbolizes divine love present in truth in the form of knowledge. This is clear from the symbolism of a *fiery flame* as divine love (discussed below) and from that of a *bramble* as truth in the form of knowledge. A bramble symbolizes truth in the form of knowledge because all bushes of every kind symbolize knowledge, the larger bushes symbolizing religious knowledge and perceptions. A bramble, as it produces flowers and berries, symbolizes truth in the form of knowledge.

The church's truth in the form of knowledge is actually the literal meaning of the Word, and in addition, every religious representation or symbol known to Jacob's descendants. In its outward form all of this is called truth in the form of knowledge, but in its inward form it is spiritual truth.

Truth was invisible to Jacob's descendants in its inner or spiritual form, though, because they cared only about what is external and refused to learn about anything deeper. That is why the Lord appeared in a bramble. When the Lord appears to someone, his appearance depends on the person's nature, because we can receive what is divine only in accordance with our nature.

Likewise when the Lord appeared on Mount Sinai, he appeared to the people as a fire burning to the heart of the sky, and as shadow, cloud, and darkness (Deuteronomy 4:11; 5:22, 23, 24, 25; Exodus 19:18). He would have had an entirely different appearance had the people watching from the foot of the mountain not been what they were. Because they cared only about what is external, Moses is said to have entered a cloud when he approached the Lord on Mount Sinai (Exodus 20:21; 24:2, 18; 34:2, 3, 5). Cloud stands for the outer level of the Word (see the preface to Genesis 18 and §§4060, 4391, 5922, 6343 at the end), so it also stands for a religious representation viewed in its outward form.

[2] The fact that the Lord appears to an individual according to that individual's nature can be seen from the following: To inhabitants of the third or inmost heaven the Lord appears as a sun that radiates an indescribable light, because the inhabitants there possess love for him and the goodness that goes with it. To inhabitants of the second or middle heaven he appears as the moon, because the love they have for the Lord there is more aloof and dimmer, since they concentrate on love for their neighbor. In the first or outermost heaven, though, the Lord appears as neither sun nor moon but only as light, which still far outshines the light of the world.

Since the Lord appears to each of us according to our nature, he necessarily appears to the inhabitants of hell as dusky cloud and darkness. As soon as heaven's light, which comes from the Lord, falls on any hell, things there turn gloomy and dark.

This evidence now shows that the Lord appears to us each in keeping with our character because he appears to us in keeping with the way we receive him. Since Jacob's descendants were focused solely on what is external, the Lord appeared to Moses in the bramble, and also in a cloud when Moses approached the Lord on Mount Sinai.

[3] A flame means divine love because in its first origin love is actually the fire and flame that come from the Lord as the sun. The fire or flame of this sun is what gives each of us the core essence of life. It is the actual fire of life, which fills our inner depths with warmth, as can be seen from love itself. The more love grows in us, the warmer we become, and the more love shrinks in us, the colder we turn.

[4] That is why the Lord appeared as fire and flame when he appeared in visions. In Ezekiel, for instance:

> The appearance of the four living creatures [which were guardian beings] was like *embers of burning fire, like the appearance of lamps.* The *fire* was moving among the living creatures, so that it had *brilliance,* and *from the fire went out lightning.* Above the expanse that was over their head was a seeming appearance of sapphire stone, like a throne. And on the likeness of a throne was what looked like the *appearance of a person on it, high above.* And I saw the *form of a burning ember,* like the form of *fire* within it all around, from the appearance of his hips and up; but from the appearance of his hips and down I saw the seeming *appearance of fire,* which had a *brilliance all around.* (Ezekiel 1:13, 26, 27, 28)

No one can deny that every detail of this vision exists to symbolize and represent something divine. However, it is impossible to see the holy secret embedded there without knowing what is meant by the guardian beings, the embers of burning fire like the appearance of lamps, the throne, the appearance of a person on it, the hips above and below which there was fire, and the brilliance cast by the fire. The guardian beings are the Lord's providence (see §308). The throne is heaven—strictly speaking, divine truth radiating from the Lord, which forms heaven (§5313). The appearance of a person on the throne, high above, is obviously the Lord in his divine humanity. The hips are marriage love and all the heavenly love it generates (§§3021, 4277, 4280, 4575, 5050–5062). This love was represented by the form of a burning ember, like the form of fire, which had a brilliance all around. [5] In Daniel:

> I was looking, until thrones were overturned, and the Ancient One sat. His clothing was like white snow, and the hair of his head was like clean

> wool. His throne was a *fiery flame,* his wheels a *burning fire; a river of fire was pouring forth and going out before him.* (Daniel 7:9, 10)

Here too the divine goodness of the Lord's divine love appeared as a fiery flame. In John:

> The one sitting on the white horse—his eyes were *like a fiery flame.* (Revelation 19:12)

Revelation 19:13, 16 says explicitly that the one sitting on the white horse is the Lord as the Word, so the fiery flame is divine truth in the Word, which comes from the Lord's divine goodness. In the same author:

> In the middle of the seven lampstands, one like the *Son of Humankind,* wearing a robe—his head and hair white, like white wool, like snow, but his eyes, like a *fiery flame.* (Revelation 1:13, 14)

Here too, eyes like a fiery flame stand for divine truth radiating from the Lord's divine goodness.

[6] The meaning of a fiery flame as divine truth radiating from the Lord is also evident in David:

> Jehovah's voice flows in like a *fiery flame.* (Psalms 29:7)

Jehovah's voice stands for divine truth.

To represent divine truth radiating from the Lord's divine goodness, it was commanded that a lampstand be made of pure gold *with seven lamps,* that it be put in the meeting tent near the table for the loaves of showbread, and that *the lamps burn continually before Jehovah* (Exodus 25:31–end; 37:17–24; 40:24, 25; Leviticus 24:4; Numbers 8:2; Zechariah 4:2). The lampstand with its seven lamps represented divine truth radiating from the Lord's divine goodness.

[7] To represent divine goodness itself as well, it was commanded that there be an eternal flame on the altar:

> *The fire shall burn on the altar and not be put out;* the priest shall kindle wood on it at every dawn. *Fire shall continually burn on the altar and not be put out.* (Leviticus 6:12, 13)

The ancients were very familiar with the role of fire as a representation of divine love. This can be seen from the fact that the use of the representation spread from the ancient church to distant nations whose worship was idolatrous. Those nations established a sacred, perpetual fire and gave charge of it to young women called Vestal virgins, as everyone knows.

[8] In a negative sense, fire and flame symbolize unclean kinds of love, such as the love of revenge, cruelty, hatred, and adultery, or more broadly, the lusts produced by self-love and materialism. The negative sense can also be seen from many passages in the Word, of which let me quote just the following. In Isaiah:

> Here, they have become like stubble; *fire has seared them;* they do not rescue their soul *from the hand of the flame. There is no ember to grow hot,* [no] *fire* to sit before. (Isaiah 47:14)

In Ezekiel:

> Here, now, I myself will *ignite in you a fire* that will consume in you every green tree and every dry tree; *the blazing flame will not be put out,* so all faces from south to north will be burned. (Ezekiel 20:47)

The fire and flame in these verses symbolize cravings for evil and falsity, which blot out all religious goodness and truth, with the result that the church is devastated. [9] In Luke:

> The rich man said to Abraham, "Father Abraham, take pity on me and send Lazarus to dip the tip of his finger into the water and cool my tongue, because *I am tormented in this flame."* (Luke 16:24)

People who do not realize that the fire of life in us has a different source than physical fire cannot help thinking that "hellfire" means fire like that in the world. In reality, though, scriptural fire does not mean physical fire but the fire of love and therefore the fire of human life, radiating from the Lord as the sun. When this fire passes into adversaries of the Lord, it turns into the fire of corrupt desires, which (again) are vengeful, hateful, cruel desires welling up out of self-love and materialism. This fire is what torments the inhabitants of the hells, because when desire of that kind is unbridled, they all attack each other and abuse each other in dire, unspeakable ways. Everyone wants to be supreme and to steal others' belongings by tricks both hidden and open. When both sides lust for this, mutually destructive hatred springs up, leading to savagery, which is committed mainly through the use of image-changing power and magic arts. These arts are innumerable and are completely unknown in the world.

[10] People who disbelieve in spiritual things—especially people who worship the material world—can never be persuaded to accept that the

warmth in living beings which actually constitutes their inner life has a different source than the world's warmth. They cannot see, much less acknowledge, that heavenly fire is what radiates from the Lord as the sun or that this fire is pure love. Neither, then, can they understand countless Scripture verses in which no other kind of fire is meant, and they cannot understand countless elements in the body, which is an organ designed to receive that fire.

And he looked, and here, the bramble was burning with fire symbolizes 6833
a perception that truth in the form of knowledge was full of a goodness that comes from divine love. This can be seen from the symbolism of *looking* as perceiving (discussed in §§2150, 3764, 4567, 4723, 5400), from that of a *bramble* as truth in the form of knowledge (discussed directly above at §6832), and from that of *fire* as divine love (discussed in §§934 at the end, 4906, 5071, 5215, 6314, 6832). *Burning with fire,* then, means being full of a goodness that comes from divine love.

And the bramble was not being consumed at all symbolizes divine 6834
truth united with divine goodness on the earthly plane, as the following shows: A *bramble* symbolizes truth in the form of knowledge, as discussed above at §§6832, 6833. In this verse, where the subject is the Lord, it symbolizes divine truth on the earthly plane. The earthly plane is symbolized because that is where truth in the form of knowledge resides. And *not being consumed* by fire means not being annihilated by the goodness that comes of divine love. For the meaning of fire as the goodness that comes of divine love, see just above at §6832. So the phrase means that they became one; divine truth became one with divine goodness on the earthly level. This is the symbolism of the clause in the highest sense, which treats of the Lord.

Here is the situation: Divine goodness born of divine love is the actual fire of the other world's sun. This fire burns so hot that if it fell on anyone—even an angel of the inmost heaven—without a tempering medium in between, that individual would lose all sensation and perish. Such is the ardor of the Lord's divine love.

When the Lord was in the world, though, and united his human essence to his divine, he took the fire of this love into his human part and merged it with the truth there in making himself the divine law. That is what is meant by the union of divine truth with divine goodness on the earthly plane.

And Moses said, symbolizes something perceived from the law imparted 6835
by the Divine. This can be seen from the symbolism of *saying* in the Word's

narratives as a perception (discussed frequently) and from the representation of *Moses* as the law imparted by the Divine (discussed above at §6827).

6836 *I will turn aside, then, and see this great sight* means reflecting on this revelation, as the following shows: *Turning aside and seeing* means reflecting, because in a spiritual sense, *turning aside* is shifting away from the thoughts one is thinking, and *seeing* is perceiving. To do both at the same time is therefore to reflect. And a *sight,* [or vision,] symbolizes revelation, as explained in §6000. It is called a *great* sight because in the highest sense the flame in the bramble symbolizes divine truth united with divine goodness in the Lord's human side (§6834).

6837 *Why the bramble does not burn up* means that such is the nature of the union. This can be seen from the remarks above at §6834.

6838 Exodus 3:4, 5, 6. *And Jehovah saw that he turned aside to see, and God called to him from the middle of the bramble and said, "Moses! Moses!" and he said, "Here I am." And he said, "You are not to come near here; slip your shoes off your feet, because the place that you are standing on is holy ground." And he said, "I am the God of your father: the God of Abraham, the God of Isaac, and the God of Jacob." And Moses covered his face, because he was afraid of looking at God.*

And Jehovah saw that he turned aside to see symbolizes a reflection received from the Lord. *And Jehovah called to him* symbolizes an inflow from the Divine. *From the middle of the bramble* means out of truth in the form of knowledge. *And said, "Moses! Moses!" and he said, "Here I am,"* symbolizes being prompted inwardly and listening to the prompting. *And he said, "You are not to come near here,"* means that he was no longer to think about the Divine in sensory terms. *Slip your shoes off your feet* means that sense impressions—the outermost aspect of the earthly level—were to be set aside. *Because the place that you are standing on is holy ground* means that otherwise nothing divine can enter. *And he said, "I am the God of your father,"* symbolizes the Divine acknowledged by the ancient church. *The God of Abraham, the God of Isaac, and the God of Jacob* symbolizes divinity itself and divine humanity, and consequently the Lord. *And Moses covered his face* means that his inner reaches would be protected. *Because he was afraid of looking at God* means so that they would not be injured by the presence of divinity itself.

6839 *And Jehovah saw that he turned aside to see* symbolizes a reflection received from the Lord. This is established by the symbolism of *turning aside to see* as reflection, as discussed above at §6836. For *Jehovah* being the Lord, see §§1343, 1736, 2921, 3023, 3035, 5663, 6303.

This passage also shows what the Word's literal meaning is like. It says Jehovah saw that Moses turned aside to see, as if Jehovah did not already know Moses would turn aside to see, as if in fact he had not inspired and moved him to do so. Yet because it accords with the appearance, that is what the literal text says. The inner meaning teaches how it should really be understood, which is that the Lord influenced his mind to reflect on it. This shows what the Word's literal meaning is like in comparison to the inner meaning. It also shows that the literal statements naturally adapt to the comprehension of the uneducated, who do not believe anything unless it agrees with the appearance. What does not appear to be true they do not believe because they cannot explore matters deeply. If the Word had not had this type of literal meaning, then, it would not have been accepted.

People who focus on sensory information and people preoccupied with worldly concerns cannot grasp anything deeper. They want to *see* before they believe. What they cannot see seems foreign to them, and when they think about it for themselves, they reject it as something to be denied or at least doubted.

And Jehovah called to him symbolizes an inflow from the Divine. This 6840
can be seen from the symbolism of *calling* as an inflow. In an inner sense, calling does not mean calling with words, as in the shallow, narrative sense, but rather calling by an inflow into the will. This sort of calling is inward, because Jehovah (the Lord) acts on the will and spurs it to do what pleases him. When this inward summons is expressed in the narrative, which contains nothing but outward images, it is expressed as either commanding or calling or addressing or something similar.

From the middle of the bramble means out of truth in the form of 6841
knowledge. This is evident from the discussion in §§6832, 6833 of the symbolism of a *bramble* as truth in the form of knowledge.

And said, "Moses! Moses!" and he said, "Here I am," symbolizes being 6842
prompted inwardly and listening to the prompting. This can be seen from the symbolism of being called by Jehovah in Scripture narratives as an inflow from the Divine (§6840). The actual call is expressed in the words *and Jehovah said, "Moses! Moses!"* These words imply all those that follow, though, starting with the instructions that Moses not come near but slip his shoes off his feet. As a result the clause symbolizes being prompted; and Moses' answer, *here I am,* symbolizes listening to the prompting.

And he said, "You are not to come near here," means that he was no lon- 6843
ger to think about the Divine in sensory terms. This can be seen from the symbolism of *coming near* Jehovah as thinking about the Divine. When a

person is said to come near the Lord, it means thinking about the Divine, because we cannot approach the Divine with our body the way we approach other people, only with our mind and therefore in thought and will. There is no other route to the Divine, because the Divine transcends the realm of space and time. In us the Divine is present in what are called states—specifically, states of love and states of faith, and therefore states of the two mental faculties of will and thought. These are the means by which we can approach the Divine. That is why *you are not to come near here* means that he was not to think about the Divine in terms of the outward sense impressions symbolized by the shoes he was first to slip off.

I say "no longer" because the outer, earthly senses are the last thing to be reborn and are therefore the last thing to accept an inflow from the Divine. The state described here was not yet one in which the outer senses could accept either [rebirth or an inflow from the Divine]. To learn about a sensory perspective, see what follows next.

6844 *Slip your shoes off your feet* means that sense impressions—the outermost aspect of the earthly level—were to be set aside. This is evident from the symbolism of *shoes* as sense impressions, the outermost aspect of the earthly level (discussed in §1748), and from that of *feet* as the earthly level itself (discussed in §§2162, 3147, 3761, 3986, 4280, 4938–4952). *Slipping off* obviously means setting aside, because the term is used in regard to sense impressions. Words have to suit the subject matter, so "slipped off" has to be used for shoes, and "set aside" for sense impressions.

I need to explain the situation. Anyone can see that the shoes here represent something out of harmony with divine holiness, so that slipping them off was an act representing the setting aside of discordant elements. Otherwise, what could it matter to the Divine whether a person approached in shoes or bare feet, as long as that person was inwardly capable of approaching the Divine in faith and love? Shoes, then, symbolize a sensory perspective, and a merely sensory perspective, which is the outermost facet of the earthly plane, is such that it cannot coexist with reverent contemplation of the Divine. Therefore, since it was important to honor representative meaning at that time, Moses was not allowed to approach with shoes on.

[2] The reason the senses, the outermost facet of the earthly level, are by nature incapable of accepting anything divine is that they are immersed in what is worldly, bodily, and earthly. After all, it is the senses that directly take in impressions from that level. What they store in our memory consequently draws its character mainly from the light and heat

of the world rather than the light and heat of heaven. As a result, the senses are the last things to be able to be regenerated—to accept any heavenly light. That is why people who focus on their senses and think from them think of the Divine the same way they think about earthly matters. If evil is what they live for, they think from their senses in direct opposition to the Divine.

When people with goodness think about anything involving faith in God or love for him, then, they are lifted up out of their senses (the outermost part of the earthly plane) to an inner level. So they are lifted from earthly and worldly concerns closer to heavenly and spiritual ones.

[3] People are not aware of this because they do not realize that their inner levels are distinct from their outer levels, or that there is inner thought and still deeper thought as well as outer thought. Since they do not know any of this, they cannot reflect on it.

But see previous discussions concerning thought based on the senses: People who think from their senses have very little wisdom: 5084, 5089, 5094, 6201, 6310, 6311, 6312, 6315, 6316, 6318, 6598, 6612, 6614, 6622, 6624. We are lifted up out of our senses, and when we are lifted we come into milder light; and this happens primarily to those of us who are being reborn: 6183, 6313, 6315.

This evidence now shows what is meant by taking one's shoes off one's feet.

The earthly level in us has outer, middle, and inner parts; see §§4570, 5118, 5126, 5497, 5649. The inner part of the earthly plane is symbolized by the lower leg, the middle part by the feet, and the outer part by shoes.

Because the place that you are standing on is holy ground means that 6845
otherwise nothing divine can enter, as the following shows: A *place* symbolizes a state, as discussed in §§2625, 2837, 3356, 3387, 4321, 4882, 5605, so the *place that you are standing on* symbolizes the state a person is still in. And *holy ground* symbolizes holiness emanating from the Lord. A state marked by the holiness emanating from the Lord's divine humanity is therefore what is meant by these words.

The meaning that otherwise nothing divine can enter follows from the preceding explanation: If we were not separated from our sense impressions, which are the outermost part of the earthly plane—that is, if we were not lifted out of them to an inner level—the Divine could not flow in. The reason it cannot flow in as long as we are engrossed in sense impressions is this: Inflow from the Divine reaches all the way to the lowest elements in the divine design and accordingly to the sense impressions that form the outermost part of our earthly plane. If everything at that level is bodily and earthly, it abolishes any divine qualities that flow in, because they are not in harmony with it. Therefore, when we are about to receive something divine—something relating to faith or love—we are raised up out of our senses. Once we have been raised up out of them, the divine inflow no longer extends as far as the outer senses. Instead it extends as far as the inner plane to which we have been lifted.

Much experience has taught me the truth of this.

6846 *And he said, "I am the God of your father,"* symbolizes the Divine acknowledged by the ancient church. This can be seen from the symbolism of a *father* as the ancient church, as dealt with at §6075. The ancient church is called a father because it gave birth to the religions that followed it: the Hebrew religion, and then the religion among Jacob's offspring. The rituals and statutes that Moses commanded to Jacob's descendants were not new, after all. They already existed among the ancient churches and were merely restored among Jacob's children. They were restored there because other nations had rendered them idolatrous, and both Egypt and Babylon had turned them into magic. (Many passages in the Word show that the ancient churches had those same rituals and statutes.) This then is why a father means the ancient church and why the parts of the Word that are about the church call the ancient church a father.

The God the ancient church worshiped was the Lord in his divine humanity, and the people of that church knew that it was the Lord who was represented in every ritual of their religion. Many of them also knew that the Lord was to come into the world to make the humanity in himself divine. Moreover, no one else was meant by Jehovah in that church, because he had appeared to them as a divine human being and was always called Jehovah (§§1343, 5663). Later on he likewise appeared to Abraham (Genesis 18:2 and following verses), Joshua (Joshua 5:13, 14, 15), Gideon (Judges 6:11 and following verses), and Manoah and his wife (Judges 13:3 and following verses), and was acknowledged as God of the universe and the only being they adored.

This then is why the *God of your father* in an inner sense means the Divine acknowledged by the ancient church—in other words, the Lord. In the outward, narrative sense, though, it is referring to Abraham and Isaac and Jacob.

6847 *The God of Abraham, the God of Isaac, and the God of Jacob* symbolizes divinity itself and divine humanity, and consequently the Lord. This is plain from the representation of *Abraham, Isaac, and Jacob* as the

Lord's divinity itself and divine humanity. For the idea that Abraham represents the Lord in regard to his divinity itself, Isaac in regard to his divine rationality, and Jacob in regard to his earthly divinity, see §§1893, 2010, 2066, 2072, 2083, 2630, 3194, 3210, 3245, 3251, 3305 at the end, 3439, 3704, 4180, 4286, 4538, 4570, 4615, 6098, 6185, 6276, 6425, 6804. *God* symbolizes what is divine, and the names of the three symbolize their representative roles, so those divine aspects of the Lord are what is meant by the *God of Abraham, the God of Isaac, and the God of Jacob.*

And Moses covered his face means that his inner reaches would be protected. This is evident from the symbolism of a *face* as the inner reaches, which is discussed in §§1999, 2434, 3527, 4066, 4796, 4797, 5102. The fact that *covering* means protecting follows from the train of ideas in the inner meaning. The text says he covered his face because he was afraid of looking at God, and this means so that his inner reaches would not be injured by the presence of divinity itself. **6848**

The next section will explain.

Because he was afraid of looking at God means so that they would not be injured by the presence of divinity itself, as the following shows: *Being afraid* means so that they—the inner reaches—would not be injured, since this was the fear. And *looking at God* symbolizes the presence of divinity itself. Only when we look at the Lord inwardly (which we do through faith that comes of neighborly love) does he stand present before us. If the Lord appears to anyone in outward form, it is still the person's inner depths that are affected, because divinity penetrates to the core. **6849**

Here is how the inner depths avoid injury from the presence of divinity itself and are therefore protected: Divinity itself is pure love, and pure love is like a fire hotter than the fire of this world's sun. If divine love in its purity flowed into any angel, spirit, or person on earth, that individual would be utterly destroyed. This is why the Word so often calls Jehovah (the Lord) a devouring fire. So to keep angels in heaven from being hurt by an inflow of heat from the Lord as the sun, they are each shielded by a kind of thin cloud, adapted to the individual, that tempers the heat flowing in from that sun.

[2] We would each be destroyed if we were not preserved from the divine presence this way, as the ancients knew. That is why they were afraid to see God, as is clear in Judges:

> Gideon saw that there was an angel of Jehovah, so Gideon said, "Lord Jehovih! *For I have seen an angel of Jehovah face to face!*" And Jehovah

> said to him, "Peace to you. *Don't be afraid, because you will not die.*" (Judges 6:22, 23)

In the same book:

> Manoah said to his wife, "*We will surely die because we have seen God!*" (Judges 13:22)

And in Exodus:

> Jehovah said to Moses, "*You cannot see my face, because no human shall see me and live.*" (Exodus 33:20)

When Moses was granted to see God, then, he was put in an opening of a rock (Exodus 33:22), which represented a dim and cloudy faith that covered and protected him.

[3] How dangerous it is for angels to be observed by the Divine with no cloud to shield them can be seen clearly from this: When angels look at any spirit engaged in evil, the spirit seems to turn into an almost inanimate object, as I have had the opportunity to see many times. The reason is that an angel's gaze conveys the light and warmth of heaven, and along with these, the truth that leads to faith and the goodness urged by love. When the truth and goodness penetrate, the evil are nearly drained of life.

[4] Considering the effect of an angel's gaze, what would the Lord's gaze do? That is why the hells are absolutely remote from heaven and why hell's inhabitants choose to be remote, because if they were not, they would suffer dreadful torment.

This shows what is meant by the words "They will say to the mountains and rocks, 'Collapse on us and hide us from the face of the one sitting on the throne!'" (Revelation 6:16; Luke 23:30; Hosea 10:8).

[5] Since the presence of divinity itself is such that no angel can bear it unless protected by a cloud that tempers and modifies the rays and warmth from that sun, the Lord's humanity is obviously divine. If it were not, it could never unite so completely with divinity itself (called the Father) as to be one with it (in keeping with the Lord's words in John 14:10 and following verses, among other passages). Anything that receives divinity to this extent must be completely divine itself. Something that is not divine would be annihilated by such a union. To use a metaphor, what can be introduced into the sun's fire without perishing, unless it is sunlike? So who can be introduced into the ardor of infinite love except one whose love is just as ardent? Who, then, but the Lord alone? The Lord's words in

John make it clear that the Father is in him and that the Father is visible only within his divine humanity:

> God has never been seen by anyone; the only-born Son, *who is in the Father's embrace,* is the one who has revealed him. (John 1:18)

And again in the same author:

> You have never heard his voice or seen his form. (John 5:37)

Exodus 3:7, 8. *And Jehovah said, "I have seen clearly the affliction of my people, who are in Egypt, and have heard their cry over their taskmasters, because I know their pain. And I have come down to deliver them from the hand of the Egyptians and to bring them up from that land to a land good and broad, to a land flowing with milk and honey, to the place of the Canaanite and the Hittite and the Amorite and the Perizzite and the Hivite and the Jebusite."* 6850

And Jehovah said, "I have seen clearly the affliction of my people," symbolizes mercy toward people in the spiritual church after they had been harassed by falsity. *And have heard their cry over their taskmasters* symbolizes merciful help against spirits wanting to enslave them. *Because I know their pain* symbolizes foreseeing how much falsity they were immersed in. *And I have come down to deliver them from the hand of the Egyptians* means that he descended to them to release them from the power of falsity in the form of knowledge, which tries to destroy the church's truth. *And to bring them up from that land* means that they would be lifted up. *To a land good and broad* means to heaven, where they would find neighborly love with its goodness, and faith with its truth. *Flowing with milk and honey* means and the resulting delight and pleasure. *To the place of the Canaanite and the Hittite* symbolizes an area occupied by the evil that comes of falsity. *And the Amorite and the Perizzite* means and by evil that produces falsity. *And the Hivite and the Jebusite* means by idolatry containing a bit of goodness and truth.

And Jehovah said, "I have seen clearly the affliction of my people," symbolizes mercy toward people in the spiritual church after they had been harassed by falsity, as the following shows: In the Word's narrative books, *saying* symbolizes a perception, as mentioned often. When ascribed to *Jehovah,* or the Lord, it means omniscience rather than perception because the Lord perceives and knows absolutely everything from eternity. *Seeing clearly,* when ascribed to Jehovah, or the Lord, symbolizes mercy, because when the Lord sees anyone in misery, or *affliction,* he has mercy on that 6851 person. Admittedly, the Lord sees everyone and therefore has mercy on everyone, but the only people he is *said* to have mercy on are those who accept his mercy, who are those intent on goodness. *Affliction* symbolizes persecution (§6663), and in this case harassment by falsity, since the agents are Egyptians, who symbolize falsity in the form of knowledge (§§6651, 6679, 6683). And a *people* symbolizes people belonging to a spiritual religion, as discussed at §2928. (The scriptural term for those belonging to a heavenly religion is a *nation.*)

6852 *And have heard their cry over their taskmasters* symbolizes merciful help against spirits wanting to enslave them, as the following shows: A *cry* symbolizes entreaty, as I said at §6801. *Hearing* symbolizes obeying and perceiving, as discussed at §5017, but when Jehovah (the Lord) is the one said to hear, it means bringing merciful help to the person entreating. The case is the same with hearing as it was above at §6851 with seeing: the Lord hears everyone and therefore helps everyone, but only in keeping with the needs expressed. If people cry out and entreat him for their own sake alone, to the detriment of others (as the evil do), he does hear them, but he does not help them. When he does not help, he is said not to hear. And *taskmasters* symbolize people wanting to enslave others.

The meaning of a taskmaster as one who enslaves others is plain in Isaiah:

> The peoples will take them and lead them to their place, and they will *rule their taskmasters.* It will happen on the day when Jehovah gives you rest both from your turmoil and *from your harsh servitude that you were forced to serve,* that you will utter this parable concerning the monarch of Babylon: "*How the taskmaster has come to an end!*" (Isaiah 14:2, 3, 4)

And in Zechariah:

> I will set up a camp from the army for my house because of the one leaving and the one returning, *so that a taskmaster will not pass over them anymore.* (Zechariah 9:8)

The same word was used for people who exacted tribute (2 Kings 23:35; Deuteronomy 15:3) and for those who used forced labor to pay off tribute imposed on them.

Taskmasters are called chiefs of tribute in Exodus 1:11, and they stand for people who enslaved others (see §6659).

6853 *Because I know their pain* symbolizes foreseeing how much falsity they were immersed in, as the following shows: *Knowing,* when attributed to the Lord, symbolizes foresight. Knowing symbolizes foresight because the Lord knows absolutely everything from eternity. And *pain* symbolizes being immersed in falsity. When people with goodness are immersed in falsity, they suffer distress and anxiety and feel tormented. That is because they love truth and loathe falsity and are always thinking about salvation and about how unhappy they would be if they were completely ruled by falsity. People without goodness, on the other hand, do not care whether they subscribe to falsity or truth, because they never think about salvation or about that type of unhappiness, since they do not believe in either one. The pleasures of self-love and materialism take away any faith in life after death. These people are perpetually immersed in falsity.

In the other life, immersion in falsity looks like a person sinking in waves that tower ever higher as the amount of falsity increases, until they finally reach over the person's head. The waves appear more sparsely or densely spaced depending on the nature of the falsity.

The immersion of the wicked looks like an enveloping cloud or fog, whether darker or lighter in color, that completely cuts off the clear sky where heaven's light shines.

And I have come down to deliver them from the hand of the Egyptians **6854**
means that he descended to them to release them from the power of falsity in the form of knowledge, which tries to destroy the church's truth, as the following shows: *Coming down* means descending, as discussed below. To *deliver* means to release, because someone who releases people from falsity delivers them. A *hand* symbolizes power, as discussed in §§878, 3387, 3563, 4931–4937, 5544. And the *Egyptians* symbolize falsities in the form of knowledge that are opposed to the church's truth (as treated of at §§6651, 6679, 6683) and therefore falsity that tries to destroy such truth.

To address the idea that the Lord *comes down:* The Lord is said to come down or descend when he comes to judge (§1311) and when he visits the lower regions. This verse is about his coming down to people in the spiritual church, symbolized by the children of Israel, because they are the subject of the inner meaning. It tells how they are harassed by falsity, then undergo times of trial, and are afterward delivered, so that they can be led into heaven.

[2] However, the contents of this and the following verses hold an even greater mystery in their inner meaning. The church does not yet know that mystery, so it must be revealed. The people designated as spiritual are those who can be reborn only in regard to their intellectual part, not the part having to do with their will. The Lord therefore grafts a new

will onto their intellectual part, and this will harmonizes with the religious teachings of their church. These people, the spiritual, were saved only by the Lord's arrival in the world. The reason is that they were out of reach to the Divine as it passed through heaven, or the divine humanity as it existed before the Lord's Coming. It could not reach them because the teachings of their religion were mostly untrue, and the goodness in their will was accordingly not good (§6427).

Since it was only the Lord's Coming that could save them, they could not be taken up into heaven until then. Meanwhile they were kept in the underground realm and in places there that the Word calls pits. This realm was hemmed in on all sides by the hells with their falsities, which made life miserable for the pit-dwellers at that time. Nonetheless the Lord was guarding them.

After the Lord came into the world, though, and made the humanity in himself divine, he freed the people living in the pits and took them up to heaven. He also formed them into a spiritual heaven—the second heaven.

That is what is meant by the Lord's descent to the lower regions and by his deliverance of the people imprisoned there.

[3] This mystery is what the current and following verses actually depict in their inner meaning. See previous discussions of spiritual people, which show the following: The spiritual are in the dark regarding religious truth and goodness: 2708, 2715, 2718, 2831, 2849, 2935, 2937, 3241, 3833, 6289. Their darkness is illuminated by the Lord's divine humanity: 2716, 4402. Since they are in the dark regarding religious truth and goodness, they are heavily attacked by the hells, but the Lord constantly protects them: 6419. The spiritual cannot be reborn in regard to their will side, only their intellectual side, and it is in their intellectual side that the Lord forms a new will: 863, 875, 895, 927, 928, 1023, 1043, 1044, 2256, 4328, 4493, 5113. The spiritual were saved by the Lord's Coming into the world: 2833, 2834, 3969.

[4] In various passages the prophetic part of the Word mentions prisoners, including those in a pit, and says that the Lord delivered them. They are the ones meant in a narrow sense by the people described here [in Exodus 3]. In Isaiah, for instance:

> I, Jehovah, have called you in righteousness and will hold your hand. For I will guard you and give you as a pact for the people, as a light for the nations, to open blind eyes, *to lead the prisoner out from prison, those sitting in darkness out of the jailhouse.* (Isaiah 42:6, 7)

In the same author:

> I guarded you and gave you as a pact with the people, to restore the earth, to distribute devastated inheritances, *to say to prisoners, "Go on out!"; to those in darkness, "Show yourselves!"* They will graze on paths, and on all the slopes will be their pasture. (Isaiah 49:8, 9)

Obviously this is about the Lord. The prisoners stand in a narrow sense for spirits held in the underground realm until the Lord's Coming, when they were taken up into heaven. In a broad sense they stand for everyone of good intent who is in effect held captive by falsity but wants to struggle free of it. [5] In Zechariah:

> By the blood of your pact *I will let your prisoners out of the pit.* (Zechariah 9:11)

In Isaiah:

> The *prisoners in the pit* will surely be gathered and will be shut up *in jail.* After a multitude of days they will be visited. (Isaiah 24:22)

The prisoners in the pit stand for the same people. Again in Isaiah:

> Jehovah has anointed me to bring good news to the poor. He has sent me to bind up the broken at heart; *to declare freedom to captives, to prisoners, to one whose eyes are bound;* to proclaim a year of good pleasure for Jehovah. (Isaiah 61:1, 2)

And in another place:

> The people *walking in darkness* have seen great light; those settling *in the land of death's shadow*—light has shone on them. (Isaiah 9:2)

And to bring them up from that land means that they would be lifted up out of the place and the state in which they are troubled by falsity. This can be seen from the symbolism of *bringing up* as being lifted and from that of the *land*—here, the land of Egypt—as the place and state in which they are troubled by falsity. I have already shown that Egypt means falsity in the form of knowledge that causes trouble, and the same thing is symbolized by the *land* of Egypt. 6855

To a land good and broad means to heaven, where they would find neighborly love with its goodness and faith with its truth. This can be seen from the symbolism of the *land*—the land of Canaan this time—as the Lord's kingdom and therefore heaven, as discussed in §§1607, 3038, 6856

3481, 3705, 4447. A *good* land symbolizes neighborly love with its goodness there, and a *broad* land symbolizes faith with its truth there. For the meaning of breadth as faith with its truth, see §§3433, 3434, 4482.

6857 *Flowing with milk and honey* means and the resulting delight and pleasure, as the following shows: *Milk* symbolizes what is heavenly-spiritual, or truth-from-goodness, as discussed at §2184. Because it symbolizes truth-from-goodness, it also symbolizes the resulting delight, since the two are intertwined. And *honey* symbolizes pleasure, as discussed at §5620.

From the explanation above at §6854 you can see what is meant by bringing them up from that land to a land good and broad, flowing with milk and honey. It means that the spirits held in the pits in the underground realm till the Lord's Coming were then lifted up to heaven, where they found neighborly love with its goodness, faith with its truth, and the resulting delight and pleasure.

That is the specific symbolism of the words. More broadly they symbolize everyone in the spiritual church who undergoes trials and is delivered from them.

6858 *To the place of the Canaanite and the Hittite* symbolizes an area occupied by the evil that comes of falsity. This is established by the representation of *Canaanites* as evil resulting from a false teaching with evil origins (dealt with at §4818) and by the representation of *Hittites* as falsity that gives rise to evil (dealt with at §2913). The nations in the land of Canaan that are listed here and in other passages (such as Genesis 15:18, 19, 20, 21; Exodus 23:23, 28; 33:2; 34:11; Deuteronomy 7:1; 20:17; Joshua 3:10; 24:11; Judges 3:5) symbolize all types of evil and falsity.

I need to say what I mean in speaking of an area occupied by evil that comes of falsity and by the other kinds of evil and falsity too. Before the Lord came into the world, evil demons and spirits occupied the entire area in heaven to which the spiritual were eventually lifted up. Many of the evil prowled about freely before the Lord's arrival, harassing good spirits, especially the spiritual ones in the underground realm. After his Coming, though, they were all thrust down into their hells, and the area they had occupied was liberated and given as an inheritance to spirits whose religion was spiritual.

I have often observed that any place deserted by good spirits is immediately taken over by evil spirits, who are then driven out. Once they have been driven out, the area passes back to the spirits intent on what is good. The reason this happens is that hellish people constantly burn to destroy things in heaven, particularly anything they are directly opposed to. So if a space is abandoned anywhere, the evil instantly take it over, because it is then unprotected.

To repeat, this is what is specifically meant by the area occupied by evil and falsity, as symbolized by the place where those nations were that needed to be driven out.

Combined with the account above at §6854, this information is a great mystery that can be known only through revelation.

And the Amorite and the Perizzite means and by evil that produces falsity. This is established by the representation of an *Amorite* as evil (dealt with in §§1857, 6306) and by that of a *Perizzite* as falsity (dealt with in §§1573, 1574). 6859

Evil has two sources and falsity has two sources. One source of evil is the falsity in one's theology or religious tradition; the other is the cravings produced by love for oneself and love of worldly advantages. Falsity has its first source in the above-mentioned falsity belonging to one's theology or religious tradition and its second source in the evil craved by the above-mentioned kinds of love. These two types of evil are the ones symbolized by the Canaanite and the Amorite, and these two types of falsity are the ones symbolized by the Hittite and the Perizzite.

And the Hivite and the Jebusite means by idolatry containing a bit of goodness and truth. This can be seen from the representation of a *Hivite* as idolatry containing a bit of goodness and from that of a *Jebusite* as idolatry containing a bit of truth. 6860

This symbolism of these nations can be seen from the fact that Joshua and the elders were allowed to strike a pact with the Gibeonites (Joshua 9:3 and following verses), who became woodchoppers and water carriers for the House of God (Joshua 9:23, 27). The Gibeonites were Hivites (see Joshua 9:7; 11:19).

The representation of Jebusites as idolaters whose idolatry nonetheless contained a bit of truth can be seen from the fact that Jebusites were tolerated in Jerusalem for a long time without being expelled (Joshua 15:63; 18:16, 28; 2 Samuel 5:6–10).

Exodus 3:9, 10, 11, 12. *"And now, look: the cry of the children of Israel has come to me, and I have also seen the oppression with which the Egyptians oppress them. And now go, and I will send you to Pharaoh. And bring my people, the children of Israel, out of Egypt." And Moses said to God, "Who am I, that I should go to Pharaoh and that I should bring the children of Israel* 6861 *out of Egypt?" And he said, "Because I will be with you. And this will be the sign to you that I myself have sent you: In your bringing the people out of Egypt, you will worship God next to this mountain."*

And now, look: the cry of the children of Israel has come to me symbolizes compassion on people in the spiritual church. *And I have also seen the oppression with which the Egyptians oppress them* means because of the attempt to subdue them made by people committed to falsity. *And now go, and I will send you to Pharaoh* symbolizes a sacred influence radiating from the Lord's humanity, which would scatter the harassing falsities. *And bring my people, the children of Israel, out of Egypt* symbolizes the consequent deliverance of people in the spiritual church from the falsities vexing them. *And Moses said to God* symbolizes a perception received from his divine side, and humility. *Who am I, that I should go to Pharaoh?* means that he did not seem to himself to have reached the stage at which he could address and remove the harassing falsities. *And that I should bring the children of Israel out* means or therefore deliver people in the spiritual church. *And he said, "Because I will be with you,"* means that divinity would be present in his humanity. *And this will be the sign to you that I [myself] have sent you* symbolizes a recognition that divinity would radiate from him. *In your bringing the people out of Egypt* means when the spiritual were delivered from harassment by falsity. *You will worship God next to this mountain* means perceiving and recognizing divinity at that time by the love it brought.

6862 *And now, look: the cry of the children of Israel has come to me* symbolizes compassion on people in the spiritual church, as the following shows: A *cry* symbolizes an entreaty for help, as noted at §6801, so the statement that a cry *has come to Jehovah* (the Lord) means the same thing as hearing. Hearing means bringing merciful help, or showing compassion; see §6852. And the *children of Israel* symbolize people in the spiritual church, as treated of at §6637.

6863 *And I have also seen the oppression with which the Egyptians oppress them* means because of the attempt to subdue them made by people committed to falsity, as the following shows: The *oppression with which they oppress* symbolizes the attempt to subdue. It symbolizes an attempt rather than subjection itself because people in the Lord's spiritual church cannot be subdued by people committed to falsity, since the Lord protects them. And *Egyptians* symbolize falsity, as discussed at §6692.

6864 *And now go, [and] I will send you to Pharaoh* symbolizes a sacred influence radiating from the Lord's humanity, which would scatter the harassing falsities, as the following shows: Moses—the one who was to *go* and was being *sent*—represents the Lord as divine law (as discussed in §§6723, 6752, 6771, 6827) and therefore the Lord in regard to his human side. When the Lord was in the world, he first turned his human side into divine truth, which is the same as the divine law. (Later he completely glorified his human side, turning it into divine goodness. The difference between divine truth and divine goodness is like the difference between light coming from the sun and the fire that is in the sun.) Being *sent* means radiating, as discussed in §§2397, 4710, 6831, and here it refers to sacred truth. For the association of holiness with truth, see §6788. And *Pharaoh* represents falsity, as discussed in §§6651, 6679, 6683, 6692. The explanation adds that the harassing falsities would be scattered (by the sacred influence of the Lord's humanity) because the next part of the verse is about the deliverance of the children of Israel—that is, the deliverance of people in the Lord's spiritual church from falsity. They can never be freed from falsity except by a holy influence radiating from the Lord. This holy influence of his not only scatters troublesome falsities but also reduces everything to divine order both in the heavens and in the hells. It separates the heavens very clearly according to the kinds of goodness and the kinds of truth that come from them, and it separates the hells very clearly according to the kinds of evil and the kinds of falsity that come from them. The Lord's holy influence also positions the types of evil directly opposite to the types of goodness, and falsities directly opposite to truths, to create spiritual balance and ensure a universal state of freedom.

And bring my people, the children of Israel, out of Egypt symbolizes the 6865
consequent deliverance of people in the spiritual church from the falsities vexing them. This can be seen from the symbolism of *bringing out* as deliverance, from that of the *children of Israel* as people in the spiritual church (dealt with at §6637), and from that of *Egypt* as falsity in the form of knowledge that opposes the church's truth and therefore harasses it (dealt with at §6692).

[2] It is falsity in the form of knowledge that causes the most harassment to people in a spiritual religion. This is because they do not perceive truth on the basis of goodness but merely know about truth on the basis of doctrine. To people like this, such knowledge is the greatest plague imaginable. Items of knowledge, you see, are very general containers that sometimes seem to contradict truth, before truth has been introduced into them making them transparent; therefore they are not recognized.

In addition, items of knowledge are full of sensory illusions that cannot be shaken off by people who merely know about truth on the basis of doctrine rather than perceive it on the basis of goodness. This is primarily because they are under the sway of worldly light, which looks bright as long as heavenly light does not touch it but goes dark as soon as heaven's light falls on it. That is why such people are brilliant and clever regarding worldly matters but dim and dense regarding heavenly matters.

[3] They consider themselves enlightened when they have proved the teachings of their religion to their own satisfaction, but it is the meager light of the senses, rising out of the world's dull glimmer, that then deceives them. Any religious teachings can be proved, no matter what they are like. Jews prove theirs, mystical fanatics prove theirs, Socinians prove theirs, heretics of all stripes prove theirs. And once these teachings have been proved, they appear to their adherents to be genuinely true, seen as they are by the dim light of the senses.

Those who enjoy heaven's light, on the other hand, are enlightened by the Lord. Before trying to prove anything, they can tell whether an idea is capable of being proved true or not, simply by looking into items of knowledge spread out in order below them.

Plainly, then, the latter kind of person has deeper insight, which transcends knowledge and is distinct from it. The former kind has a lowlier viewpoint, which dwells in knowledge and is tangled up in it (§2831).

6866 *And Moses said to God* symbolizes a perception received from his divine side, and humility. This can be seen from the symbolism of *saying* as a perception (referred to many times) and from the representation of *Moses* as the Lord in the role of divine law (discussed in §§6723, 6752, 6771, 6827). His divine side is symbolized by *God.* It is clear from the next words that this clause involves humility too, since Moses says, "Who am I, that I should go to Pharaoh and bring the children of Israel out?"

Since Moses represents the Lord and humility is mentioned here, I need to say something about the humility the Lord felt when he was in the world. So far as the Lord inhabited a human nature that had not yet become divine, he had humility, but so far as he inhabited a human nature that had become divine, he could not have humility, because to that extent he was God and Jehovah. He was humble when he inhabited a human nature that had not yet become divine because the humanity he acquired from his mother was evil by inheritance and could not approach his divine side without humility. After all, when we are truly humble we shed the idea that we have any independent power to think or do anything and instead abandon ourselves wholly to the Divine. That is the condition in which we draw close to the Divine.

[2] The Lord did have divinity in him, since he was conceived from Jehovah, but the more active his maternal inheritance was in his human side, the more distant his divine side appeared. In spiritual and heavenly affairs, disparity in state is what creates distance and absence, while likeness of state is what creates closeness and presence; and it is love that creates both the likeness and the disparity.

This discussion now identifies the source of the humility the Lord felt while he was in the world. Later, though, he shed all the humanity he inherited from his mother, to the point that he was no longer her son, and he clothed himself in divinity. At that point his state of humility came to an end, because he was then one with Jehovah.

Who am I, that I should go to Pharaoh? means that he did not seem to 6867
himself to have reached the stage at which he could address and remove the harassing falsities, as can be seen from the following: *Who am I?* means that he had not reached that stage. *Going to Pharaoh* means addressing the harassing falsities, since *Pharaoh* symbolizes falsity that causes trouble (§§6651, 6679, 6683). It means removing them too because the sacred influence of the Lord's humanity (discussed above at §6864) removes falsity and evil, which cannot begin to bear his presence.

The reason I say he did not seem to himself to be able is that the question was asked with humility.

And that I should bring the children of Israel out means or therefore 6868
deliver people in the spiritual church. This can be seen from the symbolism of *bringing out* as delivering (as above at §6865) and from the representation of the *children of Israel* as people in the spiritual church (discussed at §§6637, 6862, 6865).

And he said, "Because I will be with you," means that divinity would 6869
be present in his humanity, as the following shows: Moses represents the Lord in the role of divine law (as discussed in §§6723, 6752, 6771, 6827) and therefore the Lord in regard to his human side. As was shown above [§§6827, 6834, 6864], the Lord when he was in the world turned his human side into the divine law, that is, divine truth. And *I will be with you* symbolizes divinity, since Jehovah is the one speaking.

And this will be the sign to you that I myself have sent you symbolizes 6870
a recognition that divinity would radiate from him, as the following indicates: A *sign* symbolizes proof—and therefore recognition—that a thing is true. And being *sent* means radiating, as discussed in §§2397,

4710, 6831, so being sent by God means radiating from the Divine. Being sent by God also symbolizes divinity radiating, because one who issues from the Divine receives what is divine and passes it on.

6871 *In your bringing the people out of Egypt* means when the spiritual were delivered from harassment by falsity, as the following shows: *Bringing out* means delivering, as above in §§6865, 6868. The children of Israel—the *people* here—symbolize spiritual individuals, or adherents of a spiritual religion, as discussed in §§6637, 6862, 6865. *Egypt* symbolizes the falsity in the form of knowledge that harasses them, as discussed at §6692.

6872 *You will worship God next to this mountain* means perceiving and recognizing divinity at that time by the love it brought, as the following shows: *Worshiping God* symbolizes adoration of the Divine, although when said of the Lord it means perceiving and recognizing the divinity within his humanity. And a *mountain* symbolizes divine love and its goodness, as discussed in §§795, 796, 2722, 4210, 6435, 6829. This makes it clear that *you will worship God next to this mountain,* when said of the Lord, means perceiving and recognizing divinity by the love it brought.

[2] I need to explain what it means to perceive and recognize divinity by the love it brings. As to our nature we are each known by what we love. Love is the core essence of everyone's life; life itself actually comes from love. The nature of the love in us therefore determines what we are like. If it is love for ourselves and for worldly advantages, with all their attendant vengefulness, hatred, cruelty, adultery, and so on, then no matter how we appear on the outside, we are devils as to our spirit, or as to the inner self that lives on after death. However, if the love in us is for God and our neighbor and consequently for goodness and truth, for what is fair and upright, then no matter how we appear on the outside we are angels as to our spirit, which lives on after death.

But one in whom the love is divine (as it was in the Lord alone) is God. So the Lord's humanity became divine when he received his Father's love (the core essence of his life) in his humanity.

These remarks show what is meant by perceiving and recognizing divinity by the love it brought.

[3] It is an enduring truth that we are what we love in every respect. This is plain from angels in the other life, who appear to the eye to be embodiments of love. Love itself not only shines but even breathes from them, so that you would say they are nothing but love through and through. The reason is that all the inner workings in an angel (and likewise in a person on earth) are actually forms designed to receive life. Being designed

to receive life, they are designed to receive love, because love constitutes human life. Since the love that flows in and the form that receives it harmonize, then, it follows that the nature of an angel or person reflects the nature of her or his love. This is true not only of the elementary organic substances in the brain but also of the whole body, because the body is nothing but an organism made up of its elementary substances.

[4] All of this goes to show that we become entirely new when reborn, because everything in us is then organized to receive heavenly kinds of love. In humans, though, the old forms are moved aside rather than eliminated, while in the Lord the old forms inherited from his mother were completely uprooted and eliminated, and he received divine forms in place of them. Divine love does not harmonize with any form but a divine one; all other forms it casts off entirely. That is why the Lord ceased to be Mary's son once he had been glorified.

Exodus 3:13, 14, 15. *And Moses said to God, "Consider: I come to the children of Israel and tell them, 'The God of your fathers has sent me to you,' and suppose they say to me, 'What is his name?' What should I tell them?" And God said to Moses, "I Am Who I Am," and he said, "This is what you shall say to the children of Israel: 'I Am has sent me to you.'" And God said further to Moses, "This is what you are to say to the children of Israel: 'Jehovah, the God of your fathers—the God of Abraham, the God of Isaac, and the God of Jacob—has sent me to you.' This is my name forever, and this is my memorial to generation after generation."* 6873

And Moses said to God symbolizes a perception received from his divine side. *Consider: I come to the children of Israel* means about people in the spiritual church. *And tell them, "The God of your fathers has sent me to you,"* means that the Divine acknowledged by the ancient church will be with people of the spiritual church. *And suppose they say to me, "What is his name?"* symbolizes his quality. *What should I tell them?* means, what will the answer be? *And God said to Moses* symbolizes a first lesson. *I Am Who I Am* symbolizes the essential reality and emerging presence of everything in the universe. *And he said, "This is what you shall say to the children of Israel,"* symbolizes a second lesson. *I Am has sent me to you* means that the divine emergence will be present in this church. *And God said further to Moses, "This is what you are to say to the children of Israel,"* symbolizes a third lesson. *The God of your fathers* symbolizes the Divine acknowledged by the ancient church. *The God of Abraham, the God of Isaac, and the God of Jacob* symbolizes divinity itself and divine humanity, and consequently the Lord. *Has sent me to you* means that he will be present in their church.

This is my name forever means that divine humanity is the actual quality of divinity itself. *And this is my memorial to generation after generation* means that it should be worshiped in perpetuity.

6874 *And Moses said to God* symbolizes a perception received from his divine side. This can be seen from the symbolism of *saying* in the Word's narratives as a perception. Obviously *God* means divinity. The perception is described as being from his divine side because divinity is the source of all perception.

6875 *Consider: I come to the children of Israel* means about people in the spiritual church. This can be seen from the representation of the *children of Israel* as people in the spiritual church, as discussed in §§6637, 6862, 6865.

6876 *And tell them, "The God of your fathers has sent me to you,"* means that the Divine acknowledged by the ancient church will be with people of the spiritual church, as the following shows: The *God of your fathers* symbolizes the Divine acknowledged by the ancient church. For the symbolism of fathers as the people of the ancient church, see §§6050, 6075, 6846. The children of Israel—*you*—represent people of the spiritual church, as noted just above at §6875. And being *sent* means radiating, as discussed in §§2397, 4710, 6831. Here it is a promise to be with them, because it is said of the Divine acknowledged by the ancient church, who will be present in the spiritual church, as represented by the children of Israel.

[2] The Divine acknowledged by the ancient church was the Lord in his divine humanity—a concept which the people of the ancient church inherited from the earliest church and which also resulted from the fact that Jehovah appeared to them in human form. When they thought about Jehovah, then, they did not imagine him as some Universal Being of whom they would have had no idea, but as a human divinity on whom they could fix their thoughts. As a result, they could both think about Jehovah and unite with him in love.

The people of the ancient church, and especially those of the earliest church, were much wiser than the people of our own time, and yet they could not conceive of Jehovah as anything but a person whose humanity was divine. Moreover, when they thought of him that way, no inappropriate concept derived from the earthly self with its frail and wicked nature influenced their thinking. Rather, every thought of him to enter their mind was reverent.

Even angels, who have so much more wisdom than we do, cannot think of the Divine any other way, because they actually see the Lord in his divine humanity. They know that an angel, in whom everything is finite, cannot have any idea of the infinite except through a finite equivalent.

[3] The fact that people in ancient times revered Jehovah in the form of a human divinity is obvious from the angels that appeared in human form to Abraham and then Lot, to Joshua, and to Gideon and Manoah. These angels were called Jehovah and were revered as God of the universe.

If Jehovah appeared as a person to the church today, it would be a hurdle to people, who would consider it impossible for him to be the creator and Lord of the universe on account of his human appearance. In fact, they would think of him as nothing but an ordinary person.

On this subject they consider themselves wiser than the ancients, not realizing they are as far from wisdom as they can be concerning it. When you pour your thoughts into a Universal Being that is totally incomprehensible, your mind alights nowhere and your thoughts dissolve, to be replaced by the idea of nature, which you then give all the credit. That is why the worship of the material world is so common in the world today, especially in Christian parts of the world.

And suppose they say to me, "What is his name?" symbolizes his quality. 6877
This can be seen from the symbolism of a *name* as the quality of a thing, as discussed in §§1754, 1896, 2009, 2628, 2724, 3006, 6674.

Moses' question tells you something about Jacob's descendants. Not only had they forgotten Jehovah's name, they also acknowledged many gods, of which one was greater than another. That was why they wanted to know his name. They also considered it sufficient to acknowledge God's name. The reason Jacob's descendants were like this was that they concentrated on mere superficialities devoid of any inward depth. People who lack depth cannot view God any other way, because they cannot take in any light from heaven to illuminate their inner recesses.

In order for them to acknowledge Jehovah, then, they were told that the God of their fathers—the God of Abraham, the God of Isaac, and the God of Jacob—had appeared and was the one sending [Moses]. In this way they were persuaded to acknowledge Jehovah out of blind veneration for their ancestors rather than from any inward perception.

It was enough for that people to worship only the name of Jehovah, because they could accept nothing but the outer plane of religion; they could accept only that which *represented* its inner plane. Such worship was also established among them in order for any representation they engaged in to appear in its inward form in heaven. This would maintain some bond between heaven and humankind.

6878 *What should I tell them?* means, what will the answer be? This is self-evident.

6879 *And God said to Moses* symbolizes a first lesson. This is evident from the symbolism of *God's saying,* in this case *to Moses* (who represents the Lord as divine truth), and from Moses' mouth to the people (thus from divine truth radiating out of the Lord's divine humanity to people in the spiritual church), as giving a lesson. Here it is a first lesson because it teaches about the genuine God who is to be worshiped. The first step in religion is the concept that God exists and is to be worshiped. The first fact that needs to be known about the nature of God is that he created the universe and that the created universe depends on him for its existence.

6880 *I Am Who I Am* symbolizes the essential reality and emerging presence of everything in the universe. This can be seen from the fact that *I Am* means essential reality, and since he alone is essential reality, the phrase is used as a name. "I Am" comes up twice in *I Am Who I Am* because one instance symbolizes essential reality, and the other, emerging presence. So one symbolizes divinity itself, which is called the Father, and the other symbolizes divine humanity, which is called the Son, because divine humanity emerges from divinity itself. However, now that the Lord has become the divine reality (or Jehovah) even in regard to his human side, the divine presence that emerges from divine reality is the divine truth that radiates from his divine humanity. From this you can see that the divine reality cannot share itself with anyone except through the divine presence. That is, divinity itself cannot share itself except through divine humanity, and divine humanity cannot share itself except through divine truth, which is the holy influence of the Spirit. This is the import of the statement that everything was made by the Word (John 1:3).

[2] It does not appear to people as though divine truth is the kind of thing through which something else could come into existence, because they consider it to be like speech that vanishes once it leaves the mouth. The true situation, though, is quite the opposite. Divine truth issuing from the Lord is absolutely real and of such a nature that everything rose out of it and everything depends on it for continued existence. Whatever issues from the Lord is the realest thing in the universe. That includes divine truth, which is called the Word through which everything was made.

6881 *And he said, "This is what you shall say to the children of Israel,"* symbolizes a second lesson, as the following makes evident: *(God) said,* when repeated, symbolizes a new perception, as discussed in §§2061, 2238, 2260. This time the new perception is a second lesson. And the *children of Israel* represent people in the spiritual church, for whom the lesson is intended.

I Am has sent me to you means that the divine emergence will be present in it—in the church—as the following shows: *I Am* symbolizes divinity itself and divine humanity, as discussed just above at §6880. And Moses represents the Lord as divine law, that is, divine truth. For the idea that divine truth is the presence that emerges from divine humanity, because it is the influence radiating from him, again see §6880 above. Being *sent to them* means that he will be present in the spiritual church, as discussed in §6876. 6882

This is the second lesson. The first lesson was that God, who is the source of everything, is to be acknowledged. The second is that divine truth, which comes from him, is to be accepted.

And God said further to Moses, "This is what you are to say to the children of Israel," symbolizes a third lesson, as is evident from the explanation just above at §6881. 6883

The God of your fathers symbolizes the Divine acknowledged by the ancient church. This can be seen from the comments above at §6876, where the same words occur. 6884

In the outer narrative sense, the God of their fathers refers to Abraham, Isaac, and Jacob, but in an inner sense it means the Divine acknowledged by the ancient church. It stands to reason that the latter rather than the former is meant in an inner sense, because the narratives of the Word cannot reach heaven. Scriptural narrative is earthly and worldly, and the inhabitants of heaven are not awake to any ideas but spiritual ones, so they understand it in a spiritual way. The worldly element—the Word's literal meaning—turns into spiritual meaning as soon as it crosses heaven's threshold.

The truth of this can also be seen to some extent from the fact that people regularly transform what they hear into the kinds of ideas their minds always dwell on. People who focus on unclean thoughts turn what they hear into something unclean, while people who focus on clean thoughts turn it into something clean.

This then is why heaven's inhabitants do not take "the God of your fathers" to mean the God of Abraham, Isaac, and Jacob, because Abraham, Isaac, and Jacob are unknown in heaven. Rather, they take it to mean the Lord as represented by the three.

Consequently it is the Divine acknowledged by the ancient church that these words symbolize.

6885 *The God of Abraham, the God of Isaac, and the God of Jacob* symbolizes divinity itself and divine humanity, and consequently the Lord. This is established by what was shown above at §6847, where the same words occur.

6886 *Has sent me to you* means that he will be present in their church. This can be seen from the symbolism of being *sent to you* as the promise of his presence in the spiritual church, which is discussed above at §§6876, 6882.

6887 *This is my name forever* means that divine humanity is the actual quality of divinity itself. This can be seen from the symbolism of God's *name* as every means of worshiping him, collectively, and therefore as his quality, which is discussed in §§2724, 3006, 6674. Divinity itself cannot be worshiped because it cannot be approached in either faith or love. It transcends all thought, as the Lord says in John:

> God has never been seen by anyone; the only-born Son, who is in the Father's embrace, is the one who has revealed him. (John 1:18)

And in another place in the same author:

> You have never heard his voice or seen his form. (John 5:37)

Divine humanity, being the quality of divinity itself, is therefore what can be approached and worshiped.

[2] It is plain in John that divine humanity is the name of Jehovah:

> Jesus said, "Father, *glorify your name.*" So a voice went out from heaven: "I both have glorified it and will glorify it again." (John 12:28)

In this passage the Lord in his divine humanity calls himself the name of the Father. In Isaiah:

> I, Jehovah, have called you in righteousness and will hold your hand, for I will guard you and give you as a pact for the people, as a light for the nations, to open blind eyes, to lead the prisoner out from prison, those sitting in darkness out of the jailhouse. I am Jehovah: *this is my name,* and my glory I will not give to another. (Isaiah 42:6, 7, 8)

These verses and the ones before them in the same chapter talk overtly about the Lord. Plainly he is the one meant by the name of Jehovah, since it says that he will not give his glory to another. Seeing that these words relate to the Lord, they mean he will give the glory to himself, since the Lord and Jehovah are one. [3] In Moses:

> Watch: I am sending an angel before you to guard you on the way and to lead you to the place that I have prepared. Be careful before him and listen to his voice, because he will not tolerate your transgressing, *since my name is within him.* (Exodus 23:20, 21)

For the angel of Jehovah here meaning the Lord in his divine humanity, see §6831. Because divine humanity is the quality of divinity itself, the passage says that Jehovah's name is within him.

In the Lord's Prayer too, "Our Father in the heavens, *may your name be held sacred"* [Matthew 6:9; Luke 11:2] stands for the Lord in his divine humanity and also for every means by which he is to be worshiped, collectively.

And this is my memorial to generation after generation means that it should be worshiped in perpetuity, as the following shows: A *memorial* symbolizes something to be remembered, and when applied to divinity it symbolizes the quality of divinity as it is worshiped. And *generation after generation* means in perpetuity. **6888**

The Word uses the expressions *forever* and *to generation after generation,* and sometimes both in the space of one verse. This is because "forever" is associated with divine goodness and "generation after generation" with divine truth. The case is similar with the symbolism of a memorial and a name. A memorial is associated with the quality of divinity as it is worshiped in regard to truth, but a name with the quality of divinity as it is worshiped in regard to both truth and goodness—though specifically as it is worshiped in regard to goodness.

The meaning of a memorial as the quality of divinity as it is worshiped is clear in Hosea:

> Jehovah is God Sabaoth; *"Jehovah" is his memorial.* You yourself must therefore return with the help of God; preserve devoutness and judgment. (Hosea 12:5, 6)

This is about the quality of worship in regard to truth, so "Jehovah" is called his memorial. In David:

> Sing to Jehovah, you saints of his, and *acclaim the memorial of his holiness!* (Psalms 30:4; 97:12)

For the association of holiness with truth, see §6788. Worship based on truth is symbolized by the memorial of his holiness.

6889 Exodus 3:16, 17, 18, 19, 20. *Go, and you are to gather the elders of Israel and say to them, "Jehovah, the God of your fathers, has appeared to me—the God of Abraham, Isaac, and Jacob—saying, 'I have faithfully visited you and what has been done to you in Egypt. And I say I will bring you up from the affliction of Egypt to the land of the Canaanite and the Hittite and the Amorite and the Perizzite and the Hivite and the Jebusite, to a land flowing with milk and honey.'" And should they hear your voice, you are to go in—you and the elders of Israel—to the king of Egypt and say to him, "Jehovah, God of the Hebrews, has met us. And now please let us go a journey of three days into the wilderness and let us sacrifice to Jehovah our God." And I myself know that the king of Egypt will not grant you [your request] to go, not even under a strong hand. And I will send out my hand and strike Egypt with all my wonders that I will do in the middle of it, and afterward he will send you away.*

Go, and you are to gather the elders of Israel symbolizes people of intelligence in the spiritual church. *And say to them* symbolizes a lesson. *Jehovah, the God of your fathers,* symbolizes the Divine acknowledged by the ancient church. *Has appeared to me* symbolizes his presence. *The God of Abraham, Isaac, and Jacob* symbolizes the Lord's divinity itself and divine humanity. *Saying, "I have faithfully visited you,"* symbolizes his coming to the people of the church. *And what has been done to you in Egypt* symbolizes the attempt to subdue them. *And I say I will bring you up from the affliction of Egypt* symbolizes being lifted up and freed from falsity in the form of knowledge. *To the land of the Canaanite and the Hittite and the Amorite and the Perizzite and the Hivite and the Jebusite* symbolizes the area of heaven that was occupied by spirits devoted to evil and falsity. *To a land flowing with milk and honey* means where delight and pleasure are to be found. *And should they hear your voice* symbolizes obedience. *You are to go in—you and the elders of Israel—to the king of Egypt* symbolizes communicating with spirits intent on falsity who persecuted them. *And say to him* symbolizes an inflow. *Jehovah, God of the Hebrews, has met us* symbolizes the Lord's divinity as the church experiences it, and his demand. *And now please let us go a journey of three days into the wilderness* symbolizes a life lived by the truth—even if it is lived in the dark—at a stage when falsity has been left completely behind. *And let us sacrifice to Jehovah our God* symbolizes the resulting worship of the Lord. *And I myself know* symbolizes foresight. *That the king of Egypt will not grant you [your request] to go* means that falsity will stand in the way. *Not even under a strong hand* means that those spirits will not be overcome by the power of people in the spiritual church. *And I will send out my hand* symbolizes power from the Divine. *And strike Egypt with all my wonders* symbolizes the means divine power uses against falsity. *That I will do in the middle of it* means which touch those spirits directly. *And afterward he will send you away* symbolizes banishment of them and deliverance.

Go, and you are to gather the elders of Israel symbolizes people of intel- 6890
ligence in the spiritual church. This can be seen from the symbolism of *elders* as the leading elements of wisdom and understanding (discussed in §§6524, 6525), and therefore as people of intelligence, and from the representation of *Israel* as the spiritual church (discussed in §§4286, 6426).

And say to them symbolizes a lesson. This can be seen from the sym- 6891
bolism of *saying to them,* when done by Moses—who represents the law imparted by the Divine—as giving a lesson, as above at §§6879, 6881, 6883.

Jehovah, the God of your fathers, symbolizes the Divine acknowledged 6892
by the ancient church. This can be seen from the explanation above at §6884, where the same words occur.

Has appeared to me symbolizes [his] presence. This is evident from the 6893
symbolism of *appearing to someone* as presence, because in an inner sense, appearing means being seen in thought, not with the eyes. Thought does bring presence, too, because when you think about someone, that person stands present before your inner eye. In the other life this happens in a very real way, because when people there think intensely about another, that other appears in their presence. That is how friends come together with them there, and also enemies, at whose hands they suffer severely.

The God of Abraham, Isaac, and Jacob symbolizes the Lord's divinity 6894
itself and divine humanity. This is established by what was shown above at §6847.

Saying, "I have faithfully visited you," symbolizes his coming to the 6895
people of the spiritual church. This is established by the symbolism of *visiting* as the Lord's Coming, just before the last days of the church—days that the Word refers to as the Last Judgment. For this meaning of visitation, see §§2242, 6588. The fact that visitation is called a coming of the Lord can be seen from these words in Matthew:

> The disciples said to Jesus, "Tell us when these things will happen, what the *sign of your coming* and of the close of the age will be." (Matthew 24:3)

The Lord was then informing the disciples about the church's last days, as can be seen from the explanations in §§3353–3356, 3486–3489, 3897–3901,

4056–4060, 4229–4231, 4422–4424. He also said that when all those things had happened, the *sign of the Son of Humankind* would appear,

> and then all the tribes of the earth will mourn. And *they will see the Son of Humankind coming in the clouds of heaven with strength and glory.* (Matthew 24:30)

[2] The statement that the Lord will come does not mean that he will appear in the clouds accompanied by angels but that people will acknowledge him from the heart, with love and faith (see §§3353, 3900). It also means that he will appear in the Word, whose inmost or highest meaning is about him alone (§4060). This is the coming meant by the Lord's Coming, which occurs at the point when the old religion is rejected and a new one is established by the Lord.

Because a new religion was to be founded among Jacob's descendants now, the text says *I have faithfully visited you.* Joseph said the same thing when he died:

> Joseph said to his brothers, "I am dying, and *God will unfailingly visit you* and bring you up from this land to the land that he swore to Abraham, Isaac, and Jacob." (Genesis 50:24)

In a literal sense, this "unfailingly" or "faithfully visiting you" symbolizes deliverance from slavery in Egypt and entry into the land of Canaan. However, this is not the spiritual but the earthly dimension contained in the Word. The spiritual dimension has to do with the Lord, his kingdom and church, and love and faith. In a spiritual sense, then, faithfully visiting means being freed from falsity and in this way being introduced to attributes of the Lord's kingdom and church. So it means the Lord's arrival with love and faith among people who will be part of the new religion.

6896 *And what has been done to you in Egypt* symbolizes the attempt to subdue them. This is clear from earlier discussions of the affliction and oppression of the children of Israel, or people in the spiritual church. This affliction and oppression are what is meant by *what has been done to you in Egypt.* To see that affliction and oppression symbolize persecution and the attempt to subdue, see §§6663, 6666, 6668, 6670, 6671, 6851, 6852, 6863.

6897 *And I say I will bring you up from the affliction of Egypt* symbolizes being lifted up and freed from persecution by falsity in the form of knowledge, as the following shows: *Bringing them up* symbolizes lifting them to inner levels, as discussed in §§3084, 4539, 5406, 5817, 6007. Being lifted to inner levels means being lifted from harassment by falsity up to the true ideas and good desires taught by faith. As a result, bringing them up also means freeing them. *Affliction* symbolizes being harassed, [or persecuted,] as discussed in §§6663, 6851. And *Egypt* symbolizes falsity in the form of knowledge, as mentioned in §§6651, 6679, 6683.

To the land of the Canaanite and the Hittite and the Amorite and the Perizzite and the Hivite and the Jebusite symbolizes the area of heaven that was occupied by spirits devoted to evil and falsity. This can be seen from what was shown above in §§6854, 6858. 6898

For Canaanites and Hittites as people devoted to evil that comes of falsity, see §6858; Amorites and Perizzites as people devoted to evil and the resulting falsity, §6859; and Hivites and Jebusites as people who practice idolatry that contains a bit of goodness and truth, §6860.

To a land flowing with milk and honey means where delight and pleasure are to be found. This can be seen from the symbolism of *milk and honey* as delight and pleasure, as explained above at §6857. 6899

And should they hear your voice symbolizes obedience. This is evident from the symbolism of *hearing* as obedience, which is discussed in §§2542, 3869, 4652–4660. 6900

You are to go in—you and the elders of Israel—to the king of Egypt symbolizes communicating with spirits intent on falsity who persecuted them, as the following shows: *Entering* symbolizes communication, because entering in a spiritual sense is sharing one's thoughts with another. Moses represents the law imparted by the Divine, as discussed at §6827. *Elders* symbolize people of intelligence, as discussed in §§6524, 6525, 6890. And Pharaoh, *king of Egypt,* represents falsity that persecutes religious truth, as mentioned in §§6651, 6679, 6683. These explanations show that *you are to go in—you and the elders of Israel—to the king of Egypt* symbolizes communicating ideas contained in the law imparted by the Divine and therefore intelligent ideas to spirits intent on falsity who persecuted them. 6901

And say to him symbolizes an inflow. This can be seen from the symbolism of *saying* as an inflow, which is dealt with in §§5743, 6152, 6291. The reason "saying" means an inflow here is that the way to communicate ideas that are contained in the law imparted by the Divine and are therefore intelligent ideas, as mentioned in §6901, is by an inflow. 6902

Jehovah, God of the Hebrews, has met us symbolizes the Lord's divinity as the church experiences it, and his demand, as the following shows: *Hebrews* symbolize the church, as treated of in §§5136, 6675, 6684. *Jehovah God* is 6903 the Lord's divinity because Jehovah in the Word means none other than the Lord (§§1736, 2921, 3023, 3035, 5041, 5663, 6303). And *meeting* in this case symbolizes a demand, because it means that he spoke with them and gave them an order. You can see that "he has met us" here includes the demand by considering that the text does not go on to report what Jehovah God said but immediately follows up with his demand.

6904 *And now please let us go a journey of three days into the wilderness* symbolizes a life lived by the truth—even if it is lived in the dark—at a stage when falsity has been left completely behind, as shown by the following: *Going* symbolizes a life, as dealt with in §§3335, 4882, 5493, 5605. A *journey,* [or path,] symbolizes truth, as dealt with in §§627, 2333. *Three days* symbolizes a full, complete stage, as dealt with in §§2788, 4495, so when it has to do with putting distance between oneself and falsity, it means a stage when falsity has been left completely behind. (Putting a journey of three days [between oneself and another] means being entirely separate; see §4010.) And a *wilderness* means a place that is uninhabited and undeveloped (as discussed in §§2708, 3900), which in a spiritual sense means a dim sight of faith. You see, this chapter is about the establishment of the spiritual church, symbolized by the children of Israel. People in that church are more or less in the dark regarding the goodness and truth taught by faith; see §§2708, 2715, 2716, 2718, 2831, 2849, 2935, 2937, 3241, 3246, 3833, 4402, 6289, 6500, 6865.

A life of truth is the kind of life that people in a spiritual religion live. When the truth they glean from the Word or rather from the teachings of their religion becomes part of their life, it is called goodness, but it is really truth in action.

6905 *And let us sacrifice to Jehovah our God* symbolizes the resulting worship of the Lord. This can be seen from the symbolism of *sacrificing* as worship in general, which is discussed at §923. In the Hebrew church, and later among Jacob's descendants, all worship fell into the category of sacrifice. The evidence for this is the fact that sacrifices happened every day, many times during each of the feasts, whenever someone was installed in office, when people were being purified, in compensation for sins or for guilt, in fulfillment of a vow, and from free will. That is why sacrifices symbolize worship in general. Obviously it is worship of the Lord that is symbolized by sacrificing *to Jehovah God,* since sacrifices represented none other than the Lord and the heavenly and spiritual kinds of divine qualities that come from him (§§1823, 2180, 2805, 2807, 2830, 3519). Besides, Jehovah God in the Word refers to no one but the Lord; see above at §6903. Jehovah means his divine reality, and God means the divine presence that emerges from his divine reality, so Jehovah means the divine goodness of his divine love and God the divine truth radiating from his divine goodness.

And I myself know symbolizes foresight. This is evident from the symbolism of *knowing,* when ascribed to Jehovah, or the Lord, as foresight—a symbolism mentioned above at §6853. 6906

That the king of Egypt will not grant you [your request] to go means that falsity will stand in the way, as the following indicates: *Not granting you [your request]* means standing in the way. One who does not grant a divine command (§6903) on being told of it and who forbids anyone to worship God stands in the way. This is typical behavior for all who have hardened themselves in falsity. Pharaoh, *king of Egypt,* represents falsity, as noted in §§6651, 6679, 6683. And to *go*—to go a journey of three days into the wilderness in order to sacrifice to Jehovah God—means to live by the truth at a stage when falsity has been left completely behind and to worship the Lord by doing so (§6904). 6907

[2] I need to explain about people intent on falsity (as represented by the king of Egypt) and the opposition they put up to people intent on truth. In the world, people intent on falsity do not openly stand in the way of people intent on truth, because the external restraint of fear hinders them. They do not want to seem to oppose the laws of the country and the church, because then they could not be seen as good citizens. Everyone wants to look fair and honest in the world's eyes, and the underhanded seek this even more than the upright do. Their purpose is to win hearts and deceive, in order to gain wealth and rank. Deep inside, though, they do stand opposed. Whenever they hear someone proclaiming religious truth from zeal rather than official duty, they sneer under their breath, and if external restraints were not inhibiting them they would laugh out loud. When people like this go to the other world, external shackles no longer hamper them, because such shackles are then removed from them so that each individual's nature can reveal itself. Then they openly oppose people intent on truth and harass them at every opportunity. This is then their highest pleasure in life. If they are warned not to behave that way because eventually they will be removed and thrust down into hell if they do not stop, they still pay no attention. They persist as before in their unrelenting onslaught, which shows to what extent falsity provides them with their central pleasure. It monopolizes their minds so thoroughly that they do not let in the slightest hint of higher thinking. That is what *the*

king of Egypt will not grant you [your request] to go symbolizes, and it is what is represented by the number of times Pharaoh put up opposition. The removal of such spirits and their being sent down into hell is represented by the death of Pharaoh and the Egyptians in the Suph Sea.

[3] People who live evil lives and therefore subscribe to falsity enjoy the light of the world, because this is the light by which they view the objects of higher thought. In people devoted to the falsity that comes of evil, worldly light is a glittering light, and the more devoted they are to it, the more brightly it glitters. The glory of the world, which rises out of self-love, kindles that light and makes it sparkle. This being so, truth appears to such people by that light as absolutely false and falsity as absolutely true. The reason truth and falsity appear so is that heavenly light cannot flow into the radiance of worldly light but instead turns dark in its presence. This is why such people are so firmly convinced of falsity as opposed to truth, because that is how they view both by the world's light.

With people devoted to the truth that comes of something good, in contrast, the world's light is not glittery but dark, while the light of heaven shines brightly. Since it shines brightly, truth looks true in it, and falsity looks false. Falsity looks true in worldly light separated from heavenly, but when heavenly light falls on it, this light not only dims the glow of falsity but extinguishes it entirely. This light, the light of heaven, gradually shines brighter and brighter in such people, until at last the light of the world cannot even be compared with it.

These comments show why it is that people dedicated to the falsity that comes of evil bring such strong convictions to bear when standing in the way of people dedicated to truth. And that opposition is the subject being addressed earlier in the current section.

6908 *Not even under a strong hand* means that those spirits will not be overcome by the power of people in the spiritual church. This can be seen from the symbolism of a *hand* as power, which is discussed in §§878, 3387, 4931–4937. *Not under a strong hand,* then, means power that will not overcome. The fact that the power meant is that of people in the spiritual church becomes plain from the next few words: "And I will send out my hand and strike Egypt with all my wonders"—meaning that those spirits are to be conquered by power from the Divine and by the measures it uses.

6909 *And I will send out my hand* symbolizes power from the Divine. This can be seen from the symbolism of a *hand* as power, which is discussed in

§§878, 3387, 4931–4937. Since Jehovah (the Lord) says this about himself, it means power from the Divine.

And strike Egypt with all my wonders symbolizes the means divine power uses against falsity. This can be seen from the symbolism of *Egypt* as falsity (mentioned many times before) and from that of *wonders* as the means divine power uses to subdue people committed to falsity who cause trouble. 6910

The symbolism of wonders as the means divine power uses to subdue people committed to falsity can be seen from the wonders or miracles done in Egypt that finally forced the Egyptians to let the children of Israel go. Every one of those wonders or miracles symbolizes a means used by divine power.

That I will do in the middle of it means which touch those spirits directly. This is established by the symbolism of the *middle* as something deep within, as noted in §§1074, 2940, 2973, and therefore as something that touches us directly. Whatever touches us directly lies within us, but what does not touch us directly lies outside, because it strikes at an angle and partly glances off. 6911

And afterward he will send you away symbolizes banishment of them (that is, of people committed to falsity) and deliverance (of people committed to truth). This can be seen from the symbolism of *sending away* or letting go as being banished. People immersed in falsity do not let anyone go and never would to eternity unless they were driven away. As a result, sending away here in an inner sense means banishment and consequent deliverance. 6912

Exodus 3:21, 22. *And I will give favor to this people in the eyes of the Egyptians, and it will happen when you go that you will not go empty-handed. And have a woman ask her neighbor and her houseguest for vessels of silver and vessels of gold and for clothes, and you must put them on your sons and on your daughters and plunder the Egyptians.* 6913

And I will give favor to this people in the eyes of the Egyptians symbolizes the fear felt by those immersed in falsity toward those in the spiritual church on account of the plagues. *And it will happen when you go that you will not go empty-handed* means no longer living impoverished of resources for the earthly mind. *And have a woman ask her neighbor and her houseguest* means that each individual's goodness will be enriched with appropriate necessities. *For vessels of silver* symbolizes knowledge of truth. *And vessels of gold* symbolizes knowledge of goodness. *And for clothes* symbolizes lower-level knowledge corresponding to these. *And you must put them on your sons* means applying them to the true ideas they had. *And on your daughters* means applying them to the good desires they had. *And plunder the Egyptians* means that these advantages are to be taken away from people devoted to falsity and therefore to evil.

6914 *And I will give favor to this people in the eyes of the Egyptians* symbolizes the fear felt by those immersed in falsity toward those in the spiritual church on account of the plagues. This can be seen from the symbolism of *giving favor* as fear on account of the plagues (discussed below), from the representation of the children of Israel—the *people* here—as those in the spiritual church (discussed in §6637), and from the representation of *Egyptians* as those immersed in falsity (mentioned many times before).

The symbolism of *giving favor in the eyes of the Egyptians* as the fear felt by those immersed in falsity on account of the plagues can be seen from an understanding of matters in an inner sense. The subject is individuals under the sway of falsity, symbolized by the Egyptians. What was true and good was to be taken from them and handed over to individuals in the spiritual church. Since the passage is about people under the sway of falsity, "favor" does not mean favor, because people absorbed in falsity and evil never show favor to anyone. If they help others—or fail to harm them—it is because they are afraid of plagues. That is the source of the favor they show. Such is the favor meant in an inner sense here. The inner meaning explains matters as they truly stand, not as they are presented in the literal meaning, and it applies the details to the subject at hand.

Further evidence for this symbolism is provided by later parts of the account concerning the Egyptians, in which they let the children of Israel go not as any favor but out of fear sparked by the final plagues (Exodus 11:1; 12:33).

[2] These two verses talk about the plundering of the Egyptians through the action the women of Israel took in borrowing silver, gold, and clothes from the Egyptian women. What this is all about cannot possibly be known without revelation concerning events in the other world, because the inner meaning embraces the kinds of experiences that angels and spirits have. So the situation needs to be explained.

See above at §6858 for a report that before the Lord's Coming a low-lying place in heaven came under occupation by evil demons and spirits, that they were later ejected, and that the area was given to spirits whose religion was spiritual. As long as the evil demons and spirits were there, they remained under the constant watch of angels from a higher heaven. This kept them from open evildoing.

Today too, heavenly angels keep an eye on certain spirits who are more deceitful than others because they mislead by pretending that they have innocence and love their neighbor. As long as they are being watched, they are held back from their appalling efforts to deceive. They are positioned directly overhead, and the heavenly angels who keep an eye on them are positioned still higher. All of this goes to show what conditions were like for the evil demons and spirits who occupied the lower area of heaven before the Lord's Coming. It shows that all the while, angels from a higher heaven were holding them back from openly doing evil.

[3] I was also allowed to learn just how they were kept back from open misconduct: they were bound by external restraints, which were fear of losing rank and reputation and fear that they would be dispossessed of their holdings in that region of heaven and thrust down into hell. At the same time, unsophisticated good spirits were attached to them. Something similar happens to people in the world. They might be devils inwardly, but the same external restraints still chain them to a pretense of honor and righteousness and to good behavior, and spirits with an unsophisticated goodness are attached to them to *keep* them chained. It was the same with evil spirits in the lower part of heaven before the Lord's Coming. Under those circumstances they too could be forced by self-preserving kinds of love to say what was true and do what was good.

It is no different with evil priests, and in fact with the worst priests, who are devils within but can proclaim the teachings of their religion with so much ardor and simulated zeal that they move the hearts of their listeners to godly devotion. Nonetheless it is love for themselves and for worldly advantages that is engrossing them, because the thought of high position and financial gain dominates in every corner of their mind. That is the fire that stirs them to preach so earnestly. They have with them evil spirits who have the same kind of love and therefore the same kind of thinking who lead them, and attached to these spirits are unsophisticated good spirits.

This shows what conditions were like in heaven before the Lord's Coming.

[4] After the Lord's Coming, however, conditions in heaven and hell changed radically. Evil demons and spirits who had occupied the lower area of heaven were thrown down, and spirits of the spiritual church were

taken up there to replace them. The evil spirits who had been thrown down were then deprived of external restraints, which, again, were fear that they would lose rank and reputation and fear that they would forfeit their holdings in that area. This left them to their own inner character, which was purely devilish and infernal, and in this way they were banished to the hells.

The way external restraints are stripped off in the other world is that the good spirits attached to evil spirits are removed. Upon their removal, the evil spirits lose any ability to pretend to be good, fair, and upright. Instead they are what they were inside in the world—that is, what they were in their thoughts and intentions, which they hid from others there. After the good spirits are removed, all the evil spirits want is to do evil.

These unsophisticated good spirits, having been removed from the evil spirits, were given over and attached to the spirits from the spiritual church who were inheriting that area in heaven. That is how the latter were enriched with truth and goodness previously belonging to evil demons and spirits. In the other life, people are enriched with truth and goodness by having spirits with truth and goodness attached to them, because it is through these spirits that communication takes place.

[5] That is what is symbolized by the promise that the children of Israel would not go out from Egypt empty-handed but that a woman should ask her neighbor and her house guest for vessels of silver and vessels of gold and for clothes, and that in this way they would plunder the Egyptians.

Anyone can see that if it had not represented something like this, the Divine would never have commanded them to use such fraud against the Egyptians. Anything like it is as remote as possible from the Divine. But since that people was entirely restricted to representation, and since this process would take place with the evil in the other life, the Divine permitted them to act as they did. It is important to realize that much of what Jehovah (or the Lord) commanded means in an inner sense not that it was commanded but that it was permitted.

6915 *And it will happen when you go that you will not go empty-handed* means no longer living impoverished of resources for the earthly mind. This can be seen from the symbolism of *going* as a life (discussed in §§3335, 4882, 5493, 5605, 6904) and from that of *you will not go empty-handed* as no longer living in poverty. *Empty* means a place where there is no truth (see §4744) and therefore where there is spiritual poverty. The fact that they had been lacking resources for the earthly mind is clear from earlier remarks. To be specific, people of the spiritual church (represented by the children of Israel) were attacked by others devoted to falsity in the form of knowledge (symbolized by the Egyptians [§§6851, 6854, 6865, 6897]). Accordingly, they were attacked over resources for the earthly mind, because the earthly mind's resources are called items of knowledge. What is more, knowledge causes particular trouble for spiritual people, because they think on the level of knowledge and not much higher; see §6865.

And have a woman ask her neighbor and her houseguest means that each individual's goodness will be enriched with appropriate necessities. This is indicated by the symbolism of a *woman* as a desire for the goodness urged by neighborly love (treated of at §6014), from that of the *neighbor* as a desire for truth felt by people who focus on knowledge, and from that of the *houseguest* as a desire for goodness in the same people. As neighbors and houseguests were to be asked, the truth and goodness symbolized are those that are nearby and that are therefore appropriate. **6916**

Information given just above in §6914 reveals what is going on here. The reason *women* were to do the asking is that a woman symbolizes the goodness urged by neighborly love, and that is what has to be enriched. After all, in order for goodness to be good, there has to be truth to give it character. That is because truth actually turns into goodness when we live by it. Whatever the truth is like, then, that is what the goodness becomes. From then on the goodness attracts and attaches to itself only such truth as agrees with its own character. So it attaches to itself only truth that is appropriate, and therefore truth in the neighborhood or in the house.

Vessels of silver symbolize knowledge of truth and *vessels of gold* knowledge of goodness, as the following shows: *Vessels* symbolize items of knowledge, as discussed in §§3068, 3079. Items of knowledge are called vessels because they are very broad and can hold countless true ideas and numerous good desires. *Silver* symbolizes what is true and *gold* what is good, as discussed in §§1551, 1552, 2954, 5658. For the idea that Egypt's silver means items of knowledge that are a suitable form of truth, see §6112. **6917**

The silver and gold vessels the Egyptians had stand for knowledge of truth and goodness even though here and above and below the Egyptians themselves symbolize false knowledge. Keep in mind that items of knowledge are neither true nor false in themselves. Rather, they become true in people who are looking for truth and false in people who are looking for falsity. The way these people apply and use the knowledge is what brings this about. What we know is like the wealth and riches we own: If we are intent on evil, our wealth and riches are harmful because we apply them to evil purposes, but if we are intent on goodness, they are useful because we apply them to good purposes. Consequently, if the wealth and riches an evil person owns are transferred to a good person, they become good. So also with items of knowledge.

[2] For instance, much of the ancient church's knowledge about representation survived among the Egyptians, as their hieroglyphics demonstrate. However, because they employed that knowledge for magic and misused it, they possessed falsity (rather than truth) in the form of knowledge. The same knowledge in the ancient church, by contrast, was true, because the people of that church applied it to divine worship in a proper manner.

For another example, take altars and sacrifices. With the Hebrew nation and later with the nations of Judah and Israel, they were true rituals because the people applied them to the worship of Jehovah. With the nations in the land of Canaan, though, they were false rituals because the people applied them to the worship of their idols. For this reason [the children of Israel] were commanded to destroy the surrounding nations' altars everywhere.

The case is the same with a great deal of other knowledge. So people devoted to evil and falsity can soak up numerous items of knowledge that are capable of being applied to good purposes and therefore of becoming goodness.

[3] That is also the symbolism of what was seized from the surrounding nations in Canaan—the riches, herds, smaller livestock, houses, and vineyards that the children of Israel took as plunder there. The point becomes even clearer from the fact that the gold and silver plundered from the surrounding nations was also put to a sacred use, as can be seen in 2 Samuel:

> There were in his hand vessels of silver and vessels of gold and vessels of bronze. *These* too *King David consecrated to Jehovah, together with the silver and gold that he had consecrated from all the nations that he had subdued:* from the Syrians, from Moab, and from the children of Ammon and from the Philistines and from Amalek and from the plunder of Hadadezer, son of Rehob, king of Zobah. (2 Samuel 8:10, 11, 12)

And in Isaiah:

> In the end, Tyre's merchandise and its harlot's wages will be *holy to Jehovah;* they will not be hoarded or kept back. Instead, *the people living in*

view of Jehovah will have its merchandise for eating, for filling up on, as will the ancient ones covering themselves up. (Isaiah 23:18)

Even these items that the women among the children of Israel borrowed from the Egyptians, plundering them, were later put to use in the construction of the ark and for many other sacred objects they employed in their worship.

And clothes symbolize lower-level knowledge corresponding to these, 6918
as can be seen from the consideration that *clothes* symbolize low-level knowledge, as discussed in §§2576, 5248. Clothes have this symbolism because they envelop something within.

And you must put them on your sons means applying them to the true 6919
ideas they had. *And on your daughters* means applying them to the good desires they had. This can be seen from the symbolism of *sons* as truth (discussed in §§489, 491, 533, 1147, 2623, 3373), from that of *daughters* as goodness (discussed in §§489, 490, 491, 2362, 2363), and from that of *putting something on them* as applying it, since what is put on anyone is applied to that person.

And plunder the Egyptians means that these advantages are to be taken  6920
away from people devoted to falsity and therefore to evil. This is established by the symbolism of *plundering* as taking away and from that of *Egyptians* as people devoted to falsity (noted many times before). The thoughts offered in §§6914, 6916 show what the situation is here.

The Spirits of Mercury (Continued)

IN the universal human, spirits from Mercury make up the memory of 6921
concepts that are not matter-based, as I showed at the end of the last chapter [§§6807–6817]. As a consequence, they love to learn concepts abstracted from anything made of matter, so they are prompter and faster than other spirits at taking everything in at a glance, thinking about it, and speaking. Matter is like a weight that has a slowing, retarding effect. It carries the mind downward, immersing it in earthly interests, which displaces it from the spiritual world, the origin of all clear sight.

From this you can see how quick these spirits are.

6922 There appeared a fairly bright flame, burning cheerfully for some time. The flame signaled the arrival of some of the quickest spirits from Mercury.

When they reached me, they immediately ran through the contents of my memory. (All spirits can do this, and the ones accompanying a person on earth possess the entire store of that person's memory; §§5853, 5857, 5859, 5860.) Still, because of their speed I could not tell what they were observing. I kept hearing them say, "Yes, that's right." When they came to sights I had seen in the heavens and in the world of spirits, they said they already knew that.

I sensed that a whole crowd of spirits associated with them stood behind me, a little to the left, on a level with the back of my skull.

6923 Another time I saw a mass of these spirits, though they were some distance away, out in front and slightly to the right. They spoke with me from there, but only through intermediary spirits, because their speech is as swift as thought, which cannot be expressed in human language without spirits to mediate. To my surprise they spoke as one but still just as promptly and quickly. Because there were so many talking at once, their speech came across to me as a wave. Remarkably, it washed toward my left eye, even though the spirits were to my right. The reason it moved in this direction was that the left eye corresponds to concepts abstracted from what is matter-based. This means that it corresponds to matters of understanding, whereas the right eye corresponds to matters of wisdom.

They also picked things up by ear just as rapidly as they spoke, and with the same speed evaluated what they heard, saying yes to this and no to that. They formed their opinions instantaneously, it seemed.

6924 There was a spirit from another planet who was able to speak promptly and quickly and was therefore good at talking with them. They passed instant judgment on the spirit's utterances, saying this was too elegant, that was too clever. So the only question they would pay attention to was whether they would hear anything from the spirit that they did not yet know. They therefore rejected anything that would cloud the issue—mainly high-flown efforts to sound elegant and erudite. Such efforts conceal the true message and substitute mere words, which are the outward, matter-based form of a concept.

6925 Spirits from Mercury do not linger long in one place, or in the atmosphere of the spirits from one world, but wander everywhere. This is because they relate to the universal human's memorized store of information, which constantly needs to be replenished. That is why they are given the opportunity to wander around acquiring knowledge wherever they go.

If in these travels they come across spirits who love the realm of matter—all that is tied to the body and the earth—they flee from them, escaping to places where they do not hear such things.

This shows that the mind of spirits from Mercury transcends the level of the senses and that they consequently enjoy relatively deep illumination. This I was also allowed to experience for myself when they were near me, speaking to me. At those times I noticed that my attention was drawn away from sense impressions, to the point where my eyesight started to dim and fade.

Spirits from that planet travel in regiments in tight formation, and 6926
when they gather, they form a kind of sphere. The Lord unites them this way so that they can act in concert and so that the thoughts of each can be shared with all and the thoughts of all with each.

The fact that these spirits wander the universe to accumulate knowledge was also made clear to me by the following experience: Once, when they appeared quite far from me, they spoke with me from there. "A group of us has now come together," they said. "Now we are going outside this solar system to outer space, where we know people exist who don't care about earthly, physical things, only about concepts abstracted from such things. Those are the people we want to be with.

"We don't know where we are going, but under the watchful eye of the Divine we are taken where we can learn new information that is compatible with what we already know.

"We also don't know how we meet the companions we bond with," they said. "This too happens under divine supervision."

Because they wander the universe this way, they have more oppor- 6927
tunity than others to learn about worlds and planets outside our solar system, so I spoke with them about this too. They said there were many other planets in the universe and people on them. They expressed surprise at anyone (a person of weak judgment, to use their words) who would imagine that the heaven of Almighty God could consist of spirits and angels from just one planet. That would be so few people (they pointed out) as to be almost none, relative to God's omnipotence, [and would be few] even if there were a million worlds and a million planets.

"We are aware of more than several hundred thousand inhabited planets in the universe," they added, "but what is that to the Divine, who is infinite?"

The spirits of Mercury differ dramatically from the spirits of our planet. 6928
The spirits of our planet—especially the ones who have just arrived in the other world—love what is tied to the body and the world, in other words,

what is tied to matter. These are the things they want to know about in the other life. To enable them to coexist with good spirits who care nothing about such matters, then, they are kept in places under the feet that the Word refers to as the underground realm. They stay there until they turn against physical, earthly things and slough them off. Once they do, they are taken up to heaven, are introduced to something more inward, and become angels.

6929 Some spirits from Mercury were once with me as I wrote explanations of the Word's inner meaning. When they perceived what I was writing, they said that it was very simplistic and that almost all the expressions I used seemed as if they were matter-bound. I was granted to answer that the people of our planet nonetheless view what I had written as rarefied, lofty, and mostly beyond their grasp. Many on this planet, I added, do not know that the inner self is what acts on the outer self and enables it to live. Judging by sensory illusions, they convince themselves that the body has independent life and consequently that the whole person will inevitably die when the physical part dies. In this way they become skeptical about life after death. Furthermore, they use the term *soul* rather than *spirit* for the part of the person destined to live on after the death of the body, and they debate what the soul is and where its seat lies. They believe the soul has to reunite with the physical body for the person to live, and so on and so on.

When the spirits from Mercury heard this, they asked whether people like this can become angels. I was allowed to answer that the people who become angels are the ones who have lived lives devoted to doing good out of neighborly love or out of faith. After becoming angels they no longer focus on matter-based superficialities but on spiritual depths, and once they reach that stage they enjoy brighter light than spirits from Mercury do.

An angel in heaven who had come from our planet and had possessed this kind of skepticism when living in the world was allowed to speak with them so they could see this was so. The experience will be described in a later section [§7077].

6930 Later the spirits of Mercury sent me a long, uneven piece of paper made of many pieces glued together. It looked as if it had been printed in the kind of press used on this planet. I asked whether they had printing too. They said that they did not but that they knew we had documents like this on our planet. They refused to say more, but I was able to perceive that they were thinking this was what the knowledge of concepts was like on this planet. They considered knowledge here to be isolated from people themselves except when people trained their eye and therefore their mind on pages like these. So they were privately mocking the people of this planet as not knowing anything except from pieces of paper; but they were set straight as to the true situation.

After a while they returned and sent me another sheet of paper, also appearing to be printed in type, like the previous one. However, this one was not so patched and messy, but instead was nice and neat. They said they had been informed further that this planet has such pages, and books made of them.

The description so far of spirits from the planet Mercury shows plainly 6931
that spirits retain what they see and hear in the other life. It shows that they can be taught things—including tenets of faith—and in this way be perfected, the same as when they were people on their planet.

The more purity spirits and angels have, the more readily and fully they absorb what they hear and the more perfectly they remember it. Since this continues to eternity, you can see that they are always growing in wisdom.

The spirits of Mercury, on the other hand, are always growing in the knowledge of concepts. This process does not bring them wisdom, because they love information (which is a means) rather than the use it can be put to (which is the goal), as was noted of them in §§6814, 6815.

More will be said about the spirits of Mercury at the end of the next 6932
chapter [§§7069–7079].

Exodus 4

Teachings on Neighborly Love

6933 THERE is a common saying that we are each our own neighbor, meaning that we each ought to take care of ourselves first. Teachings on neighborly love tell us what the case with this is. We are each our own neighbor not first but last. Ahead of us come other people of good intent, ahead of them the greater community, ahead of this our country, ahead of this the church, ahead of this the Lord's kingdom, and above all people and all things the Lord.

6934 Here is how to understand the idea that we are each our own neighbor and that we ought to consider our own interests first: We must each make sure first that we have the necessities of life—food, clothing, shelter, and other basic requirements of the culture we live in. We must secure these not only for ourselves but also for our loved ones, not just for the present moment but also for the future. Unless we obtain the necessities of life, we are not in a position to exercise love toward our neighbor; no, we are in need of everything.

6935 Our ultimate goal makes a statement about the kind of neighbor we are going to be to ourselves and about the way we are going to see to our own interests first. If our goal is to become richer than others purely for the sake of riches or self-indulgence or prominence and so on, the goal is bad. People who believe they are being their own neighbor with this kind of motivation, then, are hurting themselves to eternity. However, if our goal is to acquire financial resources for the sake of life's necessities for ourselves and our loved ones, to put ourselves in a position to do good, as teachings on neighborly love command, we are seeing to our interests for eternity.

The purpose itself makes our identity, because it is the same as our love. What we love is what we adopt as our goal.

6936 The situation can be further clarified by the following analogy: We should all look out for our body by providing it with food and clothing. This has to come first, but the goal must be a healthy mind in a healthy body. And we should also look out for our mind by providing *it* with food—that is, with ideas that nourish understanding and wisdom—so that it will be in a position to serve the Lord. If we do this, we take good eternal care of ourselves.

Suppose, though, that we look out for our body for its own sake and fail to consider the health of our mind, supplying our mind with food that undermines rather than nourishes understanding and wisdom. If we do, we take poor eternal care of ourselves.

This example shows in what way we ought to each be neighbor to ourselves: not first of all but last, because we must have not ourselves but others as our ultimate purpose. Where our purpose is, there is our first priority.

Another analogy is a person building a house. The person has to lay 6937
the foundation first, but the aim of the foundation has to be the house, and the aim of the house has to be the living in it. Likewise we each ought to see to our own interests first, yet not for our own sake but to put ourselves in a position to serve our neighbor and therefore our country, the church, and above all the Lord. If we believe we are our own neighbor first of all, we are like someone who regards the foundation rather than the house or residence in it as the ultimate purpose. Instead, living there is actually the first and ultimate purpose, and the house with its foundation is merely a means to that end.

As it is with regard to wealth, so it is with regard to worldly prestige: 6938
it is perfectly allowable for us to secure our standing in the world, but only for our neighbor's sake rather than our own. If we seek rank for our own sake, we are taking poor care of ourselves, but if we seek it for the sake of our neighbor, we are taking good care of ourselves. Those who make themselves the point of everything point themselves toward hell, while those who make their neighbor the point instead, point themselves toward heaven.

Exodus 4

1. And Moses answered and said, "But here, they won't believe me or listen to my voice, because they will say, 'Jehovah has not appeared to you.'"

2. And Jehovah said to him, "What is that in your hand?" and he said, "A staff."

3. And he said, "Cast it to the earth," and he cast it to the earth, and it became a snake, and Moses fled from it.

4. And Jehovah said to Moses, "Put out your hand and grab its tail"—and he put out his hand and seized it, and it became a staff in his palm—

5. "in order that they may believe that Jehovah, the God of their fathers, the God of Abraham, the God of Isaac, and the God of Jacob, appeared to you."

6. And Jehovah said further to him, "Now put your hand into the fold of your robe," and he put his hand into the fold and took it out, and here, his hand was leprous, like snow.

7. And he said, "Put your hand back in the fold"—and he put his hand back in the fold and brought it out of the fold, and here, it returned to being like his flesh—

8. "and it will happen if they do not believe you and do not listen to the voice of the former sign, that they will believe the voice of the latter sign.

9. And it will happen if they do not believe even these two signs and do not listen to your voice, that you are to take some of the water of the river and pour it on the dry ground, and the water that you took from the river will become blood on the dry ground."

10. And Moses said to Jehovah, "Upon my life, Lord, I am not a man of words either from yesterday or from the day before or from this moment of your speaking to your servant, because I am heavy of mouth and heavy of tongue."

11. And Jehovah said to him, "Who gives humankind a mouth, or who has made a person mute or deaf or sighted or blind? Is it not I, Jehovah?

12. And now go, and I myself will be with your mouth and teach you what you should speak."

13. And he said, "Upon my life, Lord, please send [your message] by the hand [of someone else] you might send."

14. And Jehovah's anger kindled against Moses, and he said, "Isn't there Aaron your brother, the Levite? I know that he at least will speak. And besides, look: he is going out to meet you, and he will see you and rejoice in his heart.

15. And you are to speak to him and put the words in his mouth, and I myself will be with your mouth and with his mouth and teach both of you what you must do.

16. And he will speak for you to the people, and it will happen that he will be like a mouth for you, and you will be like a god for him.

17. And you are to take in your hand this staff, with which you will perform signs."

18. And Moses went and returned to Jethro his father-in-law and said to him, "I must go, please, and return to my brothers who are in Egypt and see whether they are still living." And Jethro said to Moses, "Go in peace."

19. And Jehovah said to Moses in Midian, "Go, return to Egypt, because all the men seeking your soul are dead."

20. And Moses took his wife and his sons and had them ride on a donkey and returned to the land of Egypt. And Moses took the staff of God in his hand.

21. And Jehovah said to Moses, "As you go to return to Egypt, look at all the wonders that I have put in your hand, and you are to perform them before Pharaoh. And I myself will harden his heart, and he will not send the people away.

22. And you are to say to Pharaoh, 'This is what Jehovah has said: "Israel is my son, my firstborn.

23. And I say to you, 'Let my son go and let him serve me,' and you refuse to let him go. Watch: I am killing your own son, your firstborn."'"

24. And he was in an inn on the way, and Jehovah met him and sought to kill him.

25. And Zipporah took a flint and cut off the foreskin of her son and made it touch his feet and said, "Because a blood-soaked bridegroom you are to me."

26. And [Jehovah] ceased from [killing] him; then she said "a blood-soaked bridegroom" for circumcisions.

27. And Jehovah said to Aaron, "Go to the wilderness to meet Moses," and he went and met him on the mountain of God and kissed him.

28. And Moses told Aaron all the words of Jehovah with which he had sent him and all the signs that he had commanded him.

29. And Moses went, and Aaron, and they gathered all the elders of the children of Israel.

30. And Aaron spoke all the words that Jehovah had spoken to Moses. And he performed the signs in the eyes of the people.

31. And the people believed, and they heard that Jehovah had visited the children of Israel and that he had seen their affliction. And they bent and bowed.

Summary

6939 THE inner meaning of this chapter continues with the deliverance of people in the spiritual church. First it depicts their circumstances: that if they lacked hope and faith they would draw to themselves what was false and evil and profane. That is what the three signs symbolize.

6940 It goes on to deal with the divine law and the connecting of truth to the goodness that was in the divine law. This endowed that goodness with the power to deliver people and give them hope and faith. Moses represents the goodness in the divine law, and Aaron represents the truth in it.

6941 Lastly the chapter treats of that people, [the children of Israel,] and the fact that they would merely *represent* the spiritual church. The religion itself could not be established among them because they were devoted to what is external without what is internal. This is symbolized by Zipporah's circumcision of her son and by the blood with which she stained [Moses'] feet.

Inner Meaning

6942 EXODUS 4:1, 2, 3, 4. *And Moses answered and said, "But here, they won't believe me or listen to my voice, because they will say, 'Jehovah has not appeared to you.'" And Jehovah said to him, "What is that in your hand?" and he said, "A staff." And he said, "Cast it to the earth," and he cast it to the earth, and it became a snake, and Moses fled from it. And Jehovah said to Moses, "Put out your hand and grab its tail," and he put out his hand and seized it, and it became a staff in his palm.*

And Moses answered and said symbolizes thinking based on divine law. *But here, they won't believe me or listen to my voice* means that people of the spiritual church would not put faith in it and therefore would not accept it. *Because they will say, "Jehovah has not appeared to you,"* symbolizes the Lord's divinity within his humanity. *And Jehovah said to him* symbolizes foreseeing the nature they would develop if they lacked faith. "*What is that in your hand?" and he said, "A staff,"* symbolizes the power of the Lord's divine humanity. *And he said, "Cast it to the earth,"* symbolizes an inflow of the power of the Lord's earthly divinity into the senses. *And it became a snake* symbolizes the sensory, bodily self consequently separated from the inner self. *And Moses fled from it* symbolizes horror over a disconnected sensory level. *And Jehovah said to Moses* symbolizes what the Divine provided. *Put out your hand and grab the tail* symbolizes the power to raise [the mind] above the outermost sensory level. *And he put out his hand and seized it* symbolizes elevation toward inner levels. *And it became a staff in his palm* means that the Divine then communicated power.

And Moses answered and said symbolizes thinking based on divine law, 6943
as the following shows: *Answering and saying* symbolizes thinking. What is expressed as something outward in the literal, narrative meaning symbolizes something inward in the inner meaning. Spiritual attributes, which belong to heaven, can never be presented to people on earth in any other form. We do not grasp sheer spiritual realities, and they cannot be expressed in the words of human language, so they are depicted as the earthly phenomena corresponding to them and are given to us in that form. As a consequence, the Word is suited to people in the physical world and to people in the spiritual world. The result is communication between heaven and humankind, and communion between them as well. And *Moses* represents the Lord as divine law, as discussed in §6752. Plainly, then, *Moses answered and said* symbolizes thinking based on divine law.

Thinking on the basis of divine law means thinking on the basis of truth imparted by the Divine. In this case it means realizing that the children of Israel would not believe unless they saw signs and wonders.

But here, they won't believe me or listen to my voice means that people 6944
of the spiritual church would not put faith in it and therefore would not accept it, as the following shows: The children of Israel, whom this is about, represent people of the spiritual church, as dealt with in §§6426, 6637. *Not believing* means not putting faith in. And *not listening to the voice of* means not accepting, as dealt with in §§5471, 5475.

Because they will say, "Jehovah has not appeared to you," symbolizes the 6945
divinity that was within the Lord's humanity, as the following shows: *Saying* symbolizes a perception, as noted many times. Here it symbolizes a perception by people in the spiritual church. *Jehovah's appearing* symbolizes a manifestation of the Lord's divinity within his humanity. Obviously, appearing means being manifested. It is also plain that Jehovah means the Lord's divinity itself and divine humanity, as discussed in §§1736, 2004, 2005, 2018, 2025, 2156, 2329, 2921, 3023, 3035, 5041, 5663, 6281, 6303, 6905. The idea that Jehovah's appearing means the manifestation of the Lord's

divinity within his humanity can also be seen from the fact that his divinity is not visible to any human—not even an angel—except through his divine humanity. Nor is his divine humanity visible except through divine truth radiating from him.

The subject of the inner meaning here is the deliverance of people in the spiritual church, and they were delivered by the Lord's coming into the world (see §§2661, 2716, 3969, 6854, 6914). More specifically, they were saved by the Lord's divine humanity (§§2716, 2833, 2834).

[2] Let me say more about this situation—that unless they saw signs, people of that church would not put faith in or accept the statements of the divine law, which is represented by Moses; that is, the statements of the Word. People in a spiritual religion do not perceive truth on the basis of goodness, as the heavenly do. What they acknowledge as true instead is every teaching of their religion that they have proved to their own satisfaction, so they are somewhat in the dark (§§2718, 2831, 2849, 2935, 2937, 3833, 6427, 6500, 6865). This is quite plain from their complete inability to grasp how the Lord's humanity can be divine, or that divine love in the Lord's human side can make it divine. They fix their minds on human nature as it exists in a human being and do not let go of that image when thinking about the Lord. Such is the confusion they are in. The same thing can be seen from the fact that they also do not comprehend how we can live on after death, or then enjoy the senses, such as sight, hearing, taste, and smell, or possess a human shape there. To them the idea that we could be like this after casting off our physical body with its senses and its limbs seems foreign to the truth. They are tangled up in sense impressions and in the knowledge and illusions these impressions yield. Consequently, if they did not believe the body would reunite with the soul, they would have no belief whatever in any resurrection.

[3] All this shows clearly enough how much in the dark they are on heavenly matters. That is why faith can never be planted in them unless they are forcefully withheld from falsity by the Lord. The requisite force did not exist before his Coming but only afterward, once he had made the humanity in himself divine. So not until after the Lord's resurrection could they be released from the underground region where they were being overrun with falsity and be taken up to heaven (§6914).

This then is the reason for saying they will not believe or accept what is said by divine law, or divine truth, unless they see it is so and therefore unless they see signs; and the signs are discussed below.

And Jehovah said to him symbolizes foreseeing the nature they would develop if they lacked faith. This can be seen from the symbolism of *saying* when applied to Jehovah, or the Lord, as foresight, which is mentioned at §5361. What was foreseen was their future character if they lacked faith, as is evident from the three signs, discussed below [§§6947–6978]. In their inner meaning those signs represent the state such people would be in if they did not believe. 6946

"*What is that in your hand?" and he said, "A staff,"* symbolizes the power of the Lord's divine humanity. This can be seen from the symbolism of a *hand* as power (discussed in §§878, 3387, 4931–4937, 5327, 5328, 5544) and from that of a *staff* as power as well (discussed in §§4013, 4876, 4936). The reason the power of the Lord's divine humanity is meant is that Moses represents the Lord as divine law, or as the Word, which is divine truth radiating from his divine humanity (§6752). 6947

The power symbolized by a hand is power emanating from the rational level of the Lord's divinity, but the power symbolized by a staff is power emanating from the earthly level of the Lord's divinity. The reason a staff means power emanating from the Lord's earthly divinity is that a staff supports the body the way a foot does, and a foot symbolizes the earthly plane (§§2162, 3147, 3761, 3986, 4280, 4938–4952). "Lifting a hand" stands for power on the spiritual plane and "lifting a foot" for power on the earthly plane (see §§5327, 5328), and this being so, when Moses was performing miracles he was sometimes told to lift his hand and sometimes his staff. It all depended on the level involved in the inner meaning.

And he said, "Cast it to the earth," symbolizes an inflow of the power of the Lord's earthly divinity into the senses, as the following shows: A staff symbolizes power on the earthly level, and when mentioned in connection with the Lord, power emanating from his earthly divinity, as discussed directly above at §6947. *Casting,* or sending out, symbolizes something emanating and therefore an inflow. And the *earth* symbolizes the outer part of a person, as discussed in §§82, 913, 1411, 1733. Here it symbolizes what relates to the senses and body of a person, which are the outermost aspects, because the staff became a snake, and a snake symbolizes the sensory and bodily self. 6948

[2] By the Lord's divine power here is meant divine truth radiating from the Lord, because divine truth contains so much power that it is power itself (§§3091, 4932, 6344, 6423).

Divine truth radiating from the Lord flows into each of us through our inner reaches into our outer reaches all the way to our outer senses and our bodily responses. At each point along the way it stirs up ideas corresponding to itself in order. On the level of the senses it stimulates corresponding ideas of things as they appear in the world and on the earth; but since what exists in the world and on earth appears other than it actually is, those ideas are full of illusions. When the sensory part of our mind remains trapped in such ideas, then, our thoughts cannot help opposing the good desires and true ideas taught by faith (since those thoughts grow out of illusions) and turning inflowing divine truth into falsity.

Examples can illustrate that if we do not rise above the level of the senses but remain there and think on that level, our thoughts rise out of illusions. [3] For instance, there is the illusion that the life force in us belongs to our body, when in reality it belongs to the spirit within our body. There is the illusion that sight belongs to the eye, hearing to the ear, and speech to the tongue and mouth, when in reality it is the spirit that sees, that hears, that speaks, by means of those bodily organs. There is the illusion that life is fixed in us, when in reality it flows in. There is the illusion that the soul cannot possess a human form or human senses and responses. There is the illusion about heaven and hell that the former lies above and the latter below us, when in reality they exist within us. There is the illusion that physical objects influence our inner realm, when in reality outer things never flow into inner things, only the other way around. There is the illusion that we cannot live on after death unless we live in our body. Not to mention illusions about physical phenomena, which inspire so many mutually contradictory hypotheses.

[4] Who cannot see that illusions and the falsities they generate overshadow the truth? Take just the old enduring dispute over whether blood circulates, which remained in doubt a long time despite the support of an abundance of experimental evidence. Or the argument about the sun, that it revolves daily around the earth, and not only the sun but also the moon, all the planets, and the whole starry sky, once every day. Or the continuing debate about the soul, its connection with the body, and its seat there. The illusions of the senses dominate these issues, even though the truth about them is clear from many indications and effects. Then what about the kinds of things that exist in heaven, which, being spiritual, are not visible except in corresponding objects and events?

[5] These remarks now show what our sensory level is like, regarded in itself and left to itself: it is swallowed up by illusions and consequent

false thinking and therefore opposes religious truth and goodness. That is why, when we are immersed in the senses and the dim light they give off, we are benighted concerning any subject that belongs to the spiritual world—that is, concerning subjects lit with light from the Divine. It is also why the dim light of the senses turns into pure darkness when the light from heaven falls on it. After all, truth lit by divine light cannot coexist with illusions and the falsities that result from them but extinguishes them and accordingly brings thick darkness upon them.

And it became a snake symbolizes the sensory, bodily self separated from the inner self. This is established by the symbolism of a *snake* as a person whose reasoning is based on sensory information (discussed in §§195, 196, 197, 6398, 6399) and therefore as the sensory level of a person. Since a snake symbolizes the sensory level, it also symbolizes the bodily level, because the sensory level receives everything it has from the body's senses. And since the sensory level regarded in itself has the character described directly above in §6948, a snake as the sensory level also symbolizes all evil in general (§§251, 254, 257). **6949**

That the snake here means the sensory, bodily self *separated from the inner* or rational self is evident from Moses' fleeing before it, which symbolizes horror over it. Another piece of evidence is the state this sign depicts, which is the state that people in the spiritual church would be in if they lacked faith, because their inner dimension would then be closed off. Only enough of heaven's light would flow in to make it possible for them to think and therefore speak from a disconnected sensory level.

[2] A disconnected sensory level is the platform for thought in everyone who defends falsity against truth and evil against goodness—in short, everyone who lives a life of evil and so of unbelief (since those who live evil lives believe nothing).

People like this have greater skill than others at reasoning and also a greater skill with persuasion, especially of the uneducated. This is because they rely on sensory illusions and worldly appearances when they speak. They also know how to blot out or hide the truth with illusions. For this reason, snakes also symbolize cleverness and cunning. When the sensory level is united with the inner dimension, though, or when it is properly subordinated to the rational level, a snake symbolizes shrewdness and watchfulness (§§197, 4211, 6398).

And Moses fled from it symbolizes horror over a disconnected sensory level. This can be seen from the symbolism of *fleeing* as horror, since one who is horrified by something flees from it, and from that of a snake, **6950** which is what Moses fled from, as a disconnected sensory level (discussed directly above at §6949).

6951 *And Jehovah said to Moses* symbolizes what the Divine provided, as the following shows: *Saying,* when attributed to *Jehovah,* or the Lord, symbolizes foresight, as noted above at §6946; and as it symbolizes foresight, it also symbolizes providence, since the two are tightly connected. What the Lord foresees, he provides for. He foresees what is evil and provides what is good. *Jehovah said,* then, symbolizes providence here because he now turns the snake into a staff, or evil into goodness. And *Moses* represents the Lord as divine truth. So providence from the Divine is attributable to the Lord in his humanity when he was in the world.

6952 *Put out your hand and grab the tail* symbolizes the power to raise [the mind] above the outermost sensory level. This is evident from the symbolism of a *hand* as power (dealt with above at §6947) and from that of a snake's *tail* as the outermost sensory level. A snake is the sensory level (see above at §6949), so its tail is the outermost or lowest part. *Putting out* and *grabbing* symbolize elevation, because one who puts out a hand and grabs something creeping on the earth lifts it up.

Because a snake symbolizes a disconnected sensory level and therefore reasoning about religious truth on the basis of sensory illusions, the snake's tail symbolizes falsity itself. Falsity is outermost or lowest, and people who focus on falsity and therefore on what is outermost and lowest face very much downward and out toward the surface, at the world and the earth. They do not look upward or inward, to heaven and the Lord.

[2] This symbolism of a snake's tail is clear in John:

> The locusts *had tails like scorpions,* and *stings were in their tails,* and their power is to harm people. (Revelation 9:10)

Tails like scorpions and stings in the tails mean skillful reasoning that relies on false ideas, which they use to persuade people, causing injury in the process. That is why the passage says that their power is to harm people. [3] In the same author:

> *The horses' tails were like snakes, having heads,* and by them they do harm. (Revelation 9:19)

Once again, tails like snakes here stand for reasoning that relies on falsity and does damage, only worse, because the verse says that the tails were horses' tails and had heads. Horses symbolize the intellect, as does a head, so these tails symbolize even more skillful reasoning based on illusions and accordingly on falsity that contradicts truth. This kind of reasoning is the lowest possible, because the more skillfully reason argues against truth, the lower it sinks. [4] In the same author:

> *The dragon's tail dragged a third of the stars in heaven* and threw them onto the earth. (Revelation 12:4)

The dragon's tail too stands for reasoning that stems from falsity. The stars in heaven stand for concepts of goodness and truth. Throwing them onto the earth stands for destroying them. The dragon is a snake that leads people astray by rationalizations based on falsity. It is also the snake, using the tree of knowledge—that is, knowledge based on sense impressions and therefore on illusions—that led astray the "mother of all living things" (Eve) in the garden [Genesis 3:20]. This too is clear from John:

> The big dragon, the *ancient snake,* which is called the Devil and Satan, which leads the whole inhabited world astray, was thrown [onto the earth]. (Revelation 12:9)

[5] More generally a tail means a disconnected sensory level that looks not up but down, not to heaven but to the earth. So it means falsity. This can be seen in Isaiah:

> Jehovah will cut *head* and *tail,* branch and reed off from Israel. The elder and honored one is the *head; but the prophet—the teacher of a lie—is the tail.* (Isaiah 9:14, 15)

Obviously the tail stands for falsity, which the Word here calls a lie. In the same author:

> Egypt will have no work *that can produce head and tail,* branch and reed. (Isaiah 19:15)

A reed stands for what is lowest. In Moses:

> So Jehovah will make you *into the head* and *not into the tail* so that you will be only upward and will not be downward when you obey the commandments of your God. (Deuteronomy 28:13)

[6] The tail stands for the lowest part, which faces down, or out to the surface, that is, toward the world and the earth, not to heaven and the Lord. The Lord raises our inner reaches upward, together with our sensory functioning, when we commit to the goodness urged by faith and neighborly love. If we are committed to evil and falsity, though, our inner reaches, together with our sensory functioning, look downward and therefore solely

to what we find in the world. As a result, we shed our human nature and put on the nature of a beast, which faces down, gazing only at what it finds on the earth. People who look downward will what is evil and think what is false, but people lifted upward by the Lord will what is good and think what is true. The Lord raises them up in a very real way, extracting them from evil and falsity. Angels can actually feel the sensation. It is like a pull toward a center of gravity, the center being located where the Lord is present in his sun. With angels, the head points up to this center, but with the hellish, the feet point up there, so angels look up and the hellish down (§§3641, 3642). [7] In the same author:

> The stranger who is in your midst will *rise above you* farther and farther *up.* But you will *sink* farther and farther *down. [The stranger] will become the head, but you will become the tail.* (Deuteronomy 28:43, 44)

The meaning is similar. In Isaiah:

> Say to him, "Be careful and be quiet, don't be afraid or let your heart go soft *because of the two tails of those smoking firebrands*—because of the wrath of Rezin and Syria and of Remaliah's son." (Isaiah 7:4)

Rezin, king of Syria, stands for concepts of what is evil. Syria stands for concepts of what is good (see §§1232, 1234, 3680), so in a negative sense it stands for concepts of what is evil. Remaliah's son, king of Samaria, stands for concepts of what is false. The two of these are tails because they lie at the bottom. Smoking firebrands stand for wrath.

6953 *And he put out his hand and seized it* symbolizes elevation toward inner levels, as the following shows: *Putting out a hand and seizing something* that lies below means being raised to higher levels, or inner levels (to put the same thing another way), as above at §6952. And a *hand* symbolizes inner power, as also mentioned above at §6952. And a snake, which is what he seized, symbolizes the level of the senses and reasoning that springs from there, as discussed above at §6949. When the sensory level is lifted up toward inner levels, power is communicated from the Divine, as will be seen in the next section.

6954 *And it became a staff in his palm* means that the Divine then communicated power, as the following shows: The snake that *became a staff* symbolizes the sensory level, as discussed above at §6949. A *staff* symbolizes power on the earthly level, and a *palm,* inner power, both of them being from the Divine, as discussed at §6952.

Here is the situation: On our own we look only downward, to the world and the earth, because on our own we are immersed in evil and falsity. When we face that direction, the sensory dimension is in control, and inner levels do nothing to oppose it, because they follow the force of the current and yield to it.

It is not under our own power but under the Lord's that we look up, to heaven and to him, and what brings this about is elevation. When our inner levels are raised up, our sensory level is too. The dim light on the sensory level then becomes dark, though, because heaven's light predominates. When that happens, goodness and truth from the Lord flow in, and we welcome them. This is what is meant by the communication of power from the Divine.

However, the only people who can be elevated in this way are those who have lived the life of goodness urged on us by faith and neighborly love.

It really is possible to be lifted up to inner levels, as I have been allowed to learn from personal experience, because I have felt it happen a thousand times.

Exodus 4:5, 6, 7. *"In order that they may believe that Jehovah, the God of their fathers, the God of Abraham, the God of Isaac, and the God of Jacob, appeared to you." And Jehovah said further to him, "Now put your hand into the fold of your robe," and he put his hand into the fold and took it out, and here, his hand was leprous, like snow. And he said, "Put your hand back in the fold"—and he put his hand back in the fold and brought it out of the fold, and here, it returned to being like his flesh.* 6955

In order that they may believe that Jehovah appeared to you means in order to put their faith in the Lord's divine humanity. *The God of their fathers* means that this was the Divine acknowledged by the ancient church. *The God of Abraham, the God of Isaac, and the God of Jacob* symbolizes the Lord's divinity itself and divine humanity. *And Jehovah said further to him* symbolizes foreseeing the nature that people in the spiritual church would develop if they lacked faith. *Put your hand into the fold of your robe* symbolizes adoption of truth. *And he put his hand into the fold* symbolizes the actual deed. *And took it out* symbolizes what resulted. *And here, his hand was leprous, like snow* symbolizes profanation of truth. *And he said,* symbolizes providing for the nature that people in the spiritual church would develop if they possessed faith. *Put your hand back in the fold* symbolizes adoption of truth. *And he put his hand back into the fold* symbolizes the actual deed. *And brought it out of the fold* symbolizes the result. *And here, it returned to being like his flesh* symbolizes goodness at that point.

In order that they may believe that Jehovah appeared to you means in order to put their faith in the Lord's divine humanity, as the following shows: *Believing* means putting faith in something—not faith that Jehovah 6956 (the Lord) appeared in a visible way but faith in the Lord in a spiritual sense. And *Jehovah's appearing* symbolizes a manifestation of the Lord in his divine humanity, as discussed at §6945. *That they may believe that Jehovah appeared to you,* then, means in order to put their faith in the Lord's divine humanity.

6957 *The God of their fathers* means that this was the Divine acknowledged by the ancient church. This is established by the discussion in §§6876, 6884 of the symbolism of the *God of their fathers* as the Divine acknowledged by the ancient church. This was the Lord in his divine humanity, as may also be seen there.

6958 *The God of Abraham, the God of Isaac, and the God of Jacob* symbolizes the Lord's divinity itself and divine humanity, as may be seen from the evidence at §6847, where the same words occur.

6959 *And Jehovah said further to him* symbolizes foreseeing the nature that people in the spiritual church would develop if they lacked faith. This is established by the symbolism of *Jehovah said* as foresight, as above at §6946. Why does it mean foreseeing the nature that people in the spiritual church would develop if they lacked faith? Because what follows is about people in the spiritual church, represented by the children of Israel, and the nature they would later develop if they lacked faith [§§6960–6978]. To be specific, they would become profaners of truth. The first miracle, the staff turned into a snake, symbolizes a state in which they would become entirely sense- and body-oriented. The current miracle, the hand turned leprous, symbolizes profanation, because that comes next if a spiritual religion persists in its unbelief.

[2] People in a spiritual religion put faith in the teachings of their church during their youth and early adulthood, but at that point they take their faith from their parents and teachers, not from themselves. If they later fall away from their faith, then, they profane the truth slightly if at all. Profanation of this kind can be removed by divine means, and doubters can then be cleared of their guilt.

However, suppose we develop our own faith in the church's teachings and in the Word, by confirming it all for ourselves, and then afterward fall away, privately denying what we had previously believed. Worse, suppose we live lives that violate the truth we had proved to ourselves and either reinterpret it in our favor or totally reject it. We then profane truth. We profane it because we mix and bind truth and falsity together deep within ourselves. Under these circumstances we have hardly any remaining traces of truth or goodness, so in the other world we eventually come to resemble skeletons and have as little life remaining as bones have in comparison with living, organic flesh. Yet the fate of people who profane goodness is harsher than the fate of those who profane truth. People in the Lord's spiritual church are able to profane truth but not goodness to the same extent.

[3] Since leprosy symbolizes profanation of truth, and this is the theme in what follows next, first see what has already been said and shown about profanation: People inside the church can profane what is holy, but people outside the church cannot: 2051, 3399. Holy things can be profaned only by people who have first acknowledged them: 1008, 1010, 1059, 3398, 3898, 4289. Profanation also consists in acknowledging and believing what is true and good while nonetheless living a life opposed to truth and goodness: 4601. We are withheld from profanation as far as possible: 301, 302, 303, 1327, 1328, 3398, 3402. The fate of profaners is the worst of all in the other life: 6348.

Put your hand into the fold of your robe symbolizes adoption of truth. **6960**
This can be seen from the symbolism of a *hand* as power (treated of above at §6947) and from that of the *fold of a robe* as love. What is connected with the chest corresponds to love, because in it lies the heart, which corresponds to heavenly love, and the lungs, which correspond to spiritual love (§§3635, 3883–3896, 4112, 4113, 4133). Since the fold of a robe therefore corresponds to love, it also symbolizes what is a person's own, because what we love is our own. Consequently, this putting one's hand into the fold of one's robe means adopting something as one's own. It is the adoption of truth that is meant, as is plain from what follows and from the fact that truth holds all spiritual power (§6948).

[2] The passages below demonstrate that the fold of one's robe means what is unique to an individual, therefore what is a person's own, and as a consequence adoption and union through love. In Micah:

> Do not rely on a companion or trust a leader; *from the one lying on the fold of your robe* guard the doors of your mouth. (Micah 7:5)

"One lying on the fold of your robe" stands for someone bound to this person by love. For that reason a wife is also called the *wife on the fold of her husband's robe* (Deuteronomy 28:54; 2 Samuel 12:8), and a husband is called the *husband on the fold of his wife's robe* (Deuteronomy 28:56). This is because each belongs to the other. In David:

> My prayer will *rebound onto the fold of my robe.* (Psalms 35:13)

This means that it will rebound onto himself. In the same author:

> Remember, Lord, the reproach of your servants, *my carrying* all the great peoples *in the fold of my robe.* (Psalms 89:50)

This stands for carrying them on his person, as his own. In Isaiah:

> He pastures his flock like a shepherd; he gathers the lambs into his arm and *carries them in the fold of his robe.* (Isaiah 40:11)

The meaning is similar. [3] In Luke:

> Give, and something will be given to you; good measure pressed down, shaken, and overflowing will be *put into the fold of your robe.* (Luke 6:38)

Being put into the fold of their robe means being given to them as their own. In the same author:

> Then it happened that Lazarus died and was taken away by the angels into the *fold of Abraham's robe.* (Luke 16:22)

To be taken away into the fold of Abraham's robe stands for being taken to the Lord (who is meant by Abraham) because of being bound to him by love. [4] In John:

> One of the disciples, *whom Jesus loved,* was reclining *on the fold of Jesus' robe.* He, settling down *onto Jesus' breast,* says to him, "Lord, who is it?" (John 13:23, 25)

Reclining on the fold of his robe obviously stands for being loved by him and united to him by love. In the same author:

> God has never been seen by anyone; the only-born Son, *who is in the fold of the Father's robe,* is the one who has revealed him. (John 1:18)

Being in the fold of the Father's robe means being one with him.

[5] In the following passages the fold of the robe stands for what belongs to us that we have adopted *without* love. In Isaiah:

> I will repay, *I will repay into the fold of their robe* your wickedness and the wickedness of your fathers at the same time. I will measure out their wage *into the fold of their robe.* (Isaiah 65:6, 7)

In Jeremiah:

> Jehovah is showing mercy toward thousands and *repaying the parents' wickedness into the fold of their children's robe* after them. (Jeremiah 32:18)

In David:

> *Repay into the fold of our neighbors' robe* seven times the insult with which they insulted you, Lord. (Psalms 79:12)

Repaying something into the fold of someone's robe stands for repaying it to those people themselves.

And he put his hand into the fold symbolizes the actual deed—that is, of adopting truth. This can be seen from the remarks just above. 6961

And took it out symbolizes what resulted. This can be seen from the symbolism of taking his hand out of the fold to look at it as observing what it is like and therefore what resulted. 6962

And here, his hand was leprous, like snow symbolizes profanation of truth. This can be seen from the symbolism of a *hand* as power (as above at §6947) and as truth, since spiritual power consists in truth (§§6948, 6960), and from the symbolism of *leprosy* as profanation—specifically, profanation of truth (discussed below). 6963

The narrative part of the Word treats at length of leprosy, its varying appearance in the skin, and how to judge its nature from that appearance; of lepers, that they should either be shut in, leave the congregation, or be freed of their leprosy; and of leprosy in clothes, vessels, and even houses.

Leprosy is discussed so much not because of its status as a disease but because of its spiritual meaning, symbolizing profanation of truth. It is also because Jews and Israelites were more capable than others of profaning truth. [2] Imagine if they had known the depths of the Word and the real truth represented by the religious rituals they practiced. Imagine if they had put their faith in that truth and yet had lived lives according to their native disposition—lives of self-love and materialism, hatred and mutual revenge, and cruelty to surrounding nations. Under those circumstances they could not have helped profaning the truth they had once put their faith in. After all, to believe the truth and live contrary to it is to profane it. That is why they were also withheld as far as possible from the knowledge of inner truth (§§3398, 3479), to the point where they did not even know they would live on after death. Neither did they believe the Messiah was coming in order to save their souls forever but rather to promote their nation over all other nations everywhere. Because their nation was like that, and still is today, they continue to be withheld from belief [in the truth] even when they live in the middle of the Christian world. This then is why leprosy in all its forms is described in such great detail.

[3] The symbolism of leprosy as profanation of truth is evident from the rules laid down for leprosy in Moses, Leviticus 13:1–end. The inner meaning of the description there covers every aspect of truth's profanation, such as the nature of that profanation if it is fresh, if it is old, if it goes deep in the person or lies on the surface, if it can be healed, if it cannot, what the means of healing are, and so on. None of this could ever become known to anyone except through the inner meaning of the Word. Since leprosy depicts something profane, though, it is not allowable to explain each of the details in the description of leprosy individually. Heaven cringes just at the sound of the word *profane.* Let me quote only the following, then:

> [4] If leprosy blooms vigorously in the skin, and leprosy covers the whole infected skin from the person's head to the person's toe, under the thorough view of the priest's eyes, and the priest sees that here, leprosy has covered the whole of the person's flesh, then he shall declare the infection clean. It has all turned white; the person is clean. But on the day when living flesh appears in the person, he or she shall be unclean. (Leviticus 13:12, 13, 14)

Unless it were known from the inner meaning how this matter stands, it would seem paradoxical that a person entirely leprous from head to toe should be clean. However, a person leprous from head to toe means people who know inner truth but do not acknowledge or believe it. They engage not in inward but in outward profanation, which is removed from them, so that they are clean. On the other hand, people who know religious truth and do believe it but live contrary to it engage in inward profanation. So do people who start by believing and end by denying. That is why the passage says that on the day when living flesh appears in the person, he or she shall be unclean; living flesh means acknowledgment and belief. See the concepts cited above at §6959.

6964 *And he said,* symbolizes providing for the nature that people in the spiritual church would develop if they possessed faith. This can be seen from the symbolism of *Jehovah said* as providence, as above at §6951. What was provided for was the nature they would develop if they possessed faith, as the next few sections make plain [§§6965–6968]. You see, the return of Moses' hand to being like his flesh means that they would then have spiritual goodness. The opposite is the fact that his hand turned leprous when he put it into the fold of his robe, which means that people in the spiritual church would succumb to profaning truth if they lacked faith, as discussed above in §§6959, 6963.

Put your hand back in the fold symbolizes adoption of truth. This can be seen from the symbolism of *putting his hand into the fold* as adoption of truth, which is discussed at §6960. 6965

And he put his hand back into the fold symbolizes the actual deed; see above at §6961. 6966

And brought it out of the fold symbolizes the result; again, see above, at §6962. 6967

And here, it returned to being like his flesh symbolizes goodness from truth at that point. This can be seen from the symbolism of *flesh* as the property distinctive to someone's will when it has been brought to life by the property distinctive to the Lord's divine humanity—that is, from the symbolism of flesh as heavenly autonomy (discussed at §3813). Moreover, since flesh symbolizes heavenly autonomy, it symbolizes good that is done out of love for the Lord and for one's neighbor. In people whose religion is spiritual, though, it symbolizes goodness from truth. This is because the goodness they have grows out of the truth taught by their religion and follows its guidance. When this truth becomes part of their lives, it is called goodness. 6968

Exodus 4:8, 9. *And it will happen if they do not believe you and do not listen to the voice of the former sign, that they will believe the voice of the latter sign. And it will happen if they do not believe even these two signs and do not listen to your voice, that you are to take some of the water of the river and pour it on the dry ground, and the water that you took from the river will become blood on the dry ground.* 6969

And it will happen if they do not believe you means if they lack faith. *And do not listen to the voice of the former sign* means if they fail to obey the pronouncement from the Word, then from being spiritual and rational they would become nonspiritual and nonrational. *That they will believe the voice of the latter sign* means that they would put faith in the Word's prediction that they would become profaners of truth. *And it will happen if they do not believe even these two signs* means if they lacked any faith at all that these things would come about. *And do not listen to your voice* means and if they show no obedience. *You are to take some of the water of the river* symbolizes falsity in the form of knowledge. *And pour it on the dry ground* means letting it spread on the earthly plane. *And the water that you took* symbolizes a reversal of the state. *Will become blood on the dry ground* symbolizes rendering all truth false and being destitute of it on the earthly plane as a consequence.

6970 *And it will happen if they do not believe you* means if they lack faith. This can be seen from the symbolism of *believing* as putting faith in something, as above at §6956. Putting faith in something does not here mean in signs that they would be delivered from Egypt, because that is a faith in something worldly. Rather it means believing that if they did not remain in the truth, they would become merely sense-oriented and body-oriented and would eventually become profaners of truth. That is the meaning of the two signs. The inner sense does not treat of worldly events, as the outer, narrative sense certainly does, but of spiritual events.

Faith regarding worldly issues is totally different from faith regarding spiritual issues. For example, take a belief that people will do as they say, that an individual is being truthful or not, that one course of action rather than any other is necessary for success, that a spoken or written statement is trustworthy or not, and countless other beliefs like these. These are matters of faith about something worldly, as is the faith here that the children of Israel were to be delivered from slavery in Egypt.

In contrast, believing that heaven exists; that hell exists; that we will live on after death, the good in eternal happiness and the evil in unhappiness; that the life we lived awaits each of us; that faith and neighborly love constitute spiritual life, and that this is the life possessed by angels in heaven; that the Lord has all power in the heavens and on earth, as he says in Matthew 28:18; that from him we live; that the Word teaches heavenly and divine truths; and so on—all these are matters of faith about something spiritual and are symbolized here by *believing.*

6971 *And do not listen to the voice of the former sign* means if they fail to obey the pronouncement from the Word, then from being spiritual and rational they would become nonspiritual and nonrational, as the following shows: *Listening* symbolizes obeying, as discussed in §§2542, 3869, 5017. A *voice* symbolizes a pronouncement from the Word, as discussed below. And the *former sign* symbolizes the idea that from being spiritual and rational they would become nonspiritual and nonrational. This last is evident from the symbolism of the snake that Moses' staff turned into when he cast it onto the earth—the former sign—as the sensory, bodily self (§6949) and therefore not the spiritual or the rational self. People who operate on the plane of the senses and of the body do not operate on the plane of reason or, consequently, of the spirit. They think what is false and wish what is evil. A person who acts this way is not rational, let alone spiritual. To acknowledge and believe truth and to live a good life is spirituality itself embedded in rationality, because these actions come from the Divine. To acknowledge and believe falsity and to live an evil life, though, is the opposite. (For the idea that people who are entirely absorbed in what is sensory and bodily are like this, see §§6844, 6845, 6948, 6949.)

[2] The people who become entirely taken up with the senses and the body are those who once knew about the spiritual world but have since rejected the knowledge. They have adopted false assumptions that oppose truth, and in their lives they look only to worldly, bodily, and earthly goals. As a result, they believe that we should sweeten our lives with every indulgence. "What more do we have while we are alive?" they say. "When we die, we die. If there is life after death, who has come back from it to tell us? We don't know what is going to live on after the life has gone out of someone." If anyone tries to reason them into contemplating eternal life, they think, "Nothing worse will happen to me than to others," and immediately slide back into their prior state of life. In people like this, access to heaven's light and its inflow is shut off. On their earthly level, heavenly light becomes like the dark, but worldly light turns radiant (§6907). This radiance gleams all the brighter, the more darkly clouded heaven's light becomes for them. So they cannot see the evil in their lives as anything but good, or falsity therefore as anything but true. This then is why a person becomes sense- and body-oriented.

Briefly put, once we have opened and then closed the entry for light to flow in from heaven, we are forced to look down rather than up. This is a result of the divine plan to prevent us from using falsity to sully and consequently profane truth that we once acknowledged and that remains in our inner self.

[3] The case is similar with non-Christians who go back on their religious tradition, but their lot is better than the lot of people inside the church. This is because they do not possess truth from the Word and therefore do not possess genuine truth, only truth bound up with numerous illusions, which cannot be profaned as gravely.

Regarding the symbolism of a *voice* as a pronouncement from the Word: Keep in mind that the term often appears in conjunction with concepts unrelated to a voice. For instance, it is connected with a sign here: "If they do not *listen to the voice* of the former *sign*, they will *believe the voice* of the latter *sign.*" There are other passages too, as for instance in Nahum:

> The *voice of a whip* and the *voice of the sound of a wheel!* (Nahum 3:2)

And in David:

> The *rivers* lifted *their voice* above the *voices* of many majestic *waters.* (Psalms 93:3, 4)

[4] The symbolism of a voice as a pronouncement, and in a positive sense as a pronouncement from the Word—in which case it is called the voice of Jehovah—can be seen in David:

> *Jehovah's voice* has power. *Jehovah's voice* has glory; *Jehovah's voice* is shattering cedars. *Jehovah's voice* is cutting down fiery flames. *Jehovah's voice* makes the wilderness tremble. *Jehovah's voice* sends the does into labor and strips the forests bare. (Psalms 29:3, 4, 5, 7, 8, 9)

And in another place in the same author:

> To the one riding on the heaven of heavens of ancient times. *Watch: he will lift his voice, a voice of strength.* (Psalms 68:33)

Here the voice stands for divine truth and consequently for the Word, and for a pronouncement from it.

For other symbolisms of a voice, see §219, and for the fact that it applies to truth, §3563.

6972 *That they will believe the voice of the latter sign* means that they would put faith in the Word's prediction that they would become profaners of truth, as the following shows: *Believing* means putting faith in something, as discussed just above at §6970. A *voice* symbolizes a pronouncement, as discussed at §6971, so it also symbolizes a prediction. And leprosy, the *latter sign,* symbolizes profanation of truth, as discussed above at §6963.

For a definition of profanation, see §6959 and the sections referred to there.

6973 *And it will happen if they do not believe even these two signs* means if they lacked any faith at all that such things would come about, as the following shows: *Believing* symbolizes putting faith in something, specifically in the spiritual meaning, as discussed above at §6970. And the *two signs* symbolize the fact that they would come under the sway of the senses and the body and that eventually they would become profaners of truth. These are symbolized by the snake that Moses' staff turned into when he cast it onto the earth (§6971) and by the hand that became leprous when he put it into the fold of his robe (§6963). *Not believing these two signs,* then, means lacking any faith at all that such things would come about.

And do not listen to your voice means and if they show no obedience, as the following demonstrates: *Listening* symbolizes obedience, as discussed in §§2542, 3869, 5017. A *voice* symbolizes a pronouncement and prediction, as discussed in §§6971, 6972. And Moses, whose voice they were to listen to, represents the Lord as divine law, or as divine truth, and therefore as the Word, since it contains divine truth. This makes it plain that "if they do not listen to your voice" means and if they show no obedience. **6974**

[2] Here and earlier (verses 1 and 8) the text says, "if they do not believe and if they do not listen." The two seem alike, since one who does not believe also does not listen, but they are different. Believing, which symbolizes faith, is mentioned in reference to faith and its truth, so it relates to the intellect. Listening, on the other hand, which symbolizes obedience, is mentioned in reference to neighborly love and the good that comes of it, so it relates to the will. In the Word, particularly the prophetic part, wherever the idea of truth is expressed in its own vocabulary, the idea of goodness is expressed in its own vocabulary as well. This is on account of the heavenly marriage (the marriage of goodness and truth) present throughout the Word; see §§683, 793, 801, 2173, 2516, 2712, 4137 at the end, 6343.

You are to take some of the water of the river symbolizes falsity in the form of knowledge. This is evident from the symbolism of the *water of the river*—Egypt's river, the Nile—as falsity in the form of knowledge. Water means truth (see §§2702, 3424, 4976) and in a negative sense falsity (§790). The river of Egypt means falsity in the form of knowledge (§6693). **6975**

And pour it on the dry ground means letting it spread on the earthly plane. This can be seen from the symbolism of *pouring* as letting it spread and from that of *dry ground* as the earthly plane. *Dry ground* is the term for a desert and also for land, and the land of Egypt symbolizes the earthly mind (rife with falsity) and therefore the earthly plane (§§5276, 5278, 5280, 5288, 5301). Dry ground is an even more apt symbol for the same thing. **6976**

And the water that you took symbolizes a reversal of the state. This is clear from the next phrase, "will become blood on the dry ground," **6977** which symbolizes rendering all truth false and being destitute of it on the earthly plane. When this happens, one's state is completely reversed. The current phrase, then, implies a reversal of the state, so that is also what it is said to symbolize.

The state of the earthly level truly is reversed entirely when it is occupied by nothing but falsity. Rarely does this happen to people while they are living in the world, only in the next life, where it happens to everyone thrown into hell.

It happens rarely while we are living in the world because during that time we are always kept in a state in which we can be reformed if we voluntarily refrain from evil. After death, though, our life follows us, and we continue in the state we had acquired throughout the course of our life in the world. [2] At that point people consumed with evil can no longer be reformed. To prevent them from communicating with any community in heaven, all truth and goodness are taken from them, and as a result they remain surrounded by evil and falsity, which proliferate there. The more capacity a person has developed in the world for accepting evil and falsity, the more these proliferate (although they are not allowed to exceed the bounds acquired). That is the reversal of state meant here. The nature of the reversal is such that the people can no longer improve on the inside, only on the outside. Outward emendation is achieved through fear of punishment. When they have endured frequent punishment, they eventually refrain, not voluntarily but under coercion; nonetheless the *desire* to do evil remains. Again, this desire is curbed by fear, which is a forceful external means of correction.

Such is the state of the evil in the other life.

6978 *Will become blood on the dry ground* symbolizes rendering all truth false and being destitute of it on the earthly plane as a consequence, as the following shows: *Blood* symbolizes sacred truth radiating from the Lord, and in a negative sense, truth falsified and profaned, as dealt with at §4735. The previous section explained this situation. And *dry ground* symbolizes the earthly plane, as dealt with just above at §6976.

The symbolism of blood as the falsification and profanation of truth is especially clear in Nahum:

> Doom to the *blood-soaked city!* It is all full of lying and plunder, and [the killing of] prey will not leave off. The voice of a whip, and the voice of the sound of a wheel, and a neighing horse, and a jolting chariot! A horse rider rushing up, and the glint of a sword, and the gleam of a spear, and a throng of those stabbed, and a pile of corpses, and no end of bodies;

> they stumble over their bodies. [Doom,] because of the abundance of the whorings of a whore of good grace—the mistress of sorceries, selling out nations through her whorings and clans through her sorceries. (Nahum 3:1, 2, 3, 4)

[2] The blood-soaked city symbolizes a theology that teaches what is false, so the blood symbolizes truth that has been falsified and profaned. This is plain from the inner meaning of all the words in the description, not only in the verses quoted here but also in the verses that follow them, because the description continues through the whole chapter. A city is a theology. "All full of lying and plunder" means full of falsity and the evil it gives rise to. The voice of a whip and the voice of the sound of a wheel mean the use of illusions to defend what is false. A neighing horse and a jolting chariot mean using corrupt intellectual powers and corrupt teachings. A horse rider rushing up, the glint of a sword, and the gleam of a spear mean a battle against truth. A throng of those stabbed means that the result is countless falsities and people devoted to falsity. A pile of corpses and no end of bodies mean that the result is countless evils and people devoted to evil. The whorings of a whore are the actual falsifications, as are the sorceries.

Exodus 4:10, 11, 12. *And Moses said to Jehovah, "Upon my life, Lord, I am not a man of words either from yesterday or from the day before or from this moment of your speaking to your servant, because I am heavy of mouth and heavy of tongue." And Jehovah said to him, "Who gives humankind a mouth, or who has made a person mute or deaf or sighted or blind? Is it not I, Jehovah? And now go, and I myself will be with your mouth and teach you what you should speak."* 6979

And Moses said to Jehovah symbolizes a perception from the Divine. *Upon my life, Lord* symbolizes the certainty. *I am not a man of words* means that he could not speak. *Either from yesterday or from the day before* means not from eternity. *Or from this moment of your speaking to your servant* means and not to eternity either, despite the inflow of the Divine into his humanity. *Because I am heavy of mouth and heavy of tongue* means that no sound of speech or words of speech from his divine side are heard or understood. *And Jehovah said to him* symbolizes a divine inflow. *Who gives humankind a mouth?* symbolizes verbalization. *Or who has made a person mute?* symbolizes no verbalization. *Or deaf* means no perception and no consequent obedience. *Or sighted or blind* symbolizes belief through knowledge and lack of belief through lack of knowledge. *Is it not I, Jehovah?* means that these conditions result from the life force that flows in from the Divine. *And now go* symbolizes life from his divine side. *And I myself will be with your mouth and teach you what you should speak* symbolizes the divinity of absolutely everything that emanates from the divine humanity.

6980 *And Moses said to Jehovah* symbolizes a perception from the Divine, as the following shows: In the narrative books of the Word, *saying* symbolizes perceiving, as noted many times. *Moses* represents the Lord and the divine law present in his human side when he was in the world, as discussed in §§6723, 6752, 6771, 6827. The Divine, the source of the perception, is symbolized by *Jehovah.* This shows that *Moses said to Jehovah* symbolizes a perception the Lord received in his human side from his divine side.

6981 *Upon my life, Lord* symbolizes the certainty. This can be seen from the fact that *upon my life* is a stock phrase asserting that a thing is so and consequently that it is a certainty.

6982 *I am not a man of words* means that he could not speak. This can be seen from the symbolism of *[not] a man of words* as his lacking the gift of speech and therefore being unable to speak.

This idea needs explaining. On the highest level of meaning the current passage is about the Lord, because Moses represents the Lord as divine law and therefore as divine truth. Truth as it issues straight from the Divine is audible to no one, not even an angel. For something divine to be heard, it first has to become human, and it becomes human when it passes through the heavens. After it passes through the heavens it is presented in a human form and turns into speech. The actual speaking is done by spirits, who in that state are called the Holy Spirit. The Holy Spirit is said to emanate from the Divine [John 14:26; 15:26] because the holy influence of the spirit, or the sacred truth that that spirit then speaks, comes from the Lord.

You can see, then, that truth issuing straight from the Divine cannot be presented to anyone as words or speech except through the Holy Spirit.

This is meant in the highest sense by the fact that Moses, representing the Lord as divine truth, says he is not a man of words, and that he was given the aid of his brother Aaron, who was to serve as a mouth for Moses, while Moses was to serve as a god for Aaron.

6983 *Either from yesterday or from the day before* means that not from eternity (could he speak). This is established by the symbolism of *from yesterday or from the day before* as from eternity. The reason it means from eternity is that it means a certain time—a time in the past—and when time is connected with the Lord, or the Divine, it symbolizes not time but eternity.

Nature possesses two properties that do not exist in heaven, let alone in the Divine, and they are space and time. On the particular point that these do not exist in heaven but that they are replaced by states, space by a state of being, and time by a state of emergence, see §§2625, 3938. On the broader point that space and time in heaven are states, see §§1274, 1382, 2625, 2788, 2837, 3254, 3356, 3387, 3404, 3827, 4321, 4814, 4882, 4901, 4916, 5605, 6110. In the Divine, which transcends the heavens, still less are space and time to be found, and not even states. Instead of space there is infinity, and instead of time there is eternity. These two qualities are what time and space in the world correspond to and what a state of being and a state of emergence in the heavens correspond to.

[2] In the Word, "yesterday and the day before" does not mean yesterday and the day before but past time in general. This can be seen from passages where the phrase appears, such as in Joshua:

> The waters of the Jordan returned to their place and went *as yesterday and the day before* over all its banks. (Joshua 4:18)

In 1 Samuel:

> It happened that everyone who had known Saul *from yesterday and the day before,* when they saw that here, he was prophesying with the prophets, . . . (1 Samuel 10:11)

In 2 Samuel:

> The tribe of Israel said to David, "*Both yesterday and the day before,* when Saul was king over us, you were leading Israel out and back." (2 Samuel 5:2)

In these passages and others, "yesterday and the day before" means earlier, or in times past.

Now since "yesterday and the day before" means past time, and since the highest sense treats of the Lord, who as divine law or divine truth is represented by Moses, plainly the phrase means from eternity.

The eternal idea symbolized by yesterday is expressed this way in David:

> A thousand years in your eyes are like *yesterday* when it has passed. (Psalms 90:4)

6984 *Or from this moment of your speaking to your servant* means and not to eternity either, despite the inflow of the Divine into his humanity, as the following shows: *From this moment* or from today symbolizes eternity, as discussed in §§2838, 3998, 4304, 6165, so it means *to* eternity, since it involves future time. *Speaking* symbolizes an inflow, as discussed in §§2951, 5481, 5743, 5797. The Divine as the source of the inflow is symbolized by *your* speaking, that is, Jehovah's. And a *servant* symbolizes the Lord's humanity when it had not yet become divine, as discussed at §2159—although when it had become divine it was the Lord, since it was one with Jehovah.

6985 *Because I am heavy of mouth and heavy of tongue* means that no sound of speech or words of speech from his divine side are heard or understood. This can be seen from the symbolism of a *mouth* as the sound of speech and from that of a *tongue* as the words of speech. A mouth symbolizes the sound of speech because it is the organ that produces sound, and a tongue symbolizes the words of speech because it is the organ that forms words. Anyone can see the difference between the sound and the words of speech and can see that we speak of the sound as being heard and of the words as being understood.

This concept can be expressed only as "heavy of mouth and heavy of tongue" in the literal, narrative meaning, which deals with Moses, a human being, who could talk but only with difficulty. When the literal meaning becomes the inner meaning, though, angels perceive the idea in relation to the topic at hand. Since this verse is about the Divine, they take it to mean that no sound of speech can be heard, no words of speech can be understood directly from him, only indirectly through spirits, in keeping with the remarks above at §6982.

6986 *And Jehovah said to him* symbolizes a divine inflow. This is established by the symbolism of *he said* as an inflow, which is mentioned in §§5743, 5797, 6152, 6291. It means an inflow from the Divine because it was *Jehovah* who said it.

6987 *Who gives humankind a mouth?* symbolizes verbalization. This can be seen from the symbolism of a *mouth* as the sound of speech, which is discussed above at §6985. Because it symbolizes the sound of speech, it symbolizes verbalization.

What a mouth symbolizes in particular can be seen only from correspondence. The mouth with its lips corresponds to inner speech, which is the speech of thought. Human thought is either active or passive. Active thought is the kind we engage in when talking, and this can be called verbal thought. Passive thought is the kind we engage in when not talking. The difference between the two is evident to those who ponder the question. The *mouth given to humankind* symbolizes active, verbal thought and therefore verbalization.

In regard to the active thought symbolized by a mouth, it is important to know that this type of thought itself actually speaks, in its own way. When engaging in its kind of speech, active thought stimulates the physical organs corresponding to it.

[2] A thought seems to contain the words used to utter it, but this is an illusion; it actually contains only the sense of the words. We can hardly tell what this sense is like, because it is in the language of our spirit, a universal language like that spoken by spirits in the other life. When speech in this language flows into the corresponding physical organs, it generates audible speech, which differs vastly [in nature] from the thought that produces it. The magnitude of the difference is obvious from the fact that it takes us only a moment to think a thought that requires time to verbalize or write out. That would not be so if the thought were formed of words, the way oral speech is.

It is because of the correspondence between the language of thought and the language of the mouth that we know how to speak the universal language when we enter the company of spirits after death. That is, we know how to talk with spirits no matter what language they spoke in the world. We can barely tell we are not speaking the same way there as we spoke in the world. Yet the words of spirits' language are not words like those we used in the body but are rather ideas that made up the thoughts we had; and each idea holds a wealth of content. A spirit therefore needs only an instant to articulate something that a person can scarcely put into words over the course of half an hour, and yet that same idea contains much that can never be expressed in physical language.

[3] Angels in heaven, though, speak differently than spirits do. The language of angels in heaven is made up of intuitional concepts that philosophers call immaterial ideas. The language of spirits is made up of mental images they call material ideas. A single angelic idea therefore holds a great deal that spirits cannot verbalize even in long strings of their own ideas and much that they could never express.

However, when spirits become angels, they have the same fluency in the angelic language that we have in the spirits' language when we become spirits after death, and for the same reason.

This shows what active thought is: the language of the human spirit.

6988 *Or who has made a person mute?* symbolizes no verbalization. This can be seen from the symbolism of *muteness* as no verbalization, because it is the opposite of a mouth, which symbolizes verbalization, as explained just above at §6987.

By verbalization here I do not mean vocal utterance, or speech, because this is earthly utterance. Rather, I mean acclaiming the Lord and preaching faith in him, because this is spiritual utterance. On an inner level, then, a *mute person* plainly symbolizes people who cannot acclaim the Lord or consequently preach faith in him because they do not know about him. This is the situation of non-Christian nations and also of the uneducated within the Christian world. The fact that these people are symbolized by a mute is clear in Isaiah:

> Then the lame will spring up like a deer, and *the tongue of the mute will sing,* because water will burst forth in the wilderness, and rivers in the wilderness plain. (Isaiah 35:5, 6)

"The tongue of the mute will sing" means that the people mentioned above will acclaim the Lord and the tenets of faith in him. "Water will burst forth in the wilderness, and rivers in the wilderness plain" means that they will learn concepts of truth and goodness. A wilderness is a situation in which religious concepts are lacking because they are unknown.

[2] The mute individuals healed by the Lord also symbolize people outside the church who were delivered from falsity and the resulting evil by his coming into the world. These are symbolized by a mute person in Matthew, for instance:

> Here, they brought him a *mute person* possessed by a demon, but *the demon being cast out, the mute spoke.* (Matthew 9:32, 33)

And by another mute person in the same author:

> They brought Jesus a man possessed by a demon, blind, and *mute,* and he healed him, so that the blind and *mute man both spoke* and saw. (Matthew 12:22)

The same is symbolized by another *mute person* possessed by a demon in Mark 9:17–30.

[3] Be aware that the miracles the Lord performed all symbolize the state of the church and of the human race, which was saved by his coming into the world. To be specific, people who welcomed a faith marked

by neighborly love were delivered from hell then. That is what the Lord's miracles hold within them.

To speak more generally, all the miracles described in the Old Testament symbolize the state of the church and of the Lord's kingdom. This distinguishes divine miracles from devilish or magical miracles, no matter how much the latter resemble the former on the outside, as the miracles of the magicians in Egypt did.

Or deaf means no perception of truth and therefore no obedience. **6989**
This can be seen from the symbolism of a *deaf* person as those who do not perceive what is true and therefore do not obey it. In the abstract, then, it symbolizes no perception of truth and therefore no obedience. The reason a deaf person has this symbolism is that hearing corresponds to both perception and obedience. It corresponds to perception because what we hear we perceive inside, and to obedience because we know what to do by having heard. This correspondence of hearing (and of the ear) may be seen in §§3869, 4652–4660, 5017. From this it is evident what the deaf symbolize.

The deaf in the Word also symbolize people outside the church who do not know the truth belonging to the [true] faith (since they do not have the Word) and so cannot live by that truth but welcome it after being taught, and live according to it. They are meant in Isaiah:

> Then the eyes of the blind will be opened, and *the ears of the deaf will be opened.* (Isaiah 35:5)

In the same author:

> *You who are deaf, listen!* And you who are blind, look and see! (Isaiah 42:18, 19, 20)

In the same author:

> *On that day the deaf will hear the words of the book,* and out of the darkness and out of the shadows the eyes of the blind will see. (Isaiah 29:18)

In the same author:

> Lead forth a blind people, which has eyes, and the *deaf, who have ears!* (Isaiah 43:8, 9)

The deaf here mean people who arrived by way of the Lord's Coming at a state in which they could accept the truth belonging to the faith—that is, perceive it and obey it. The same people are symbolized *by the deaf whom the Lord healed* as told in Mark 7:31–end; 9:25.

As this is what the deaf symbolize, the people among whom the representative religion was established were forbidden to *curse a deaf person* or put a stumbling block before a blind person (Leviticus 19:14).

6990 *Or sighted or blind* symbolizes belief through knowledge and lack of belief through lack of knowledge, as the following shows: Being *sighted,* [or seeing,] symbolizes understanding and believing, as discussed in §§897, 2325, 2807, 3863, 3869, 4403–4421, so it symbolizes belief resulting from knowledge. In the original language the word means "open"—open of eye—so it means having sight as a result of knowledge, since knowledge opens one's eyes. And *blind* symbolizes lack of belief from lack of knowledge, because a blind person is not sighted.

In the Word the blind also symbolize people who are outside the church and therefore live in ignorance of the truth that constitutes the faith but who accept the faith once they learn about it; see §2383. The same people are also symbolized by the blind whom the Lord healed, as told in Matthew 9:27–31; 12:22; 20:29–end; 21:14; Mark 8:22–26; 10:46–end; Luke 18:35–end; John 9:1–end.

6991 *Is it not I, Jehovah?* means that these conditions result from the life force that flows in from the Divine. This can be seen from the fact that the kinds of conditions symbolized by the mute, the deaf, and the blind, by a mouth, and by the sighted arise in us as a result of the life force that flows in from *Jehovah,* or the Lord. From that inflowing life arise both the evil and the goodness in every one of us. However, the evil arises from us, the goodness from the Lord. Evil arises from us because we take the life that flows in from the Lord—that is, the goodness and truth—and turn it into evil and falsity. So we turn it into the opposite of life, which is called spiritual death. The situation resembles that of light from the sun, which turns various colors—vibrant and clear in some objects, lifeless and murky in others—as a result of the way those objects receive it.

It appears, though, as if the Lord introduces evil too, since he gives life. In keeping with the appearance, then, the Word attributes evil to Jehovah (the Lord). Many passages attest to this, including the current statement that he makes a person mute, deaf, and blind; because these conditions exist as a result of the inflow of life from the Divine, it says that Jehovah causes them.

The inner meaning, on the other hand, explains and teaches how the matter truly stands, not how it appears.

And now go symbolizes life from his divine side. This is established by the symbolism of *going* as living a life, which is discussed in §§3335, 4882, 5493, 5605. It symbolizes life from his divine side because Moses represents the Lord. 6992

And I will be with your mouth and teach you what you should speak symbolizes the divinity of absolutely everything that emanates from the divine humanity, as the following shows: *Being with someone's mouth,* when promised by Jehovah, means being in the words that person utters. For the symbolism of a *mouth* as verbalization, see above at §§6987, 6988. What is more, the current speech is addressed to Moses, who represents the Lord and the divine law present in his divine humanity, so *I will be with your mouth* symbolizes the divinity of that which emanates from the divine humanity. And *teaching you what you should speak* means emanating. *Teaching* and *speaking* mean flowing in, and when ascribed to the Lord's divine side, they mean emanating. From the divine humanity itself of the Lord emanates divine truth, which is called the Holy Spirit. Since the Lord was divine truth itself when he was in the world, he taught about love and faith, and he did not then do so through the Holy Spirit, as he teaches in John: 6993

> There was not the Holy Spirit yet because Jesus was not yet glorified. (John 7:39)

However, once the Lord even in regard to his human side became Jehovah, or divine goodness (after the resurrection), he was no longer divine truth. Rather, divine truth emanated from his divine goodness.

The Holy Spirit is divine truth emanating from the Lord's divine humanity. It is not some spirit or spirits existing from eternity. This is quite plain from the Lord's words in the quotation above saying that there was not the Holy Spirit yet. It is also plain [from the consideration] that the Spirit itself cannot emanate, only the holy influence of the Spirit, or rather the holy influence that emanates from the Lord and is verbalized by the Spirit. See also §6788.

[2] From this train of thought it now follows that in the Lord the entire Trinity of Father, Son, and Holy Spirit is complete, and consequently that there is one God, not three who are distinct persons but are nonetheless said to constitute a single deity.

The purpose behind the mention of Father, Son, and Holy Spirit in the Word was for people to acknowledge both the Lord and the divinity in him. Humankind was in such thick darkness (and still is today) that otherwise people would not have acknowledged any divinity in the Lord's humanity. The concept, being totally incomprehensible to them, would have been utterly beyond belief. Besides, it is true that a Trinity exists, but it exists in one individual: the Lord. The various Christian religions even acknowledge that the Trinity dwells entirely in him. The Lord also taught explicitly that he was one with the Father (John 14:9, 10, 11, 12) and (again in John) that the holy thing the Holy Spirit speaks belongs not to the Spirit but to the Lord:

> The Paraclete—the Spirit of Truth—*will not speak from himself but will speak whatever he hears.* He will give me glory, *because he will take from what is mine and proclaim it to you.* (John 16:13, 14)

John 14:26 equates the Paraclete with the Holy Spirit.

6994 Exodus 4:13, 14, 15, 16, 17. *And he said, "Upon my life, Lord, please send [your message] by the hand [of someone else] you might send." And Jehovah's anger kindled against Moses, and he said, "Isn't there Aaron your brother, the Levite? I know that he at least will speak. And besides, look: he is going out to meet you, and he will see you and rejoice in his heart. And you are to speak to him and put the words in his mouth, and I myself will be with your mouth and with his mouth and teach both of you what you must do. And he will speak for you to the people, and it will happen that he will be like a mouth for you, and you will be like a god for him. And you are to take in your hand this staff, with which you will perform signs."*

And he said, "Upon my life, Lord," symbolizes an assertion. *Please send [your message] by the hand [of someone else] you might send* means that divine truth radiating from the divine humanity must be expressed indirectly. *And Jehovah's anger kindled against Moses* symbolizes compassion. *And he said, "Isn't there Aaron your brother, the Levite?"* symbolizes teachings about goodness and truth. *I know that he [at least] will speak* symbolizes preaching. *And besides, look: he is going out to meet you* symbolizes acceptance. *And he will see you* symbolizes perception. *And rejoice in his heart* symbolizes a feeling of love. *And you are to speak to him* symbolizes an inflow. *And put the words in his mouth* means that what he announces will issue from the divine humanity. *And I myself will be with your mouth* means that divine truth will come from divinity itself by way of the divine humanity. *And with his mouth* means that [divinity] will consequently be with that which develops out of it. *And teach both of you what you must do* means that the Divine will consequently be present in absolutely everything that happens. *And he will speak for you to the people* means that he will be the doctrine for the spiritual church. *And it will happen that he will be like a mouth for you* symbolizes divine truth that also comes from the Lord, but indirectly. *And you will be like a god for him* symbolizes divine truth that comes directly from the Lord. *And you are to take in your hand this staff* symbolizes divine power in both. *With which you will perform signs* symbolizes the resulting enlightenment and confirmation of the truth.

And he said, "Upon my life, Lord," symbolizes an assertion. This can be seen from the fact that *upon my life* is a stock phrase asserting that a thing is so, as above at §6981. 6995

Please send [your message] by the hand [of someone else] you might send means that divine truth radiating from the divine humanity must be expressed indirectly, as the following shows: Moses, the speaker of these words, represents the Lord in regard to the Word, or in regard to divine truth, as discussed at §6752. *Sending,* when the Lord is said to do it, means radiating, as discussed in §§2397, 4710. And sending *by the hand [of someone else]* means through another person who will be given the power—the power to put into words the divine truth radiating from the Lord's divine humanity. Since it means through another who will be given the power, it means indirectly. 6996

I showed above in §§6982, 6985 that divine truth issuing directly from the Lord's divine humanity cannot be heard or understood by any human, not even an angel. In order for divine truth to be heard and understood, then, it has to pass through some kind of medium, and the medium it passes through is heaven. Afterward it passes through the angels and spirits present with us.

[2] This fact is abundantly clear from the consideration that we cannot even hear the spirits who are with us talking to each other. If we did hear them, we would not understand them, because the language of spirits lacks the kind of words we use and is common to all tongues.

Furthermore, spirits cannot hear angels, and if they could, they would not understand them, because angelic language is still more universal. In fact, angels of the inmost heaven are even harder to hear and understand, because their language is a language not of ideas but of feelings that embody heavenly love.

If these languages lie so far beyond our reach that we cannot possibly hear or understand them, what about divine "language," which infinitely transcends the languages in the heavens? I am calling it divine language, but I mean divine truth emanating from the Lord's divine humanity.

This being the case, you can see that if divine truth emanating from the Lord is to be heard and understood, it must reach us by passing through different kinds of medium. The final medium is the spirit accompanying us, who flows in either through our thoughts or through audible words.

[3] The fact that divine truth coming directly from the Lord cannot be heard or understood is also evident from correspondences and the representations they give rise to. What a person on earth says is presented in an entirely different form to spirits, and what spirits say, in an entirely different form to angels. This is clear from the spiritual and literal meanings of the Word: the literal meaning, which is suited to a person on earth, serves to symbolize and represent the contents of the spiritual meaning. Consider that the spiritual meaning is not perceptible to a person on earth, except to the extent that it can be presented and explained in terms of the world and nature. Still less is the angelic meaning perceptible. What then about divine truth coming directly from the Lord's divinity? After all, this truth infinitely transcends an angel's ability to understand and is not perceptible in heaven except to the extent that it passes through heaven, taking on a form suited and adapted to the perception of the inhabitants. This is accomplished through a remarkable inflow that is totally incomprehensible to anyone.

The intent of this discussion is to show that divine truth radiating from the Lord cannot be heard or understood by anyone unless it passes through various kinds of medium.

6997 *And Jehovah's anger kindled against Moses* symbolizes compassion. This is evident from the symbolism of *Jehovah's anger* not as anger but as the opposite of anger: mercy, and in this case compassion.

Jehovah clearly does not have any anger, since he is love itself, goodness itself, and mercy itself, and anger is the opposite of these. It is also a failing, and failings have nothing to do with God. When the Word attributes anger to Jehovah, or the Lord, then, angels do not perceive the idea of anger but the idea either of mercy or of removing evil from heaven. Here they perceive the idea of compassion because it is addressed to *Moses,* who represents the Lord in regard to divine truth when he was in the world.

[2] The Word ascribes anger to Jehovah, or the Lord, because of the very broad truth that everything, both bad and good, comes from God. This truth is necessary for children, youths, and the uneducated, but eventually it has to be illuminated by the concept that evil comes from

humankind. It appears as though evil comes from God, and [the Word] speaks in these terms in order for the young and the simple to learn to fear God. Otherwise they might be destroyed by the evil they themselves commit. Later they will be able to love him, because fear has to come before love if love is to contain holy fear. (Fear becomes holy when incorporated into love, because love is holy.) At that point their fear is no longer that the Lord will become angry and punish them but that they might act against Goodness itself, because that would torment their conscience.

[3] Punishment is also what forced the people of Israel and Judah into a perfunctory observance of the statutes and commandments. Because of the punishments, they believed that Jehovah habitually grew angry with them and disciplined them, when in reality they themselves brought on their suffering and separated themselves from heaven through their idolatry. That is where the punishment came from, as Isaiah even says:

> *Your offenses are causing a division between you and your God; and your sins hide his face from you.* (Isaiah 59:2)

Since the people of Israel and of Judah cared only about outward appearances, not the inner reality, they were kept in the belief that Jehovah was angry and punished them. People who are observant only on the outside, not on the inside, do everything from fear and nothing from love.

[4] This discussion now reveals what is meant in the Word by Jehovah's anger and wrath, namely, punishment. In Isaiah, for instance:

> Look: The name of Jehovah comes from afar, *as does his burning anger* and the weight of [his oracular] burden; *his lips are full of outrage,* and his tongue is like *burning fire.* (Isaiah 30:27)

The anger stands for a rebuke and a warning not to be destroyed by evil. In the same author:

> *In a flood of anger* I hid my face from you for a moment. (Isaiah 54:8)

The flood of anger stands for times of trial, in which evil causes anguish and torment. In Jeremiah:

> I myself will fight with you by an outstretched hand and by a strong arm and *in anger* and *in fury* and *in great outrage. May my fury not go forth like fire and burn, so that there is no one quenching it,* because of the wickedness of your deeds! (Jeremiah 21:5, 12)

In the same author:

> . . . to fill [the houses] with the corpses of people whom I have struck *in my anger* and *in my wrath.* (Jeremiah 33:5)

In Zephaniah:

> I will pour out on them *my outrage, all the wrath of my anger,* because in the *fire of my zeal* the whole earth will be consumed. (Zephaniah 3:8)

In David:

> He sent against them the *wrath of his anger,* his *outrage,* and *fury,* and anguish, and a *delegation of evil angels.* (Psalms 78:49)

[5] Not to mention many other passages. In those passages as in these, anger, wrath, fury, and fire mean the punishment and damnation into which we cast ourselves when we plunge into evil. As a consequence of the divine design, goodness brings its own reward, which is why evil carries its own punishment and in fact is bound up with its punishment. Punishment and damnation are also meant by the *day of Jehovah's anger* (Isaiah 13:9, 13; Lamentations 2:1; Zephaniah 2:3; Revelation 6:17; 11:18), by the *wine of God's anger* and the *goblet of God's anger* (Jeremiah 25:15, 28; Revelation 14:10; 16:19), and by the *winepress of God's anger and fury* (Revelation 14:19; 19:15).

[6] The symbolism of anger as punishment and damnation is also evident in Matthew:

> Brood of vipers, who has shown you *that you must flee from the anger to come?* (Matthew 3:7)

In John:

> Those who do not believe in the Son will not see life; *instead, God's anger rests on them.* (John 3:36)

In Luke:

> In the last days there will be great anguish on the earth and *anger on this people.* (Luke 21:23)

These passages clarify that Jehovah's anger symbolizes punishment and damnation.

The reason anger means compassion and mercy is that all punishment of the evil springs from the Lord's mercy toward the good, which seeks to prevent the evil from hurting them. However, the Lord does not call punishment down on them; they call it down on themselves, because in the other life, evil is bound up with its own punishment. It is especially when the Lord is showing mercy to the good that the evil inflict punishment on themselves, because their evil then multiplies, which means that their punishments do too. That is why angels take Jehovah's anger, which symbolizes punishment of the evil, to mean mercy.

[7] This reveals the nature of the Word in its literal meaning and the nature of divine truth in its broadest form: each accords with appearances. The reason is that by our own nature we believe what we can see and grasp with our senses, and what we cannot see or grasp with our senses we disbelieve and therefore do not accept.

It is for this reason that the Word in its literal meaning accords with appearances; but close to its heart it contains genuine, hidden truth, while deep in its inmost heart it contains divine truth itself, which issues directly from the Lord. As a consequence, it also contains divine goodness, or the Lord himself.

And he said, "Isn't there Aaron your brother, the Levite?" symbolizes 6998
teachings about goodness and truth. This can be seen from the representation of *Aaron* as the Lord in regard to divine goodness, or in regard to priesthood. Here, though, before Aaron has been initiated into the priesthood, he represents teachings about goodness and truth, which is why the text adds that he would be like a mouth for Moses and that Moses would be like a god for him. Moses, you see, represents the Lord in regard to the divine truth that comes directly from him, so Aaron represents divine truth that comes indirectly from him. This truth consists of teachings about goodness and truth. The truth that Moses represents here is truth that people are unable to hear or understand (§6982), but the truth that Aaron represents is truth people are capable of both hearing and understanding. That is why Aaron is called a mouth and why Moses is called his god. It is also why Aaron is called a *Levite,* since a Levite symbolizes the church's teachings about goodness and truth, which minister to and serve the priesthood.

I know that he [at least] will speak symbolizes preaching, as can be 6999
seen from the symbolism of *speaking.* When the teachings represented by Aaron are said to speak, it symbolizes preaching, because this is the role of the teachings—that is, of the person who represents the teachings and who is called a mouth, which means verbalization (§6987).

And besides, look: he is going out to meet you symbolizes acceptance. 7000
This can be seen from the symbolism here of *going out to meet* as standing

ready to accept—to accept the divine truth represented by Moses—and therefore as acceptance of that truth.

Angels and spirits who receive divine truth radiating from the Lord and pass it along are said to go out to meet it, once the Lord has prepared them to accept it.

7001 *And he will see you* symbolizes perception. This is established by the symbolism of *seeing* as understanding and perceiving, as dealt with in §§2150, 2807, 3764, 3863, 4567, 4723.

7002 *And rejoice in his heart* symbolizes a feeling of love. This can be seen from the symbolism of *rejoicing in one's heart* as delight and pleasure that stem from a loving feeling. All rejoicing comes from a feeling of love.

I am ascribing a loving feeling to teachings about goodness and truth rather than to people with those teachings because of the way angels speak. They speak as I have because they dislike talking about specific individuals. Talk about personalities would distract their minds from a comprehensive insight into matters and therefore from grasping large numbers of considerations simultaneously. So angels attribute delight and pleasure, passion, and so on to teachings. Besides, religious teachings hold these feelings when we apply them to ourselves. That is because they hold divine truth radiating from the Lord, and divine truth radiating from the Lord holds love and therefore delight and pleasure.

7003 *And you are to speak to him* symbolizes an inflow. This is established by the discussion in §§2951, 5481, 5743, 5797 of the symbolism of *speaking* as an inflow.

7004 *And put the words in his mouth* means that what he announces will issue from the divine humanity, as the following shows: Moses, who was to put the words in Aaron's mouth, represents the Lord in regard to the divine truth that emanates from his divine humanity, as explained before. A *mouth* symbolizes audible speech and verbalization, as explained above at §6987. So *putting [the words] in* his mouth means making him a spokesman, but when the Lord is said to do it, what it means is to issue, [or emanate,] because the Word, which is uttered by a spirit or angel, issues from the Lord's divine humanity. Aaron represents teachings about goodness and truth that are verbalized.

[2] Here is the situation: From the Lord issues divine truth directly and indirectly. The truth that issues directly from him completely transcends the ability of angels to understand it. The truth that issues indirectly, though, is adapted to angels in the heavens and also to humans, because it passes through heaven, from which it takes on an angelic quality and a human

quality. The Lord also flows *directly* into this truth and in this way leads angels and people both indirectly and directly; see §6058. Everything in general and in particular comes from the original source of existence, and the divine design was established in such a way that the first source of existence is present indirectly and directly in what develops out of it. So it is as fully present on the outermost level of the divine design as on the first. Divine truth itself is the only substance there is. What develops out of it consists merely in forms resulting from it. This too makes it plain that the Divine also flows into everything in general and in particular, because everything was created out of divine truth. After all, divine truth is the only essence (§6880) and is therefore the source of everything. Divine truth is what John calls the Word:

> In the beginning there was the Word, and the Word was with God, and the Word was God. Everything was made by him, and nothing that was made was made without him. (John 1:1, 3)

Through this kind of inflow the Lord leads us by providing for us not only in the most general way but also in every particular, even in the smallest particulars of all. This then is the reason for saying that what is announced must issue from the divine humanity.

[3] The fact that there is a direct inflow from the Lord everywhere there is an indirect inflow from him and consequently he flows in as fully on the outermost level of the divine design as on the first level—this was told to me from heaven, and I was given a vivid perception of the matter. Likewise the idea that what results from the indirect inflow, through heaven and the angels there, does not amount to much, comparatively, and the idea that the Lord at the same time uses a direct inflow to lead heaven and to keep everything there connected and orderly.

And I myself will be with your mouth means that divine truth will 7005
come from divinity itself by way of the divine humanity. This can be seen from the representation of Moses as the Lord in regard to divine truth (discussed before) and from the symbolism of *being with your mouth* as being within the divine truth that radiates from the divine humanity. Divinity itself, called the Father, is meant by *I myself,* or Jehovah. *I myself will be with your mouth,* then, clearly means that divine truth comes from divinity itself by way of the divine humanity. This is the same as saying that the holy influence of the Spirit comes from the Son, and the Son from the Father, as the church teaches, although the teaching must be understood to mean that these three exist in the Lord, where they are one.

7006 *And with his mouth* means that [divinity] will consequently be with that which develops out of it. This is evident from the representation of Aaron as teachings about goodness and truth (discussed at §6998) and from the symbolism of being *with his mouth* as the divinity with and within those teachings. Because they develop out of divine truth, which comes directly from the divine humanity (as discussed directly above at §7005), being with his mouth means being with that which develops out of [divine truth].

Teachings about goodness and truth come indirectly and directly from the Lord's divine humanity; see above at §7004.

7007 *And teach both of you what you must do* means that the Divine will consequently be present in absolutely everything that happens, as the following shows: *Teaching* means flowing in, and when ascribed to the Divine, as it is here, it means emanating, as above at §6993. And *what you must do* means what will happen. "In absolutely everything" is meant because the text is talking about the Divine.

Something needs to be said here about the idea that the Divine is present in absolutely everything that happens to us. This is not at all how it appears to us, because we think that if the Divine were present in each and every event, nothing bad would happen, no one would go to hell, justice would always triumph, the honest would meet with better worldly success than the dishonest, and so on. Because we witness the opposite, we do not believe that the Divine is present in everything. As a result, we assign credit for the details to ourselves and our own prudence, and only the broadest oversight to the Divine. The rest we describe as fortune or chance, which we see as blind forces of the material world.

[2] The reason we think this way is that we do not know the following secrets of heaven: The Lord leaves us each our freedom, because if we do not have freedom, we cannot possibly reform. Compulsion does not reform us, because it does not enable anything to take root in us. Forced action is not our will; free action is. Yet goodness and truth must take root in our will if we are to have them for our own. Nothing that lies outside our will is part of us. So since we are each left to our freedom, we are allowed to think evil and do evil, so far as external fears do not block us. It is for the same reason that the dishonest apparently exult and glory more on earth than the honest do; but the glory and exultation of the dishonest is outward and belongs to the body. In the other life it turns into hellish misery, while the glory and exultation of the honest, which is inward and belongs to the spirit, abides and becomes heavenly happiness.

[3] What is more, distinction and wealth contain worldly rather than eternal good fortune, which is why the dishonest achieve them as often as the honest do. If the honest do not achieve them, it is to prevent such things from turning them away from goodness. People equate worldly benefits and success with God's blessing, so when they witness the opposite, in their weakness they succumb to errors about divine providence.

They also draw conclusions from what they see in the present, failing to consider that divine providence looks to eternity. Its main goal is to organize everything in heaven and also in hell in such a way that heaven always resembles a single human being and hell stands opposite, creating a balance. This system cannot come into being except through divine providence in the smallest details of all, which means that the Divine must constantly govern and redirect our freedom.

[4] As for the rest, see earlier statements and evidence concerning divine providence: The Lord's providence is impossible at the universal level unless it exists in the smallest details: 1919 at the end, 4329, 5122 at the end, 5894 at the end, 6481–6486, 6490. The Lord's providence looks to eternity: 5264, 6491. The Lord foresees what is evil and provides what is good: 5155, 5195, 6489. The Lord turns the evil he foresees into good: 6574. Chance events are actually part of providence: 5508, 6493, 6494. Our own prudence is like a little dust scattered in the air, while providence is like the entire atmosphere: 6485. There are many fallacies undermining the concept that divine providence extends to the details: 6481.

And he will speak for you to the people means that he will be the doctrine for the spiritual church, as the following shows: Aaron, who the text says would speak for Moses to the people, represents doctrinal teachings about goodness and truth (discussed at §6998). *Speaking* symbolizes acclamation [of the Lord] and preaching (mentioned at §6999). And the children of Israel, the *people* here, represent the spiritual church (discussed at §6426). 7008

And it will happen that he will be like a mouth for you symbolizes doctrinal truth, which also comes from the Lord, but indirectly. This is established by the representation of Aaron, who was to be like a mouth for Moses, as doctrinal teachings (discussed at §6998), and by the symbolism of *being like a mouth for* Moses as the verbalization or preaching of them, as discussed at §6987. The reason this is called doctrinal truth that also comes from the Lord, but indirectly, is that the doctrinal truth Aaron represents is the truth as heard and understood by angels and people on earth. This truth is what emanates indirectly from the Lord. The truth 7009

Moses represents is what emanates directly from the Lord and is not heard or understood by people or even angels; see §§6982, 6985, 6996, 7004.

7010 *And you will be like a god for him* symbolizes divine truth that comes directly from the Lord. This can be seen from the representation of Moses as the Lord in regard to divine truth, as discussed at §6752. The fact that it is divine truth coming directly from the Lord is symbolized by his *being like a god for* Aaron. In the Word, "God" means the Lord in regard to divine truth, and "Jehovah" means the Lord in regard to divine goodness.

For the idea that the Word refers to the Lord as God when the subject is truth and as Jehovah when the subject is goodness, see §§2586, 2769, 2807, 2822, 3921 at the end, 4402. For the idea that angels are called gods because of the truth with which the Lord endows them, §4402. And for the idea that in a negative sense the gods of the surrounding nations mean falsity, §§4402 at the end, 4544.

7011 *And you are to take in your hand this staff* symbolizes divine power in both. This is evident from the symbolism of a *staff* as power, as discussed in §§4013, 4015, 4876, 4936—specifically, when the staff is in someone's hand. A hand, you see, symbolizes spiritual power, and a staff, earthly power. Just as the earthly plane has no power except from the spiritual, a staff has no power unless it is in someone's hand, so this verse says to *take it in his hand.*

When mentioned in connection with the Lord, a hand means power emanating from the rational level of his divinity, and a staff means power emanating from the earthly level of his divinity; see §6947. I speak of divine power *in both*—in the [two] kinds of truth mentioned above [§§7009, 7010]—because power is ascribed to truth (§§3091, 6344, 6423, 6948).

7012 *With which you will perform signs* symbolizes the resulting enlightenment and confirmation of the truth. This can be seen from the symbolism of a *sign* as confirmation of the truth (noted at §6870). A sign also symbolizes enlightenment because the way truth is confirmed is through enlightenment from the Lord when a person studies the Word with the purpose of learning what is true.

Regarding enlightenment and the resulting confirmation of truth: It needs to be realized that people who focus on outward appearances devoid of inward content, as the people of Judah and Israel did, cannot be enlightened and therefore cannot confirm the truth. People who focus on the outward appearance and at the same time on the inward significance, though, are enlightened when they read the Word. In that enlightenment they see the truth, which they then confirm more and more.

Remarkably, the kind of enlightenment we individually enjoy depends on the desire we have for truth, and the desire we have for truth depends on how much goodness we practice in our lives. That is why people who have no desire for truth on its own account, only as a means of achieving affluence, receive no light at all when they read the Word. They only confirm themselves in their theology, whatever its teachings are like, whether they are distortions (as heretical [Christian] teachings are) or are diametrically opposed to the truth (as Jewish teachings are). Such people seek not the kingdom of God but the world, not faith but fame, not heavenly but only earthly riches [Matthew 6:19–20, 33]. If they happen to be struck with a lust for learning truth from the Word, they keep discovering falsity rather than truth, and eventually, grounds for denying all truth.

The purpose of these remarks has been to explain what enlightenment and the resulting confirmation of truth are.

Exodus 4:18, 19, 20. *And Moses went and returned to Jethro his father-in-law and said to him, "I must go, please, and return to my brothers who are in Egypt and see whether they are still living." And Jethro said to Moses, "Go in peace." And Jehovah said to Moses in Midian, "Go, return to Egypt, because all the men seeking your soul are dead." And Moses took his wife and his sons and had them ride on a donkey and returned to the land of Egypt. And Moses took the staff of God in his hand.* 7013

And Moses went and returned symbolizes a continuation of his life before. *To Jethro his father-in-law* means of simple goodness. *And said to him, "I must go, please, and return to my brothers who are in Egypt,"* symbolizes being lifted up to an inward, more spiritual life on the earthly plane. *And see whether they are still living* symbolizes a perception of that life. *And Jethro said to Moses, "Go in peace,"* symbolizes assent and good wishes. *And Jehovah said to Moses in Midian* symbolizes enlightenment and confirmation from his divine side in that state. *Go, return to Egypt* symbolizes spiritual life on the earthly plane. *Because all the men seeking your soul are dead* symbolizes the removal of falsities that were trying to destroy a life of truth and goodness. *And Moses took his wife* symbolizes the goodness attached to it. *And his sons* symbolizes the resulting true ideas. *And had them ride on a donkey* symbolizes knowledge that would serve a new understanding. *And returned to the land of Egypt* means within the earthly mind. *And Moses took the staff of God in his hand* means that all this resulted from divine power.

7014 *And Moses went and returned* symbolizes a continuation of his life before. This can be seen from the symbolism of *going* as living a life (remarked on in §§4882, 5493, 5605), from that of *returning* as living where one did before, and from the representation of *Moses* as the Lord in regard to the law imparted by the Divine, or to truth from the Divine (discussed in §§6771, 6827). When Moses was with Jehovah on Mount Horeb, where Jehovah appeared within a flame, he represented the Lord as divine truth. Now that he is with Jethro, his father-in-law, who is the goodness in a religion possessing the truth that goes with simple goodness, he represents the Lord in regard to truth from his divine side.

Here and elsewhere in the Word, the inner meaning describes all the stages of the Lord's life in the world, and the way he made his human side divine while here. Clearly there were gradual stages. As a child the Lord was childlike, and later he grew in understanding and wisdom, always incorporating divine love into these, until even in regard to his human side he became divine love—that is, divine beingness, or Jehovah. Since the Lord put on divinity in this gradual way, he first turned himself into truth from his divine side, then into divine truth, and finally into divine goodness. These were the steps of the Lord's glorification, and they are described here and elsewhere in the Word's inner meaning.

7015 *To Jethro his father-in-law* means of simple goodness—that is, a continuation of a life of simple goodness, as the following shows: *Jethro,* priest of Midian, represents the goodness in a religion possessing the truth that goes with simple goodness, as noted at §6827. This is the goodness meant by simple goodness. And a *father-in-law* symbolizes the source of the union between goodness and truth, as noted at §6827.

7016 *And said [to him], "I must go, please, and return to my brothers who are in Egypt,"* symbolizes being lifted up to an inward, more spiritual life on the earthly plane, as the following shows: *Going and returning* symbolizes the next stage of life, and in this case the next stage of life involves being lifted to an inward, more spiritual life, closer to the Divine. When the Lord as represented by Moses is said to go and return, it means being lifted to divine beingness, or to Jehovah, who was within the Lord and from whom the Lord came. The children of Israel, the *brothers* here, represent the Lord's spiritual kingdom and therefore a spiritual religion, as discussed in §§6426, 6637. And *Egypt* symbolizes the earthly plane, as explained in §§6147, 6252. This makes it clear that *I must go and return to my brothers who are in Egypt* symbolizes being lifted up to an inward, more spiritual life on the earthly plane. Moses' residence in

Midian symbolized a life spent among people devoted to the truth that comes of simple goodness and therefore devoted to simple goodness itself (§7015). So his residence now among the children of Israel symbolizes a life spent among people devoted to the truth and goodness of a spiritual religion, which is more inward and spiritual than the life before. On the point that the goodness and truth of a spiritual religion reside on the earthly plane, see §§4286, 4402.

And see whether they are still living symbolizes a perception of that 7017
life. This can be seen from the symbolism of *seeing* as understanding and perceiving (discussed in §§2325, 2807, 3764, 3863, 4403–4421, 4567, 4723, 5400) and from the symbolism of *living* as spiritual life (discussed at §5407).

By "a perception of that life" I mean a perception beforehand. When we propose something to ourselves, we perceive it as if it were present. We put our mind into the appropriate state, which stirs our desires and enables us to enjoy the thing as if it were present. In this way intermediate goals unite with the ultimate goal, creating in effect a unified goal.

And Jethro said to Moses, "Go in peace," symbolizes assent and good 7018
wishes. This can be seen from the symbolism of *Jethro said to Moses* as an answer. The assent is symbolized by *go in peace,* and so are the good wishes.

And Jehovah said to Moses in Midian symbolizes enlightenment and 7019
confirmation from his divine side in that state. This can be seen from the fact that Jehovah was telling Moses he should return to Egypt even though he had given Moses this command before (Exodus 3:10 and following verses, and above in the current chapter, at verse 12 and following verses). What is more, Moses had already responded to the command by preparing for the trip. Clearly, then, the command here symbolizes enlightenment and confirmation from the Divine.

The idea that the enlightenment and confirmation came during that state—a state marked by the truth that goes with simple goodness—is symbolized by Jehovah's saying this to Moses *in Midian.* Midian is the truth that goes with simple goodness; see §§3242, 4756, 4788, 6773.

Go, return to Egypt symbolizes spiritual life on the earthly plane. This 7020
can be seen from the symbolism of *going* and *returning* as an inward, more spiritual life (discussed above at §7016) and from that of *Egypt* as the earthly plane (discussed in §§6147, 6252).

Because all the men seeking your soul are dead symbolizes the removal 7021
of falsities that were trying to destroy a life of truth and goodness, as the

following shows: *Being dead* means being removed, because people who have died have also been removed. Egyptians, the *men* here, symbolize people who subscribe to falsity (discussed at §6692). And *those seeking your soul* symbolize people who try to destroy life. I speak of a life of truth and goodness because spiritual life is a life of faith with its truth and of neighborly love with its goodness. This shows that *all the men seeking your soul are dead* symbolizes the removal of falsities that were trying to destroy a life of truth and goodness.

[2] A *soul* in the Word refers to any living thing. Even animals there are credited with a soul, but it is more properly spoken of in connection with a human being, and in that connection it has varied meanings. People themselves are called souls in reference to their life in general. They are called souls specifically in regard to their intellectual life (or their intellect) and to their volitional life (or their will). In a spiritual sense a soul means living energy in the truth that leads to faith and the goodness that comes from neighborly love. Broadly speaking it means the actual person in regard to her or his spirit, which lives on after death. The word appears in this sense in Matthew:

> Don't be afraid of those who can kill the body *but cannot kill the soul.* (Matthew 10:28)

In the same author:

> What does it profit you if you gain the whole world *but lose your soul,* or what will you give as an adequate exchange for *your soul?* (Matthew 16:26)

In Luke:

> The Son of Humankind did not come to destroy *people's souls* but to save them. (Luke 9:56)

In Ezekiel:

> You profaned me among my people, *to kill souls* that should not die and *to keep souls alive* that should not live. (Ezekiel 13:19)

In these passages a soul stands for a person's spiritual life, which is the life of a person's spirit after death. Killing the soul, losing one's soul, and destroying the soul stand for dying spiritually, or being damned.

7022 *And Moses took his wife* symbolizes the goodness attached to it. This is clear from the representation of Moses as the Lord in respect to the law or truth imparted by the Divine (explained before) and from the symbolism of a *wife* as goodness that is attached (explained in §§4510, 4823).

Here is why Moses' wife in an inner sense (and also in the highest sense, which has to do with the Lord) represents goodness united with truth: In every aspect of the spiritual world and the physical world there is something analogous to a marriage. The equivalent of a marriage exists where there is an active and a passive force—and there will be an active and a passive force wherever something comes into being. Nothing at all can be brought into existence without a union between these two forces.

The reason there is a virtual marriage everywhere is that everything relates to goodness and truth and therefore to the heavenly marriage of goodness and truth; and the heavenly marriage relates to the divine marriage of divine goodness and divine truth. To repeat, nothing can emerge or come into being unless there is an active and a passive force, and consequently unless there is a kind of marriage. Quite plainly, then, faith and its truth without neighborly love and its goodness cannot produce anything, nor can neighborly love and its goodness without faith and its truth. No, a union of the two is necessary to bear fruit and create the life of heaven in a person.

[2] In everything there is an image of marriage (see §§1432, 2173, 2516, 5194). At every point the Word contains a marriage of goodness and truth (§§683, 793, 801, 2516, 2712, 4137 at the end, 5138, 6343). So at every point the Word contains heaven, because heaven is that very marriage. And since the Word contains heaven at every point, it contains the Lord at every point, because the Lord is the all in all of heaven.

This discussion shows why even in the highest sense, which treats of the Lord, Moses' wife represents goodness united to truth, just like Sarah, wife of Abraham (as dealt with in §§2063, 2065, 2172, 2173, 2198), and Rebekah, wife of Isaac (§§3012, 3013, 3077).

And his sons symbolizes the resulting true ideas. This is established by 7023
the symbolism of *sons* as true ideas, which is discussed in §§489, 491, 533, 1147, 2623, 3373. I describe them as resulting because they are born of the marriage mentioned directly above.

And had them ride on a donkey symbolizes knowledge that would serve 7024
a new understanding, as the following shows: *Riding* symbolizes that which has to do with the intellect, and in this case, with a new understanding that would characterize life among the people of the spiritual church (§7016). Riding has this meaning because a horse symbolizes the intellect (concerning which, see §§2761, 2762, 3217, 5321, 6534). And a *donkey* symbolizes

truth that is subservient—in this case to the new intellect—as discussed in §§2781, 5741. It also symbolizes knowledge (§5492).

7025 *And returned to the land of Egypt* means within the earthly mind. This is established by the discussion in §§5276, 5278, 5280, 5288, 5301 of the symbolism of the *land of Egypt* as the earthly mind.

7026 *And Moses took the staff of God in his hand* means that all this resulted from divine power. This can be seen from the fact that a *staff* symbolizes power, as discussed in §§4013, 4015, 4876, 4936. The staff *of God* is therefore divine power.

See above at §7011 for the idea that a staff is earthly power and a hand spiritual power, that the earthly level receives power from the spiritual, and therefore that a staff symbolizes power when a hand is holding it.

The identification of a staff with power traces its origin to representations in the other world, where people who perform magic are seen with staffs, which really do serve them as instruments of power. For the same reason, the Egyptian magicians also had staffs that they used to perform what looked like miracles. For the same reason again, the literature of the ancients always depicts magicians as having staffs. A staff is clearly a representation of power, then, and also corresponds to power in a very real way, since people actually exercise power through staffs. When sorcerers do so, though, it is an abuse of the correspondence and is completely ineffective except within the hells they inhabit, where it is effective only because deceit and illusion reign supreme.

It is because a staff corresponds to power in a very real way that Moses was commanded to take staff in hand and perform signs. It is for the same reason that monarchs have a scepter, which is a short staff signifying their royal power.

The correspondence of a staff with power is due to the fact that a staff supports the hand and arm and therefore the body too, and the hand and arm of the universal human correspond to power (see §§878, 3387, 4931–4937, 5327, 5328, 5544, 6947, 7011).

7027 Exodus 4:21, 22, 23. *And Jehovah said to Moses, "As you go to return to Egypt, look at all the wonders that I have put in your hand, and you are to perform them before Pharaoh. And I myself will harden his heart, and he will not send the people away. And you are to say to Pharaoh, 'This is what Jehovah has said: "Israel is my son, my firstborn. And I say to you, 'Let my son go and let him serve me,' and you refuse to let him go. Watch: I am killing your own son, your firstborn."'"*

And Jehovah said to Moses symbolizes a perception from the Divine. *As you go to return to Egypt* symbolizes spiritual life on the earthly level. *Look at all the wonders that I have put in your hand* symbolizes a means of power then received from the spiritual plane. *And you are to perform them before Pharaoh* means against aggressive falsities. *And I myself will harden his heart, and he will not send the people away* symbolizes obstinacy and consequently no liberation yet. *And you are to say to Pharaoh* symbolizes an urgent message. *This is what Jehovah has said* means from the Divine. *Israel is my son, my firstborn,* means that people with spiritual truth and goodness have been adopted. *And I say to you* symbolizes a command. *Let my son go* means to abstain from persecution of the church's truth. *And let him serve me* symbolizes being taken up to heaven to perform useful deeds from there. *And you refuse to let him go* symbolizes obstinacy in the extreme. *Watch: I am killing your own son, your firstborn,* symbolizes the blotting out of faith that is devoid of neighborly love and consequently the stripping away of truth among the people concerned.

And Jehovah said to Moses symbolizes a perception from the Divine. 7028
This can be seen from the symbolism of *saying* in Scripture narratives as perception, which has been mentioned many times. Its source in the Divine is symbolized by the fact that it was *Jehovah* who said it.

The words *Jehovah said to Moses* are repeated here because a new perception is being symbolized (§§2061, 2238, 2260, 2506, 2515, 2552).

As you go to return to Egypt symbolizes spiritual life on the earthly 7029
level. This can be seen from the symbolism of *going* and *returning* as being lifted to an inward, more spiritual life, and from that of *Egypt* as the earthly level, both of which are mentioned above at §7016.

Look at all the wonders that I have put in your hand symbolizes a means 7030
of power then received from the spiritual plane. This is clear from the symbolism of *wonders,* or miracles, as the means divine power uses (discussed at §6910), and from that of a *hand* as spiritual power (explained at §7011). Clearly, then, *look at all the wonders that I have put in your hand* symbolizes a means of power received from the spiritual plane.

And you are to perform them before Pharaoh means against aggressive 7031
falsities. This can be seen from the representation of *Pharaoh* as falsity that attacks the church's truth, as discussed in §§6651, 6679, 6683, 6692. *You are to perform them before Pharaoh* means against that kind of falsity because it follows in sequence from the preceding clause. That clause, "Look at all the wonders that I have put in your hand," symbolizes a means of power

received from the spiritual level and therefore a means used against aggressive falsities. The subject matter of the inner meaning has a logical flow to which the wording of the literal meaning is secondary.

7032 *And I myself will harden his heart, and he will not send the people away* symbolizes obstinacy and consequently no liberation yet, as the following demonstrates: *Hardening* symbolizes obstinacy, and the *heart* symbolizes the will (discussed in §§2930, 3888). The combination therefore symbolizes willful stubbornness and thus stubbornness that delights in evildoing, because what we will we enjoy, and what we enjoy we love. And *not sending the people away* symbolizes an obstinate unwillingness to free them, and consequently no liberation yet.

This verse and others to follow [Exodus 7:3; 9:12; 10:1, 20, 27; 11:10; 14:4, 8, 17] say that Jehovah hardened Pharaoh's heart. This phrasing is due to appearances and to the common notion that the Divine causes everything, but it needs to be understood in the same way as attribution to Jehovah, or the Lord, of evil, anger, fury, devastation, and so on (§§2447, 6071, 6991, 6997).

[2] In regard to the obstinacy of [spirits] devoted to falsity and therefore evil, or to evil and therefore falsity: It is important to know that their stubbornness is beyond description. They never stop unless they are punished severely and, in the process, learn fear. Warnings and threats do nothing. The reason they are so obstinate is that the core pleasure of their life is evildoing. This pleasure they developed while living in the world, mainly because they loved themselves alone, not their neighbor, and accordingly had no Christian charity. Since people like this do not allow the Lord to lead them, they act on their own will, which is evil as a result of heredity and of the way they actually live. People who act on their own will do evil because they love it, since anything that relates to the will relates to love. So they take pleasure in doing evil, and the more pleasure they take, the more obstinate they are.

[3] In the world it is not apparent that this is the situation, but that is because self-love and materialism hinder such people. They are afraid that if they openly do evil they will lose their reputation and consequently their wealth and privilege. The law and fear for their life also give them pause. If those obstacles did not stand in the way, though, they would rush to destroy anyone who did not cater to them. They would plunder all others of their resources and ruthlessly kill everyone. That is what humankind is like inside. In other words, that is what people are like in their spirit, even if they do not appear so in the world.

This is quite plain to see in people in the other life. Those who were like this in the world have their outer layer taken from them and are left to their intentions and consequently to what they love. Left to what they love, they find nothing more fun than doing evil, which they pursue so obstinately that they never stop unless they are punished (as just mentioned) and are then plunged into hell.

This shows what we are like when we display no love toward our neighbor. It also shows that our life awaits each of us—not our public life, which was on the surface, visible to the world, but our spiritual life, which was within, invisible to the world.

And you are to say to Pharaoh symbolizes an urgent message. This is 7033
evident from the symbolism of *saying,* when done under divine command, as an urgent message, and from the representation of *Pharaoh* as falsity troublesome to the church's truth and therefore the people subscribing to such falsity who cause the trouble (discussed in §§6651, 6679, 6683, 6692).

This is what Jehovah has said means (an urgent message) from the 7034
Divine. This is evident from the discussion just above and the remarks that follow next.

Israel is my son, my firstborn, means that people with spiritual truth 7035
and goodness have been adopted, as the following shows: A *son,* when Jehovah (the Lord) uses the term in regard to people in the spiritual church, symbolizes someone who has been adopted, as discussed below. A *firstborn* symbolizes faith marked by neighborly love, which characterizes the spiritual church, as discussed in §§367, 2435, 3325, 4925, 4926, 4928, 4930. And *Israel* represents the spiritual church itself, as discussed at §6637.

Why does *Israel is my son, my firstborn,* mean that people with spiritual truth and goodness—people in the spiritual church—have been adopted, or acknowledged as his children? It is because the Lord saved these people by coming into the world; see §§6854, 6914. For this reason, and also because of their faith in the Lord, they are called his firstborn son. The Lord refers to the same people in John:

> And other sheep I have that are not from this fold. Those too I need to bring, and they will hear my voice, and there will come to be one flock and one shepherd. (John 10:16)

And I say to you symbolizes a command. This can be seen from the 7036
symbolism of *saying,* when done by Jehovah, as a command.

7037 *Let my son go* means to abstain from persecution of the church's truth, as the following shows: Pharaoh represents falsity persecuting the church's truth, as discussed in §§6651, 6679, 6683, 6692. *Let him go* symbolizes a command to abstain. And a *son* symbolizes people with spiritual truth and goodness who have been adopted, as discussed just above at §7035. Plainly, then, *let my son go* means to abstain from persecution of people who possess the church's truth.

7038 *And they shall serve me* symbolizes being taken up to heaven to perform useful deeds from there. This can be seen from the symbolism of *serving* Jehovah, or the Lord, as being useful. This can be seen from the symbolism of *serving* Jehovah, or the Lord, as being useful. This is about people of the spiritual church who were saved by the Lord's Coming. Some of them were in the underground realm before his Coming but afterward were taken up to heaven (§§6854, 6914), so they entered a state in which they could do something useful. *They shall serve me* consequently symbolizes being taken up to heaven to perform useful deeds from there.

Serving the Lord means performing useful deeds because true worship consists in being useful and therefore in exercising neighborly love. Anyone who believes that serving the Lord consists only in going to church, listening to sermons there, and praying, and who considers this enough, is badly mistaken. Worship of the Lord actually consists in useful behavior. To be useful while living in the world means to do your job properly whatever your position is, and in this way serve your country, its communities, and your neighbor from the heart; to deal honestly with your companion; and to help others in a prudent way, according to each individual's character. These functions are the principal acts of charity and the principal means of worshiping the Lord. Going to church, listening to sermons, and praying are also necessary but do no good without useful deeds, because they are not part of living but rather teach how to live.

All the happiness felt by angels in heaven comes from their usefulness and in proportion to their usefulness, so much so that being useful is heaven to them.

[2] The fact that happiness is proportional to usefulness, in keeping with the divine design, can be seen from correspondence between the parts of the human body and the parts of the universal human. The outer senses of sight, hearing, taste, smell, and touch are an example. These senses correspond [to those of the universal human], as demonstrated at the end of many previous chapters, so they have their pleasures, in perfect alignment

with the use they serve. The sensations of marriage love are the most pleasurable, because they serve the greatest use, leading as they do to the procreation of the human race, from which heaven is drawn. The pleasure of taste comes next and provides this level of pleasure because it supports the nourishment and therefore the health of the body, on which healthy mental function depends. The pleasure of smell is a lesser pleasure, because it serves only to refresh a person and therefore as an additional means of health. The pleasure of hearing and the pleasure of sight come in last place because they merely gather information for future use and tend to the needs of the mind's intellectual side, not so much its volitional side.

[3] From this and similar evidence, it becomes clear that usefulness determines how much happiness is given by the Lord in heaven and that being useful is the main way to worship the Lord.

This explains why John reclined on the Lord's chest at the table and why the Lord loved him more than he loved the rest [John 13:23]. It was not because of John himself but because John represented the exercise of neighborly love—in other words, useful activity. For this representation of John, see the prefaces to Genesis 18 and 22 and §3934.

[4] *And you refuse to let him go* symbolizes obstinacy in the extreme. This can be seen from the symbolism of *refusing to let him go* as no liberation, on account of obstinacy, as above at §7032.

Watch: I am killing your own son, your firstborn, symbolizes the blot- **7039**
ting out of faith that is devoid of neighborly love and consequently the stripping away of truth among the people concerned. This can be seen from the symbolism of *killing* as blotting out and from that of a *firstborn son*—the firstborn son of Pharaoh and of the Egyptians—as faith without neighborly love (discussed at §3325). Pharaoh and the Egyptians represented religious knowledge (4749, 4964, 4966, 6004), so they represented knowledge having to do with faith, since this is religious knowledge. However, they turned that knowledge into magic (6692), the consequence of which was that their deeds were evil and lacking in any neighborly love. As a result, their firstborn symbolize derivations of their religious knowledge and therefore faith without neighborly love. This symbolism of Egypt's firstborn is evident from the symbolism of Israel's firstborn as faith that does exhibit neighborly love (discussed above at §7035).

[2] I speak of faith without neighborly love, but in this case faith means knowledge related to faith, because faith itself is impossible where neighborly love is absent. In people who lack charity, any knowledge about faith

is merely subject matter for the memory, where it is stored in a form no different from that of other types of knowledge. Furthermore, the knowledge stored there contains no true information about faith, because it is sullied with false concepts and serves as a means for promoting falsity. Since this is what faith devoid of charity is like, it is blotted out among the evil in the other life, and they are stripped bare of truth. The point is to prevent truth from serving them as a means for evil and so to prevent hell from somehow gaining control over any heavenly qualities in them, which would leave them hanging between heaven and hell. This blotting out and stripping away of truth is what the killing of the firstborn in Egypt symbolizes.

Later the Egyptians perished in the Suph Sea, which represented a subsequent state of damnation, or spiritual death, for such people. After all, when the wings of faith, or truth, that had lifted them up have been taken from them, they soon drop like dead weight into hell.

7040 Exodus 4:24, 25, 26. *And he was in an inn on the way, and Jehovah met him and sought to kill him. And Zipporah took a flint and cut off the foreskin of her son and made it touch his feet and said, "Because a blood-soaked bridegroom you are to me." And [Jehovah] ceased from [killing] him; then she said "a blood-soaked bridegroom" for circumcisions.*

And he was in an inn on the way means that Jacob's descendants were concerned with superficialities devoid of inward content. *And Jehovah met him* symbolizes opposition. *And sought to kill him* means that a representative religion could not be established among them. *And Zipporah took a flint* means that their nature was demonstrated by a representative religion using truth. *And cut off the foreskin of her son* symbolizes the removal of unclean kinds of love and the resulting exposure of what lies within. *And made it touch his feet* means that the nature of the earthly plane at that time was shown. *And said, "Because a blood-soaked bridegroom you are to me,"* means that it was full of all sorts of violence and hostility against truth and goodness. *And [Jehovah] ceased from [killing] him* means that they were allowed a representational role. *Then she said "a blood-soaked bridegroom" for circumcisions* means that even though they were full of violence and hostility against truth and goodness on the inside, circumcision would still be accepted as a sign representing purification from unclean kinds of love.

7041 *And he was in an inn on the way* means that Jacob's descendants were concerned with superficialities devoid of inward content. This can be seen from Moses' representation here. In what comes before and after, the inner sense treats of the spiritual church, meant by the children of Israel. These three verses, though, treat of the church that should have been established among Jacob's descendants but could not be since they focused on superficialities devoid of inner content. In this case, then, Moses represents not the law, or the Word, but that nation, or Jacob's descendants (whose leader he was going to become), and therefore the worship of that nation too. Throughout the Word, leaders, judges, and monarchs represent the nation and people of which they are the leader, judge, or monarch, because they are its head; see §4789. That is why Moses is understood to be the one who was in an inn on the way (even though his name does not appear) and whom Jehovah then met and sought to kill, despite having previously commanded him in so many words to go and return to Egypt.

He was on the way symbolizes the original intent, and an *inn* symbolizes the outer earthly level, or the level of the senses (§5495). As just mentioned, the topic here is the religion that should have been established among Jacob's descendants, so what is being symbolized is the empty superficiality that characterized that nation. For this reason too the clause symbolizes the outer earthly level, or the level of the senses, in an isolated state. On the point that the sensory plane isolated from the inner plane is full of illusions and consequent falsities and that it opposes religious truth and goodness, see §§6948, 6949.

[2] Before I explain the rest of the passage, see what I have already shown about Jacob's descendants: They did not have a religion, only the representation of a religion: 4281, 4288, 6304. Their worship of God was merely outward worship, detached from inward, and they were forced into that worship by external means: 4281, 4433, 4844, 4847, 4865, 4899, 4903. They were not chosen; rather, they stubbornly insisted on being the church: 4290, 4293. They were by nature capable of representing something holy, even though they were consumed by bodily and worldly types of love: 4293, 4307. Such was that nation from its first origins: 4314, 4316, 4317. And there is much else I have demonstrated concerning that nation: 4444, 4459 at the end, 4503, 4750, 4815, 4818, 4820, 4825, 4832, 4837, 4868, 4874, 4911, 4913, 5057, 6877.

And Jehovah met him symbolizes opposition. This can be seen from the 7042
symbolism of *meeting* as opposition—specifically, over whether a church could be established among that nation. The opposition is directed against the Divine, as symbolized by the fact that *Jehovah* met him. In the literal meaning it seems as though Jehovah, or the Divine, put up the opposition, because it says *Jehovah met him,* but the inner meaning is that

opposition was put up against the Divine. The Divine never opposes anyone; no, it is a person or a nation that sets itself up against the Divine. When we oppose the Divine, it appears as though we encounter resistance from it, because we cannot stand what is divine.

The situation in all this can be seen from people arriving in the other world with a desire to go to heaven even though they are not of a type that can survive there. When they are granted their wish, they head off, but near the entrance to heaven they turn monstrous in their own eyes and start to suffer pain and torment, because they cannot bear the truth and goodness there. They believe that heaven and the Divine oppose them, when they are the ones who stand opposed and consequently bring their suffering on themselves.

This too shows that the Divine does not oppose anyone but that we are the ones who oppose the Divine.

7043 *And sought to kill him* means that a representative religion could not be established among them. This can be seen from the symbolism of *seeking to kill* as not accepting, which is discussed in §§3387, 3395. In this case it means not accepting or choosing that nation as one in which a representative religion would be established.

In the three verses under discussion, that nation is consistently meant by Moses, its future leader and head (see above at §7041). That nation was not chosen but rather insisted stubbornly on being the church (see §§4290, 4293). No religion was established among that nation, only a representation of a religion (4281, 4288, 6304). Sacred attributes of the church can be represented even by evil people, because a representational role has no regard to personality, only to the quality being represented (3670, 4208, 4281).

There are other passages with an inner meaning similar to this. One is Numbers 14:12, which says that Jehovah wanted to obliterate that nation entirely and raise up a new nation from Moses to replace it. Others are those speaking of Jehovah's regret that he was bringing or had brought that nation into the land of Canaan.

7044 *And Zipporah took a flint* means that their nature was demonstrated by a representative religion using truth. This can be seen from the meaning of *Zipporah* here as a representative religion and from the symbolism of *flint* as religious truth.

The use of flint knives for circumcision symbolized the fact that purification from foul kinds of love was accomplished through religious truth

(§§2039, 2046, 2799), circumcision being a practice that represented purification from those kinds of love (§2799).

The reason religious truth is the means of purification is that it teaches us what is good and what is evil and therefore what to do and what not to do. When we know such truth and choose to act on it, we are led by the Lord and are purified by his divine means.

Since religious truth teaches what is evil and what is good, *Zipporah took a flint* clearly symbolizes the use of truth to demonstrate the nature of something. The meaning of Zipporah as a representative religion can be seen from what follows in the current verses.

And cut off the foreskin of her son symbolizes the removal of unclean 7045
kinds of love and the resulting exposure of what lies within, as the following shows: *Cutting off* symbolizes removal. A *foreskin* symbolizes earthly and bodily love, which taints spiritual and heavenly love, as discussed in §§3412, [3413,] 4462. And the *son* symbolizes truth known to a representative religion. For the symbolism of a son as truth, see §§489, 491, 533, 1147, 2623, 3373. The kind of truth symbolized is truth known to a representative religion because Zipporah means such a religion; and she calls him her son and through him shows what that nation was like and therefore what its worship was like.

A *foreskin* symbolizes kinds of love that are unclean because the groin and genitals correspond to marriage love (§§5050–5062), and as they correspond to marriage love, they correspond to all heavenly and spiritual love (§§686, 4277, 4280, 5053). So a foreskin corresponds to the outermost types of love, which are called bodily and earthly. If these kinds of love are present without the inner kinds, called spiritual and heavenly, they are unclean, as they were in that nation, which was devoted to external things devoid of inward content.

I use the phrase "devoid of inward content" to mean lacking in any acknowledgment of truth or any desire for what is good and therefore in any faith or neighborly love. These qualities belong to the inner self and give rise to the exercise of neighborly love, which is outward goodness. An inner dimension of this kind—barren of faith and charity, full of evil and falsity—is described by the Lord in Matthew 12:43, 44, 45 as empty. That is why I speak of external things devoid of inward content.

Now since the outermost kinds of love are symbolized by a foreskin, their removal (symbolized by Zipporah's cutting off of the foreskin) causes their true nature to appear, so that what lies within is exposed.

7046 *And made it touch his feet* means that the nature of the earthly plane at that time was shown. This can be seen from the symbolism of *making it touch* as showing, because touch is demonstrative, and from the symbolism of the *feet* as the earthly plane (discussed at §§2162, 3147, 3761, 3986, 4280, 4938–4952).

To say that the nature of the earthly plane was shown is to say that the inner nature of that nation was shown, and the inner nature appears when an outer layer is removed.

A person's inner core is not visible in the world until the outer surface has been removed, because the outward behavior of evil people is totally at odds with their inward intentions and thoughts. They feign honor, they feign righteousness and Christian goodness, or neighborly love, in order to convince others they have these qualities inside. In addition, they are driven to pretense by fear of losing wealth, reputation, and rank, by fear of the law and its punishments, and by fear for their life. When such fears are removed, though, and they act on their inner nature, they become unhinged and plunder the goods of others. They yearn for murder and bloodshed, even against their fellow citizens, as is seen in civil war.

The fact that they are like this within is still more plainly evident from evil individuals in the other life, whose outer layers are taken away to reveal their inner layers (concerning which, see §7032). Many who looked like angels in the world are then revealed as devils.

[2] This large a discrepancy between the inner and outer levels indicates an entirely corrupt state in a person. With people of sincerity, righteousness, and goodness there is no such discrepancy. They say what they think and think what they say. It is quite the opposite in people lacking sincerity, righteousness, and goodness. With them the inner levels differ from the outer level. This was true of the Jewish nation, as the Lord describes in these words in Matthew:

> Doom to you, scribes and Pharisees—hypocrites! Because you cleanse the outside of the cup and plate, but the insides are full of plunder and excess. Blind Pharisee, cleanse first the inside of the cup and plate, so that the outside also becomes clean. Doom to you, scribes and Pharisees—hypocrites! Because you make yourselves like whitewashed tombs that do look beautiful outside but inside are full of the bones of the dead and every kind of uncleanness. Likewise, on the outside you also look righteous to people, but inside you are full of hypocrisy and wickedness. (Matthew 23:25, 26, 27, 28)

And said, "Because a blood-soaked bridegroom you are to me," means 7047
that it was full of all sorts of violence and hostility against truth and goodness, as the following shows: A *bridegroom* in this case symbolizes the representation of a church, or the outside layer of a religion, since a true representative religion is the bride. For the idea that in these three verses Moses represents that nation and the representation of a religion among its people, see above at §7041. For the idea that Zipporah means a representative religion, 7044. Since Zipporah means such a religion, and Moses represents its outside layer, Zipporah calls him a bridegroom, not her husband. A bride can represent something different from a bridegroom, but a man or husband and his wife cannot, because the marriage bond makes them one. And *blood* symbolizes violence inflicted on charity (discussed in §§374, 1005) and truth falsified and profaned (4735, 6978). So it symbolizes hostility against truth and goodness.

And [Jehovah] ceased from [killing] him means that they were allowed 7048
a representational role. This can be seen from the symbolism of *ceasing from him,* that is, ceasing from killing him, as allowing them a representational role. "Jehovah sought to kill him" meant that a representative religion could not be established with that nation (§7043), so when it now says *[Jehovah] ceased from [killing] him,* the meaning is that they were allowed a representational role. In other words, although that nation was not allowed to have a religion established among its people, it *was* allowed to have the representation of a religion established. Plainly it is one thing to represent a church and another to be a church, since even evil people can represent a church but only good people can be a church. Representing a church is purely external; see §§3670, 4208, 4281.

Then she said "a blood-soaked bridegroom" for circumcisions means that 7049
even though they were full of violence and hostility against truth and goodness on the inside, circumcision would still be accepted as a sign representing purification from unclean kinds of love. This is clear from the symbolism of a *blood-soaked bridegroom* as something full of all sorts of violence and hostility against truth and goodness (discussed above at §7047) and from that of *circumcision* as a sign representing purification from unclean kinds of love (discussed in §§2039, 2632, 3412, 3413, 4462, 4486, 4493).

This is said by Zipporah because that nation was now permitted to represent a religion, a circumstance symbolized by "[Jehovah] ceased from killing him" (§7048).

Circumcision became a sign representing purification because the cutting off of the foreskin symbolized the removal of unclean types of love and the resulting exposure of what lay within (§7045). When the inner dimension is dismissed—as it was by that nation, which was focused on what is external without what is internal—the symbolism remains. Since circumcision, or the cutting off of the foreskin, symbolizes the removal of unclean types of love and therefore purification, it was able to serve as a representational sign.

7050 It is plain in every word of these three verses that they contain secrets no one can know without the inner meaning. Who could guess the significance? Consider that immediately after Jehovah had commanded Moses to go to Egypt, while Moses was on the way, Jehovah met him and sought to kill him. Consider that when Zipporah had cut off the foreskin of her son, she made it touch his feet and said to Moses that he was a blood-soaked bridegroom to her. Consider that she then said, "a blood-soaked bridegroom" for circumcisions. Who cannot see that this passage has secrets hidden in it and that they can be revealed only through the inner meaning?

7051 People who know nothing about the Word's inner meaning inevitably believe that the nation of Israel and Judah was chosen above all other nations and was therefore better than the rest, as the people of that nation themselves believed. Surprisingly, it is not only that nation that believes it. Christians believe it too, even though they know that the people of that nation are given to unclean passions, sordid greed, hatred, and pride, and that they disdain and loathe anything inward, meaning anything that has to do with neighborly love and faith or with the Lord.

The reason Christians too believe that nation was chosen above others is that they believe we are chosen and saved out of mercy, no matter how we live, and consequently that the wicked can be let into heaven as easily as the devout and upright. They do not stop to think that the divine choice is universal, meaning that everyone who lives a good life is among the chosen. Or that the Lord's mercy extends to all who refrain from evil and try to live a good life and therefore who allow themselves to be led by the Lord and to be reborn, which happens continuously, throughout their life.

[2] For the same reason, most people in the Christian world also believe that that nation will again be chosen and will then be led back into the land of Canaan. This belief too they base on the literal meaning of such passages as the following: Isaiah 10:20, 21, 22; 11:11, 12; 29 at the end; 43:5, 6; 49:6–26; 56:8; 60:4; 61:3–10; 62; Jeremiah 3:14–19; 15:4, 14; 16:13, 15; 23:7, 8; 24:6, 7; 25:29; 29:14, 18; 30:3, 8, 9, 10, 11; 31:8, 9, 10, 17; 33:16, 20, 26; Ezekiel 16:60; 20:41; 22:15, 16; 34:12, 13; 37:21, 22; 38:12;

39:23, 27, 28; Daniel 7:27; 12:7; Hosea 3:4, 5; Joel 2:32; 3; Amos 9:8, 9, and following verses; Micah 5:7, 8. These and other passages lead even Christians to believe that that nation will again be chosen and brought into the land of Canaan. Yet Christians realize that that nation is waiting for a messiah to take it back into the land. At the same time, they know that the wait is in vain, that the kingdom of the Messiah, or the Christ, is not of this world, and consequently that the Canaan to which the Messiah will lead is heaven.

[3] Christians also fail to ponder the fact that the Word has a spiritual sense and that in a spiritual sense Israel does not mean Israel, Jacob does not mean Jacob, and Judah does not mean Judah. Rather, by those figures are meant the qualities they represent.

Again, Christians fail to ponder what the narratives tell us about that nation, its nature when it was in the wilderness, and its nature afterward in Canaan: that at heart it was idolatrous. They fail to ponder what the Prophets tell us about that nation, its spiritual whoredom, and its abominations. Its nature is described in Moses' song in these words:

> I will conceal my face from them. I will see what their posterity is. For they are a perverse generation—offspring in whom there is no faithfulness. Let me say: I will banish them to the farthest corners. I will make their memory cease from humankind, unless their enemies should say, "Our hand is high, and Jehovah has not done all this." For they are a nation that has lost all counsel, and there is no understanding in them. From the grapevine of Sodom comes their grapevine, and from the fields of Gomorrah. Its grapes are grapes of gall; clusters of bitterness are theirs. The poison of serpents is their wine, and the cruel gall of asps. Is it not hidden with me, sealed up in my treasuries? To me belongs revenge and retribution. For a time their foot will falter, because nearby is the day of their ruin, and let what is to come hurry on them! (Deuteronomy 32:20, 26, 27, 28, 32, 33, 34, 35)

Jehovah dictated this song to Moses, as may be seen in Deuteronomy 31:19, 21.

In addition, the Lord said the following about that nation, in John:

> You are from your father, the Devil, and your father's desires you wish to do; he was a murderer from the start and did not stand on truth. (John 8:44)

Not to mention many other passages.

[4] Why do Christians, knowing this, still believe that that nation will eventually turn to the Lord and then be brought into the land it once occupied? To repeat, this is because they do not know the Word's inner meaning and because they imagine that the way we live makes no difference. They do not think evil is any hindrance to our turning spiritual, being reborn, and generally making ourselves pleasing to the Lord through faith in him, even if the evil has been ingrained by constant practice and the faith is of only one short hour's duration. Furthermore, they believe that going to heaven is a matter of a pure mercy that the Lord extends to one nation and not to everyone everywhere who accepts his mercy. People who think this way do not realize that it is directly contrary to the Divine for some people (the chosen) to be born to salvation and heaven and for others (the unchosen) to be born to damnation and hell. To think this way about the Divine would be appalling, because such a policy would be the height of ruthlessness, when the reality is that the Divine is mercy itself.

These comments now make several facts clear: The nation of Israel and Judah was not chosen; still less will it be chosen in the future. It did not and could not possess a religion, only the representation of a religion. And it was preserved right to this day for the sake of the Old Testament Word (concerning which, see §3479).

7052 Exodus 4:27, 28, 29, 30, 31. *And Jehovah said to Aaron, "Go to the wilderness to meet Moses," and he went and met him on the mountain of God and kissed him. And Moses told Aaron all the words of Jehovah with which he had sent him and all the signs that he had commanded him. And Moses went, and Aaron, and they gathered all the elders of the children of Israel. And Aaron spoke all the words that Jehovah had spoken to Moses. And he performed the signs in the eyes of the people. And the people believed, and they heard that Jehovah had visited the children of Israel and that he had seen their affliction. And they bent and bowed.*

And Jehovah said to Aaron symbolizes doctrinal truth and a perception from the Divine concerning it. *Go to meet Moses* means that it would form a union with truth coming directly from the Divine. *To the wilderness* means where there had been none before. *And he went and met him on the mountain of God* symbolizes union within a loving goodness there. *And kissed him* symbolizes a desire for the union. *And Moses told Aaron all the words of Jehovah* symbolizes an inflow of truth emanating directly from the Lord's divine side into truth emanating indirectly, and instruction in each and every doctrinal teaching. *With which he had sent him* means which emanates from him. *And all the signs that he had commanded him* symbolizes enlightenment and also the resulting confirmation. *And Moses went, and Aaron* symbolizes a life in which the two are united. *And they gathered all the elders of the children of Israel* symbolizes the leading elements of wisdom in a spiritual religion. *And Aaron spoke all the words that Jehovah had spoken to Moses* symbolizes a resulting theology from the Divine. *And he performed the signs in the eyes of the people* symbolizes proofs capable of being grasped. *And the people believed, and they heard* symbolizes faith and hope. *That Jehovah had visited the children of Israel* means that people in the spiritual church would be delivered and saved by the Lord's Coming. *And that he had seen their affliction* means after such grave trials. *And they bent and bowed* symbolizes humility.

And Jehovah said to Aaron symbolizes doctrinal truth and a perception 7053
from the Divine concerning it, as the following shows: *He said* symbolizes a perception, as explained many times, so *Jehovah* said symbolizes a perception received from the Divine. And *Aaron* represents doctrinal teachings about truth and goodness, as discussed in §§6998, 7009, so he represents the truth in those teachings. All doctrine consists of truth, because doctrine is either about truth and the goodness it leads to (this is called the doctrine of faith) or about goodness and the truth it leads to (the doctrine of neighborly love). In either case it consists of truth.

Go to meet Moses means that it would form a union with truth com- 7054
ing directly from the Divine. This can be seen from the symbolism of *going to meet* as uniting and from the representation of *Moses* as truth coming directly from the Divine (dealt with above at §7010).

To the wilderness means where there had been none—no union—before. 7055
This can be seen from the symbolism of a *wilderness* as a place where there is not yet much life (dealt with at §1927) and accordingly where there is no goodness or consequent truth (§4736), since life comes from them. In this case it means where there was no union between truth coming directly from the Divine and truth coming indirectly. The promise of a union between them is symbolized by the plan for Aaron to go to the wilderness to meet Moses.

Regarding this union, it needs to be known that truth coming indirectly from the Divine can exist in us without being united to truth that comes directly from him.

[2] As the matter is unknown, though, let me illustrate it with examples. Some people, after proving to themselves that the teachings of their religion are valid, make sure they think and teach in alignment with those

teachings. The only way they know that an idea is true is if it comes from their church doctrine and has been handed down by educated and enlightened men. Truth that comes indirectly from the Divine can exist with them, but it is not united with the truth that comes directly from him. If the two were united, these people would want to know the truth for its own sake and above all for the sake of living by it. As a result, they would also have a gift for perceiving whether the teachings of their religion were true, before proving the validity of those teachings to themselves. And in every case they would be able to see whether the proofs for the teachings agreed with genuine truth.

[3] For another example, take the prophets through whom the Word was written, who wrote as the spirit from the Divine dictated, since the very words they were to write were announced in their ears. Truth coming indirectly from the Divine, through heaven, existed with them, but it did not lead to truth coming directly from him. They had no perception of the inner-level symbolism of the individual words, because as just described, perception happens when the two unite.

This union rarely exists in a person on earth, but it exists in everyone in heaven, especially the inhabitants of the third or inmost heaven. In people on earth it does not exist unless they have regenerated to the point where they can be lifted out of their senses to their rational plane and stand in the light of heaven, where angels dwell.

Both direct and indirect divine inflow do come to all of us (§§6063, 7004), but the two are not united except in people who perceive truth on the basis of goodness. After all, people in whom a direct divine inflow unites with an indirect one allow the Lord to lead them, but people in whom those inflows do not unite lead themselves and love to do so.

This discussion now shows what is meant by the wilderness here: a place where there was no such union.

7056 *And he [went and] met him on the mountain of God* symbolizes union within a loving goodness there. This can be seen from the symbolism of *meeting,* or going to meet, as union (noted just above at §7054) and from that of the *mountain of God* as divine love and its goodness (noted at §6829).

Here is the situation: Truth emanating directly from the Divine cannot unite with truth emanating indirectly except within goodness. Goodness is the soil, and truths are seeds that cannot grow in any other soil than goodness.

Goodness is also the very soul of truth. It is from goodness that truth springs, [and must spring] if it is to be true, and it is from goodness that truth has life.

[2] Truth that comes directly from the Divine is *called* truth, but it is actually goodness because it radiates from divine goodness. However, it is a goodness with which all divine truth has become one. It is called truth because in heaven it appears in the form of light, but this light is like the light in spring, which is joined to a warmth that brings everything on earth to life.

This argument too shows that truth coming directly from the Divine cannot unite with truth coming indirectly except within goodness. For the union to take place, then, we must desire truth for its own sake and especially for the sake of goodness. So we must desire it for the sake of living by it—since it is when we live by the truth that we adopt goodness.

[3] To explain even further about the union: Truth that comes directly from the Divine enters a person's will. That is its path. Truth that comes indirectly from the Divine, on the other hand, enters a person's intellect. The two cannot unite, then, unless the will and intellect are one, that is, unless the will intends what is good and the intellect supports it with truth.

Accordingly, when the two unite, the Lord seems present, and his presence is perceptible; but when they do not unite, the Lord seems absent. However, his absence is not perceptible to people who have no idea what his presence feels like.

And kissed him symbolizes a desire for the union. This is established by 7057
the symbolism of *kissing* as uniting out of desire, as discussed in §§3573, 3574, 4353, 5929, 6260.

And Moses told Aaron all the words of Jehovah symbolizes an inflow of 7058
truth emanating directly from the Lord's divine side into truth emanating indirectly, and instruction in each and every doctrinal teaching, as the following shows: *Telling* symbolizes an inflow, as mentioned at §5966. *Moses* represents truth emanating directly from the Lord's divine side, as explained at §§7010, 7054. *Aaron* represents truth emanating indirectly from the Lord's divine side, as explained at §7009. And *all the words of Jehovah* symbolize each and every doctrinal teaching. Instruction is symbolized by the fact that Moses told Aaron the words, because the means of divine instruction is an inflow, which is what *telling* symbolizes.

This evidence makes it plain that *Moses told Aaron all the words of Jehovah* symbolizes an inflow of truth coming directly from the Lord's divine side into truth coming indirectly, and instruction in each and every doctrinal teaching.

[2] To explain about instruction in each and every doctrinal teaching: This instruction takes place when truth coming directly from the Lord's divinity unites with truth coming indirectly, because that is when perception takes place; see above at §7055. The two are united primarily in angels of the third or inmost heaven, who are called heavenly angels. These angels have a keen perception of both kinds of truth and therefore of the Lord's presence. This is because they exhibit more goodness than others, since their goodness is innocent. They are consequently closest to the Lord and are bathed by a light that flashes and almost blazes, because they see the Lord as the sun and are near enough to experience its rays of light this way.

[3] I speak of truth radiating directly *from the Lord's divine side* even though the inner meaning here is about the Lord in the world when he called on his Father as a being separate from himself. I have explained a number of times before [§§1745, 1999, 2159, 6866] how this matter stands: Divinity itself, or Jehovah, was in the Lord, because the Lord was conceived from Jehovah, so that he called Jehovah his Father and called himself Jehovah's Son. At those times, though, the frail humanity he inherited from his mother was active in him. The more active it was, the more Jehovah (the divinity itself inside him) appeared to be missing. But the more active his glorified humanity was—that is, a humanity that had been made divine—the more present Jehovah (divinity itself) was in his humanity.

From this you can see what it means to say that truth that had come directly from the Divine came from the Lord's divinity.

7059 *With which he had sent him* means which emanates from him (referring to each doctrinal teaching). This can be seen from the symbolism of *being sent* as emanating, as discussed in §§2397, 4710.

7060 *And all the signs that he had commanded him* symbolizes enlightenment and also the resulting confirmation. This is evident from the symbolism of *signs* as enlightenment and confirmation of the truth, as discussed at §7012.

7061 *And Moses went, and Aaron* symbolizes a life in which the two—truth emanating directly from the Lord's divinity and truth emanating indirectly—are united. This is established by the symbolism of *going* as living a life (dealt with in §§3335, 3690, 4882, 5493), by the representation of *Moses* as truth coming directly from the Divine (dealt with in §§7010,

7054), and by the representation of *Aaron* as truth coming indirectly from the Lord (dealt with at §7009). Because they went their way together, a life in which the two are united is now being symbolized.

And they gathered all the elders of the children of Israel symbolizes the leading elements of wisdom in a spiritual religion. This can be seen from the symbolism of *elders* as the leading elements of wisdom and therefore as something that harmonizes with goodness (discussed at §6524) and from the representation of the children of Israel as a spiritual religion (discussed in §§6426, 6637). 7062

And Aaron spoke all the words that Jehovah had spoken to Moses symbolizes a resulting theology from the Divine, as the following shows: *Speaking,* when attributed to the theology that Aaron represents, symbolizes verbalization and preaching (discussed in §§6987, 6999). *Aaron* represents truth coming indirectly from the Lord's divinity and therefore theological teachings about truth and goodness (discussed in §§6998, 7009). And the *words that Jehovah had spoken to Moses* means from the Divine—that is, through truth that comes directly from the Lord's divinity, as represented by Moses (§§7010, 7054). 7063

And he performed the signs in the eyes of the people symbolizes proofs capable of being grasped, as the following shows: *Signs* symbolize proof—and therefore recognition—that something is true, as mentioned at §6870. And *eyes* symbolize the range of inner vision, or of the intellect, as discussed in §§2701, 3820, 4403–4421, 4523–4534, so *in the eyes* means within the grasp of the intellect. 7064

And the people believed, and they heard symbolizes faith and hope, as the following shows: *Believing* symbolizes spiritual belief, or faith, as discussed at §§6956, 6970. And *hearing* means obeying and also perceiving, as discussed at §5017. Here it means having hope, because people who believe and obey take hope when they perceive proof. Proof gives hope. 7065

That Jehovah had visited the children of Israel means that people in the spiritual church would be delivered and saved by the Lord's Coming, as the following shows: *Visiting* symbolizes deliverance through the Lord's coming into the world, as discussed at §6895, and consequently salvation, too. On the point that people in the spiritual church were adopted and saved through the Lord's arrival in the world, see §§6854, 6914, 7035. And the *children of Israel* represent the spiritual church, as discussed in §§6426, 6637. On the point that in the Word, *Jehovah* is the Lord, see §§1343, 1736, 2921, 3023, 3035, 5663, 6281, 6303, 6905. 7066

7067 *And that he had seen their affliction* means after such grave trials. This can be seen from the symbolism of *affliction* as trial (dealt with at §5356) and from the representation of the children of Israel as people in the spiritual church (discussed in §§6426, 6637). Concerning the way falsity afflicted or vexed the people of the spiritual church before the Lord's Coming, and so concerning their trials, see §§6854, 6914, 7035.

7068 *And they bent and bowed* symbolizes humility. This can be seen from the symbolism of *bending and bowing* as an outward effect of humility, as explained in §§2153, 6266. Bending, though, symbolizes an outward humility, felt by people dedicated to truth, while bowing symbolizes an inward humility, felt by people dedicated to goodness; see §5682.

I have often seen this fact illustrated in people motivated by truth and people motivated by goodness. People motivated by truth are rigid and stand stiff and straight. When they have to humble themselves before the Divine, they bend their body only a little. But people motivated by goodness are flexible, and when they humble themselves before the Divine, they bow all the way to the ground. Truth without goodness is totally rigid, although when it looks to goodness as its goal, the rigidity starts to soften. Goodness, however, is inherently flexible, and when truth is incorporated into goodness, it becomes goodness and therefore turns flexible itself. This is because truth cannot be rearranged in a heavenly pattern except by goodness, which means that on its own it is hard. The heavenly pattern is remarkably free and unresisting, so the goodness in which truth makes a home when properly rearranged is likewise free and unresisting, and as just mentioned, it is flexible.

The Spirits of Mercury (Continued)

7069 TO continue where I left off, the character of spirits from Mercury can be seen still more clearly from the following information.

Keep in mind that all spirits without exception were once people, since the human race is the breeding ground for heaven. Keep in mind too that these spirits are exactly what they were when they lived in the world, because one's life always follows one. This being so, the character of the people on each planet can be recognized from the character of the spirits from that planet.

Spirits in the universal human who come from Mercury relate to the 7070
memory of concepts abstracted from matter (§6808), so when anyone talks to them on subjects that are earthly, bodily, and strictly worldly, they are totally unwilling to listen. If forced to listen, they alter the information—usually into its opposite—in order to avoid it.

To learn for certain that this was their mindset, I was allowed to pres- 7071
ent images to them of meadows, freshly plowed fields, gardens, woods, and streams, but they immediately changed them. The meadows and fields they obscured and filled with images of snakes. The streams they stained, spoiling the clarity of the water. When I asked why, they said they did not want to think about things like that. They wanted to think about something real, meaning the knowledge of concepts abstracted from anything earthly and particularly knowledge of the kinds of concepts prevalent in the heavens.

Later I showed them images of the kinds of larger and smaller birds 7072
on our planet. In the other world one can present an image of such a thing as if it were actually there. Even the verbal communication of spirits and angels is full of images.

At first when they saw the images of the birds, they wanted to change them, but then they decided they liked them and eased off. This was because birds symbolize known concepts, and a realization of that fact then dawned on them. So they refrained from changing the images, as they otherwise would have done to block these from their memory.

Afterward I was allowed to present them with an image of an utterly delightful garden full of lamps and lanterns. That made them pause and stop, because lamps and lanterns symbolize truth that shines with goodness. Clearly, then, they could be induced to keep looking at physical objects if they were just given an idea of what the objects symbolized in a spiritual sense. Spiritual meaning is separate from material objects but is still represented in them.

I also talked with them about sheep and lambs, but they did not want 7073
to hear it because they perceived it as being earthly. This was because they did not understand what the innocence symbolized by lambs was. I could tell they did not understand it from this: I told them that lambs do not appear as images of lambs in heaven either but that instead of lambs (when the word comes up), the inhabitants perceive innocence.

They responded that they did not know what innocence was; they knew only the word. That is because they care only for knowledge, not for using it, which is actually the whole point of knowledge (§6815). As they do not care about the purpose of knowledge, then, they also have no inner perception from which they can see what innocence is.

7074 Some spirits from Mercury came to me on a mission from others to listen in on the discussions around me. A spirit from our planet said to them, "Tell your friends not to say anything but the truth. Don't answer questions in your usual contrary way. If any spirit from *our* planet did that, the spirit would be severely punished."

"If we were punished for that, we would *all* be punished," answered the distant group that had sent the spirits. "We cannot behave any other way, since that is our standard practice.

"When we talk to people on our own planet we do the same. But we are not trying to deceive anyone, we only want to spark a desire to learn. When we give them misleading information and obscure the question in a certain way, we stir up people's impatience to know about it; so being eager to explore the subject, they enrich their store of knowledge."

7075 I discussed the same subject with them another time, and knowing that they spoke with people on their planet, I asked how they teach the inhabitants. "We don't tell them how matters really stand," they said, "but we do give them some inkling of it so that their craving for knowledge can be nourished and grow. If we answered *all* their questions, that craving would die.

"Another reason we give misleading information," they added, "is to make the truth stand out more clearly. Truth is always visible by comparison with its opposite."

7076 It is their custom not to tell anyone what they know and yet to want to know what everyone else knows.

With their own community, though, they share everything, to the point where all know what each knows, and each knows what all know there.

7077 Because the spirits of Mercury are like this and always have abundant knowledge, they have a kind of pride (§6813). They imagine they know so much that it is almost impossible to know more. Spirits from our planet, though, have said to them, "You know a little, not a lot, and what you don't know is infinite by comparison. What you don't know in relation to what you do know is like the water in the largest ocean compared to the water in a puny spring."

To let them know this was true, a certain angelic spirit was allowed to talk with them and tell them in a general way what they did and did not know. The spirit said that what they did not know was limitless and that over the span of eternity they could not master even the general outlines of knowledge.

The spirit spoke in the language of angelic ideas, much more quickly than they spoke. Since the spirit was revealing what they did and did not know, they were dumbstruck.

Later I saw them addressed by another angel, who appeared some distance up and to the right. The angel gave a long list of things they did not know and afterward spoke with them in the language of changes in state, which they said they did not understand. The angel then told them that each change in state held infinite content, as did all the smallest elements of a state.

[2] Because they prided themselves on their knowledge, they started to feel humbler when they heard this. Their abasement was represented as the downward plunge of a whole scroll of them. (As a group they had now taken on the shape of a scroll that was some distance out in front and to the left on a level with the area below the navel.) The scroll they formed seemed to develop a hollow in the middle, though, and to lift at the ends, and I could see it quiver. They were told what this symbolized—that is, what they were thinking in their humility—and that the spirits appearing higher up, at the ends, were not yet feeling at all humble. I saw that the scroll split and the ones who were not humble were dismissed to their planet. The rest stayed.

Since the spirits of Mercury shun the spirits of our planet, who concentrate on the material realm, and since they had asked whether spirits like this could become angels (§6929), they now received the answer that the angel who had spoken with them was from this planet.

Be advised that spirits from other planets appear not within the same realm as spirits from our planet but outside it, some at a greater distance, some at a lesser, and all in different directions. The reason is that spirits from one planet do not have the same character or way of life as spirits from another, and they make up different areas of the universal human. Dissimilarity in their state of life creates that apparent separation. But the inhabitants of the inmost heaven appear [together], not separated from each other. 7078

By contrast, the spirits of Mercury do not appear in a certain region or at a certain distance but now in front, now on the left, now a little way behind. This is because they are allowed to wander the universe amassing knowledge with which to fill their memory.

Their planet is presented to spirits as being in back, and so is the worldly sun, when they think about it, since it is not at all visible. The reason it is presented as being behind them is that for inhabitants of the other life, the world's sun stands in deep darkness and is pitch black. Heaven's sun—or the Lord—appears out in front before the right eye, though, because it is the source of all the inhabitants' light. The right eye corresponds to the intellect's power of vision, as illuminated not only by truth but also by goodness (§4410). So the Lord looks on us—and enlightens us—with goodness.

7079 See further about the spirits of Mercury at the end of the next chapter [§§7170–7177].

Exodus 5

Teachings on Neighborly Love

IN preceding articles I defined what our neighbor is [§§6703–6712, 6818–6824, 6933–6938]. The next step is to define the charity or love we ought to bear toward our neighbor. 7080

Love is our very life, and the quality of our love determines the quality of our life. In fact, it determines our entire nature. 7081

Our dominant or reigning passion—our passion for whatever we take as our goal—is what makes us who we are.

This passion has many specific passions as categories and subcategories under it, which evolve out of it. Even though they may not resemble it, the ruling passion lies inside these individual passions and governs them. Through them as intermediate goals it looks toward and aims at its ultimate goal, which is the first and last goal of all. This it does both directly and indirectly.

There are two elements in the physical world that create life there, and they are warmth and light. There are also two elements in the spiritual world that create life *there,* and they are love and faith. The physical phenomenon of warmth corresponds to the spiritual phenomenon of love, and the physical phenomenon of light corresponds to the spiritual phenomenon of faith. That is why "spiritual warmth" or "spiritual fire" means love, and "spiritual light" means faith. What is more, love actually is the vital heat in us, and people recognize that love makes us warm. Faith actually is the light we see by, and people can recognize that faith enlightens us. 7082

Warmth and light in the physical world come from the world's sun, but spiritual warmth and spiritual light, or love and faith, come from heaven's sun. The sun of heaven is the Lord, and the warmth that radiates from him as the sun is love, while the light that radiates from him as the sun is faith. 7083

The fact that the Lord is the light can be seen in John:

> Jesus said, "I am the *light of the world;* whoever follows me will not walk in the dark but *have the light of life."* (John 8:12)

And the fact that the Lord is the sun can be seen in Matthew:

> When Jesus was transfigured, his *face* shone *like the sun* and his *clothes* became *like the light.* (Matthew 17:2)

7084 From this correspondence it is also possible to see how faith and love relate to each other. Faith without love resembles light without warmth, like the light in winter, but faith with love resembles light with warmth, like the light in spring. Everyone knows that everything grows and flourishes in spring light and that everything droops and dies in winter light. It is the same with faith and love.

7085 Now since love is the source of our life and determines our entire nature, and since love is spiritual connection, it follows that everyone in the other life associates with others according to different kinds of love. Our life, after all—which is our love—follows us. People motivated by love for their neighbor and love for God come together in heaven, but people motivated by love for themselves and love for worldly advantages come together in hell. This is because self-love is opposed to love for God, and love of worldly advantages is opposed to love for one's neighbor.

7086 When I speak of love for God, I mean love for the Lord, because the Trinity is in him. He is the ruler of heaven, because he has all power in heaven and on earth (Matthew 28:18).

Exodus 5

1. And afterward Moses and Aaron came and said to Pharaoh, "This is what Jehovah, God of Israel, has said: 'Send away my people and let them keep a feast to me in the wilderness.'"

2. And Pharaoh said, "Who is Jehovah, that I should listen to his voice, to send Israel away? I do not know Jehovah and will not send Israel away, either."

3. And they said, "The God of the Hebrews has met us. Please let us go a journey of three days into the wilderness, and let us sacrifice to Jehovah our God, to keep him from falling on us with contagion and sword."

4. And the king of Egypt said to them, "Moses and Aaron, why do you distract the people from their work? Go to your burdens!"

5. And Pharaoh said, "Here, the people of the land are now many, and you have made them cease from their burdens."

6. And Pharaoh on that day commanded the taskmasters over the people and their managers, saying,

7. "You must no longer give straw to the people to make bricks, as yesterday and the day before; they themselves must go and are to gather straw for themselves.

8. And the quota of bricks that they were making yesterday and the day before you must lay on them; you must not take away from it, because they are lazy. That is why they cry out, saying, 'Let us go sacrifice to our God!'

9. Let the weight of their servitude be increased on the men, and have them do it and not look to lying words."

10. And the people's taskmasters went out, as did their managers, and said to the people, saying, "This is what Pharaoh has said: 'I am not giving you any straw.

11. You yourselves, go take yourselves straw from wherever you find it, because nothing will be taken away from your [required] servitude at all.'"

12. And the people scattered out into all the land of Egypt to gather stubble for straw.

13. And the taskmasters were exerting pressure, saying, "Complete your work—the matter of a day in its day—as when there was straw."

14. And there were beatings for the managers of the children of Israel, whom Pharaoh's taskmasters put over them, saying, "Why don't you complete your assignment to make bricks both yesterday and today as you did yesterday and the day before?"

15. And the managers of the children of Israel came and cried out to Pharaoh, saying, "Why do you do this to your servants?

16. No straw is given to your servants, and 'Make bricks,' they say to us, and here, your servants are beaten and your people has sinned."

17. And he said, "Lazy you are, lazy! That is why you say, 'Let us go sacrifice to Jehovah.'

18. And now go serve, and straw will not be given to you, and you must yield the quota of bricks."

19. And the managers of the children of Israel saw themselves beset by evil, saying, "You must not take away from your [quota of] bricks at all, day by day."

20. And they came across Moses and Aaron standing before them as they went out from Pharaoh.

21. And [the managers] said to them, "Jehovah look on you and judge! For you have made our scent stink in the eyes of Pharaoh and in the eyes of his servants, to put a sword into their hand to kill us."

22. And Moses went back to Jehovah and said, "Lord, why have you done evil to this people? Why is this, [that] you sent me?

23. And ever since I came to Pharaoh to speak in your name, he has done evil to this people, and you have decidedly not delivered your people."

Summary

7087 THE inner meaning of the current chapter continues to describe how people in the spiritual church were overrun with falsity. First it talks about the [spirits] overrunning them, who paid no attention whatever to the urgent warning from the Divine. Then it says that the [spirits] afterward persecuted them still more, introducing falsities that were deceptive fabrications. The people of the spiritual church could not dispel these falsities or shake off their persecutors, so they complained to the Divine.

Inner Meaning

7088 EXODUS 5:1, 2, 3, 4. *And afterward Moses and Aaron came and said to Pharaoh, "This is what Jehovah, God of Israel, has said: 'Send away my people and let them keep a feast to me in the wilderness.'" And Pharaoh said, "Who is Jehovah, that I should listen to his voice, to send Israel away? I do not know Jehovah and will not send Israel away, either." And they said, "The God of the Hebrews has met us. Please let us go a journey of three days into the wilderness, and let us sacrifice to Jehovah our God, to keep him from falling on us with contagion and sword." And the king of Egypt said to them, "Moses and Aaron, why do you distract the people from their work? Go to your burdens!"*

And afterward Moses and Aaron came symbolizes divine law and teachings derived from it. *And said to Pharaoh* symbolizes an urgent message delivered by them to people who oppose the church's truth. *This is what Jehovah, God of Israel, has said,* means that it comes from the Lord's divine humanity. *Send away my people* means that they should stop attacking them. *And let them keep a feast to me in the wilderness* means so they can worship the Lord with a glad heart in the dim state of faith that is theirs. *And Pharaoh said,* symbolizes negative thinking. *Who is Jehovah, that I should listen to his voice?* means about the Lord, that they would take note of his urgent message. *To send the people away* means to the effect that they should stop. *I do not know Jehovah* means that they do not care about the Lord. *And will not send Israel away, either* means that neither will they end their harassment. *And they said, "The God of the Hebrews has met us,"* means that the God himself of the church has issued a demand. *Please let us go a journey of three days into the wilderness* means for them to be in a state entirely separate from falsity, even though their sight of faith is dim. *And let us sacrifice to Jehovah our God* means so they can worship the Lord. *To keep him from falling on us with contagion and sword* means in order to escape being damned by evil and falsity. *And the king of Egypt said to them* symbolizes the response from people committed to falsity. *Moses and Aaron, why do you distract the people from their work?* means that their divine law and teachings will not exempt them from heavy loads. *Go to your burdens!* means that they must live lives of combat.

And afterward Moses and Aaron came symbolizes divine law and teachings derived from it. This can be seen from the representation of *Moses* as the Lord in the role of divine law (discussed at §6752) and from that of *Aaron* as teachings about goodness and truth (discussed at §6998). **7089**

Divine law, which Moses represents, means the Word as it is in its inner sense and therefore as it is in the heavens. Teachings mean the Word as it is in its literal sense and therefore as it is on earth. How great the difference is between them can be seen from the explanations of the Word's inner meaning so far.

As illustration, take the Ten Commandments, to which the term the *law* specifically refers. Their literal sense is that we must honor our parents, not kill, not commit adultery, not steal, and so on. The inner sense, though, is that we must worship the Lord, not hate, not distort the truth, and not claim for ourselves what belongs to the Lord. That is how these four commandments are understood in heaven, and the others are also understood in their own way. The heavens do not know any Father but the Lord, so they take the requirement to honor one's parents as a requirement to worship the Lord. The heavens also do not understand killing, because they live forever there, but they take killing to mean hating others or injuring someone's spiritual life. Again, the heavens do not know what adultery is, so they instead perceive the commandment's equivalent, which is not to distort truth. In place of [not] stealing they perceive not taking anything (such as goodness or truth) from the Lord and claiming it for oneself.

[2] This is what "the law"—and the entire Word—is like in the heavens, so this is what it is like in its inner meaning. In fact, it is even deeper, since most of what is thought and said in the heavens cannot be expressed in the words of human language because it is a spiritual, not a physical, world there. Features of the spiritual world transcend features of the physical world just as the intangible transcends the tangible. Still, because what is tangible corresponds to spiritual features, they can be explained [to people on earth] in physical terms and consequently in earthly language but not in spiritual language. Spiritual language is a language not of physical words but of spiritual words, which are thoughts turned into words in the spiritual atmosphere. They are represented by the variegation of heavenly light, which is actually divine understanding and wisdom emanating from the Lord.

This discussion shows what is meant by "divine law" in its true sense, as represented by Moses, and what is meant by "teachings," as represented by Aaron.

7090 *And said to Pharaoh* symbolizes an urgent message delivered to people who oppose the church's truth, as the following shows: *Saying*—since it was done by Moses and Aaron on divine command—symbolizes an urgent message, as it also does at §7033. And *Pharaoh* represents knowledge that opposes the church's truth, as noted in §§6651, 6679, 6683, so he also represents people who oppose that truth.

The subject here and in what follows is people of the spiritual church who were saved by the Lord's coming into the world and until then were held in an underground realm, where they were tormented by falsity—in other words, by hellish beings devoted to malicious falsity. This realm lies underfoot, surrounded by the hells. In front of it live hellish beings who distorted what was true and adulterated what was good. On the right live those who invert the divine design and strive to gain power by doing so. Behind it live evil demons, who secretly plotted evil against their neighbor out of self-love. Deep under them live those who absolutely despised the Divine and worshiped the material world, ridding themselves of anything spiritual. Those are the types who surround the inhabitants of the underground realm, which provided refuge for people of the spiritual church until the Lord's Coming. They were persecuted there but were nonetheless protected by the Lord and taken up to heaven with the Lord when he rose again. For more on this, see what was said and shown earlier, in §§6854, 6914, 6945, 7035.

[2] The underground realm that provided refuge for people of the spiritual church until the Lord's Coming is mentioned a number of times in the Word, as in Isaiah:

> Sing, you heavens, because Jehovah has acted. *Shout for joy, you underground realm!* Break into song, you mountains, you forest and every tree in it, because Jehovah has redeemed Jacob and rendered himself glorious in Israel. (Isaiah 44:23)

This is about people in the underground realm and their salvation by the Lord. Jacob and Israel are the spiritual church, Jacob being the outer aspect of that church and Israel the inner aspect (§§3305, 4286, 6426). In Ezekiel:

> I will make you go down with those going down into the *pit,* to an ancient people, and settle you *in the underground realm* in desolate places. (Ezekiel 26:20)

In the same author:

> . . . *to the underground realm,* in the midst of the children of humankind, to those going down into the pit. So *in the underground realm* all the trees of Eden will comfort themselves, the choice and foremost of Lebanon, all drinking the water. (Ezekiel 31:14, 16)

This is the underground realm, where people whose religion was spiritual were.

[3] Even today people in the church are let down into the underground realm if they have filled their thinking with worldly or earthly notions and have caused religious truth to be connected to such notions. They too undergo conflict there, which lasts until the worldly and earthly dimension

has been detached from religious truth and factors that will prevent any future connecting of the two have been put in place.

It is when this process reaches its end that they are taken up from that realm to heaven. Not until worldly and earthly elements are removed can they possibly be among angels, because these elements are shadows and stains incompatible with the light and purity of heaven.

The worldly and earthly elements can be detached and removed only by a war on falsity, and here is how the battle goes: The people there are attacked by illusions and resulting falsities, which are spewed out by the hellish beings surrounding them but are refuted by the Lord through heaven. At the same time, truth is introduced. All this appears to be happening inside the people undergoing the conflict.

[4] This is why it is appropriate to describe the spiritual church as militant. Religion is rarely militant in anyone in the world today, though, because religious people living in the world do not bear up under the struggle. This is due to the evil crowd in whose midst they live and to the flesh they inhabit, which is weak. In the next life we can be held firmly by the bonds of conscience, but not as firmly in the world. In the world, if we are driven to desperation (as we usually are during these fights), we immediately break the bonds of conscience; if we break them, we succumb; and if we succumb in this way, it is all over for our salvation. That is why the Lord allows few in the church today to enter into a fight for truth against falsity. These battles are spiritual trials.

See also some earlier explanations of the underground realm and of the devastation there in §§4728, 4940–4951, 6854.

7091 *This is what Jehovah, God of Israel, has said,* means from the Lord's divine humanity—that is, an urgent message from it delivered to those who oppose the church's truth. This can be seen from the fact that *Jehovah, God of Israel,* means the Lord in his divine humanity. For the Lord being Jehovah in the Word, see §§1343, 1736, 2921, 3023, 3035, 5041, 5663, 6281, 6303, 6905. He is called God of Israel because Israel symbolizes the Lord's spiritual kingdom (§§6426, 6637), and by his coming into the world the Lord saved the people of that kingdom, or of the spiritual church (§§6854, 6914, 7035).

The reason the God of Israel means the Lord in his divine humanity is that people of the spiritual church have an earthly concept of everything spiritual and heavenly and also of what is divine. So unless they thought of the Divine as a physical person, they could form no emotional bond with him. If they did not think of the Divine as a physical person, they would form either no concept at all or some outrageous one, defiling what is divine. That is why the God of Israel means the Lord as regards his divine humanity and even the earthly aspect of his divinity.

(In the highest sense, Israel and Jacob mean the Lord in regard to his earthly divinity, Israel meaning the Lord in regard to his inner earthly divinity, and Jacob in regard to his outer earthly divinity; see §4570. People of a spiritual religion were and are saved through the Lord's divine humanity; §§2833, 2834. And the spiritually religious person for whom Israel stands operates on the inner earthly level; §§4286, 4402.)

[2] These considerations now show why the Word refers to the Lord as Jehovah, God of Israel, and Jehovah, the Holy One of Israel. Anyone can see that the Divine is given these names only because they match some sacred quality that is not visible in the literal meaning.

The fact that the Lord in regard to his earthly divinity is meant by the God of Israel is evident from many passages in the Word and is plainly evident in the following:

> Moses and Aaron, Nadab and Abihu, and the seventy elders of Israel *saw the God of Israel,* under whose feet was something like a work of sapphire stone, and it looked like the substance of the sky for cleanness. (Exodus 24:9, 10)

This was the Lord, not Jehovah (called the Father), as the Lord's words in John make plain:

> God has never been seen by anyone. (John 1:18)

> You have never heard his voice or seen his form. (John 5:37)

[3] In Isaiah:

> I will give you the treasures of the dark and the secret riches of hideaways so that you may recognize that I am Jehovah, the *one who calls you by your name: God of Israel.* (Isaiah 45:3)

In Ezekiel:

> Over the head of the guardian beings was a seeming appearance of sapphire stone, like a throne. And on the likeness of a throne was what looked like the *appearance of a person* on it, high above. And it had the appearance of fire and of a rainbow and of brilliance all around. (Ezekiel 1:26, 27, 28)

These sights are called the glory of *Jehovah* and of the *God of Israel* in Ezekiel 1:28; 8:4; 9:3; 10:19, 20.

[The Lord is referred to as God of Israel] again where the same author treats of the new temple in Ezekiel 43:2; 44:2; and in many other passages too, such as Isaiah 17:6; 21:10, 17; 24:15; 41:17; Psalms 41:13; 59:5; 68:8, 35; 69:6; 72:18; and others. He is also called the *Holy One of Israel,* in Isaiah 1:4; 5:19; 10:20; 17:7; 30:11, 12, 15; 49:7; 60:9, 14; Ezekiel 39:7.

[4] Another piece of evidence that the God of Israel and the Holy One of Israel is the Lord in his divine humanity is the fact that he is called Redeemer, Savior, and Maker. He is called *Redeemer* in Isaiah:

> *Our redeemer is Jehovah Sabaoth; his name is the Holy One of Israel.* (Isaiah 47:4)

and in Isaiah 41:14; 43:14; 48:17; 54:5. He is called *Savior* in Isaiah 43:3, and *Maker* in Isaiah 45:11.

These passages too show that in the Old Testament Word, Jehovah means no one but the Lord, because he is called *Jehovah God* and the *Holy One of Israel, Redeemer, Savior,* and *Maker.* He is called Jehovah the Redeemer and Savior in Isaiah:

> . . . so that all flesh may know that *I, Jehovah,* am your *Savior* and *your Redeemer,* the Mighty One of Jacob. (Isaiah 49:26)

In the same author:

> . . . so that you may know that I, *Jehovah,* am *your Savior* and *your Redeemer,* the Powerful One of Israel. (Isaiah 60:16)

Likewise in Isaiah 43:14; 44:6, 24; 54:8; 63:16; Psalms 19:14.

[5] It says in Isaiah that the Lord saved Israel, or the people of the spiritual church:

> I will mention Jehovah's mercies, the praises of Jehovah, according to all that Jehovah has repaid us. Abounding in goodness to the *house of Israel,* he said, "*Surely they are my people,* offspring who do not lie." *And so he became a savior to them.* In all their anguish, he had anguish; and *the angel of his presence delivered them. In his love* and his forbearance *he redeemed them* and *picked them up* and *carried them all the days of old.* (Isaiah 63:7, 8, 9)

7092 *Send away my people* means that they should stop attacking them, as the following shows: *Sending away,* when it is said to Pharaoh, who represents falsity that attacks religious truth, means stopping the attack. And the children of Israel—*my people*—represent adherents of a spiritual religion, as discussed in §§6426, 6637.

And let them keep a feast to me in the wilderness means so they can worship the Lord with a glad heart in the dim state of faith that is theirs, as the following shows: *Keeping a feast* symbolizes worship from a glad heart, as discussed below. For the idea that the Lord was the one to whom they were to keep a feast and who is meant here by *to me*—Jehovah—see just above at §7091. And a *wilderness* symbolizes a dim state of faith, as discussed in §§2708, 7055. For the idea that people whose religion is spiritual are somewhat in the dark concerning faith, see §§2708, 2715, 2716, 2718, 2831, 2849, 2935, 2937, 3241, 3246, 3833, 6289, 6500, 6945. **7093**

[2] *Keeping a feast* symbolizes worship from a glad heart because the feast was to be kept at the distance of a three-day journey from Egypt and therefore in a state free from attack by falsity, or in a state of liberation. Those who are delivered from falsity and from the anguish in which falsity places them thank God—and therefore hold a feast to him—with a glad heart.

Besides, the feasts established among the people (which happened three times a year) are said to have been established in memory of their deliverance from slavery in Egypt. In a spiritual sense that means the feasts were established in memory of their deliverance from attack at the hands of falsity, by means of the Lord's coming into the world.

That is why the people were commanded to be glad during the feasts, as is clear in Moses, where he describes the Feast of Booths:

> In the feast of booths, on the first day you shall take the fruit of a noble tree, palm fronds, and the branch of a dense tree, and river willows, and you are to *be glad before Jehovah your God for seven days.* (Leviticus 23:40)

[3] The fruit of a noble tree, the palm fronds, the branch of a dense tree, and the river willows symbolize joy over goodness and truth permeating a person from the inmost core to the outside. A loving goodness, which is at the core, is symbolized by the fruit of a noble tree. Good done out of faith is symbolized by the palm fronds. Truth in the form of knowledge is symbolized by the branch of a dense tree. And truth gained through the senses, which is the outermost kind, is symbolized by the river willows. The people could not have been ordered to take them up without a reason originating in the spiritual world, and that reason is completely invisible except in the inner meaning.

[4] Their gladness during the Feast of Weeks is also clear in Moses:

> You shall keep the Feast of Weeks to Jehovah your God, *and you are to be glad before Jehovah your God*—you and your son and your daughter and your male slave and your female slave and the Levite who is within your gates. (Deuteronomy 16:10, 11)

These words too in their inner meaning symbolize gladness over goodness and truth from the inmost core to the outside.

[5] The following passages also show that feasts were happy times and that keeping a feast therefore means worshiping with a glad heart. In Isaiah:

> *You will have song* like that of a night spent in holy observance of a *feast.* (Isaiah 30:29)

In Nahum:

> Look! On the mountains, the feet of the *one who brings good news, who proclaims peace. Celebrate your feasts, Judah;* fulfill your vows! For belial will no longer continue to pass through you; he will be entirely cut off. (Nahum 1:15)

In Zechariah:

> To the house of Judah, the fasts will serve *for joy* and *for gladness,* and *for good feasts.* Only be sure to love truth and peace. (Zechariah 8:19)

In Hosea:

> I will put an end to *all its joy, its feast,* its new moon celebration. (Hosea 2:11)

In Amos:

> I will turn *your feasts* into mourning and all your songs into a lament. (Amos 8:10)

[6] This meaning of keeping a feast—that is, worship from a heart glad that they had been delivered from slavery in Egypt (or in a spiritual sense, that they had been delivered from attacks of falsity)—is quite plain from the Feast of Passover. The children of Israel were ordered to celebrate Passover every year on the day they left Egypt, and the reason for celebrating was that they had been delivered from slavery. That is, the reason for celebrating was that people of the spiritual church were delivered from

falsity and therefore from damnation. Since the Lord delivered them by his Coming and took them up with him into heaven when he rose again, the resurrection also happened during Passover. The same thing is symbolized by the Lord's words in John:

> Now is the judgment of this world; now will the ruler of this world be thrown out. But I, if I am raised up from the earth, will draw everyone to myself. (John 12:31, 32)

And Pharaoh said, symbolizes negative thinking. This can be seen from the symbolism of *saying* as thinking, which is mentioned at §3395. The fact that it means negative thinking on the part of the aggressive spirits represented by Pharaoh is plain from what follows next: far from stopping, Pharaoh oppressed the children of Israel still more [Exodus 5:6–9]. 7094

Who is Jehovah, that I should listen to his voice? means about the Lord, that they would take note of his urgent message; that is, it means negative thinking about this. The meaning can be seen from the symbolism of the *voice* here as an urgent message, since it refers to what Moses and Aaron said to Pharaoh (a symbolism mentioned at §7090), and from that of *listening* as obeying (discussed at §§2542, 3869, 5017). *Listening to his voice,* then, means obeying or taking note of the message. 7095

The reason the Lord is the one whose message Pharaoh declined to take note of is that in the Word, Jehovah means none other than the Lord; see above at §7091.

To send the people away means to the effect that they should stop. This can be seen from the symbolism of *sending away* as stopping, as above at §7092. What was to stop was the attack on adherents of the spiritual church, who are the *people* here. For the idea that the children of Israel stand for members of a spiritual religion, see §6426. 7096

I do not know Jehovah means that they do not care about the Lord. This can be seen from the symbolism of *not knowing* as not caring, because people who do not care say they do not know. For the idea that *Jehovah* means the Lord, see above at §7091. 7097

Here is the story behind the fact that Pharaoh says he does not know Jehovah: Since ancient times Egyptians did know Jehovah, because the ancient church had existed also in Egypt, as is quite plain from the fact that Egyptians observed the representative and symbolic practices of that church. Egyptian hieroglyphics are nothing else. Hieroglyphics had a spiritual symbolism, and Egyptians knew that the hieroglyphics had an actual correspondence too. Egyptians started to use them in their sacred worship, worshiping the very symbols and eventually even turning them into magic. In doing so they associated themselves with the devilish mob in hell, so they completely destroyed the ancient church in themselves.

That is why Egyptians in the Word symbolize the church's knowledge perverted, and also falsity opposed to the church's truth.

[2] Once the worship of God had been corrupted this way in Egypt, the people there were no longer allowed to worship Jehovah either, or in the end even to know that Jehovah was the God of the ancient church. This was in order to prevent them from profaning Jehovah's name.

Jehovah's name was indeed known at that time, before it was declared anew to Abraham's descendants through Moses on Mount Horeb [Exodus 3:15]. This is plainly evident from the fact that Balaam, who was from Syria, not only knew Jehovah but also worshiped him and sacrificed to him (Numbers 22, 23, 24).

This discussion now shows why Pharaoh said, "Who is Jehovah, that I should listen to his voice, to send the people away? I do not know Jehovah."

[3] However, since Pharaoh represents spirits in the hells who are devoted to falsity and who harass people of the spiritual church, something needs to be said about them.

Most of the spirits in the hells who harass people of the spiritual church are of the type who said [when they lived in the world] that faith by itself brings salvation but who nevertheless lived a life contrary to faith. After our body dies, our life remains the same, so the evil these spirits conceived, plotted, and carried out remains. To defend their wicked lives, then, they take what they had claimed were the tenets of faith and either adapt them or totally reject them.

The true tenets of faith are taken away from them, though, to prevent them from misusing them, and once they have been deprived of religious truth, they seize on falsity that directly contradicts it. This falsity they then use to persecute people in possession of truth, and such persecution becomes the core pleasure of their life. Many of them proceed to learn magic in order to gain power. That is the course of people who had deceived their neighbor by using various tricks they dreamed up in the world and who were led by their success to credit everything afterward to their own shrewdness.

[4] People who have developed this kind of attitude acknowledge the Father, the creator of the universe, but they do not acknowledge the Lord. Of the Lord they say what Pharaoh says here of Jehovah: "Who is Jehovah? I do not know Jehovah." Just as the atmosphere of heaven is permeated

throughout with acknowledgment of and love for the Lord, so the atmosphere of the hells is permeated throughout with denial of and hatred for the Lord. The inhabitants cannot bear to hear his name.

These spirits of hell by their very nature are incapable of being stopped by warnings and threats, so strong is the pleasure they take in life from tormenting the upright and turning them aside from acknowledgment of the Lord and faith in him. This central pleasure of theirs only grows when they receive a warning to stop, because it leads them to believe that the people they are molesting will soon meet their doom.

These now are the people meant specifically by Pharaoh and the Egyptians.

And will not send Israel away, either means that neither will they end their harassment. This can be seen from remarks above at §§7092, 7096. 7098

And they said, "The God of the Hebrews has met us," means that the God himself of the church has issued a demand. This can be seen from the symbolism of *Hebrews* as the people of the church (discussed in §§6675, 6684, 6738) and from that of *meeting* as issuing a demand (discussed in §6903). 7099

Please let us go a journey of three days into the wilderness means for them to be in a state entirely separate from falsity, even though their sight of faith is dim. See §6904, where the same words occur. 7100

And let us sacrifice to Jehovah our God means so they can worship the Lord. See §6905, where (again) the same words occur. 7101

To keep him from falling on us with contagion and sword means in order to escape being damned by evil and falsity, as the following shows: *To keep him from falling on us* means to keep people from bringing (damnation) on themselves. *Contagion* symbolizes damnation by evil, as discussed below. And a *sword* symbolizes the devastation of truth, and punishment for falsity, as discussed at §2799, so it too symbolizes damnation. To be punished for falsity after being stripped of truth is damnation. 7102

[2] The Word mentions four kinds of devastation and punishment: sword, famine, the evil wild animal, and contagion. A *sword* symbolizes being stripped of truth and punished for falsity. *Famine* symbolizes being stripped of what is good and punished for evil. An *evil wild animal* symbolizes being punished for the evil that rises out of falsity. *Contagion* symbolizes being punished for the evil that rises not out of falsity but out of evil. As these symbolize punishment, they symbolize damnation, because damnation is the punishment of people who have held fast to an evil course.

Here is what Ezekiel says about these four types of punishment:

> When I send *my four evil judgments*—the *sword* and *famine* and the *evil wild animal* and *contagion*—on Jerusalem, to cut human and animal off from it, . . . (Ezekiel 14:21)

In the same author:

> I will send *famine* on you, and the *evil wild animal,* and I will leave you bereft, and *contagion* and blood will pass through you; the *sword* especially I will bring on you. (Ezekiel 5:17)

[3] The symbolism of contagion as being punished for and damned by evil is clear from the following passages. In Ezekiel:

> Those who are in the wastelands will *die by the sword,* and those who are on the face of the field I will give to the *wild animal* to devour them, and those who are in strongholds and caverns will *die by contagion.* (Ezekiel 33:27)

Dying by the sword in the wastelands stands for being purged of truth and therefore damned by falsity. Giving those on the face of the field to the wild animal for devouring stands for the damnation of people immersed in the evil that comes of falsity. The death by contagion of those in strongholds and caverns stands for being damned by evil that fortifies itself with falsity. [4] In the same author:

> The *sword outside,* and *contagion* and *famine inside!* Those who are in the field will *die by the sword,* but those who are in the city—*famine* and *contagion* will consume them. (Ezekiel 7:15)

The sword stands for being stripped of truth and damned by falsity. The famine and contagion stand for being stripped of goodness and damned by evil. The sword is said to be outside and the famine and contagion inside because truth is stripped off the surface but goodness is stripped away within. When people live by falsity, though, their damnation is symbolized by "those in the field will die by the sword"; and when they live lives of evil that they defend with falsity, their damnation is symbolized by "those in the city—famine and contagion will consume them." [5] In Leviticus:

> *I will bring on you a sword* exacting the vengeance in the pact. Wherever you gather into your cities, *I will send contagion into your midst* and

> deliver you into the hand of the foe, while I break the staff of bread for you. (Leviticus 26:25, 26)

Here too the sword stands for being purged of truth and damned by falsity. The contagion stands for being damned by evil. The famine, depicted as a threat to break the staff of bread for the people, symbolizes the stripping away of goodness. The cities into which they gathered, like the city mentioned above, symbolize falsity that they use to defend evil. For the meaning of cities as truth and in a negative sense as falsity, see §§402, 2268, 2712, 2943, 3216, 4492, 4493. [6] In Ezekiel:

> Because you have defiled my sanctuary with all your abominations, a third of you will *die of contagion* and be consumed [by *famine*] in your midst. Then a third will *fall to the sword* around you. Finally, a third I will scatter to every wind, so much so that I *unsheathe a sword* after them. (Ezekiel 5:11, 12)

The [contagion and] famine stand for being damned by evil, the sword for being damned by falsity. Scattering them to every wind and unsheathing a sword after them stand for dispersing truth and seizing on falsity. [7] In Jeremiah:

> If they offer burnt offering or minha, I will not be favoring those things, but with *sword, famine,* and *contagion* I myself will *consume them.* (Jeremiah 14:12)

In the same author:

> I will strike the residents of this city, both human and animal; *by great contagion they will die.* Afterward I will deliver Zedekiah, king of Judah, and his servants and the people and the survivors in this city *from the contagion* and *from the sword* and *from the famine* into the hand of Nebuchadnezzar. Those who remain in this city will die *by the sword* and *by famine* and *by contagion.* But those who go out and defect to the Chaldeans besieging you will live, and their soul will become spoils. (Jeremiah 21:6, 7, 9)

In the same author:

> I will send against them *sword, famine,* and *contagion,* until they are consumed from the earth. (Jeremiah 24:10)

Once more the sword symbolizes a stripping away of truth; the famine, a stripping away of goodness; and the contagion, damnation. In addition, sword, famine, and contagion have this symbolism in the following passages: Jeremiah 27:8; 29:17, 18; 32:24, 36; 34:17; 38:2; 42:17, 22; 44:13; Ezekiel 12:16.

[8] Since these three follow one another in order, they were the options the prophet Gad presented to David. That is to say:

> Whether seven years of *famine* should come, whether for three months he should flee before his foes, or whether there should be three days of *contagion* in the land. (2 Samuel 24:13)

Fleeing before his foes takes the place of the sword here.

In Amos:

> *I sent contagion among you* as in Egypt; with the *sword* I killed your young men, along with your captured horses. (Amos 4:10)

Contagion as in Egypt stands for a stripping away of goodness through falsity (the use of falsity being what "as in Egypt" refers to). The killing by sword of the young men along with the captured horses stands for a stripping away of truth. Young men symbolize truth; and horses symbolize intellectual traits (§§2761, 2762, 3217, 5321, 6534). [9] In Ezekiel:

> *Contagion* and *blood* will pass through you. (Ezekiel 5:17)

In the same author:

> I will send against it *contagion* and *blood* in its streets. (Ezekiel 28:23)

In this case the contagion stands for goodness that has been adulterated, and the blood for truth that has been rendered false. For the meaning of blood as truth rendered false, see §§4735, 6978. [10] In David:

> You will not be afraid of the horror at night, of the arrow [that] flies by day, *of contagion* that creeps in the dark, of death [that] ravages at midday. (Psalms 91:5, 6)

The horror at night stands for falsity that is hidden. The arrow [that] flies by day stands for falsity out in the open. Contagion that creeps in the dark stands for evil that is hidden. Death [that] ravages at midday stands for evil out in the open. Clearly the contagion means evil and the damnation that evil brings because it is called death. All that distinguishes death from contagion here is the description of death as ravaging at midday and of contagion as creeping in the dark. In the same author:

> He straightened out a path for his anger, he did not withhold their soul from death, and their life he closed with *contagion.* (Psalms 78:50)

This is about Egyptians. The contagion stands for evil of every kind and the damnation it brings.

And the king of Egypt said to them symbolizes the response from peo- **7103**
ple committed to falsity, as the following shows: *Saying,* when Pharaoh addresses Moses and Aaron, symbolizes negative thinking, as above at §7094, so it symbolizes a thought in response. And Pharaoh, or the *king of Egypt,* represents falsity in the form of knowledge, as discussed in §§6651, 6679, 6683, 6692, so he represents people who subscribe to falsity.

Moses and Aaron, why do you distract the people from their work? means **7104**
that their divine law and teachings will not exempt them from heavy loads, as the following shows: *Moses* represents the Lord in regard to divine law, as dealt with in §§6723, 6752. *Aaron* represents the Lord in regard to teachings based on that law, as dealt with in §§6998, 7009. *Distracting* means exempting. And *work* symbolizes a heavy load, because the people's work consisted of labors and burdens (as below) and therefore of heavy loads as a result of the combat symbolized on an inner level by the work and burdens.

Go to your burdens! means that they must live lives of combat. This **7105**
can be seen from the symbolism of *going* as living (discussed in §§3335, 4882, 5493, 5605) and from that of *burdens* as onslaughts of falsity (discussed at §6757) and therefore as combat against falsity.

Exodus 5:5, 6, 7, 8, 9. *And Pharaoh said, "Here, the people of the land* **7106**
are now many, and you have made them cease from their burdens." And Pharaoh on that day commanded the taskmasters over the people and their managers, saying, "You must no longer give straw to the people to make bricks, as yesterday and the day before; they themselves must go and are to gather straw for themselves. And the quota of bricks that they were making yesterday and the day before you must lay on them; you must not take away from it, because they are lazy. That is why they cry out, saying, 'Let us go sacrifice to our God!' Let the weight of their servitude be increased on the men, and have them do it and not look to lying words."

And Pharaoh said, symbolizes what the spirits attacking the church's truth want. *Here, the people of the land are now many* symbolizes the large number of people in the spiritual church. *And you have made them cease from their burdens* means that they had not persecuted them enough. *And Pharaoh on that day commanded* symbolizes a desire to attack the church's truth during that state. *The taskmasters over the people and their managers, saying,* symbolizes the people who most directly inflict persecution and their most immediate victims. *You must no longer give straw to the people* symbolizes concepts on the lowest level, the most general concepts of all. *To make bricks* means for the fabrications and falsities that will be put in. *As yesterday and the day before* means in a change from the previous state. *They themselves must go and are to gather straw for themselves* means for them to acquire those lowliest concepts for themselves. *And the quota of bricks that they were making yesterday and the day before you must lay on them* means that they were to put in as many fabrications and falsities as before. *You must not take away from it* means without reduction. *Because they are lazy* means that they are not sufficiently beaten down. *That is why they cry out, saying, "Let us go sacrifice to our God!"* means that this is the cause of such grand thoughts about such [contemptible] worship. *Let the weight of their servitude be increased on the men* means that the assault is to intensify. *And have them do it* means to make it happen. *And not look to lying words* means to keep them from resorting to the truth.

7107 *And Pharaoh said,* symbolizes what the spirits attacking the church's truth want, as the following shows: *Saying* symbolizes what a person wants, as discussed below. And *Pharaoh* represents spirits who attack the church's truth (treated of in §§6651, 6679, 6683) and therefore who attack people in the spiritual church, since these in a sense possess the church's truth. The reason *saying* means wanting, or what a person wants, is that it involves the words that come after; when we want something, we put it into words.

Since "she says" or "he says" involves the words that come after, it symbolizes various things, such as a command (§7036), an urgent message (5012, 7033, 7090), communication (3060, 4131, 6228), thinking (7094), and in its proper sense, a perception (1791, 1815, 1819, 1822, 1898, 1919, 2080, 2862, 3509, 5687).

7108 *Here, the people of the land are now many* symbolizes the large number of people in the spiritual church. This is established by the symbolism of the *people of the land* as people of the spiritual church, as treated of at §2928. After all, a *people* symbolizes those dedicated to faith and its truth (§§1259, 1260, 3581), and the *land* symbolizes the church (§§662, 1066, 1068, 1262, 1733, 1850, 2117, 2118 at the end, 3355, 4447, 4535, 5577).

And you have made them cease from their burdens means that they had not persecuted them enough. This can be seen from the symbolism of *burdens* as times of being persecuted by falsity and therefore as times of combat, as discussed in §§6757, 7104, 7105. *Making them cease* from their burdens, then, means that they had not persecuted them enough. 7109

And Pharaoh on that day commanded symbolizes a desire to attack the church's truth during that state, as the following shows. *Commanding* symbolizes a demand, and because a desire to do harm lurks within the demands of the evil (since it is the source of those demands), *he commanded* also symbolizes that desire. *Pharaoh* represents spirits who attack the church's truth, as mentioned in §§6651, 6679, 6683. And a *day* symbolizes a state, as discussed in §§23, 487, 488, 493, 893, 2788, 3462, 3785, 4850. 7110

The taskmasters over the people and their managers, saying, symbolizes the people who most directly inflict persecution and their most immediate victims, as the following shows: *Taskmasters* symbolize individuals who enslave others, as discussed at §6852, and since they enslave others by persecuting them, taskmasters also symbolize people who inflict persecution. However, they symbolize the ones who most directly inflict persecution, as discussed below. And *managers* symbolize their most immediate victims. The managers were from among the children of Israel, but the taskmasters were from among the Egyptians, as subsequent verses show. In an inner sense, then, managers mean the most immediate victims, and taskmasters mean those who most directly persecute them. 7111

[2] Who they are can be seen from those spirits in the other life that inflict persecution and introduce falsity and evil and from those that receive all this and pass it along. The persecutors who introduce falsity and evil are the hells, but to achieve their goals they send out some of their number as emissaries through whom they can act. The emissaries show up not far from their victims. The point of this is to bring to a focus the thoughts and intentions of many spirits, which would otherwise be diffused. These emissaries show up in certain places assigned to them in the world of spirits, and the locations where they appear indicate which hell they come from. Some appear overhead at various distances and angles; some show up next to the head on the right or left or in back; some can be seen below the head on a level with various parts of the body from head to toe. They bring with them the spewings that flow in from hell. As far as the spirits or people on earth [who are being targeted] can sense or tell, it is all happening inside themselves; that is, they believe the thoughts and intentions are their own.

These emissaries are called delegates, and an earlier description of them from personal experience may be seen at §§4403, 5856, 5983–5989. Because they most directly inflict the persecution, they are symbolized by the taskmasters.

The spirits who receive the persecution from them and pass it along, though, are the managers, and they are go-betweens. As mentioned just above, the managers were from among the children of Israel, but the taskmasters were from among the Egyptians.

[3] "Managers" was the name for those among the people of Israel and Judah who would say what to do and give commands. They would therefore sit in with the judges and elders in the gates and report to the people the judges' decisions and the decrees of the leader. The following passages illustrate this. In Moses:

> Judges and *managers* you shall put in all your gates, according to your tribes, who shall judge the people with righteous judgment. (Deuteronomy 16:18)

In the same author:

> When they go out to war, the priest shall speak to the people and admonish them not to be afraid. Then the *managers shall say* that anyone who has built a house should return, as should the fearful. (Deuteronomy 20:1, 2, 3, 5, 8, 9)

In Joshua:

> Joshua commanded the *managers to say to the people* to get provisions ready before they crossed the Jordan. (Joshua 1:10, 11)

In the same author:

> At the end of three days it happened that the *managers* passed through the middle of the camp and *commanded* that when [the people] saw the ark of Jehovah's covenant, they too should set out. (Joshua 3:2, 3)

As rulers of the people, managers were distinct from the people's chieftains (see Deuteronomy 1:15), from the elders (Deuteronomy 31:28), and from the judges (Joshua 8:33).

7112 *You must no longer give straw to the people* symbolizes concepts on the lowest level, the most general concepts of all. This is evident from the symbolism of *straw* or hay as truth in the form of knowledge (discussed at §3114) and indeed concepts on the lowest level, the most general of all.

The food that is lowliest in a spiritual sense is hay or straw, because it is for animals.

Concepts that are full of sensory illusions are the ones I am describing as being on the lowest level. They are concepts that the evil misuse to corrupt what is good and true and in the process promote what is evil and false. Because of the illusions involved, you see, such concepts can be twisted to favor false principles and evil cravings. The same concepts are also the most general concepts of all, which are capable of supporting falsity and evil unless they are filled in with less general truth and even detailed truth. The more they are filled in with truth, the less they support falsity and evil.

These concepts are what are used for harassment of the upright in the other life by people who in the world championed faith alone but lived an evil life. However, angels dispel such ideas, which is why the text now says that straw was no longer to be given to make bricks; that is, these spirits would not add such concepts to the fabrications and falsities they would introduce.

[2] As an inner meaning of the current clause, this interpretation admittedly seems remote from the literal meaning. Keep in mind, though, that there is nothing in the physical world that does not correspond to some attribute of the spiritual world; and everything that we understand in earthly terms, the angels with us understand in spiritual terms. They do not know what straw is or what bricks are. They knew about them when they lived in the world but forgot them on arrival in heaven because in heaven they put on a spiritual frame of mind. That is why, when angels discern the images of such things in our minds, they turn them into the corresponding spiritual qualities.

The meaning of straw or grass as lowest-level concepts and of bricks as fabrications and falsities can be seen from much evidence. That is the precise meaning of plant matter [§§59, 75, 91, 5201, 6767] and of anything relating to straw [3114, 3146, 5495], while seeds, barley, wheat, and similar substances stand for inner truth and goodness [29, 3332, 3941, 5212, 6139, 6154, 6158]; and stones, because they are not fabricated, stand for truth [1296, 1298].

To make bricks means for the fabrications and falsities that will be put in. This can be seen from the symbolism of *making bricks* as fabricating falsities, which is discussed in §§1296, 6669. 7113

In the literal, narrative meaning, the children of Israel made bricks, so it is as if they invented the falsities themselves, but in the inner meaning the symbolism is that spirits of hell subscribing to those falsities introduced them. As was said earlier [§§7090, 7111], the falsities seem to belong to the person subjected to them, so the literal meaning accords with appearances; but the inner meaning explains it. The literal meaning is rife with such appearances; see §§5094, 6400, 6948.

7114 *As yesterday and the day before* means in a change from the previous state. This can be seen from the symbolism of *yesterday and the day before* as the past, which is noted at §6983. And since all periods of time symbolize states (§§2625, 2788, 2837, 3254, 3356, 4814, 4882, 4901, 4916), *yesterday and the day before* symbolizes the previous state.

7115 *They themselves must go and are to gather straw for themselves* means for them to acquire those lowliest concepts for themselves. This is clear from the symbolism of *gathering* as acquiring and from that of *straw* as the lowliest concepts (discussed just above at §7112).

7116 *And the quota of bricks that they were making yesterday and the day before you must lay on them* means that they were to put in as many fabrications and falsities as in the previous state, as the following shows: A *quota* means an amount, and in this case, the same amount. *Bricks* symbolize fabrications and falsities, as mentioned just above at §7113. *Yesterday and the day before* symbolizes the previous state, as also discussed just above, at §7114. And *laying it on them* means putting them in, since it has to do with the fabrications and falsities.

These comments show that *the quota of bricks that they were making yesterday and the day before you must lay on them* means that they were to put in as many fabrications and falsities as in the previous state.

7117 *You must not take away from it* means without reduction, as is self-evident.

7118 *Because they are lazy* means that they are not sufficiently beaten down. This can be seen from the symbolism of being *lazy* as not being sufficiently overrun with falsity and therefore not being sufficiently beaten down.

How this matter stands can again be gleaned from people in the other life who are being troubled by falsity. The spirits who trouble them work as hard as they can to prevent the upright spirits they are besieging from thinking about the Lord. As soon as the slightest conscious thought of the Lord slips into the mind of the upright, the spirits immediately take it away, which they know how to do very well.

However, thoughts about the Lord still dominate the minds of the people under attack and are therefore too deep to come out in the open, since they flow in through heaven. As soon as these people are not being attacked, then, they start thinking about the Lord. Anything that flows into us from heaven and reigns supreme in us reveals itself whenever it has the freedom to do so.

This discussion clarifies the inner meaning of the current words: "because they are lazy; that is why they cry out, saying, 'Let us go sacrifice to our God!'"

That is why they cry out, saying, "Let us go sacrifice to our God!" means 7119
that this is the cause of such grand thoughts about such [contemptible] worship, as the following shows: *Crying out* symbolizes thought in this case. Saying and speaking symbolize thoughts (§§2271, 2287, 7094), so crying out does too, only it symbolizes forceful thoughts accompanied by a full intent to act, which is why I am describing them as such grand thoughts. *Sacrificing to our God* symbolizes worship of the Lord, as discussed in §§6905, 7101. It is described as such [contemptible] worship, though, because Pharaoh said he did not know Jehovah (7095, 7097), because Egyptians loathed sacrifice (1343), and because Moses said they would go a journey of three days into the wilderness (6904, 7100).

Let the weight of their servitude be increased on the men means that the 7120
assault is to intensify, as the following shows: *Increasing in weight* means growing in intensity. When *servitude* is mentioned by people who inflict falsity on others, it symbolizes an intent to subdue them, as discussed in §§6666, 6670, 6671. So it symbolizes an assault, since it is by assaulting their victims that they intend to subdue them. And *men* symbolize people of the spiritual church. There are two words in the original language that mean "person." One is *adam* and the other is *enosh.* A person called *adam* means a person whose religion is heavenly, but a person called *enosh* means a person whose religion is spiritual. The idea of "men" is expressed as *enosh* here because the text is talking about people of the spiritual church.

And have them do it means to make it happen, as is self-evident. 7121

And not look to lying words means to keep them from resorting to the 7122
truth. This can be seen from the symbolism of *looking to* as resorting to and from that of *lying words,* when mentioned by believers in falsity, as truth. People who believe in falsity, being perverse, refer to truth as falsity (and therefore as lying words) and to falsity as truth.

The inner meaning of these verses has now described the onslaught of falsity to which the upright in the other life can be subjected and has explained the way in which they are persecuted.

The purpose for which the onslaught is allowed is the removal of falsity and introduction of truth, which could never happen if these people were not attacked. After death, everything we thought in the world, everything we intended or wished or said or did, clings to us and remains in our [inner and outer] levels of memory. Nothing is erased. On the point that these experiences are imprinted on our [two] levels of memory—especially our inner memory, which is the memory proper to our spirit—see §§2469, 2470, 2474, 2475. This being the case, grime and filth and also evil and falsity from our life in the world inevitably cling and cause the truth we learned and the good qualities we adopted to hide, because truth and goodness cannot emerge among them. [2] As a consequence, before truth and goodness can show themselves and bring us into company with heaven's inhabitants, the evil and falsity have to unmask themselves so that we can see and recognize them and in this way learn what is true and good.

This change cannot possibly occur without a fight against the evil and falsity in us. The fight is a real one: evil spirits stir up falsity and evil, and angels pardon it if our motive is good, and instill truth. We perceive this fight as taking place inside us, just the way we perceive our spiritual trials, which feel exactly as though they happen inside us, even though they are battles between angels and evil spirits outside us. On this subject, see §§3927, 4249, 4307, 5036, 6657.

Much experience has taught me for certain that this is how matters stand.

The intent of this discussion has been to show why people of the spiritual church are harassed by falsity—this harassment being the theme in the inner meaning of the current verses so far and in what follows.

7123 Exodus 5:10, 11, 12, 13. *And the people's taskmasters went out, as did their managers, and said to the people, saying, "This is what Pharaoh has said: 'I am not giving you any straw. You yourselves, go take yourselves straw from wherever you find it, because nothing will be taken away from your [required] servitude at all.'" And the people scattered out into all the land of Egypt to gather stubble for straw. And the taskmasters were exerting pressure, saying, "Complete your work—the matter of a day in its day—as when there was straw."*

And the people's taskmasters went out, as did their managers symbolizes the sending out and presence of the spirits who most directly inflict persecution and of their most immediate victims. *And said to the people, saying,* symbolizes a perception. *This is what Pharaoh has said* means about the persecution. *I am not giving you any straw* means that these spirits will no longer supply the extremely general concepts. *You yourselves, go take yourselves straw from wherever you find it* means that the victims should acquire them anywhere else they could. *Because nothing will be taken away from your [required] servitude at all* symbolizes the putting in of falsities without any reduction in amount. *And the people scattered out into all the land of Egypt* means that they sent their earthly mind out in all directions. *To gather stubble for straw* means in order to find any truth in the form of knowledge. *And the taskmasters were exerting pressure* means that the ones most directly inflicting persecution insisted. *Saying, "Complete your work—the matter of a day in its day,"* means on their supporting so-called falsity in every state. *As when there was straw* means just as they had supported their so-called truth.

And the people's taskmasters went out, as did their managers symbolizes 7124
the sending out and presence of the spirits who most directly inflict persecution and of their most immediate victims, as the following shows: *Going out* symbolizes being sent out, because the spirits symbolized by the taskmasters are sent out to serve as a means of communication. This can be seen from the remarks above at §7111. Going out also means making oneself present to another in a form adapted to that other (see §5337), so it symbolizes presence as well. *Taskmasters* symbolize the spirits who most directly inflict persecution. And *managers* symbolize the ones who most directly receive the persecution and pass it along, as discussed in §7111.

And said to the people, saying, symbolizes a perception. This is evident 7125
from the symbolism in the Word's narratives of *saying* as a perception, as discussed in §§1791, 1815, 1819, 1822, 1898, 1919, 2080, 2862, 3509, 5687.

This is what Pharaoh has said means about the persecution. This is 7126
evident from the representation of *Pharaoh* as spirits who persecute those whose religion is spiritual (discussed a number of times before) and accordingly as persecution.

I am not giving you any straw means that these spirits will no longer 7127
supply the [extremely] general concepts. This can be seen from the symbolism of *not giving any* as no longer supplying and from that of *straw* as the most general concepts of all (discussed at §7112).

I described this situation above [§§7112, 7115], but I need to explain further. Who are the people in the other life who foist straw—or the most general concepts of all—on the upright people they persecute? The main ones are those in the church who convinced themselves that faith alone brings salvation but who lived a life of evil rather than a life of religion. There they continue to be what they had been here: skilled at arguing for faith alone, which they claim saves us no matter how we had lived. Their proofs, though, are mere rationalizations harmonizing with a foregone conclusion. Anything, even the greatest falsity, can be proved logically and can be presented to the uneducated as truth through the arts of elocution and argumentation. [2] Their primary means to this end are the most general concepts of all from the Word which, without its inner meaning, can be manipulated to favor any opinion whatever.

That is what they foist on people of the spiritual church, and it is what they use to persecute those people. Still, it is nothing but straw or hay for making bricks. The truly essential element, which is neighborly love, they leave out. They do say that deeds of charity are the fruits of faith, but they dismiss them as worthless and make the case that no matter what kind of life we have lived, we are saved by faith alone, even in the last hour of life. So they maintain that we are saved by faith without its fruits and therefore without a life of faith and neighborly love.

[3] When the upright are confronted with such assertions in the other world, they have arguments they can use to defend themselves in the fight, however long it lasts. After all, they can see that the line of reasoning is wrong when the essential ingredient of neighborly love is left out in this fashion and when they see that their opponents do not care about how to live. Everything in the other world shows them all this as clear as day.

This then is what is meant by concepts on the lowest level, the most general concepts of all, and it is symbolized by straw.

People who persuaded themselves that faith alone brings salvation but lived a wicked life are in a fairly deep hell off to the right and out in front a little. I have heard them harassing the upright from there with their reasoning, but the upright, led by the Lord through angels, have rejected the arguments as hollow. They have also uncovered the errors lurking within the confirmations and proofs drawn from the general statements of the Word.

7128 *You yourselves, go take yourselves straw from wherever you find it* means that the victims should acquire them anywhere else they could. This can be seen from the symbolism of *taking from wherever they found it* as acquiring them anywhere else they could, and from the symbolism of *straw* as concepts on the lowest level, the most general concepts of all (discussed at §7112 and directly above at §7127).

7129 *Because nothing will be taken away from your [required] servitude at all* symbolizes the putting in of falsities without any reduction in amount. This can be seen from the symbolism of *nothing at all being taken away,* which means without reduction, and from that of *servitude* as an assault by falsity (discussed above at §7120) and therefore also as harassment.

And the people scattered out into all the land of Egypt means that they sent their earthly mind out in all directions. This can be seen from the symbolism of *scattering out* as sending out and from that of the *land of Egypt* as the earthly mind (discussed in §§5276, 5278, 5280, 5288, 5301). 7130

A person has two minds. One is the earthly mind, the other is the rational mind. The earthly mind belongs to the outer self, while the rational mind belongs to the inner self. The contents of the earthly mind are called knowledge, while the contents of the rational mind are called the reasoning of the intellect. Another distinction between them is that the contents of the earthly mind stand mostly in the world's light, which is called physical illumination, but the contents of the rational mind stand in heaven's light, which is spiritual light.

To gather stubble for straw means in order to find any truth in the form of knowledge. This can be seen from the symbolism of *stubble for straw* as truth in the form of knowledge. Stubble is the kind of truth that is suited to the knowledge symbolized by straw. The reason this kind of truth is meant by stubble is that it is a stalk topped by seed, and seeds in the Word symbolize truth and goodness. The stalk under the seeds, then, symbolizes a general holder for truth, so it symbolizes truth in the form of knowledge. Concepts about faith and neighborly love are indeed truths, but general truths, and are therefore vessels for holding specific and detailed truths. Anyone can see this. It is a truth in the form of knowledge, for example, that charity for one's neighbor is an essential component of religion, that faith can exist only where there is neighborly love, that truth and goodness can be united but not truth and evil nor goodness and falsity, besides many other similar ideas that are truths in the form of knowledge. Plainly they can be filled in with countless other truths, since whole volumes can be written about them without exhausting the details, which are the inner truths of faith. After all, these detailed truths are visible only in heaven's light and are incompatible with earthly words. The case is the same for these truths as for neighborly love, which is a spiritual desire that is for the most part inexpressible in words. All that can be verbalized is its broadest outlines, or that part which wears earthly clothing and can be compared to different features of the world. 7131

The purpose of these remarks has been to show what general concepts are.

7132 *And the taskmasters were exerting pressure* means that the ones most directly inflicting persecution insisted. This can be seen from the symbolism of *taskmasters* as the people who most directly inflict persecution (discussed at §7111) and from that of *exerting pressure* as insisting.

7133 *Saying, "Complete your work—the matter of a day in its day,"* means on their supporting so-called falsity in every state, as the following shows: *Completing your work* means supporting falsity. Making bricks symbolizes fabrications and falsities that are put in (see §7113), and since this is the work the people were to complete, it means [insisting] that they support the fabrications and falsities. I describe the falsities as so-called because the wicked people speaking do not acknowledge falsity as false but call it true. And the *matter of a day in its day* means in every state. For the meaning of a day as a state, see §§23, 487, 488, 493, 893, 2788, 3462, 3785, 4850.

7134 *As when there was straw* means just as they had supported their so-called truth. This is established by the symbolism of *straw* as general concepts, which are containers for truth, as discussed in §§7112, 7131. I describe the truth as so-called because the words are those of wicked people, who do not acknowledge truth as true.

7135 Exodus 5:14, 15, 16, 17, 18. *And there were beatings for the managers of the children of Israel, whom Pharaoh's taskmasters put over them, saying, "Why don't you complete your assignment to make bricks both yesterday and today as you did yesterday and the day before?" And the managers of the children of Israel came and cried out to Pharaoh, saying, "Why do you do this to your servants? No straw is given to your servants, and 'Make bricks,' they say to us, and here, your servants are beaten and your people has sinned." And he said, "Lazy you are, lazy! That is why you say, 'Let us go sacrifice to Jehovah.' And now go serve, and straw will not be given to you, and you must yield the quota of bricks."*

And there were beatings for the managers of the children of Israel means that the people who most directly received the persecution and passed it along were harmed by the falsities that were introduced. *Whom Pharaoh's taskmasters put over them* symbolizes spirits brought in by the persecutors. *Saying, "Why don't you complete your assignment to make bricks?"* means that they are not receiving and passing along the falsities that were introduced, as they had been charged to do. *As you did yesterday and the day before* means as in the previous state. *Both yesterday and today* symbolizes the state that will exist from then on. *And the managers of the children of Israel came* symbolizes the people who most directly received and passed along [the harassment]. *And cried out to Pharaoh* symbolizes outrage registered with the persecutors. *Saying, "Why do you do this to your servants?"* means that thus they could not carry out the duty laid on them. *No straw is given to your servants* means that concepts containing truth are no longer being supplied. *And "Make bricks," they say to us* means that they still have to endure the introduced falsities. *And here, your servants are beaten* means that the falsities are therefore hurting them. *And your people has sinned* means that [the persecutors] were consequently guilty of doing evil. *And he said,* symbolizes an answer. *Lazy you are, lazy!* means that they have not been beaten down enough. *That is why you say, "Let us go sacrifice to Jehovah,"* means that this is why they think about such [contemptible] worship. *And now go serve* symbolizes ongoing harassment. *And straw will not be given to you* means without such concepts. *And you must yield the quota of bricks* symbolizes falsities that must be introduced in full measure.

And there were beatings for the managers of the children of Israel means 7136
that the people who most directly received the persecution and passed it along were harmed by the falsities that were introduced, as the following shows: The *beatings,* because they were administered by the taskmasters, who meant the persecutors, symbolize harm done by falsities. Being beaten in a spiritual sense does not mean being beaten but suffering harm to the truth and goodness we possess, that is, to what constitutes our spiritual life. It is like the word *die,* which in a spiritual sense does not mean to die but to be deprived of truth and goodness, to wallow in falsity and evil, and so to be damned. And the *managers* symbolize the people who most directly receive persecution and pass it along, as discussed at §7111. And the *children of Israel* represent people of the spiritual church (as discussed in §§6426, 6637), with whom the people symbolized by the managers communicated.

Whom Pharaoh's taskmasters put over them symbolizes spirits brought 7137
in by the persecutors, as the following shows: *Putting [the managers] over them,* since it is accomplished by bringing in spirits (as discussed below), symbolizes this process. And the *taskmasters* symbolize spirits who inflict persecution, as discussed at §7111.

What the situation in all this is cannot be known except from experience with such happenings in the other world.

I said above that the taskmasters symbolize the spirits who most directly inflict persecution, while the managers symbolize those who most directly receive the persecution and pass it along (see §7111). The people who most directly receive and communicate it are simple, upright spirits, whose main function this is. The persecutors, using techniques known only in the other life, put these spirits into a community with which they are establishing communication. (The spirits who do this are those who inflict persecution and who are symbolized by the taskmasters.) As a result, the hells have a means of communication on their side, and so do the victims of the persecution on theirs.

The fact that this is how it works I have seen and experienced hundreds of times, if not a thousand.

This information shows that the inner-level symbolism of the current phrase cannot be known except from experience with such happenings in the other world.

7138 *Saying, "Why don't you complete your assignment to make bricks?"* means that they are not receiving and passing along the falsities that were introduced, as they had been charged to do, as the following shows: The managers to whom these words are addressed symbolize the spirits who most directly receive and pass along [falsities], as discussed at §7111. *Completing the assignment* symbolizes doing as one has been charged to do. And *making bricks* symbolizes receiving fabrications and falsities, as mentioned at §7113.

7139 *As you did yesterday and the day before* means as in the previous state. This can be seen from the discussion in §§6983, 7114 of the symbolism of *yesterday and the day before* as the previous state.

7140 *Both yesterday and today* symbolizes the state that will exist from then on, as the following shows: *Yesterday* symbolizes the previous state, as directly above. And *today* symbolizes that which never ends, as discussed in §§2838, 3998, 4304, 6165, so it symbolizes something that will last and therefore a future the same as the past.

7141 *And the managers of the children of Israel came* symbolizes the people who most directly received and passed along [the harassment]. This can be seen from the discussion above in §7136 of the symbolism of the *managers of the children of Israel* as those who most directly receive and pass along the harassment.

7142 *And cried out to Pharaoh* symbolizes outrage registered with the persecutors, as the following shows: *Crying out* in this case means registering outrage—outrage that they had been beaten (or hurt by the falsities introduced) and that they were not being given straw to make bricks (or that all they received and introduced were fabrications and falsities). And

Pharaoh represents those who inflict persecution, as dealt with in §§6651, 6679, 6683, 7126.

Saying, "Why do you do this to your servants?" means that thus they could not carry out the duty laid on them. This can be seen from the symbolism of a *servant* as someone who assists and carries out duties. Because such people serve, they are called servants, as happens throughout the Word. (For someone who obeys being called a servant, see §1713, and for the meaning of serving as study, §§3824, 3846.) The words that come next imply that they could not keep up this service, so *why do you do this to your servants?* clearly means that thus they could not carry out the duty laid on them. 7143

No straw is given to your servants means that concepts containing truth are no longer being supplied, as the following shows: *Straw* symbolizes the most general concepts of all, as discussed at §7112. I refer to them as concepts containing truth because general concepts are like containers that can be filled with truth (§§4345, 4383, 5208, 7131). *Not being given* means not being supplied. And *servants* symbolize people who assist and carry out their duties, as discussed directly above at §7143. 7144

And "Make bricks," they say to us means that they still have to endure the introduced falsities. This is evident from the symbolism of *making bricks* as receiving fabrications and falsities introduced by the wicked, as discussed at §7113. Here it means enduring them. 7145

And here, your servants are beaten means that the falsities are therefore hurting them. This can be seen from the symbolism of being *beaten* as being hurt by falsities, as discussed at §7136. 7146

And your people has sinned means that [the persecutors] were consequently guilty of doing evil. This can be seen from the symbolism of *sinning* as becoming guilty of evil, and in view of their guilt, as the fact that they deserved to pay a penalty. 7147

Let me explain the contents of this and the preceding verses in a general way. People in the underground realm are attacked by falsities and evils introduced by the hells surrounding them, the purpose being to remove evil and falsity, instill truth and goodness, and so bring the inhabitants into a state in which they can be taken up into heaven; see §§7090, 7122. Toward the end, though, they are harassed worse than ever, because truth is then taken away from them, and pure falsity is allowed to attack them, till they reach a point of despair. It is part of the divine plan for persecution and times of trial to culminate in despair; see §§1787, 2694, 5279, 5280.

Pharaoh acted the way he did so that the children of Israel could represent this state experienced by people in the spiritual church. What is more, he waited till the persecution was near its end, that is, till the children of Israel were about to be delivered and led to the land of Canaan.

[2] It is important to know how the persecution is conducted. The hells introduce falsity and evil into the spirits' thoughts, while heaven—or rather the Lord through heaven—introduces truth and goodness. This happens because people and spirits do not think on their own; everything flows in. That is not at all how it feels, so it seems unbelievable, but it is still absolutely true. On this subject, see previous reports and explanations from experience in §§2886, 4151, 4249, 5846, 5854, 6189–6215, 6307–6327, 6466–6495, 6598–6626.

From these remarks you can see how to understand the idea that persecution is conducted through the introduction of falsity and that it increases to a point of despair.

7148 *And he said,* symbolizes an answer. This can be seen from the discussion in §7103 of the symbolism of *saying* as an answer.

7149 *Lazy you are, lazy!* means that they have not been beaten down enough. This can be seen from the symbolism of being *lazy* as not being beaten down enough by falsity, as discussed at §7118.

7150 *That is why you say, "Let us go sacrifice to Jehovah,"* means that this is why they think about such [contemptible] worship. This is evident from the remarks above at §7119, where similar words occur.

7151 *And now go serve* symbolizes ongoing harassment. This can be seen from the symbolism of *serving* as being harassed by falsity, which is discussed in §§7120, 7129. *Go serve,* then, means ongoing harassment. They complained about their servitude, but the answer they received was that they were to continue serving.

7152 *And straw will not be given to you* means without such concepts. This can be seen from the symbolism of *straw* as extremely general concepts and therefore as concepts containing truth, as discussed in §§7112, 7144. The fact that the people will be without those concepts is symbolized by *will not be given.*

7153 *And you must yield the quota of bricks* symbolizes falsities that must be introduced in full measure. This can be seen from the discussion above at §7116, where similar words occur.

These now are the contents of the inner meaning for the current set of verses. To a person on earth the details might seem unimportant and random, but all of them are nonetheless essential aspects of the matter at hand and fit together in the most beautiful way. Angels perceive that this is so, because they see the series of ideas and the connections among them in heaven's light. By that light they see the countless secrets involved, formed as they are of inner truth, which produces an overall structure of great beauty and delight. People on earth are completely incapable of seeing it this way, because inner truth is hidden from them, and as a result they cannot piece the parts together. Instead it all looks random to them and therefore, as just mentioned, unimportant.

Exodus 5:19, 20, 21. *And the managers of the children of Israel saw them-* 7154
selves beset by evil, saying, "You must not take away from your [quota of] bricks at all, day by day." And they came across Moses and Aaron standing before them as they went out from Pharaoh. And [the managers] said to them, "Jehovah look on you and judge! For you have made our scent stink in the eyes of Pharaoh and in the eyes of his servants, to put a sword into their hand to kill us."

And the managers of the children of Israel saw themselves beset by evil means that they were close to being damned. *Saying, "You must not take away from your [quota of] bricks at all,"* means because there was to be no reduction in the number of falsities introduced. *Day by day* means in every state. *And they came across Moses and Aaron* symbolizes thoughts about the divine law and about teachings that grow out of it. *Standing before them as they went out from Pharaoh* means that these became visible when falsity was not attacking as strongly. *And [the managers] said to them* symbolizes a perception. *Jehovah look on you and judge!* symbolizes divine arrangements. *For you have made our scent stink in the eyes of Pharaoh and in the eyes of his servants* means that everyone committed to falsity greatly loathes our obedient attitude on account of [the law and its teachings]. *To put a sword into their hand to kill us* means that this is why they burn so ardently to destroy religious truth through falsity.

And the managers of the children of Israel saw themselves beset by evil 7155
means that they were close to being damned, as the following shows: *Seeing* symbolizes a perception, as discussed in §§2150, 3764, 4567, 4723, 5400. The *managers* symbolize the people who most directly receive the persecution and pass it along, as discussed in §§7111, 7136. And *evil* symbolizes damnation, because viewed in itself, evil is hell (§6279) and therefore damnation.

The reason *being beset by evil* means being close to damnation is that the people who most directly received the persecution and passed it along suffered harm (symbolized by the beatings they were given by the taskmasters, §7136) and were persecuted to the point of despair by the constant introduction of falsity (§7147). This is why the clause *they saw themselves beset by evil* means that they sensed they were close to being damned. After all, people who are in despair think they cannot bear to be assaulted any longer, so they imagine they have no choice but to surrender and become captives to falsity. Such is the state of despair. That point, however, is when they start to be lifted up and to be led out of the dark into the light.

7156 *Saying, "You must not take away from your [quota of] bricks at all,"* means because there was to be no reduction in the number of falsities introduced. This can be seen from the symbolism of *not being taken away at all* as no reduction (as also above at §7129) and from that of making *bricks* as enduring the falsities introduced (discussed in §§7113, 7145).

7157 *Day by day* means in every state, as can be seen from the discussion in §7133 of the symbolism of *day by day,* meaning in every state.

7158 *And they came across Moses and Aaron* symbolizes thoughts about the divine law and about teachings that grow out of it, as the following shows: *Coming across* means thinking about, because "they came across them" here means that they happened upon them and spoke with them, which in an inner sense means thinking about the quality they represent. For the meaning of speaking as thinking, see §§2271, 2287, 2619. *Moses* represents the divine law, as discussed at §6752. And *Aaron* represents teachings about goodness and truth, as discussed in §§6998, 7009, 7089.

7159 *Standing before them as they went out from Pharaoh* means that these became visible when falsity was not attacking as strongly. This can be seen from the symbolism of *standing before them* (when the divine law and its teachings are said to do it) as becoming visible and from the symbolism of *going out from Pharaoh* as a time when falsity was not attacking as strongly. For the meaning of Pharaoh as falsity on the attack, see §§7107, 7110, 7126, 7142.

[2] *And [the managers] said to them* symbolizes a perception. This can be seen from the symbolism of *saying* in Scripture narrative as perceiving, as mentioned many times.

7160 *Jehovah look on you and judge!* symbolizes divine arrangements. This is evident from the symbolism of *Jehovah look [on you] and judge* as divine arrangements, because what Jehovah looks on and judges he arranges. *Looking* symbolizes divine perception, or more properly, foresight, while *judging* symbolizes divine management, or more properly, providence. Since that is what the current clause symbolizes on an inner level, it was customary to say, "Jehovah look [on you] and judge!" to someone at fault for something bad that had happened.

For you have made our scent stink in the eyes of Pharaoh and in the eyes of his servants means that everyone committed to falsity greatly loathes our obedient attitude on account of [the law and its teachings], as the following shows: *Making something stink* symbolizes loathing, as discussed below. And a *scent* symbolizes a perception of something pleasing, as discussed in §§925, 1514, 1517, 1518, 1519, 3577, 4626, 4628, 4748. Because a scent symbolizes a perception of something pleasing, it symbolizes a perception of faith and neighborly love, since these perceptions are pleasing (§§1519, 4628, 4748). Since they are pleasing, a scent symbolizes an obedient attitude that is most pleasing, because an attitude of obedience is the core value of faith and neighborly love. That is why the scent here symbolizes obedience. 7161

[2] As a scent means everything that is pleasing to the Lord, a stink means that which is displeasing to the Lord, so it means something loathsome or abhorrent. In fact, a stench actually corresponds to objects of loathing and abhorrence, which are marked by falsity and evil. Because a bad odor means something that is loathed, the Word uses it in expressions of loathing, as in Samuel:

> *Israel became foul smelling* to the Philistines. (1 Samuel 13:4)

In the same author:

> Achish said of David that he had *made himself extremely foul smelling* among his people, in Israel. (1 Samuel 27:12)

In the same author:

> When the children of Ammon saw *that they had become foul smelling* to David, . . . (2 Samuel 10:6)

In the same author:

> Ahithophel told Absalom to let all Israel hear "*that you have become foul smelling* to your father." (2 Samuel 16:21)

In these passages, "foul smelling" stands for what is loathed. In Isaiah:

> Let the stabbing victims among the surrounding nations be thrown out and the *stench of their corpses rise* and the mountains melt with blood. (Isaiah 34:3)

The stench stands for abhorrent evil. Likewise in Amos 4:10 and in David, Psalms 38:4, 5.

[3] *In the eyes of Pharaoh and in the eyes of his servants* means in the perception of everyone committed to falsity, as can be seen from the symbolism of *eyes* as perception (§4339) and from the representation of *Pharaoh* as people committed to falsity (mentioned in §§6651, 6679, 6683, 7107, 7110, 7126, 7142). The reason the scent of the children of Israel is said to reek in the Egyptians' eyes is that everyone devoted to falsity and evil loathes what is good and feels that truth stinks.

[4] The fact that people immersed in evil and therefore in falsity stink is obvious from hells that are called corpselike and hells that are called feces-laden. (The former are populated by assassins and people implacably bent on revenge, the latter by adulterers and people who had set their sights on unclean sensual pleasures.) When these hells open up, they give off unbearable fumes (§4631), but the only individuals who smell the fumes are those who can access the inner depths of their spirit. Inhabitants of those hells sense the odors as pleasant, so they love to live among the fumes (§4628). They are like the creatures that spend their time in dead bodies and excrement, where they find the joy of their lives.

When spirits like this travel outside the realm of those stenches, they find sweet, pleasant smells to be offensive and highly objectionable.

This discussion shows how to understand the idea that people committed to falsity harbor great loathing for points of the divine law and of its teachings, as represented by Moses and Aaron, who are being said to have made the scent of the children of Israel stink in the eyes of Pharaoh and in the eyes of his servants.

7162 *To put a sword into their hand to kill us* means that this is why they burn so ardently to destroy religious truth through falsity, as the following shows: A *sword* symbolizes falsity fighting and inflicting devastation, as discussed in §§2799, 6353, 7102. And *killing* symbolizes destroying all that faith and neighborly love imply, as discussed at §6767. The children of Israel, who the text is saying would be killed, symbolize aspects of faith and neighborly love, because neighborly love and faith are the essentials of the spiritual religion they symbolize (§6637).

7163 Exodus 5:22, 23. *And Moses went back to Jehovah and said, "Lord, why have you done evil to this people? Why is this, [that] you sent me? And ever since I came to Pharaoh to speak in your name, he has done evil to this people, and you have decidedly not delivered your people."*

And Moses went back to Jehovah and said, symbolizes a complaint lodged by the divine law. *Lord, why have you done evil to this people?* means that spirits governed by truth and goodness have been harassed with falsity too much. *Why is this, [that] you sent me?* means even though the law emanating from the Divine seems to decree otherwise. *And ever since I came to Pharaoh to speak in your name* means when statements in the divine law appeared to demand it of spirits caught up in falsity. *He has done evil to this people* means then spirits governed by religious truth and goodness seemed to be injured by the introduction of falsities. *And you have decidedly not delivered your people* means that they were not released from a state of being harassed by falsity.

And Moses went back to Jehovah and said, symbolizes a complaint lodged by the divine law, as the following shows: *Going back to Jehovah* means reporting a complaint to the Divine about the persecution of people intent on truth and goodness, inflicted by people intent on falsity and evil. The symbolism of "going back to Jehovah" as a complaint is clear from what follows. *Moses* represents the divine law, as discussed in §§6723, 6752, 6771, 6827, 7014, so truth in the divine law is what is complaining that people guided by falsity have this kind of control over people guided by truth. **7164**

Lord, why have you done evil to this people? means that spirits governed by truth and goodness have been harassed with falsity too much, as the following shows: *Doing evil* means allowing spirits to be harassed with falsity too much. That is what evildoing is in a spiritual sense when it is said to be inflicted on spirits in possession of truth and goodness. And the children of Israel—the *people* here—represent adherents of a spiritual religion and therefore individuals in possession of the church's truth and of its good qualities, as just above in §7162. **7165**

Why is this, [that] you sent me? means even though the law emanating from the Divine seems to decree otherwise, as the following makes evident: *Why is this?* means, why does this happen when it is decreed otherwise? Moses, who says this about himself, represents the law imparted by the Divine, as mentioned just above at §7164. And *being sent* means emanating, as discussed in §§4710, 6831. So *Why is this, [that] you sent me?* means that the law emanating from the Divine seems to decree otherwise. **7166**

Because this is said in complaint against harassment at the hand of falsity, it appears as though the law imparted by the Divine decreed otherwise, and that is why I say that it seems to decree otherwise, although in reality it does not. The law imparted by the Divine is the ordained law, and the ordained law for people in a state of harassment at the hand of falsity is that they will be plagued to the point of despair. Unless they reach the point of despair, the infestation fails to achieve its ultimate purpose.

The idea that spiritual trials intensify to the point of despair is obvious from the Lord's trials in Gethsemane (Matthew 26:38, 39; Mark 14:33, 34, 35, 36; Luke 22:44) and afterward on the cross (Matthew 27:46), which lasted till he reached a state of despair. The Lord's trials are a model for the trials of the faithful, so the Lord says that those who want to follow him should take up their cross (Matthew 10:38; 16:24). The Lord's glorification is a model for our rebirth (§§3138, 3212, 3296, 3490, 4402, 5688), and the primary means of rebirth is spiritual trials.

7167 *And ever since I came to Pharaoh to speak in your name* means when statements in the divine law appeared to demand it of spirits caught up in falsity, as the following shows: *Coming to speak* means delivering a demand, though here it symbolizes an apparent demand. Demands from the Divine are not delivered explicitly to inhabitants of the hells; rather, they receive lectures through spirits, which appear to them to be demands from the Divine. *Pharaoh* represents spirits caught up in falsity who inflict persecution, as mentioned in §§6651, 6679, 6683, 7107, 7110, 7126, 7142. And Jehovah's *name* symbolizes all the faith and neighborly love with which the Lord is worshiped, as discussed in §§2724, 3006, 6674. It therefore symbolizes the whole of the divine law, because divine law is identical with attributes of charity and faith. After all, divine law is divine truth radiating from the Lord, and what radiates from the Lord is divine goodness and truth, divine goodness being love and charity, and divine truth being faith.

7168 *He has done evil to this people* means then spirits governed by religious truth and goodness seemed to be injured by the introduction of falsities, as the following demonstrates: *Doing evil* symbolizes injury through the introduction of falsities. Here it symbolizes apparent injury, because no one being persecuted and tested can actually be injured by the introduction of falsities, since the Lord keeps such a person safe. And the children of Israel—the *people* here—represent those who possess the church's truth and its good qualities, as above at §7162.

7169 *And you have decidedly not delivered your people* means that they were not released from a state of being harassed by falsity. This can be seen from the symbolism of being *delivered* as being released from a state in which one is attacked by falsity. The previous verses have been about attacks by falsity, so being delivered here means being released from that persecution. *Your people* means spirits with religious truth and goodness who have been harassed; see just above at §§7165, 7168.

The Spirits and Inhabitants of Mercury (Continued)

SPIRITS from Mercury appeared to the left in a ball and later in a long, stretched-out scroll. Wondering where they wanted to go—to our planet or another—I soon noticed that they bent back to the right and spun close to the planet Venus on the side that faces away from the sun. When they arrived they said they did not want to be there, because the people are bad. So they circled around to the other side of the planet, which faces the sun, and then they said they wanted to stay because the people there are good. 7170

After this was done, I felt a major change in my brain and strong activity generated there.

This evidence led me to the conclusion that the spirits of Venus on that side of the planet harmonized with the spirits of Mercury. It also indicated that the spirits of Venus related to the memory of matter-based concepts, which harmonizes with the memory of non-matter-based concepts formed by spirits from Mercury. That is why I felt stronger activity from the spirits of Mercury when they were there.

It is worth knowing that the world's sun and its light are completely invisible to any spirit, since its light is like thick darkness to spirits. That sun lingers in spirits' perception only from the sight they had of it while they lived in the world. It presents itself to their mind's eye as a dark blot far behind them, and slightly above head level. 7171

The planets within the system around that sun show up in fixed positions relative to the sun. Mercury appears to the back and a little to the right. Venus appears to the left and a little behind. Mars appears out in front and to the left. Jupiter too appears out in front and to the left but farther away. Saturn appears straight in front and far, far away. The moon appears fairly high up to the left. Other planets' satellites also appear on the left side of their planet.

That is how those bodies are positioned in the thinking of spirits and angels. In addition, spirits appear near their planet but outside it.

7172 I once saw that spirits from our planet were with spirits from Mercury, and I heard them conversing together. Among other things, the spirits from our planet were asking them whom they believed in. "In God," they answered, but when the spirits from our planet pressed them further about the God they believed in, they refused to say, because it is their habit not to answer questions directly.

Then the spirits of Mercury turned the tables and asked the spirits of our planet whom *they* believed in. They said in the Lord God.

"We can tell you don't believe in any God," the spirits of Mercury retorted. "You are in the habit of saying with your lips that you believe, without actually believing." Spirits from Mercury have keen powers of perception because they are constantly using those powers to investigate what others know.

The spirits from our planet were some of those who during their time in the world had proclaimed the faith the church had taught them but had not lived a life of faith. When they heard what the spirits from Mercury said, they fell silent because they were then given an awareness leading them to acknowledge that the words were true.

7173 Certain spirits had learned from heaven that the spirits of Mercury were once promised a vision of the Lord, so the spirits around me asked the spirits of Mercury whether they remembered the promise. "Yes," they said, "but we don't know whether it was promised so firmly as to remove all doubt."

While they were discussing this among themselves, the sun of heaven appeared to them. (The sun of heaven, which is the Lord, is visible only to inhabitants of the third or inmost heaven. Everyone else sees the light from it and also the moon, as explained in §§1529, 1530, 1531, 4060.) On seeing the sun they said it was not the Lord God, because they did not see a face.

The spirits kept talking to each other, although I do not know what they were saying. Then suddenly the sun appeared again, and at its center was the Lord, ringed with a sunlike halo. At this sight the spirits of Mercury sank down in profound humility.

Then the Lord appeared in the sun to spirits of this planet as well—spirits who had seen him in the world when they were people there. One after another in a long procession testified that he was the Lord; and they testified to this in front of the entire gathering.

Then the Lord also appeared in the sun to spirits from the planet Jupiter, who stated clearly and audibly that he was the one they saw on their planet when the God of the universe appeared to them.

After seeing the Lord, some were led out front and to the right. As 7174
they went, they said they had seen a much clearer, purer light than ever before and that no one could ever see a brighter light. At the time it was evening here. The spirits saying this were numerous.

A little later I was shown one of the women who live on Mercury. She 7175
had a pretty face but a smaller one than the women on our planet have. She was thinner, too, but the same height. On her head she wore a length of linen simply but nicely arranged.

I also saw a man from that planet, and he too had a thinner body than the men on our planet. The man I saw wore a dark blue garment fitted tightly to his body without pleats or flaps anywhere.

However, inhabitants of that planet spare little thought for their bodies. This was evident to me from the fact that when they go to the other world and become spirits, they want to appear not as people, the way spirits from our planet do, but as crystal balls. They want to appear in this form in order to divest themselves of anything that suggests matter. Besides, the knowledge of non-matter-based concepts is represented in the other life by crystals.

Their breeds of bulls and cows were also shown to me. Now, the 7176
cattle were not very different from the cattle on our planet, but they were smaller, somewhat approaching the look of our does and bucks.

Asked how the world's sun appears from their planet, they said it was 7177
large. They said they could tell by the mental image other spirits have of the Sun that it looks larger from their planet than from others.

They went on to say they had a moderate climate, not too warm or cold. I was then allowed to tell them that their lack of extreme heat was a provision of the Lord's, since their planet was closer to the Sun than other planets. After all, heat results not from proximity to the Sun but from the depth and therefore the density of the atmosphere. This is evident from the cold temperatures on high mountains even in warm climates. Warmth also varies in proportion to the angle of incidence of the Sun's rays, as is evident from the winter and summer seasons in every region.

That is what I was privileged to learn about the spirits and inhabitants of Mercury. At the end of the next chapter I will tell about spirits of the planet Venus [§§7246–7254].

Exodus 6

Teachings on Neighborly Love

NO one can tell what goodness is, understood in a spiritual sense, without knowing what love for one's neighbor and love for God are. 7178
And no one can tell what evil is without knowing what love for oneself and love for worldly advantages are.

Furthermore, no one can tell what religious truth is from an inward recognition of it without knowing what goodness is and without committing to it. Nor can anyone tell what falsity is without knowing what evil is.

None of us, then, can examine ourselves unless we learn what is good from the two good kinds of love and learn from goodness what is true, and unless we learn what is evil from the two evil kinds of love and learn from evil what is false.

We have two capacities, one called the intellect and the other called 7179
the will. We have been given a will for the sake of love and of the good it seeks, and an intellect for the sake of faith and of the truth it espouses. Love and its goodness relate to the will, while faith and its truth relate to the intellect.

Each capacity communicates with the other in an extraordinary way.

The two capacities unite in people devoted to goodness and therefore to truth, and they also unite in people devoted to evil and therefore to falsity. In both groups the two capacities form a single mind. Not so with people whose beliefs are true but whose lives are evil, and with people whose beliefs are false but whose lives appear to be good.

We are not allowed to split our mind and tear the two capacities apart; 7180
we are not allowed to understand and speak truth while intending and committing evil. If we did that, one capacity would gaze up toward heaven and the other would gaze down toward hell, which would leave us hanging between the two. We need to know, though, that it is our will that carries us away; our intellect caters to our will.

This discussion shows how faith and love work and what our condition is like if the two are separated.

7181 Nothing is more necessary for us than to know whether we have heaven or hell inside us, since we will live in one or the other forever. In order to learn the answer to this question we need to learn what good and evil are, because goodness constitutes heaven and evil constitutes hell. Teachings about neighborly love define both.

7182 I speak of love for God, by which I mean love for the Lord, because no one else is God. The Father is in him (John 14:9, 10, 11), and the holy influence of the Spirit comes from him (John 16:13, 14, 15).

Exodus 6

1. And Jehovah said to Moses, "Now you will see what I will do to Pharaoh, because with a strong hand he will send them away, and with a strong hand he will drive them from his land."

2. And God spoke to Moses and said to him, "I am Jehovah.

3. And I appeared to Abraham, to Isaac, and to Jacob as God Shaddai, and by my name 'Jehovah' I was not known to them.

4. And I have also resurrected my pact with them, to give them the land of Canaan, the land of their immigrant journeys, in which they resided as immigrants.

5. And I have also heard the groan of the children of Israel, that the Egyptians force servitude on them. And I have remembered my pact.

6. Therefore say to the children of Israel, 'I am Jehovah, and I will lead you out from under the burdens of the Egyptians and free you from servitude to them. And I will redeem you with an outstretched arm and great judgments.

7. And I will take you to me as a people and will be to you as God, and you will know that I am Jehovah your God, leading you out from under the burdens of Egypt.

8. And I will bring you to the land where I lifted my hand, to give it to Abraham, Isaac, and Jacob, and I will give it to you as an inheritance. I am Jehovah.'"

9. And Moses spoke this way to the children of Israel, and they did not listen to Moses because of their anguish of spirit and because of their hard servitude.

10. And Jehovah spoke to Moses, saying,

11. "Come, speak to Pharaoh, king of Egypt, and have him send the children of Israel away from his land."

12. And Moses spoke before Jehovah, saying, "Look: The children of Israel did not listen to me, and how will Pharaoh listen to me, since I am foreskinned of lips?"

13. And Jehovah spoke to Moses and to Aaron and commanded them for the children of Israel and for Pharaoh, king of Egypt, to lead the children of Israel out of the land of Egypt.

14. These are the heads of the house of their fathers: The sons of Reuben, Israel's firstborn: Hanoch and Pallu, Hezron and Carmi; these are the clans of Reuben.

15. And the sons of Simeon: Jemuel and Jamin and Ohad and Jachin and Zohar and Shaul, the son of a Canaanite woman. These are the clans of Simeon.

16. And these are the names of the children of Levi according to their births: Gershon and Kohath and Merari. And the years of Levi's life were one hundred thirty-seven years.

17. The sons of Gershon: Libni and Shimei, according to their clans.

18. And the sons of Kohath: Amram and Izhar and Hebron and Uzziel. And the years of Kohath's life were one hundred thirty-three years.

19. And the sons of Merari: Mahli and Mushi. These are the clans of Levi according to their births.

20. And Amram took Jochebed his father's sister to himself for his woman, and she bore him Aaron and Moses. And the years of Amram's life were one hundred thirty-seven years.

21. And the sons of Izhar: Korah and Nepheg and Zichri.

22. And the sons of Uzziel: Mishael and Elzaphan and Sithri.

23. And Aaron took Elisheba, daughter of Amminadab, sister of Nahshon, to himself for his woman. And she bore him Nadab and Abihu, Eleazar and Ithamar.

24. And the sons of Korah: Assir and Elkanah and Abiasaph. These are the clans of the Korahites.

25. And Eleazar son of Aaron took himself one of the daughters of Putiel for a woman for himself, and she bore him Phinehas. These are the heads of the fathers of the Levites according to their clans.

26. This is the Aaron and Moses to whom Jehovah said, "Lead the children of Israel out of the land of Egypt according to their armies."

27. They were the ones speaking to Pharaoh, king of Egypt, to lead the children of Israel out of Egypt. This is that Moses and Aaron.

28. And it happened on the day Jehovah spoke to Moses in the land of Egypt

29. that Jehovah spoke to Moses, saying, "I am Jehovah; speak to Pharaoh, king of Egypt, everything that I speak to you."

30. And Moses said before Jehovah, "Look: I am foreskinned of lips, and how will Pharaoh listen to me?"

Summary

7183 THE previous chapter dealt with people of the Lord's spiritual kingdom, describing how they were attacked by falsity and eventually found themselves on the verge of despair over those attacks. Now they are buoyed by hope and the sure promise of deliverance. This is the theme of the current chapter's inner meaning, the hope and promise being symbolized by what Jehovah says to Moses.

7184 The chapter goes on to depict the Lord's spiritual kingdom in regard to its faith, its neighborly love, its theology, and its acceptance of divine law. Reuben and Simeon and their clans represent facets of faith; Levi and his clans, facets of neighborly love; Aaron and his clans, facets of theology; and Moses, facets of divine law.

Inner Meaning

7185 EXODUS 6:1. *And Jehovah said to Moses, "Now you will see what I will do to Pharaoh, because with a strong hand he will send them away, and with a strong hand he will drive them from his land."*

And Jehovah said to Moses symbolizes instruction about divine law. *Now you will see what I will do to Pharaoh* means perceiving clearly what will happen to the persecutors. *Because with a strong hand he will send them away* means that they will keep away from their victims, which will require all their might and power. *And with a strong hand he will drive them from his land* means that with all their might and power they will make their victims flee from their vicinity.

And Jehovah said to Moses means instruction about divine law. This can be seen from the symbolism of *Jehovah said* as instruction by the Divine (discussed below) and from the representation of *Moses* as divine law (discussed in §§6723, 6752, 7014). **7186**

The reason *Jehovah said to Moses* symbolizes instruction about divine law is this: At the end of the previous chapter [§§7165–7169], people of the spiritual church believed the divine law was promising them immediate deliverance from persecution. In reality, though, the divine plan is to bring about a gradual removal of the persecuting evil spirits and a gradual deliverance of people in the spiritual church. There is no other divine plan. So there is no other divine law, either, since all divine law embodies that plan—so much so that it does not matter whether you say the divine law or the law of the divine plan. [2] The people of the spiritual church are now learning about this law and its sure promise that they are to be delivered when the time and state decreed by the plan are at hand.

Moses—representing the divine law as it exists among people of a spiritual religion when they are under assault—understood the divine law to promise them immediate deliverance from persecution. This is plain from his speech at the end of the previous chapter: "Why have you done evil to this people? Why is this, [that] you sent me? And you have decidedly not delivered your people" [Exodus 5:22, 23]. The symbolism of these words is that these people have been harassed with falsity too much, even though the law emanating from the Divine seems to decree otherwise, so that they have not been released from a state of being harassed; see §§7165, 7166, 7169.

[3] Why is it that people of the spiritual church who are in the underground realm are freed from harassment in gradual stages, not all at once? It is because that is the only way the evil and falsity clinging to them can be removed and be replaced with goodness and truth. The process requires many changes of state, so it takes place in gradual stages.

Those who believe that we can be admitted to heaven instantly and that all it takes is the Lord's mercy are greatly mistaken. If this were true, absolutely everyone in hell would be lifted up to heaven, because the Lord has mercy toward everyone. No, the orderly plan is for us each to take our life with us as we lived it in the world; our life here determines our state there. It is also orderly for the Lord's mercy to flow into all of us but for us to receive it in various ways, and for people mired in evil to reject it. Having learned to reject it in the world, they keep the habit in the other life, where they cannot change for the better. A tree lies where it has fallen [Ecclesiastes 11:3]. Part of the plan, then, is that people who lived good lives but who also exhibit crude, impure qualities tainted by self-love and materialism cannot associate with the inhabitants of the heavens until those qualities have been removed.

These remarks show that deliverance from persecution takes place in gradual stages.

7187 *Now you will see what I will do to Pharaoh* means perceiving clearly what will happen to the persecutors, as the following shows: *Seeing* symbolizes perception, as discussed in §§2150, 3764, 4567, 4723, 5400, and here it symbolizes clear perception, since it applies to instruction from the Divine. *What I will do* means what will happen. And *Pharaoh* represents those who inflict persecution by introducing falsity, as mentioned in §§6651, 6679, 6683, 7107, 7110, 7126, 7142.

7188 *Because with a strong hand he will send them away* means that they will keep away from their victims, which will require all their might and power. This can be seen from the symbolism of a *strong hand* as all might and power (for the symbolism of a hand as power, see §§878, 3387, 4932, 5327, 5328, 6947, 7011) and from the symbolism of *sending them away* as keeping away from them.

Here is the situation: When punishment frightens the hellish away from evildoing, they eventually stop persecuting others, preferring to leave them alone and run. However, since the sole pleasure of their life is doing evil and causing trouble, they are unable to desist unless they use all their might and power to remove themselves. Whatever provides our highest pleasure in life is something we love and is therefore part of our life. It carries us away irresistibly, unless the unpleasantness of being punished outweighs the pleasure of doing evil. That is why the evil are punished in the other world.

7189 *And with a strong hand he will drive them from his land* means that with all their might and power they will make their victims flee from the vicinity. This can be seen from the symbolism of *with a strong hand* as with all their might and power (discussed directly above at §7188), from that of *driving them away* as making them flee, and from that of *his land* as the vicinity. The land where adherents of the spiritual church come under attack by falsity is near the hells that are causing the persecution and is called the underground realm (see §7090). *From his land,* then, means from the vicinity.

Exodus 6:2, 3, 4, 5, 6, 7, 8. *And God spoke to Moses and said to him, "I am Jehovah. And I appeared to Abraham, to Isaac, and to Jacob as God Shaddai, and by my name 'Jehovah' I was not known to them. And I have also resurrected my pact with them, to give them the land of Canaan, the land of their immigrant journeys, in which they resided as immigrants. And I have also heard the groan of the children of Israel, that the Egyptians force servitude on them. And I have remembered my pact. Therefore say to the children of Israel, 'I am Jehovah, and I will lead you out from under the burdens of the Egyptians and free you from servitude to them. And I will redeem you with an outstretched arm and great judgments. And I will take you to me as a people and will be to you as God, and you will know that I am Jehovah your God, leading you out from under the burdens of Egypt. And I will bring you to the land where I lifted my hand, to give it to Abraham, Isaac, and Jacob, and I will give it to you as an inheritance. I am Jehovah.'"* 7190

And God spoke to Moses symbolizes a thought that is new but continuous with previous ideas. *And said to him, "I am Jehovah,"* symbolizes confirmation by the Divine, which is irreversible. *And I appeared to Abraham, to Isaac, and to Jacob as God Shaddai* symbolizes trials endured by the Lord's human side and by the faithful, and comfort afterward. *And by my name "Jehovah" I was not known to them* means that in a state of trial, people whose religion was spiritual did not think about what comes from God in their religion. *And I have also resurrected my pact with them* symbolizes union anyway at that time through the Lord's divine humanity. *To give them the land of Canaan* means that this union would lift them into heaven. *The land of their immigrant journeys, in which they resided as immigrants* means where the attributes of faith and neighborly love they learned about and incorporated into their lives are found. *And I have also heard the groan of the children of Israel* symbolizes the grief and pain they suffer as a result of the struggle. *That the Egyptians force servitude on them* means with spirits intent on falsity who strive to subdue them. *And I have remembered my pact* symbolizes being released from their grasp because of the union. *Therefore say to the children of Israel* means that the divine law will give members of the Lord's spiritual kingdom a perception. *I am Jehovah* symbolizes confirmation by the Divine. *And I will lead you out from under the burdens of the Egyptians* means that the Lord will release them from persecution at the hand of spirits devoted to falsity. *And free you from servitude to them* symbolizes full release from those spirits' efforts to subdue them. *And I will redeem you with an outstretched arm* symbolizes bringing them out of hell by divine power. *And great judgments* means in keeping with the laws of order from the Lord's divine humanity. *And I will take you to me as a people* means that they will be added to the number of inhabitants in heaven who serve the Lord there. *And will be to you as God* means that they will also receive what is divine. *And you will know that I am Jehovah your God* symbolizes an awareness at that point that the Lord is the only God. *Leading you out from under the burdens of Egypt* means who delivered them from harassment at the hand of falsity. *And I will bring you to the land where I lifted my hand, to give it to Abraham, Isaac, and Jacob* symbolizes being taken by divine power up into heaven, where the Lord's divine humanity is everything. *And I will give it to you as an inheritance* symbolizes the Lord's life there forever. *I am Jehovah* symbolizes confirmation from the Divine.

7191 *And God spoke to Moses* symbolizes a thought that is new but continuous with previous ideas. This can be seen from the fact that in the flow of the text we very often read "Jehovah said" and "Jehovah spoke." The current chapter includes examples: verse 1 reads "Jehovah said to Moses," the current verse reads *God spoke to Moses,* and we read similar phrases in verses 10, 13, 28, and 29. Likewise elsewhere. The repetition actually signals the start of a new thought, but one that should be connected with preceding ideas. For "Jehovah said" meaning a new perception, see §§2061, 2238, 2260.

Keep in mind that the Word in its original language lacks punctuation marks. Phrases like this one accordingly served in place of punctuation, and the word *and* served for minor breaks or divisions—which is why it occurs so often. Angelic speech is also continuous. It does have pauses, but it has a marvelous way of connecting what comes before a pause with what comes after. Angelic ideas are amazingly complex and include countless aspects that are inexpressible in words and incomprehensible to us as long as we are in the world. So the ends of previous sentences can be connected with the beginnings of subsequent sentences in a thoroughgoing way that turns multiple series into a single series.

As surprising and hard to believe as the concept may be, angelic speech presents an image of heaven's structure. All angelic speech therefore exhibits its songlike harmony ending in a single syllable—and consequently in unity—at every pause. The reason this happens, I was told, is that everything in heaven harks back to the one God as its focal point.

This evidence too showed me that all thought and therefore all speech flows in from the Lord through heaven, which is the source of this harmony in speech that ends in a unified cadence.

And said to him, "I am Jehovah," symbolizes confirmation by the Divine, which is irreversible, as needs no explanation. After all, Jehovah (that is, the Lord) can confirm something only by invoking himself. He cannot call on heaven as a witness because it is far below him; still less can he call on anything in the world. No, if there is to be divine confirmation, eternal and irreversible, it must come from the Divine itself. **7192**

This confirmation—*I am Jehovah*—appears many times in Moses, as for instance in Exodus 12:12; Leviticus 18:5, 6; 19:12, 14, 18, 28, 30, 32, 37; 20:8; 21:12; 22:2, 3, 8, 30, 31, 33; 26:2, 45; Numbers 3:13, 41, 45. In the Prophets we find "says Jehovah," which likewise means confirmation from the Divine, as for example in Isaiah 3:15; 14:22, 23; 17:6; 22:14, 25; 43:12; 52:5; Jeremiah 2:22; 3:1, 10, 13, 20; 8:12; 12:17; 13:25; 15:6, 20; 16:16; 23:7, 24, 29, 31; and many other places.

The Divine also offers confirmation by invoking his divine humanity (another way of invoking himself) in Isaiah:

> God has sworn by his right hand and by the arm of his strength. (Isaiah 62:8)

And I appeared to Abraham, to Isaac, and to Jacob as God Shaddai symbolizes trials endured by the Lord's human side and by the faithful, and comfort afterward, as the following shows: *Appearing,* or being seen, when it applies to Jehovah, symbolizes a perception received from the Divine, as dealt with in §§2150, 3764, 4567, 5400. *Abraham, Isaac, and Jacob* represent the Lord's divinity itself and divine humanity, as dealt with in §§6804, 6847. Here, though, since Jehovah is speaking and saying he appeared to them, they symbolize the Lord's human side, that is, his humanity before he made it divine. Abraham symbolizes the heavenly plane of that humanity, Isaac the spiritual plane, and Jacob the earthly plane. **7193**

[2] The reason they stand for the Lord's human side here, not for his divinity itself and divine humanity, is that the subject is times of trial. The Lord's human side could be tested before he made it divine, but his divine humanity could not, let alone his divinity itself. What is divine is beyond all challenge. The hellish beings who try us cannot even go near heavenly angels, because when they do they are seized with horror and anguish and become almost lifeless. If they cannot approach heavenly angels—and it is something divine with the angels that makes this

impossible—much less can they approach the Divine itself, which is infinitely far above the angelic.

This makes it plain that the Lord took on a weak human nature from his mother so that he could be tested and through his trials reduce everything in heaven and in hell to order, at the same time glorifying his human side, or making it divine.

[3] For the symbolism of God Shaddai as times of trial and comfort afterward, see §§1992, 3667, 4572, 5628.

I speak of comfort afterward because the divine design calls for the pain of such challenges to be followed by solace, exactly the same way evening and night are followed by morning and the dawn. The one even corresponds to the other, because there are cycles of states in the other life just as there are cycles of time in this world. States of trial and persecution and states of desolation are evening and night there, and states of consolation and celebration are morning and the dawn there.

The same words *(I appeared to Abraham, to Isaac, and to Jacob)* also symbolize trials endured by the faithful and comfort afterward because human rebirth, which takes place by means of trials, is an image of the Lord's glorification (§§3138, 3212, 3296, 3490, 4402, 5688). What applies to the Lord in the Word's highest sense, then, applies to the faithful in a secondary, inward sense.

7194 *And by my name "Jehovah" I was not known to them* means that in a state of trial, people whose religion was spiritual did not think about what comes from God in their religion, as the following shows: The *name "Jehovah"* symbolizes every means of worshiping God, collectively, as discussed in §§2724, 3006, 6674, and therefore everything that comes from God in the religion. Strictly speaking, the name of Jehovah means the Lord's divine humanity (§§2628, 6887), and since this is the conduit and source of all faith and all love—which is what comes from God in the religion—it means all divine worship, collectively. And *not being known* symbolizes lack of awareness or lack of thought about it—that is, about what comes from God in the religion—at least during a state of trial (as symbolized by God Shaddai). That is why the verse says that he was known to Abraham, Isaac, and Jacob but not by his name "Jehovah."

This is the inner meaning of the words above, but the outer, narrative meaning is different. The latter meaning makes it clear that Abraham, Isaac, and Jacob worshiped God Shaddai rather than Jehovah (see §§1992, 3667, 5628) and that Abraham did not know Jehovah (§§1356, 2559). The reason Jehovah's name is used in the narratives about Abraham, Isaac, and Jacob is that this part of the Word was written by Moses, who *was* informed of Jehovah's name. Jehovah's name comes up in those narratives because of the inner meaning. Throughout the Word, Jehovah is mentioned when the subject is love and its goodness, while God is mentioned when the subject is faith and its truth (§§709, 732, 1096, 2586, 2769, 2807, 2822, 3921 at the end, 4402).

And I have also resurrected my pact with them symbolizes union anyway at that time through the [Lord's] divine humanity. This is established by the symbolism of a *pact* as union (discussed in §§665, 666, 1023, 1038, 1864, 1996, 2003, 2021, 6804) and by the representation of Abraham, Isaac, and Jacob, with whom the pact was made, as the Lord's divine humanity (mentioned in §§6804, 6847). These considerations reveal what the most direct inner meaning of the clause is: that divinity itself is one with the divine humanity. This gives rise to a secondary meaning: that divinity itself unites with adherents of a spiritual religion by means of the divine humanity. As has been shown a number of times before, people of the spiritual church were saved by the Lord's divine humanity; see §§6854, 6914, 7035, 7091 at the end. 7195

I speak of union *anyway at that time* to connect this clause with the previous one, in that the union occurred during a state of trial even though these people were not thinking about what comes from God in their religion. The Lord is more immediately present in a state of trial than outside one, even if the case seems otherwise; see §840.

To give them the land of Canaan means that this union would lift them into heaven. This is established by the symbolism of the *land of Canaan* as the Lord's kingdom in the heavens and as the church, which is discussed in §§1607, 3038, 3481, 3705, 4447, 6516. Their being lifted into heaven is obviously symbolized by giving them that land, since people who are given heaven are lifted up. 7196

The land of their immigrant journeys, in which they resided as immigrants means where the attributes of faith and neighborly love they learned about and incorporated into their lives are found, as the following shows: The *land* symbolizes the Lord's kingdom in the heavens and on earth, as noted directly above at §7196, so it also symbolizes what constitutes the Lord's kingdom, which everyone knows is faith and neighborly love. These two as well are symbolized by the land of Canaan, then, in a passage about learning and living (which is what immigrating symbolizes). 7197

And *immigrating* symbolizes learning and living, as discussed in §§1463, 2025, 3672. Clearly, then, the *land of their immigrant journeys, in which they resided as immigrants* means where the attributes of faith and neighborly love they learned about and incorporated into their lives are found.

[2] To expand on this subject: In the next life we each receive heaven according to the traits of faith and neighborly love within us, because neighborly love and faith create heaven in us. However, when I say that neighborly love and faith create heaven, I mean that a *life* of neighborly love and faith does.

Be very clear, though, that a life containing heaven is a life incorporating the religious truths and goodness we have learned about. Unless these are the standards and principles of our life, we look for heaven in vain, no matter how we have lived. Without them we are like a reed swaying with every breeze. We bend as readily to evil as to goodness, because we have no firmly established truth or goodness in us that angels can use for holding us to what is true and good and turning us aside from the falsity and evil that hellish spirits are constantly introducing. In other words, what makes heaven is a life of Christian goodness, not worldly goodness.

7198 *And I have also heard the groan of the children of Israel* symbolizes the grief and pain they suffer as a result of the struggle. This can be seen from the symbolism of a *groan* as grief and pain as a result of struggle and from the representation of the *children of Israel* as people of the spiritual church, who find themselves overrun with falsity and are therefore in a struggle.

7199 *That the Egyptians force servitude on them* means with spirits intent on falsity who strive to subdue them. This can be seen from the symbolism of *Egyptians* as spirits intent on falsity (discussed in §§6692, 7097, 7107, 7110, 7126, 7142) and from that of *forcing servitude on them* as striving to subdue them (discussed in §§6666, 6670, 6671).

7200 *And I have remembered my pact* symbolizes being released from their grasp because of the union, as the following shows: *Remembering* the pact—the pact with Abraham, Isaac, and Jacob, to give them the land of Canaan—symbolizes deliverance or release from the persecution meant by the servitude in Egypt, and elevation to heaven. And a *pact* symbolizes union, as noted above at §7195.

Why do I describe the union as the reason these people were to be liberated and taken up to heaven? Faith and love are what bind us to the Lord, because the truth taught by faith and the goodness urged by love radiate from him, and what radiates from the Lord is his, so much so that it *is* the Lord. People who accept faith and love, then, unite with him, and people who unite with him are necessarily taken up to him, that is, to heaven.

Therefore say to the children of Israel means that the divine law will give members of the Lord's spiritual kingdom a perception, as the following shows: Moses, who is being told to speak to the children of Israel, represents divine law, as dealt with in §§6723, 6752. *Saying* symbolizes perceiving, as dealt with in §§1791, 1815, 1819, 1822, 1898, 1919, 2080, 2506, 2515, 2619, 2862, 3509, 5877. In this case it means enabling to perceive, because divine law is what is described as saying. And the *children of Israel* represent members of the Lord's spiritual kingdom, as dealt with in §§6426, 6637. **7201**

I am Jehovah symbolizes confirmation by the Divine. This is evident from comments above at §7192. **7202**

And I will lead you out from under the burdens of the Egyptians means that the Lord will release them from persecution at the hand of spirits devoted to falsity. This is clear from the symbolism of *leading out* as releasing, from that of *burdens* as persecution at the hand of falsity, and as combat (treated of in §§6757, 7104, 7105), and from that of *Egyptians* as spirits who inflict persecution by introducing falsity (mentioned just above at §7199). **7203**

And free you from servitude to them symbolizes full release from [those spirits'] efforts to subdue them. This can be seen from the symbolism of *servitude* as efforts to subdue, as discussed in §§6666, 6670, 6671. **7204**

And I will redeem you with an outstretched arm symbolizes bringing them out of hell by divine power, as the following shows: *Redeeming* symbolizes bringing out of hell. The term can be used in connection with servitude, evil, or death and means being released from these things and therefore from hell; and it is the Lord in his divine humanity who is called the Redeemer. (See §6281.) And an *outstretched arm* symbolizes divine power. For the symbolism of an arm as power, see §§878, 4932, 4933, 4934, 4935. An outstretched arm means omnipotence, or divine power, because when an extended arm appears in the heavens it represents power from the Divine, but when the arm is bent rather than extended it represents power in the usual sense. This then is why the Word often uses the phrases an *outstretched arm* and a *strong hand* to express divine power, as in Jeremiah: **7205**

> I myself made the earth, the human, and the animal that is on the face of the earth by *my great power* and by *my outstretched arm.* (Jeremiah 27:5)

In the same author:

> Oh, Lord Jehovih, here you have made heaven and earth by *your great power* and by *your outstretched arm;* no word is too wondrous for you. You brought your people Israel out of the land of Egypt by signs and miracles, and *by a strong hand,* and *by an outstretched arm.* (Jeremiah 32:17, 21)

In Ezekiel:

> I will bring you out from the peoples and gather you from the lands to which you have scattered *by a strong hand* and *by an outstretched arm.* (Ezekiel 20:34)

In David:

> He brought Israel out from the midst of the Egyptians by a *strong hand* and an *outstretched arm.* (Psalms 136:11, 12)

Other passages are Deuteronomy 4:34; 5:15; 7:19; 9:29; 11:2; 26:8; 1 Kings 8:42; 2 Kings 17:36.

7206 *And great judgments* means in keeping with the laws of order from the Lord's divine humanity. This can be seen from the symbolism of *judgments* as truth (discussed in §§2235, 6397) and in the highest sense, in which they are ascribed to the Lord, as divine truth. Divine truth is actually the laws of order from the Lord's divine humanity, because all order comes from the Lord, which means that all the laws of order come from him. These laws govern all of heaven and consequently the universe as well. The laws of order—or truth coming from the Lord that governs all of heaven and the universe—are what John calls the Word through which everything was made (John 1:1, 2, 3). This is because the Word is divine truth radiating from the divine goodness of the Lord's divine humanity. That is why everything in the spiritual world and in the physical world relates to truth, as anyone who reflects on it can see.

[2] In their most immediate sense, these great judgments mean truth used in judging the spirits who inflicted persecution by introducing falsity—spirits symbolized by the Egyptians and by Pharaoh. They also mean truth used in judging spirits who are released from the persecution—spirits symbolized by the children of Israel. Out of these judgments comes damnation for people devoted to the falsity that rises out of evil, and out of these judgments comes salvation for people devoted to the truth that rises out of goodness. Not that truth coming from the Lord damns anyone.

All truth radiating from the Lord comes from his divine goodness, so it is purely merciful, but because we do not accept his mercy, we lay our own selves open to damnation, since we are then devoted to evil and the evil condemns us. On the other hand, truth from the Lord does not save us if we believe we are saved by the religious truth we know rather than by mercy. After all, we are mired in evil and on our own are in hell, but the Lord's mercy withholds us from evil, maintains us in goodness, and does so with mighty power.

As for the idea that judgments symbolize both the damnation of the evil and the salvation of the good, this is plain from Scripture passages treating of the Last Judgment, such as Matthew 25:31–45 and elsewhere.

And I will take you to me as a people means that they will be added to 7207
the number of inhabitants in heaven who serve the Lord there. This can be seen from the symbolism of *taking them as a people* (when Jehovah, or the Lord, is said to do it) as receiving them among the inhabitants of heaven. Heaven's inhabitants are called the Lord's people, even while they are still living in the world, because their souls even then are in heaven; see §§687, 697, 3255, 4067, 4073, 4077.

The reason these words mean that the people of the spiritual church will be added to the number of inhabitants in heaven who serve the Lord there is this: Before the Lord's Coming they were held in the underground realm, but they were taken up to heaven when the Lord rose again, at which point they were added to the number of inhabitants who serve the Lord there; see §§6854, 6914, 7091 at the end.

And will be to you as God means that they will also receive what is 7208
divine. This is evident from the symbolism of *being to them as God* (when this is said of Jehovah, or the Lord) as receiving what is divine. Everyone in heaven gets to receive what is divine: divine goodness and truth, and therefore wisdom and understanding, and accordingly a life made happy by usefulness—in other words, by the exercise of neighborly love. These things are symbolized by *I will be to you as God.*

And you will know that I am Jehovah your God symbolizes an aware- 7209
ness at that point that the Lord is the only God. This can be seen from the symbolism of *knowing* as being aware. The reason *I am Jehovah your God* means that the Lord is the only God is that in the Word none but the Lord is meant by Jehovah (§§1343, 1736, 2921, 3023, 3035, 5663, 6281, 6303, 6905). It is also because in heaven they know and perceive that the Lord is the Lord of heaven and consequently the Lord of the universe; that, as he says in Matthew, he has all power in the heavens and on earth

(Matthew 28:18); that Jehovah does not give his glory to anyone but himself (Isaiah 42:8); that he is one with the Father (John 14:9, 10, 11); and that the Holy Spirit is a holy influence from him (John 16:13, 14, 15). So they know and perceive that the Lord is the only God.

7210 *Leading you out from under the burdens of Egypt* means who delivered them from harassment at the hand of falsity. This is clear from the remarks above at §7203, where similar words occur.

7211 *And I will bring you to the land where I lifted my hand, to give it to Abraham, Isaac, and Jacob* symbolizes being taken by divine power up into heaven, where the [Lord's] divine humanity is everything, as the following shows: *Bringing them to the land* of Canaan symbolizes taking them up to heaven. (For the meaning of the land of Canaan as the Lord's kingdom, or heaven, see above at §7196.) *Lifting one's hand,* when Jehovah (the Lord) is said to do it, means by divine power. (For the symbolism of a hand as power, see §§878, 4931–4937, 5327, 5328, 6947, 7011.) And *Abraham, Isaac, and Jacob* represent the Lord's divinity itself and his divine humanity, as mentioned in §§6804, 6847. Here they represent the Lord's divine humanity because this is the all-in-all of heaven.

The divine humanity is the all-in-all of heaven because no one there, not even an angel of the third or inmost heaven, can have any idea of divinity itself. As the Lord says in John:

> God has never been seen by anyone. (John 1:18)
>
> You have never heard the Father's voice or seen his form. (John 5:37)

Angels are finite, and nothing finite can have any idea of what is infinite. So in heaven, if their mental image of God did not have a human appearance, they would have no image at all or else an inappropriate one. They would then be unable to unite with the Divine either through faith or through love. This being so, heaven's inhabitants perceive the Divine in a human form. That is why the divine humanity is everything to the insights they have in the heavens and is therefore the all-in-all of faith and love, which are the source of union, which in turn is the means of salvation (§6700).

7212 *And I will give it to you as an inheritance* symbolizes the Lord's life there forever. This can be seen from the symbolism of an *inheritance,* when it refers to heaven, as the Lord's life, as discussed at §2658. Moreover, everything given as an inheritance is a permanent possession of the person to whom it is given, and in heaven it is an eternal possession, since the inhabitants live forever. As a consequence, the Lord's life there forever is what is being symbolized.

The Lord's life fills heaven, so heaven's inhabitants dwell in that life, because they dwell in truth and goodness that radiate from the Lord. The goodness within truth is the Lord himself, and the truth that has goodness within it is life from the Lord, the source of everyone's life. Clearly, then, people who dwell in goodness and therefore in truth—as everyone in the heavens does—dwell in the Lord's life.

I am Jehovah symbolizes confirmation from the Divine, as the comments above at §§7192, 7202 show. 7213

Exodus 6:9, 10, 11, 12, 13. *And Moses spoke this way to the children of Israel, and they did not listen to Moses because of their anguish of spirit and because of their hard servitude. And Jehovah spoke to Moses, saying, "Come, speak to Pharaoh, king of Egypt, and have him send the children of Israel away from his land." And Moses spoke before Jehovah, saying, "Look: The children of Israel did not listen to me, and how will Pharaoh listen to me, since I am foreskinned of lips?" And Jehovah spoke to Moses and to Aaron and commanded them for the children of Israel and for Pharaoh, king of Egypt, to lead the children of Israel out of the land of Egypt.* 7214

And Moses spoke this way to the children of Israel symbolizes an urgent message from the divine law to members of the Lord's spiritual kingdom. *And they did not listen to Moses* means that they were not moved by faith and obedience to accept it. *Because of their anguish of spirit* means on account of their state of near despair. *And because of their hard servitude* means from being attacked by pure falsity. *And Jehovah spoke to Moses, saying,* symbolizes a continuation. *Come, speak to Pharaoh, king of Egypt,* symbolizes a warning to people who inflict harassment through pure falsity. *And have him send the children of Israel away from his land* means to go away and leave them alone. *And Moses spoke with Jehovah, saying,* symbolizes the law imparted by the Divine, and thinking based on it. *Look: The children of Israel did not listen to me* means that spiritual people did not accept what was announced to them. *And how will Pharaoh listen to me?* means that people immersed in falsity will not accept it. *Since I am foreskinned of lips* means that to them I am impure. *And Jehovah spoke to Moses and to Aaron* means being taught anew from divine law and from religious teachings. *And commanded them for the children of Israel* means concerning what is required of members of the Lord's spiritual kingdom. *And for Pharaoh, king of Egypt,* symbolizes a warning to people who inflict harassment through pure falsity. *To lead the children of Israel out of the land of Egypt* means that they are to be delivered.

7215 *And Moses spoke this way to the children of Israel* symbolizes an urgent message from the divine law to members of the Lord's spiritual kingdom. This is clear from the symbolism of *speaking* as an urgent message (since [Moses] was telling the people what Jehovah had commanded him), from the representation of *Moses* as divine law (discussed in §§6723, 6752), and from the representation of the *children of Israel* as the Lord's spiritual kingdom (discussed in §§6426, 6637).

7216 *And they did not listen to Moses* means that they were not moved by faith and obedience to accept it. This is established by the symbolism of *listening* as being moved by faith and obedience to accept something. For the meaning of listening as possessing faith in our will and in our actions and having obedience, see §§2542, 3869, 4652–4660, 5017.

7217 *Because of their anguish of spirit* means on account of their state of near despair. This can be seen from the symbolism of *anguish of spirit* as a state of near despair, since the spirits of people in such a state are anguished. This state is symbolized by the burden Pharaoh laid on the children of Israel in requiring them to seek out their own straw for making bricks, as the end of the previous chapter showed [§§7163–7169].

Evidence that anguish of spirit means a state of near despair is the fact that people who are in a state bordering on despair feel deep anxiety, and their spirit is actively in anguish.

In an outer sense, anguish of spirit is a feeling of tightness in the chest, which makes it feel hard to breathe. In an inner sense, though, it consists in anxiety over being deprived of religious truth and charitable goodness and in a consequent state of near despair. Pinched breathing on one hand and anxiety over being deprived of religious truth and charitable goodness on the other correspond to one another, as a physical effect in the body and its spiritual cause in the mind. This can be seen from explanations in §§97, 1119, 3886, 3887, 3889, 3892, 3893.

[2] People lacking in faith and charity cannot believe that being deprived of spiritual truth and goodness gives birth to such anxiety and consequently such distress. They consider it a weakness and mental sickness to feel anguish on that account. That is because they dismiss the reality of faith and charity and therefore of anything involving their soul or heaven. The only real things to them are wealth and status and therefore bodily and worldly concerns. "What are faith and charity?" they ask themselves. "They are nothing but words! In fact, what is conscience? To agonize over these is to

agonize over the hallucinations of a private delirium, which the patient imagines are something when they are nothing. Wealth and status, now—we see with our own eyes what *they* are. And the pleasure they give us proves they exist, because they cause an expansive feeling in our whole body and fill it with joy." That is how merely earthly people think and how they talk among themselves. Spiritual people think and talk differently. Their primary life is the life of the spirit and the life of spiritual qualities—namely, faith and charity. When they think they have been deprived of the truth and goodness belonging to faith and charity, then, they feel pangs like the pangs of death, because they see spiritual death—damnation—before their eyes. As mentioned above, to merely earthly people they seem weak and mentally ill, but they are strong and mighty. People who are merely earthly, on the other hand, appear strong and mighty to themselves, and they truly are strong of body, but they are totally weak in spirit, because they are spiritually dead. If they saw what their spirit was like, they would acknowledge this, but they do not see it till their body has perished.

And because of their hard servitude means from being attacked by pure **7218**
falsity. This can be seen from the symbolism of *servitude* as being attacked by falsity, which is dealt with in §§7120, 7129. *Hard* servitude, then, means being attacked by pure falsity. When we are attacked by pure falsity and do not have truth that is capable of dispelling the falsity to revive us, and yet our life is one of religious truth and charitable goodness, we feel extreme anguish. As long as we are in that state, we experience a kind of hard servitude, and that is why hard servitude symbolizes such attacks.

[2] It needs to be realized that all thoughts flow in from elsewhere, but that when spirits go through a state of evening and night they are in a state of forced thought. They are compelled to think about falsities that are being introduced and cannot free themselves at all from the compulsion. However, when they go through a state of morning and afternoon they are in a state of free thought. They can then think about things they love and therefore about the truth and goodness that go with faith and charity, since this is what they love. For the idea that what springs from love is free, see §§2870–2893.

And Jehovah spoke to Moses, saying, symbolizes a continuation. This **7219**
can be seen from the discussion above at §7191.

Come, speak to Pharaoh, king of Egypt, symbolizes a warning to peo- **7220**
ple who inflict harassment through pure falsity. This is evident from the symbolism of *speaking,* when done on divine command, as a warning and from the representation of *Pharaoh* as people who inflict harassment

through falsity (noted at §§7107, 7110, 7126, 7142). Since they inflict it through pure falsity, Pharaoh is called *king of Egypt* here, because a monarch in a positive sense symbolizes truth and in a negative sense falsity (§§2015, 2069).

7221 *And have him send the children of Israel away from his land* means to go away and leave them alone. This is evident from the symbolism of *sending away* as going away and leaving someone alone, from the representation of the *children of Israel* as people whose religion is spiritual (mentioned often), and from the symbolism of the *land* of Egypt as a state of persecution. These particulars make it plain that *have him send the children of Israel away from his land* means that they should leave the people of the spiritual church alone and not persecute them.

7222 *And Moses spoke with Jehovah, saying,* symbolizes the law imparted by the Divine, and thinking based on it. This can be seen from the symbolism of *speaking* as thought (discussed in §§2271, 2287, 2619) and from the representation of *Moses* as the law imparted by the Divine (discussed in §§6771, 6827).

7223 *Look: The children of Israel did not listen to me* means that spiritual people did not accept what was announced to them. This is established by the representation of the *children of Israel* as spiritual people, or people of the Lord's spiritual church (discussed in §§6426, 6637), and by the symbolism of *not listening* as not being moved by faith and obedience to accept the message (mentioned above at §7216). Obviously it is what was announced to them (about being delivered) that they did not accept.

7224 *And how will Pharaoh listen to me?* means that people immersed in falsity will not accept it. This is established by the symbolism of *not listening* as not accepting (as directly above at §7223) and by the representation of *Pharaoh* as people immersed in falsity (noted in §§6651, 6679, 6683, 7107, 7110, 7126, 7142). Pharaoh represents people immersed in falsity who inflict persecution and therefore represents more than one person, because a king is head of his people and accordingly symbolizes the same thing as his people; see §4789.

7225 *Since I am foreskinned of lips* means that to them I am impure, as the following shows: Being *foreskinned* or uncircumcised symbolizes being impure. Circumcision represented purification from disgusting kinds of love, or from love for oneself and love of worldly advantages; see §§2039, 2632, 2799, 4462, 7045. So men who were not circumcised and were called foreskinned represented people who had not been purified of these two kinds of love and were therefore impure (§§3412, 3413, 4462, 7045).

And the symbolism of *lips* has to do with doctrine, as discussed in §§1286, 1288, so being foreskinned of lips symbolizes being impure in regard to doctrinal teachings. The term *foreskinned* can apply to doctrine or to life, so Jeremiah speaks of a *foreskinned ear:*

> To whom shall I speak and testify and they will listen? Look, now, *their ear is foreskinned* and they cannot hear. Look, now, Jehovah's word has become a reproach; they do not want it. (Jeremiah 6:10)

The same author also refers to a *foreskinned heart:*

> The whole house of Israel are *foreskinned at heart.* (Jeremiah 9:26)

In Ezekiel:

> You bring in foreign sons, *foreskinned at heart* and *foreskinned in the flesh,* to be in my sanctuary. (Ezekiel 44:7, 9)

In Moses:

> Then *their foreskinned heart* will be brought low. (Leviticus 26:41)

[2] These passages show that what is foreskinned or uncircumcised is impure. Since all impurity rises out of impure love (love of worldly advantages and self-love), anything uncircumcised symbolizes something that blocks the inflow of goodness and truth. Where impure love exists, inflowing goodness and truth are extinguished, because they are opposites, just as heaven and hell are. A foreskinned ear therefore symbolizes disobedience, and a foreskinned heart the rejection of goodness and truth. Goodness and truth are most especially rejected when the impure kinds of love have built a wall of falsity around themselves.

[3] It is for the sake of the inner meaning that Moses refers to his stutter as his being foreskinned of lips, to symbolize the fact that believers in falsity (represented by Pharaoh) would not take note of the divine law's message to them. The reason they would not take note of it is that people who believe in falsity refer to truth in the divine law as false and to falsity that opposes such truth as true, because they are totally perverse. As a result they cannot help perceiving doctrinal truth as impure. Heavenly kinds of love also seem impure to them. Moreover, when they go near some community of heaven, they reek horribly, and when they catch the scent, they suppose it is coming from the heavenly community, though in reality it comes from themselves. A bad odor does not smell bad unless contrasted with its opposite.

7226 *And Jehovah spoke to Moses and to Aaron* means being taught anew from divine law and from religious teachings, as the following shows: *Speaking* symbolizes being taught anew, because the next words teach them what they have to do. *Moses* represents divine law, as discussed in §§6723, 6752. And *Aaron* represents teachings about goodness and truth, as discussed at §6998. For the difference between divine law and religious teachings, see §§7009, 7010, 7089.

7227 *And commanded them for the children of Israel* means concerning what is required of members of the Lord's spiritual kingdom. This can be seen from the symbolism of *commanding* as what is required and from the representation of the *children of Israel* as members of the Lord's spiritual kingdom (noted many times before).

7228 *And for Pharaoh, king of Egypt,* symbolizes a warning to people who inflict harassment through pure falsity, as the following shows: Speaking, when done on divine command to people intent on falsity, symbolizes a warning, as above at §7220. And *Pharaoh,* when he is also called *king of Egypt,* represents people who inflict harassment through pure falsity, as mentioned above at §7220.

7229 *To lead the children of Israel out of the land of Egypt* means that they are to be delivered, as is self-explanatory.

7230 Exodus 6:14–25. *These are the heads of the house of their fathers: The sons of Reuben, Israel's firstborn: Hanoch and Pallu, Hezron and Carmi; these are the clans of Reuben. And the sons of Simeon: Jemuel and Jamin and Ohad and Jachin and Zohar and Shaul, the son of a Canaanite woman. These are the clans of Simeon. And these are the names of the children of Levi according to their births: Gershon and Kohath and Merari. And the years of Levi's life were one hundred thirty-seven years. The sons of Gershon: Libni and Shimei, according to their clans. And the sons of Kohath: Amram and Izhar and Hebron and Uzziel. And the years of Kohath's life were one hundred thirty-three years. And the sons of Merari: Mahli and Mushi. These are the clans of Levi according to their births. And Amram took Jochebed his father's sister to himself for his woman, and she bore him Aaron and Moses. And the years of Amram's life were one hundred thirty-seven years. And the sons of Izhar: Korah and Nepheg and Zichri. And the sons of Uzziel: Mishael and Elzaphan and Sithri. And Aaron took Elisheba, daughter of Amminadab, sister of Nahshon, to himself for his woman. And she bore him Nadab and Abihu, Eleazar and Ithamar. And the sons of Korah: Assir and Elkanah and Abiasaph. These are the clans of the Korahites. And Eleazar son of Aaron took himself one of the daughters of Putiel for a woman for himself, and she bore him Phinehas. These are the heads of the fathers of the Levites according to their clans.*

[2] *These are the heads of the house of their fathers* symbolizes the leading elements of religion. *The sons of Reuben, [Israel's firstborn]: Hanoch and Pallu, Hezron and Carmi* symbolizes traits of an intellectual faith. *These are the clans of Reuben* symbolizes the truth encompassed in that faith. *And the sons of Simeon: Jemuel and Jamin and Ohad and Jachin and Zohar* symbolizes traits of an active faith [within the church]. *And Shaul, the son of a Canaanite woman,* symbolizes traits of an active [faith] outside the church. *These are the clans of Simeon* symbolizes the truth and goodness that belong to an active faith. *And these are the names of the children of Levi according to their births: Gershon and Kohath and Merari* symbolizes traits of neighborly love. *And the years of Levi's life were one hundred thirty-seven years* symbolizes its nature and state. [3] *The sons of Gershon: Libni and Shimei, according to their clans* symbolizes new categories of goodness and resulting truth—the first group of them to develop. *And the sons of Kohath: Amram and Izhar and Hebron and Uzziel* symbolizes the second group to develop. *And the years of Kohath's life were one hundred thirty-three years* symbolizes the nature and state [of the quality he represents]. *And the sons of Merari: Mahli and Mushi* symbolizes the third group to develop. *These are the clans of Levi according to their births* means that these are the types of goodness and truth that develop out of neighborly love. *And Amram took Jochebed his father's sister to himself for his woman* symbolizes union between goodness that develops [out of neighborly love] and a related type of truth. *And she bore him Aaron and Moses* means that from the union they received the church's theology and the law imparted by the Divine. [4] *And the years of Amram's life were one hundred thirty-seven years* symbolizes the nature and state [of the goodness he represents]. *And the sons of Izhar: Korah and Nepheg and Zichri* symbolizes a further development in the second group, of goodness and consequent truth. *And the sons of Uzziel: Mishael and Elzaphan and Sithri* symbolizes another further development in that group, of goodness within truth. *And Aaron took Elisheba, daughter of Amminadab, sister of Nahshon, to himself for his woman* symbolizes the church's theology and how the goodness and truth in that theology united. *And she bore him Nadab and Abihu, Eleazar and Ithamar* symbolizes new categories of faith and neighborly love that develop out of the union, and their nature. [5] *And the sons of Korah: Assir and Elkanah and Abiasaph* symbolizes another round of development in the second group. *These are the clans of the Korahites* symbolizes goodness and truth and their nature. *And Eleazar son of Aaron* symbolizes teachings that develop out of the basic theology of neighborly love. *Took himself one of the daughters of Putiel for a woman for himself* symbolizes a union of goodness and

truth in those teachings. *And she bore him Phinehas* symbolizes a new category that develops as a result. *These are the heads of the fathers of the Levites according to their clans* symbolizes the leading elements of religion, as regards neighborly love and the faith it gives rise to.

7231 Because this passage is nothing but names, there is no need to explain it in detail. Besides, I have already shown what Reuben, Simeon, Levi, Aaron, and Moses represent [§7184]. Their sons and grandsons named here are simply later-developing qualities. (For Reuben representing a faith that belongs to the intellect, see §§3861, 3866, 4731, 4734, 4761; for Simeon representing a faith that belongs to the will and action, 3869, 3870, 3871, 3872, 4497, 4502, 4503, 5482, 5626, 5630; for Levi representing neighborly love, 3875, 3877, 4497, 4502, 4503; for Aaron representing the church's theology, 6998, 7009, 7089; and for Moses representing the law imparted by the Divine, 6771, 6827.)

The reason Reuben, Simeon, Levi, and their offspring are mentioned here and not the rest of the tribes' ancestors with their offspring in order can be known only from the inner meaning. Of course the current chapter presents this list in order to inform the reader about the birth of Aaron and Moses, but the genealogy of Levi would have been enough for that. The genealogy of Reuben, Simeon, and their offspring contributes nothing whatever to that purpose.

[2] No, the reason revealed by the inner meaning alone is that the text is talking about the spiritual church represented by the children of Israel. The spiritual church in us starts with a faith consisting in knowledge and then in comprehension, as represented by Reuben and his offspring. Later, as the church grows in us, that faith passes into our will and from our will into action. At that point we have an intent to act on the truth taught by faith and do act on it because the Word commands us to. This stage of faith is represented by Simeon. Eventually we sense the feeling of neighborly love in our will, which by now has become a new will, so that we want to do good out of charity for our neighbor, not out of faith as we did before. When we regenerate to that point, we are part of the spiritual church, because we then have the church inside us. This love for our neighbor and the feeling it calls up in us is what Levi represents.

This then is why the clans of Reuben and of Simeon are enumerated, and finally the clan of Levi, who (again) represents neighborly love, the true spiritual element of religion.

Aaron represents the outer part of the spiritual church and Moses the inner part. The inner part of the church is called the law imparted by the Divine, and the outer part is called the theology derived from it. The law imparted by the Divine, or the inner part of the church, is the same as the Word in its inner meaning, and the theology derived from it is the Word in its outer meaning. These are represented by Moses and Aaron; see §7089.

Exodus 6:26, 27, 28, 29, 30. *This is the Aaron and Moses to whom Jehovah said, "Lead the children of Israel out of the land of Egypt according to their armies." They were the ones speaking to Pharaoh, king of Egypt, to lead the children of Israel out of Egypt. This is that Moses and Aaron. And it happened on the day Jehovah spoke to Moses in the land of Egypt that Jehovah spoke to Moses, saying, "I am Jehovah; speak to Pharaoh, king of Egypt, everything that I speak to you." And Moses said before Jehovah, "Look: I am foreskinned of lips, and how will Pharaoh listen to me?"* 7232

This is the Aaron and Moses means that from them come the divine theology and law among those people. *To whom Jehovah said,* symbolizes a command from [divine theology and law]. *Lead the children of Israel out of the land of Egypt* means that people of the Lord's spiritual kingdom would be delivered. *According to their armies* means by categories and subcategories of goodness within truth. *They were the ones speaking to Pharaoh, king of Egypt,* symbolizes a warning from them to spirits who cause trouble through pure falsity. *To lead the children of Israel out of Egypt* means to leave them alone and stop troubling them. *This is that Moses and Aaron* means that this comes from the law imparted by the Divine and from the resulting theology. *And it happened on the day Jehovah spoke to Moses in the land of Egypt* symbolizes the state the church was in when the law imparted by the Divine gave a command to members of the Lord's spiritual kingdom, while they were still in the vicinity of hell's inhabitants. *That Jehovah spoke to Moses, saying,* symbolizes being taught by the Divine. *I am Jehovah* symbolizes divine confirmation. *Speak to Pharaoh, king of Egypt, everything that I speak to you* symbolizes warnings delivered by inflow from the Divine to spirits who inflict persecution through pure falsity. *And Moses said before Jehovah* symbolizes thoughts about divine law on the part of people devoted to falsity. *Look: I am foreskinned of lips* means that it seems impure. *And how will Pharaoh listen to me?* means that people devoted to falsity will therefore not accept it.

This is the Aaron and Moses means that from them come the divine theology and law among those people. This can be seen from the representation of *Aaron* as the church's theology (discussed in §§6998, 7009, 7089) and from that of *Moses* as divine law (discussed in §§6723, 6752). Among 7233 people of the spiritual church, these two—divine law and theology—rise mainly out of the Word, though with a nod to the faith and neighborly love adopted by their founders. When I say it comes *from them,* I do not mean from Aaron and Moses but from the neighborly love and faith represented by Levi, Simeon, and Reuben, as discussed just above [§7231].

[2] Further on this subject, it is important to realize that the theology of the spiritual church is not a theology of real divine truth. This is because people whose religion is spiritual have no perception of divine truth, as people whose religion is heavenly do. In place of perception they have conscience, which is formed out of the truth and goodness acknowledged within their religion, no matter what that truth and goodness are like. (For the fact that people of the spiritual church are somewhat in the dark concerning religious truth, see §§86, 2708, 2715, 2716, 2718, 2831, 2935, 2937, 3241, 3246, 3833, 6289, 6500, 6865, 6945.) That is why all people in a spiritual religion acknowledge the decrees of its founders as the true tenets of faith. They do not seek further in the Word to find out whether those tenets are really true, and if they do seek, they do not discover the truth unless they have been reborn. Even then they must possess specific enlightenment. The reason they do not discover it is that although their intellect may be enlightened, their new will is not moved by any other goodness than the kind formed through union with the truth accepted within their religion. The will that is properly their own, you see, is a ruinous one, and their new will is formed in the intellectual side of their mind (see §§863, 875, 1023, 1043, 1044, 1555, 2256, 4328, 5113). The separation of their own will from this new will in the intellectual side leaves them with a feeble light resembling the light shed by the moon and stars at night, in comparison with the light shed by the sun during the day. A consequence is that in the Word's inner meaning, the moon stands for goodness that comes of spiritual love, while the sun stands for goodness that comes of heavenly love (§§30–38, 1529, 1530, 1531, 2495, 4060).

[3] This being the case with a spiritual religion, it is no wonder that to most people faith rather than neighborly love is the essential ingredient of religion, and that they discount teachings about neighborly love.

The fact that people take their teachings from Scripture does not ensure they are divine truth, because all manner of teachings can be hatched from the Word's literal meaning. A doctrine that caters to the lower passions can easily be seized on. So falsity can be seized on instead of truth, as is the case with the teachings of Jews, Socinians, and many others. This does not happen if a teaching is formed out of the inner meaning.

The inner meaning is not only the sense hidden within the outer meaning, as I have been demonstrating, but is also the sense that springs from a range of passages in their literal meaning properly compared with each other. This meaning is apprehended by people whose intellect is enlightened by the Lord. An enlightened intellect can tell the difference between apparent and real truth, and above all between falsity and truth, even if it lacks the ability to judge between one real truth and another.

However, our intellect cannot be enlightened unless we believe that love for the Lord and charity for our neighbor are the main, essential ingredients of religion. If we proceed from those acknowledgments, then as long as our heart is in them we see countless truths and even secrets revealed before us—and see them with inner acknowledgment—depending on the degree to which we are enlightened by the Lord.

To whom Jehovah said, symbolizes a command. This can be seen from 7234
the discussion in §7036 of the symbolism of *Jehovah said* as a command.

Lead the children of Israel out of the land of Egypt means that people 7235
of the Lord's spiritual kingdom would be delivered—delivered from the vicinity of spirits ruled by falsity. This can be seen from the symbolism of *leading out* as delivering, from the representation of the *children of Israel* as members of the Lord's spiritual kingdom (discussed in §§6426, 6637, and 6862, 6868, 7035, 7062, 7198, 7201, 7215, 7223), and from the symbolism of the *land of Egypt* as the place where falsities used for harassment are found.

According to their armies means by categories and subcategories of 7236
goodness within truth. This is clear from the symbolism of an *army* as the truth that leads to faith, which is discussed at §3448. In a spiritual religion, though, goodness is essentially nothing but truth, because truth is called goodness when a person lives by it. So when the word *army* is used of people in a spiritual religion who have been reborn, it symbolizes goodness that comes from truth, or goodness within truth.

The text speaks of the children of Israel as needing to be led out according to their armies because it refers to a time when they would leave Egypt, or in an inner sense, when they would emerge from battle against falsity. It therefore refers to a point at which they had just finished service as spiritual soldiers.

Strictly speaking, being led out according to their armies means being divided up according to goodness within truth. As a result, it means being divided into groups by type of goodness, the purpose being to represent the Lord's kingdom in the heavens. The nature of each person's goodness in general and in particular determines how all are divided up there, and it determines what place in the universal human they are allotted.

[2] The fact that everyone in the heavens is divided up by type of goodness shows how many different types of goodness there are and how varied they are. Goodness is so diverse that no one ever has the same kind as another. Even if millions of people were multiplied forever, one person's goodness would not be the same as another's, any more than one person would have the same face as another. And in the heavens, goodness shapes the angels' faces.

The reason variety never ends is that every form consists of various distinct parts. After all, if two parts were exactly the same, they would have to be one, not two. For the same reason, the material world contains nothing that is the same in every respect as anything else.

[3] The factor that makes goodness so diverse is truth. Truth united with goodness gives goodness its quality. What makes truth so manifold and various that it can diversify goodness in this way? It is the fact that true ideas are countless, that inner truth takes a different form than outer truth, and that illusions of the outer senses latch on, as do falsities rising out of corrupt desires. As true ideas are so numerous, then, you can see that their union [with goodness] would produce so many different strains that one could not possibly be the same as another. The concept is quite clear to anyone who knows that a mere twenty-three different [letters] combined in various ways can yield the words of all languages, with unending variety, even if there were thousands of languages. What then of components that number in the thousands and millions, as truths do?

This also proves the common rule in the world that there are as many opinions as heads, that is, as many different ideas as there are people.

7237 *They were the ones speaking to Pharaoh, king of Egypt,* symbolizes a warning from them to spirits who cause trouble through pure falsity. This is clear from the remarks at §7228 above, where similar words occur.

7238 *To lead the children of Israel out of Egypt* means to leave them alone and stop troubling them, as the following shows: Being *led out* symbolizes being delivered, as above at §7235, so it means that the spirits should leave them alone and stop troubling them. The *children of Israel* represent people in a spiritual religion, as mentioned just above at §7235. And *Egypt* symbolizes falsity used to cause trouble, as mentioned before.

7239 *This is that Moses and Aaron* means that this comes from the law imparted by the Divine and from the resulting theology. This is established by the representation of *Moses* as the law imparted by the Divine (discussed in §§6771, 6827) and by that of *Aaron* as the resulting theology (discussed in §§6998, 7009, 7089).

And it happened on the day Jehovah spoke to Moses in the land of Egypt symbolizes the state the church was in when the law imparted by the Divine gave a command to members of the Lord's spiritual kingdom, while they were still in the vicinity of hell's inhabitants. This can be seen from the following: A *day* symbolizes a state, as discussed in §§23, 487, 488, 493, 893, 2788, 3462, 3785, 4850, 6110, and in this case it symbolizes the state of the church, since that is the current subject. *Jehovah spoke* symbolizes a command, in this case to members of the Lord's spiritual kingdom. *Moses* represents the law imparted by the Divine, as discussed in §§6771, 6827. And the *land of Egypt* symbolizes the place where people of the Lord's spiritual kingdom were attacked by falsities. The attacks took place in the underground realm, which is near the hells; see §7090. The land in Egypt that the children of Israel occupied, called Goshen, symbolizes that realm, but the land the Egyptians occupied symbolizes the surrounding hells, which administered the attacks by falsity. 7240

That Jehovah spoke to Moses, saying, symbolizes being taught by the Divine. This can be seen from the symbolism of *Jehovah spoke* as being taught anew (noted at §7226) and from the representation of *Moses* as the law imparted by the Divine (discussed in §§6771, 6827). 7241

I am Jehovah symbolizes divine confirmation. This can be seen from statements above in §§7192, 7202. 7242

Speak to Pharaoh, king of Egypt, everything that I speak to you symbolizes warnings delivered by inflow from the Divine to spirits who inflict persecution through pure falsity, as the following shows: *Speaking* to people devoted to falsity symbolizes a warning, as above at §7220. *Pharaoh, king of Egypt,* represents spirits who inflict persecution through pure falsity, as discussed at §§7220, 7228. And *everything that I speak to you* symbolizes what flows in from the Divine. 7243

And Moses said before Jehovah symbolizes thoughts about divine law on the part of people devoted to falsity. This can be seen from the symbolism of *he said* as thoughts (mentioned at §7094) and from the representation of *Moses* as divine law (discussed in §§6723, 6752). The way these words lead into the next shows that they stand for thoughts about divine law on the part of people devoted to falsity, because when "he said" occurs and symbolizes thoughts, it includes what comes after it. Here it includes the idea that divine law seems impure to people devoted to falsity. 7244

7245 *Look: I am foreskinned of lips* means that it seems impure—that is, divine law seems impure to people devoted to falsity. *And how will Pharaoh listen to me?* means that people devoted to falsity will therefore not accept it. This can be seen from the discussion above in §§7224 and 7225, where the same words occur.

In an inner sense, Moses' description of himself as foreskinned of lips means that divine law seems impure to people who subscribe to falsity, in keeping with the explanation at §7225. In the narrative sense, though, Moses as head of Jacob's descendants stands for those descendants and for anything of religion existing with them, as above at §7041. On that level of meaning, his being foreskinned of lips means that the worship of God among that nation was such. You see, that nation's worship was impure, because its people worshiped what is external and entirely rejected anything internal, meaning faith and neighborly love. In fact, they even spurned any knowledge of profound concepts, such as all the symbolism and representation involved in ritual. This being their character, their worship was impure, because they worshiped Jehovah out of self-love and materialism rather than love for him and for their neighbor. Moses' description of himself as foreskinned of lips in its narrative sense symbolizes this worship, but in an inner sense it has the symbolism given in the explanation above at §7225.

The Inhabitants and Spirits of Venus

7246 ON Venus there are two kinds of people, with opposite dispositions: fierce, almost brutal people, and gentle, humane people. Those who are fierce and almost brutal appear on the side of the planet facing this way, while those who are gentle and humane appear on the opposite side.

Bear in mind, though, that they appear there in keeping with the state of their life, because the state of one's life creates all appearances of location and space.

7247 As spirits picture it, Venus appears on the left, slightly behind and somewhat distant from this planet. I say "as spirits picture it" because no spirit can see the world's sun or any planet. Rather, spirits simply have the idea that these bodies exist, and the bodies appear the way the spirits picture them. The world's sun shows up as a dark blot behind the back.

The planets always appear in the same places, rather than wandering as they do in the world; see §7171.

7248 Concerning the inhabitants of that planet who appear on this side after they die and become spirits, I was told that they take great delight in pillage, and the greatest possible delight in eating plundered food. The pleasure they feel when thinking about eating plundered food was communicated to me, and I sensed that it was supreme.

Our own planet has also had inhabitants with a similarly fierce nature. This is evidenced by the histories of various nations, by the inhabitants of Canaan (1 Samuel 30:16), and by the nation of Judah and Israel, even in David's time, when its people went on yearly raids, looting the surrounding nations and rejoicing in the plunder.

[2] As for inhabitants of this type on Venus, they enjoy pillage, but that does not mean they are cruel. They drown the victims of their raids, but they save the ones they can, and the ones they drown they later bury. This is a sign that they possess a degree of humanity. They are unlike Jews who liked to toss aside their murder victims, leaving them out to be eaten by wild forest animals and birds, and sometimes to use cruel and savage methods of putting their enemies to death (2 Samuel 12:31).

I was able to perceive how much Jews had enjoyed such behavior by an aura communicated to me from a large number of them, who quickly ran close and then ran away.

7249 I was also told that most of the inhabitants of that planet are giants and that inhabitants of our own planet come up only to their navel.

I heard too that the inhabitants appearing on this side of the planet are stupid, not asking what heaven is or what eternal life is but caring only about concerns involving their land and their livestock.

7250 People who are still like this when they reach the other life are completely overcome there with falsity and evil. Their hells appear around their planet and do not communicate with the hells of our planet's evil spirits. This is because they have an entirely different mindset and character, which means that their evils and falsities are also of an entirely different kind.

However, the ones who are capable of being saved are taken to places set aside for the process of devastation, where they are reduced to the depths of despair. There is no other way to remove that kind of evil and falsity. While they are in a state of despair, they shout that they are animals, brutes, an abomination, detestable, and therefore damned. Some of them also cry out against heaven in that state, but they are forgiven for this because it comes of desperation. The Lord makes sure they do not transgress certain limits in their torrent of criticism. Once they have suffered the furthest extreme of the process, their bodily urges die, so to speak, and as a result they are finally saved.

7251 I was also told concerning them that when they lived on their planet, they believed in a Supreme Creator without any mediator. They are the ones who undergo the devastation described above, and they are finally saved once they have learned and accepted the idea that the Lord is the only God, Savior, and Mediator. I once heard them confessing that without the Mediator they could never have been saved because they were unclean and unworthy.

I also saw some of them taken up to heaven after they had suffered the worst, and when they had been welcomed there, I sensed such a tender gladness in them that it wrung tears from my eyes.

7252 The inhabitants and spirits of Venus who appear on the other side of the planet have a disposition that is almost exactly the opposite, since they are gentle and humane. Some of the spirits from there were allowed by the Lord to come to me, and they appeared just above my head. In conversation with me they said that when they were in the world they acknowledged our Lord as their only God and that they do so even more fully now. They said that on their planet they saw him walking among them, and they also presented an image showing how he looked to them.

7253 In the universal human, these spirits relate to the memory of matter-based concepts corresponding to the memory of non-matter-based concepts that the spirits of Mercury constitute. See the description of Mercury's spirits at §7170.

7254 The end of the next chapter will tell about the inhabitants and spirits of Mars [§§7358–7365].

Exodus 7

Teachings on Neighborly Love

SINCE that which is good makes heaven in us, and that which is evil makes hell, it is absolutely essential to know what goodness is and what evil is. As already mentioned [§7178], goodness is the result of love for the Lord and charity for one's neighbor, and evil is the result of self-love and love of worldly advantages, so it follows that love alone tells us what is good and what is evil. 7255

Everything in the universe that is in harmony with the divine design relates to goodness and truth, while everything in the universe that opposes the divine design relates to evil and falsity. This is because goodness and truth, which come from the Divine, go to make up the divine design. In fact they *are* the divine design. 7256

The goodness that comes of love for the Lord is called heavenly goodness, and the goodness that comes of charity for one's neighbor is called spiritual goodness. I must explain below the nature and extent of the difference between heavenly goodness embodying love for the Lord and spiritual goodness embodying charity for one's neighbor. 7257

Teachings about the heavenly goodness that embodies love for the Lord are profusely abundant and deeply secret. Teachings about the spiritual goodness that embodies charity for one's neighbor are also abundant and secret, but less so than teachings about the heavenly goodness that embodies love for the Lord. 7258

It is plain that teachings about charity are abundant, since charity cannot be the same in one person as in another, and one neighbor is not the same as another.

Because teachings about neighborly love were so abundant, the ancients (among whom these teachings were the core teachings of the church) divided charity for their neighbor into many categories and subcategories. To each category they assigned a name, teaching how charity ought to be exercised toward the members of one category and toward the members of another. In this way they reduced the teachings about neighborly love to order and made it possible to understand the different ways in which that love was to be exercised. 7259

7260 The names they assigned the beneficiaries of neighborly love were numerous. Some they called the blind, some the lame, some the maimed, some the poor, some the wretched and afflicted, some the orphaned, some the widowed. More broadly they referred to them as hungry people to whom they should give something to eat, thirsty people to whom they should give something to drink, foreigners they should gather in, naked people they should clothe, sick people they should visit, and people in jail they should come to. Regarding these categories, see §§4954–4959.

7261 The ancients who were part of the church received these names from heaven and took them to refer to people who were spiritually such. Their teachings on neighborly love taught them the identity of these people and the form neighborly love should take toward each.

7262 That is why the same names come up in the Word, where they symbolize people who are such in a spiritual sense.

In itself the Word is nothing but a lesson on love for the Lord and charity for one's neighbor, as the Lord also teaches:

> You shall love the Lord your God with all your heart and with all your soul and with all your mind; *this is the first and great commandment.* A second is similar to it: You shall love your neighbor as yourself. *On these two commandments depend the Law and the Prophets.* (Matthew 22:37, 38, 39, 40)

The Law and the Prophets are the whole Word.

7263 The reason the same names come up in the Word is that people whose worship was outward would exercise charity toward the kind of people called by those names, while people whose worship was inward would exercise it toward the kind meant spiritually. The simple-thinking would therefore understand and follow the [Lord's] Word in a simple way and the wise in a wise way. A further purpose was for the outward practice of charity to introduce the simple-thinking to the inward practice of it.

Exodus 7

1. And Jehovah said to Moses, "See, I have made you a god to Pharaoh, and Aaron your brother will be your prophet.

2. You will speak everything that I command you. And Aaron your brother will speak to Pharaoh, and [Pharaoh] is to send the children of Israel from his land.

3. And I will harden Pharaoh's heart and multiply my signs and my portents in the land of Egypt.

4. And Pharaoh will not listen to you. And I will lay my hand on the Egyptians and lead my armies—my people, the children of Israel—out of the land of Egypt with great judgments.

5. And the Egyptians will know that I am Jehovah, in my stretching my hand out over Egypt, and [when] I lead the children of Israel out of their midst."

6. And Moses did so, as did Aaron; as Jehovah had commanded them, so they did.

7. And Moses was a son of eighty years, and Aaron a son of eighty-three years, in their speaking to Pharaoh.

8. And Jehovah spoke to Moses and Aaron, saying,

9. "When Pharaoh says to you, saying, 'Show a portent for yourselves,' then you shall say to Aaron, 'Take your staff and throw it down before Pharaoh; it will become a water snake.'"

10. And Moses came to Pharaoh, as did Aaron, and they did so, as Jehovah had commanded, and Aaron threw his staff down before Pharaoh and before his servants, and it became a water snake.

11. And Pharaoh too called sages and sorcerers, and they did so too—the magicians of Egypt, with their spells.

12. And they each threw their staff down, and these became water snakes. And Aaron's staff swallowed up their staffs.

13. And Pharaoh's heart hardened, and he did not listen to them, as Jehovah had spoken.

14. And Jehovah said to Moses, "Pharaoh's heart has turned leaden; he has refused to send the people away.

15. Go to Pharaoh in the morning (watch: he walks out to the water) and stand to meet him by the bank of the river, and take in your hand the staff that turned into a snake.

16. And you shall say to him, 'Jehovah, God of the Hebrews, has sent me to you, saying, "Send my people away, and let them serve me in the wilderness," and here, you have not listened so far.

17. This is what Jehovah said: "In this you will know that I am Jehovah: Here, I am striking with the staff that is in my hand on the waters that are in the river, and they will turn to blood.

18. And the fish that are in the river will die, and the river will reek, and the Egyptians will labor to drink water from the river.'""

19. And Jehovah said to Moses, "Say to Aaron, 'Take your staff and stretch your hand out over the waters of Egypt, over their streams, over their rivers, and over their pools, and over every gathering of their waters, and they will be blood. And there will be blood in all the land of Egypt and in containers of wood and in containers of stone.'"

20. And Moses and Aaron did so, as Jehovah had commanded, and he lifted the staff and struck the waters that were in the river before the eyes of Pharaoh and before the eyes of his servants, and all the waters that were in the river turned to blood.

21. And the fish that were in the river died, and the river reeked, and the Egyptians could not drink water from the river. And there was blood in the whole land of Egypt.

22. And the magicians of Egypt did the same with their spells. And Pharaoh's heart hardened, and he did not listen to them, as Jehovah had spoken.

23. And Pharaoh looked away and came to his house and did not take even this to heart.

24. And all the Egyptians dug around the river [for] water to drink, because they could not drink from the waters of the river.

25. And seven days were fulfilled after Jehovah's striking the river.

26 [= NRSV 8:1]. And Jehovah said to Moses, "Come to Pharaoh, and you shall say to him, 'This is what Jehovah says: "Send my people away and let them serve me.

27 [= 8:2]. And if you refuse to send them away, watch: I [will] afflict your whole border with frogs.

28 [= 8:3]. And the river will cause frogs to creep out, and they will go up and come into your house and into your bedroom and onto your bed and into the house of your servants and of your people and into your ovens and into your kneading troughs.

29 [= 8:4]. And onto you and onto your people and onto all your servants the frogs will come up."'"

Summary

7264 THE inner meaning of what follows is about the devastation and eventually the damnation of spirits devoted to falsity and evil. The process by which they are devastated is depicted by eleven plagues inflicted on the Egyptians and their land.

7265 In the current chapter the inner meaning is about the first three steps of devastation. *First:* Sheer illusion started to take over in them, leading to false thoughts. This is depicted by the snake that Aaron's staff turned into. *Second:* Real truth became falsity in them, and falsity became truth. This is depicted by the blood that the water turned into. *Third:* They argued against religious truth and goodness on the basis of falsity. This step is depicted by the frogs from the river.

Inner Meaning

7266 EXODUS 7:1, 2, 3, 4, 5, 6, 7. *And Jehovah said to Moses, "See, I have made you a god to Pharaoh, and Aaron your brother will be your prophet. You will speak everything that I command you. And Aaron your brother will speak to Pharaoh, and [Pharaoh] is to send the children of Israel from his land. And I will harden Pharaoh's heart and multiply my signs and my portents in the land of Egypt. And Pharaoh will not listen to you. And I will lay my hand on the Egyptians and lead my armies—my people, the children of Israel—out of the land of Egypt with great judgments. And the Egyptians will know that I am Jehovah, in my stretching my hand out over the Egyptians, and [when] I lead the children of Israel out of their midst." And Moses did so, as did Aaron; as Jehovah had commanded them, so they did. And Moses was a son of eighty years, and Aaron a son of eighty-three years, in their speaking to Pharaoh.*

And Jehovah said to Moses symbolizes instruction. *See, I have made you a god to Pharaoh* symbolizes divine law and its power over people devoted to falsity. *And Aaron your brother will be your prophet* symbolizes the doctrine that results. *You will speak everything that I command you* symbolizes receiving the divine inflow and passing it along. *And Aaron your brother will speak to Pharaoh* symbolizes receiving the inflow from there and passing it along to people devoted to falsity. *And [Pharaoh] is to send the children of Israel [from his land]* symbolizes [an inflow telling them] to stop inflicting harassment. *And I will harden Pharaoh's heart* symbolizes obstinacy on the part of evil-from-falsity. *And multiply my signs and my portents* symbolizes warnings of every kind, and not a single one missing. *In the land of Egypt* means where the harassers are. *And Pharaoh will not listen to you* means that believers in falsity will not accept it. *And I will lay my hand on the Egyptians* means that they will consequently be forced by divine power to comply. *And lead my army—my people, the children of Israel—out* means that people dedicated to goodness and truth are to be delivered. *Of the land of Egypt* means from persecution. *With great judgments* means in keeping with the laws of order. *And the Egyptians will know that I am Jehovah* means that they will be afraid of the Divine. *In [my] stretching my hand out over the Egyptians* means when they notice God's power over them. *And [when] I lead the children of Israel out of their midst* means and when they see people of the spiritual church delivered, as they will. *And Moses did so, as did Aaron; as Jehovah had commanded [them], so they did* means that what was said was also done. *And Moses was a son of eighty years* symbolizes the state and nature of the law imparted by the Divine. *And Aaron a son of eighty-three years* symbolizes the state and nature of the theology. *In their speaking to Pharaoh* means when these commands have been delivered.

7267 *And Jehovah said to Moses* symbolizes instruction—in this case, instruction in how to proceed with people devoted to falsity who inflict harassment. This can be seen from the symbolism of *Jehovah said* as instruction, as discussed at §7186.

7268 *See, I have made you a god to Pharaoh* symbolizes divine law and its power over people devoted to falsity, as the following shows: *Making you a god* symbolizes divine truth (in other words, divine law) and its power. Where the Word talks about truth and the power of truth, it uses the name God, but where it talks about goodness it uses the name Jehovah; see §§300, 2586, 2769, 2807, 2822, 3910, 3921 at the end, 4287, 4295, 4402, 7010. And *Pharaoh* represents people devoted to falsity who inflict harassment, as mentioned in §§6651, 6679, 6683.

Further information regarding the symbolism of *God:* In the highest sense God is divinity as it exists above the heavens, but in an inward sense God is divinity as it exists *in* the heavens. Divinity as it exists above the heavens is divine goodness, but divinity as it exists in the heavens is divine truth. From divine goodness comes divine truth, which creates and organizes heaven. What is properly called heaven is simply divinity given form there, because the angels in heaven are human forms receiving what is divine and making up the overall form, which is the form of a human.

[2] Divine truth in the heavens is what the Old Testament Word means by God. That is why the term for God in the original language is the plural Elohim. It is also why angels in the heavens, being receptacles of divine truth, are called gods, as for instance in David:

> Who in heaven will compare themselves to Jehovah, will be like Jehovah *among the children of gods?* (Psalms 89:6, 7, 8)

In the same author:

> Give Jehovah—you *children of gods*—give Jehovah glory and strength! (Psalms 29:1)

In the same author:

> I have said, "*You are gods,* and you are all children of the Highest One." (Psalms 82:6)

In John:

> Jesus said, "Is it not written in your law, 'I have said, "*You are gods*"'? So he called those people *gods* to whom the Word came." (John 10:34, 35)

Then there are passages in which the Lord is called God of the gods and Lord of the lords—passages such as Genesis 46:2, 3; Deuteronomy 10:17; Numbers 16:22; Daniel 11:36; Psalms 136:1, 2, 3.

These passages reveal in what sense Moses is called a god—a god to Pharaoh here and a god to Aaron in Exodus 4:16—namely, that he represented divine law, which is divine truth and is called the Word. That is why Aaron is called his prophet here and his mouth in the earlier passage; Aaron is being referred to as someone who declares divine truth in such a way that listeners can understand it, even though it actually comes directly from the Lord and transcends all understanding. Moreover, since a prophet means someone who teaches and declares divine truth in a way that listeners can understand, it also means the teachings of the church themselves. This is mentioned in the next section.

And Aaron your brother will be your prophet symbolizes the doctrine that results. This can be seen from the symbolism of a *prophet* as doctrinal truth and therefore as teachings from the Word, which is discussed at §2534. *Aaron* represents the church's doctrine, or teachings about goodness and truth that come from the Word; see §§6998, 7009, 7089. 7269

Since a prophet symbolizes doctrinal teachings, in a narrower sense it symbolizes someone who teaches doctrine, in keeping with the discussion directly above at the end of §7268.

7270 *You will speak everything that I command you* symbolizes receiving the divine inflow and passing it along, as the following shows: Moses, who is to speak, represents divine truth, and Aaron represents teachings derived from that truth, as discussed at §7089. *Speaking* symbolizes an inflow and reception of the inflow, as mentioned at §5797. And *commanding* also symbolizes an inflow, as discussed in §§5486, 5732. Here it symbolizes receiving the inflow.

This shows that *speaking* symbolizes an indirect inflow of divine truth into doctrine, or into a teacher of doctrine. After all, the assumption is that in speaking Jehovah's commands, Moses (divine truth) would be relaying them to Aaron (doctrine, or a teacher of doctrine) and therefore to one who would pass them along. It also shows that *commanding* symbolizes a direct divine inflow into divine law (represented by Moses).

[2] How to understand all this can be seen from earlier comments in §§7009, 7010 to the effect that Moses represents truth that comes directly from the Divine and that Aaron represents truth that comes indirectly.

If you do not know how the pattern of sequential levels works, you also cannot see how inflow works, so I need to explain briefly. Truth that comes directly from the Lord comes from divine infinity itself, so not a whit of it can be taken in by any finite living entity, including angels. For this reason the Lord created sequential levels that could be used as a means of communicating the divine truth that comes directly from him. However, the first level in sequence after this divine level is still too full to be received by any finite living entity, including angels. The Lord therefore created yet another level, through which some share of the divine truth that comes directly from him could be received. This level is divine truth as it exists in heaven. The first two levels are above the heavens like brilliant fiery rings around the sun, which is the Lord. Such is the sequential pattern down to the heaven closest to the Lord, which is the third heaven, populated by the innocent and wise. From there the levels continue in sequence to the lowest heaven and from the lowest heaven to the sensory, bodily level of a human being, which is the outermost level to receive the inflow.

[3] This shows that there is a continuous sequence of levels from the first origin (the Lord) through to the lowest level in us and in fact to the lowest realm of the physical world. The lowest level in us and in the physical world is relatively sluggish and therefore cold, relatively vague and therefore dim. It also shows that through this sequence everything has an unbroken connection with the original source of existence.

Spiritual inflow operates according to the sequence of levels; the divine truth that radiates directly from divine goodness flows in on one level after another. Along the way, at each new level in order, it grows more general and therefore vaguer and dimmer; it grows slower and therefore more sluggish and colder.

These remarks clarify what the divine pattern of sequential levels and so of inflows is like.

[4] It is really important to know, though, that the divine truth that flows into the third heaven—the heaven closest to the Lord—also flows right down to the lowest levels of the pattern, without any sequential modification. Even on the lowest level it exercises direct control over everything and makes all necessary provisions itself, on behalf of the first origin. This holds the sequential levels together in good order and connection.

The truth of this is somewhat clear from a law not unknown to scholars in the world that there is only one substance that truly subsists, and that everything else is formed from it. That one, unique substance exists throughout the entities formed from it, not only as the form of the entity but also as what is unformed, as it is at its original source. Otherwise an entity formed from it could never subsist or act. But this is said for those who will understand.

And [Pharaoh] is to send the children of Israel [from his land] symbol- 7271
izes [an inflow telling them] to stop inflicting harassment, as the following shows: Pharaoh, to whom this was to be said, represents people who use falsity to inflict harassment, as dealt with in §§7107, 7110, 7126, 7142. *Sending them [from his land]* means that they should stop. And the *children of Israel* symbolize people of the spiritual church, as in §§6426, 6637, 6862, 6868, 7035, 7062, 7198.

And I will harden Pharaoh's heart symbolizes obstinacy on the part of 7272
evil-from-falsity. This can be seen from the symbolism of *hardening* as obstinacy. The fact that it is on the part of evil-from-falsity is symbolized by *Pharaoh's heart.* In a positive sense a heart symbolizes the goodness associated with heavenly love (§§3313, 3887, 3889), so in a negative sense it symbolizes the evil of hell. The reason it is evil arising from falsity is that Pharaoh represents people devoted to falsity.

Evil-from-falsity is evil that traces its origin to false premises. Take for example the premise that people are rendered holy by outward acts, such as (among the people of Israel and of Judah) sacrifices, ritual washing, and the spattering of blood, rather than by neighborly love and faith. This led them to believe they were holy even though they lived lives of hatred, revenge, plundering, violence, and so on. These evils are what are called evil-from-falsity because they trace their origin to false premises.

[2] For another example, take people who believe that faith alone saves them and that deeds of neighborly love contribute nothing to their salvation. Take people who believe they are saved even in the final hour of death, no matter how they have lived the entire course of their life. I am talking about people led by these premises to live lives devoid of neighborly love, lives of contempt, of enmity and hatred for anyone who fails to worship them, of lust for revenge, of longing to deprive others of their goods, of ruthlessness, deceit, and trickery. These evils too are evil-from-falsity, because falsity persuades such people either that the evils are not evil or, even if they are, they will be wiped away. All that is required, they believe, is to proclaim with apparent trust before their last breath that the Lord intercedes and that his suffering on the cross wiped away their sins.

[3] For yet another example, take someone who turns in prayer to dead human beings as saints and who therefore worships these people and even their images. The evil in this worship is evil-from-falsity.

People who do the kind of evil that arises out of falsity always believe the falsity to be true, so they consider the evil to be either not evil or at least not capable of damning them.

People who believe sins can be pardoned by other human beings, and people who believe they can make it into heaven no matter what sins they have indulged in—no matter how bad they smell spiritually—also [commit evil-from-falsity].

In short, there are as many different kinds of evil based on falsity as there are false beliefs and false ideas of worship. These evils damn a person, but not to the same extent as evil that originates in evil. Evil that originates in evil stems from perverted longings that arise out of self-love or materialism.

7273 *And multiply my signs and my portents* symbolizes warnings of every kind, and not a single one missing. This is clear from the symbolism of *signs and portents* as confirmations of truth (treated of in §§3900, 6870, 7012) and as a means used by divine power (§6910). Here they symbolize warnings, because as a result of them, [the Egyptians] saw both the falsity of their thinking and the divine power and were accordingly warned.

The reason for saying that believers in falsity receive warnings of every kind, and not a single one missing, is that people devoted to evil are not damned the instant they arrive in the other world. They are not condemned until they have been "visited," or examined. The reason for examining them is to enable them to recognize for themselves that they cannot help being damned, because they have not lived any other way. It also enables [other] spirits and angels to see the same. As a consequence, they can no longer be excused in their own eyes or in the eyes of others. [2] The method by which they are examined is the one laid down by divine truth, which naturally means that nothing whatever is missing.

The method of divine truth that applies to the evil who are being damned is different from that which applies to the good who are being saved. The difference is that the method for the evil who are being damned involves divine truth detached from divine goodness and therefore detached from mercy, because these people did not accept divine goodness and consequently rejected mercy. The other method, for the good who are being saved, involves divine truth united with divine goodness and therefore with mercy, because these people accepted divine goodness and consequently the Lord's mercy.

Step by step, as the evil are being examined with this method, they are also being judged and damned.

From this you can see that they receive warnings of every kind—so that not one is missing—before being condemned to hell. That is what is symbolized by the signs and miracles worked in Egypt before the firstborn were killed and the Egyptians died in the Suph Sea. (The Suph Sea is hell.)

In the land of Egypt means where the harassers are. This is established 7274
by the symbolism of the *land of Egypt* as the place where spirits who subscribe to falsity and inflict harassment are found, as dealt with at §7240.

And Pharaoh will not listen to you means that believers in falsity will 7275
not accept it. This can be seen from an earlier discussion at §7224, where similar words occur.

And I will lay my hand on the Egyptians means that they will conse- 7276
quently be forced by divine power to comply, as the following shows: A *hand* symbolizes power, as discussed in §§878, 4931–4937, 5327, 5328, 7011, 7188, 7189, and since Jehovah is speaking about himself, calling it *his* hand, it symbolizes divine power. And the *Egyptians* symbolize believers in falsity who inflict harassment, as mentioned before. This makes it plain that *I will lay my hand on the Egyptians* means that believers in falsity will be forced by divine power to comply.

And lead my army—my people, the children of Israel—out means that 7277
people dedicated to goodness and truth are to be delivered, as the following shows: *Leading out* means delivering. An *army* symbolizes goodness

within truth, of all kinds. The symbolism of a *people* has to do with individuals dedicated to spiritual truth and goodness (discussed in §§1259, 1260, 3295, 3581, 4619) and consequently with adherents of a spiritual religion (§§2928, 7207). And the *children of Israel* represent such adherents of a spiritual religion (mentioned above at §7271) and therefore people committed to goodness and truth.

7278 *Of the land of Egypt* means from persecution. This is established by the symbolism of the *land of Egypt* as the location of spirits devoted to falsity who inflict persecution, as mentioned at §§7240, 7274, and so as persecution itself. After all, a land means the nation there, and a nation in an inner sense means a characteristic of that nation, so here it symbolizes persecution.

7279 *With great judgments* means in keeping with the laws of order, as can be seen from the earlier discussion at §7206.

7280 *And the Egyptians will know that I am Jehovah* means that they will be afraid of the Divine. This can be seen from the symbolism of *knowing that I am Jehovah* as being afraid of the Divine (discussed below) and from that of *Egyptians* as spirits devoted to falsity who inflict persecution.

About the fear the Divine will inspire in spirits who subscribe to falsity and inflict persecution: It is important to know that fear is the only way to control the hellish and keep them under restraint.

Fear is a bond that the upright and the evil have in common. The upright, though, have internal fear—fear for their salvation, or fear that their souls will be destroyed. They are afraid of doing anything that would violate their conscience, that is, anything that would violate the truth and goodness that make up their conscience. So they fear violating what is just and fair, which means they fear doing anything to harm their neighbor. This fear becomes holy fear so far as it is joined with charitable desires and especially so far as it is joined with love for the Lord. It is then like the fear children have for parents they love. Under those circumstances, the greater the sway of love and its goodness over a person, the less visible the fear, but the less the sway of goodness, the more visible the fear, which turns into anxiety. Such is the fear of God that the Word mentions many times.

[2] The fear the evil feel, on the other hand, is no internal fear, no fear for their salvation, so it is no conscientious fear. Such fear they totally rejected in the world, both by the way they lived and by distorted principles justifying their way of life. Rather than internal fear they have external fear, or fear of being deprived of rank, wealth, and consequent

prestige, fear of being punished by the law, and fear of losing their life. Those are the fears that people devoted to evil feel while they are in the world.

When they reach the other world and become impervious to control or restraint by internal fear, they are held back by external fear, which is imposed on them through punishments. Those are what frighten them away from doing evil. Eventually they develop fear of the Divine, but again it is a shallow fear, devoid of any urge to stop doing evil from a desire for goodness. What motivates them instead is a terror of punishments that finally come to horrify them.

[3] All this now shows that fear is the only way to keep people under restraint and that the external fear of punishment is the only way to control the evil. Clearly that is the reason for the torment the evil undergo in hell.

You see, when the wicked go to the other world and are left to their passions—the external restraints they had in the world having been taken from them—they are like wild animals. They want nothing more than to dominate and to destroy anyone who does not coddle them. This is the highest pleasure of their life. After all, the more we love ourselves, the more we hate people who do not cater to us, and the more we hate people, the more we enjoy destroying them. But in the world we hide this.

In [my] stretching my hand out over the Egyptians means when they 7281
notice God's power over them, as the following shows: A *hand* ascribed to the Divine symbolizes divine power, as stated above at §7276. It is clear from this that the meaning of sitting at the right hand of God is omnipotence. And *Egyptians* symbolize believers in falsity who inflict persecution, as discussed before.

And [when] I lead the children of Israel out of their midst means and 7282
when they see people of the spiritual church delivered, as they will. This is evident from the symbolism of *leading out* as being delivered (as above at §7277) and from that of the *children of Israel* as people of the spiritual church (mentioned above at §7271).

And Moses did so, as did Aaron; as Jehovah had commanded [them], so 7283
they did means that what was said was also done. This is self-evident.

And Moses was a son of eighty years symbolizes the state and nature of 7284
the law imparted by the Divine. This can be seen from the representation of *Moses* as the law imparted by the Divine (discussed in §§6771, 6827) and from the symbolism of *eighty years* as the state and nature of the law imparted by the Divine, specifically among the people of the spiritual

church at the time of this first visitation. The symbolism of eighty here would be difficult to articulate because it involves the whole state and nature of the law imparted by the Divine as it existed among them at that time. Eighty means a state of trial (see §1963), but in that case it involves the same thing as forty. However, as it is also the product when ten and eight are multiplied, one must seek there too for the symbolism of the number. For the meaning of ten, see §§576, 1906, 1988, 2284, 3107, 4638; and for that of eight, §§2044, 2866.

For the general principle that all numbers have symbolic meaning, and that they symbolize the state and nature of something, see §§482, 487, 575, 647, 648, 755, 813, 1963, 1988, 2075, 2252, 3252, 4264, 4495, 4670, 5265, 5291, 5335, 5708, 6175.

7285 *And Aaron a son of eighty-three years* symbolizes the state and nature of the theology, as the following shows: *Aaron* represents the church's teachings, as discussed in §§6998, 7009, 7089. And the number *eighty-three* symbolizes the state and nature—the state and nature of that theology. Its state and nature cannot be known in detail, though, unless the number is reduced to its factors and is then applied to the people whose theology it was. For more about numbers in Scripture, see directly above at §7284.

7286 *In their speaking to Pharaoh* means when these commands have been delivered. This can be seen from the symbolism of *speaking* as a command (noted at §7240) and from the representation of *Pharaoh* as believers in falsity who inflict harassment (noted in §§7107, 7110, 7126, 7142).

7287 Exodus 7:8, 9, 10, 11, 12, 13. *And Jehovah spoke to Moses and to Aaron, saying, "When Pharaoh says to you, saying, 'Show a portent for yourselves,' then you shall say to Aaron, 'Take your staff and throw it down before Pharaoh; it will become a water snake.'" And Moses came to Pharaoh, as did Aaron, and they did so, as Jehovah had commanded, and Aaron threw his staff down before Pharaoh and before his servants, and it became a water snake. And Pharaoh too called sages and sorcerers, and they did so too—the magicians of Egypt, with their spells. And they each threw their staff down, and these became water snakes. And Aaron's staff swallowed up their staffs. And Pharaoh's heart hardened, and he did not listen to them, as Jehovah had spoken.*

And Jehovah spoke to Moses and to Aaron, saying, symbolizes instruction. *When Pharaoh says to you* means if they have doubts about the Divine. *Saying, "Show a portent [for yourselves],"* means and therefore want proof. *Then you shall say to Aaron* symbolizes an inflow and the communication of that inflow. *Take your staff and throw it down before Pharaoh* symbolizes a display of power. *It will become a water snake* means through the fact that sheer illusion and consequent falsity will predominate in them. *And Moses came to Pharaoh, as did Aaron, and they did so, as Jehovah had commanded* means that it was carried out. *And Aaron threw his staff down before Pharaoh and his servants, and it became a water snake* means that sheer illusion and consequent falsity took over in them. *And Pharaoh too called sages and sorcerers* symbolizes misuse of the divine design. *And they did so too—the magicians of Egypt, with their spells* means that by this misuse they seemed to do the same, twisting the purposes of the divine plan. *And they each threw their staff down, and these became water snakes* symbolizes power derived from the divine design to make people's perception of truth grow dull. *And Aaron's staff swallowed up their staffs* means that this power was taken away from them. *And Pharaoh's heart hardened* symbolizes obstinacy. *And he did not listen to them* means that spirits engaged in evil-from-falsity were unreceptive. *As Jehovah had spoken* means as predicted.

And Jehovah spoke to Moses and to Aaron, saying, symbolizes instruction. This is clear from the discussion in §§6879, 6881, 6883, 6891 of the symbolism of *Jehovah's speaking, saying,* as instruction. 7288

When Pharaoh says to you means if they have doubts about the Divine. This can be seen from the next words, "If Pharaoh says, 'Show a portent,'" which plainly imply doubt about the Divine, since to desire a portent is to be skeptical until there is empirical proof. 7289

Saying, "Show a portent [for yourselves]," means and therefore want proof. This can be seen from the symbolism of *portents* and signs as proof of the truth, as mentioned in §§3900, 6870. 7290

About the portents and signs described in the next verses, it is necessary to know that they were performed for the kind of people whose worship was shallow and who did not wish to learn about inward worship. People whose worship was like this had to be compelled by external means. That is why miracles were performed for the people of Israel and Judah, since they had only external worship and no internal worship. In addition, as they had no desire to worship inwardly, they had to engage in external worship so that on the outside they could represent something holy and there could be communication with heaven through some vestige of religion. After all, anything that has correspondence, representation, or symbolism unites the physical world with the spiritual. This then was the reason so many miracles were performed for that nation.

[2] In contrast, for people whose worship is internal—people with neighborly love and faith—miracles are not performed, because they are

harmful; they force belief, and what is forced does not remain but rather dissolves. The inner attributes of worship, which are faith and neighborly love, must be rooted in freedom because a person then takes ownership of them, and what is owned in this way remains. Anything rooted as a result of duress, on the other hand, stays outside the inner self in the outer self. The only way anything enters the inner self is through ideas that are truly understood, which means through reason. The soil of the inner self that accepts the seed is enlightened rationality. That is why no miracles happen today.

From this it is evident that miracles can be harmful. They compel belief and cement into the outer self the conviction that certain ideas are so. If the inner self afterward takes an idea proved valid by miracles and denies it, the inner and outer selves come into opposition and conflict. Eventually, when the concepts gleaned from miracles melt away, falsity and truth form a bond, and profanation results. This shows how damaging miracles would be today in the church in which the inner depths of worship have been revealed. That is also what is meant by the Lord's words to Thomas:

> Because you have seen me, Thomas, you have believed; fortunate are those who do not see, and believe. (John 20:29)

Fortunate too, then, are those who believe without miracles.

[3] However, miracles do not hurt people who worship outwardly without worshiping inwardly. No opposition of inner and outer self can exist in them, so no conflict can occur either and consequently no profanation.

The fact that miracles also do not add anything to one's faith is plain enough from the complete and utter ineffectiveness of the miracles among the Israelite people in Egypt and in the wilderness. Although that people shortly before had seen many miracles in Egypt—after they had seen the Suph Sea parted and the Egyptians drowned in it, a pillar of cloud going before them by day and a pillar of fire by night, manna raining down from the sky daily; although they had seen Mount Sinai covered in smoke and heard Jehovah speaking from it, among other things—nonetheless in the midst of such wonders they fell away from all belief and turned from worshiping Jehovah to worship a calf (Exodus 32:1–end). This shows how effective miracles are.

[4] Still less effective would they be today, when no one acknowledges that anything comes from the spiritual world and everyone denies any miraculous event that cannot be attributed to the physical world. A

negative attitude toward any divine inflow or governance over the earth prevails. As a result, if people in the church today saw genuine, divine miracles, they would start by dragging the miracles down into the physical realm and muddying them there. They would afterward reject them as mirages and end by scoffing at anyone who attributed them to the Divine rather than to physical causes. The complete ineffectiveness of miracles can also be seen from the Lord's words in Luke:

> If they don't listen to Moses and the Prophets, neither will they be persuaded if someone rises from the dead. (Luke 16:31)

Then you shall say to Aaron symbolizes an inflow and the communica- 7291
tion of that inflow, specifically between divine law (represented by Moses) and theology (represented by Aaron). This can be seen from the symbolism of *saying*, when Moses is addressing Aaron, as an inflow and the communication of the inflow, as at §6291. In this case, saying has the same symbolism as speaking, and what is symbolized is both inflow and the communication of that inflow. (For this symbolism of speaking, see §7270.) The inflow and the communication of it can be expressed in Scripture narrative only as saying and speaking.

The divine law represented by Moses flowed into the theology represented by Aaron because divine law is inner truth whereas theology is outer truth. The overarching rule is that inner levels flow into outer levels, not the reverse. That is because inner qualities are purer and finer, while outer qualities are coarser, since they are aggregates of inner qualities.

Take your staff and throw it down before Pharaoh symbolizes a display 7292
of power. This can be seen from the symbolism of a *staff* as power (discussed in §§4013, 4015, 4876, 4936, 6947, 7011, 7026) and from that of *throwing it down before Pharaoh* as displaying it. What is thrown down before someone's eyes is displayed.

It will become a water snake means through the fact that sheer illusion 7293
and consequent falsity will predominate in them. This can be seen from the symbolism of a *snake* as the sensory, bodily plane (discussed at §6949) and therefore as illusions. A sensory, bodily plane that is separated from the rational plane, or not subordinate to it, is full of illusions—so full that it is hardly anything but illusion (see §§6948, 6949).

It is a water snake that is meant here because the word for this "snake" in the original language is the same as the word for a whale, the biggest fish in the ocean. A whale symbolizes knowledge in general, so when

Egyptians symbolize falsities based on illusion, the word means a snake, and specifically a water snake, because the word can also be used for a whale living in the water—the waters of Egypt being falsities.

[2] The use of "whale" to refer to Pharaoh, or Egypt, can be seen in Ezekiel:

> Speak, and say, "This is what Lord Jehovih has said: 'Here, now, I am against you, Pharaoh, king of Egypt, *you great whale,* who lies in the middle of his rivers.'" (Ezekiel 29:3)

In the same author:

> Son of humankind, raise a lamentation over Pharaoh, king of Egypt, and tell him, "You have become like a young lion of the nations. *And you are like whales in the seas,* and you have emerged with your rivers, you have churned your rivers." (Ezekiel 32:2)

A whale here symbolizes knowledge in general, which, since it rises out of the sensory self, is a means of corrupting religious concepts. A whale means knowledge in general because a fish means a particular type of knowledge (§§40, 991). Since whales symbolize knowledge that corrupts religious truth, they also symbolize rationalizations based on illusion, which give rise to false concepts. [3] That is what they symbolize in David:

> You yourself split open the sea with your strength; *you broke the heads of the whales on the waters.* (Psalms 74:13)

The same thing is also symbolized by Leviathan in Isaiah:

> On that day Jehovah, with his steely and great and mighty sword, will exact punishment on *Leviathan the stretched-out serpent* and on *Leviathan the coiled serpent,* and he will kill the *whales* that are in the sea. (Isaiah 27:1)

And in David:

> *You shattered the heads of Leviathan;* you gave him as food to the people of Ziim. (Psalms 74:14)

In a positive sense, in Job 41:1–34, Leviathan stands for reasoning based on truth. Reasoning based on truth is the opposite of rationalizations based on falsity.

[4] Now as whales symbolize truth-twisting rationalizations based on illusion, water snakes—represented by the same word in the original language—symbolize the illusional falsities themselves on which the

rationalizations are based and by which the truth is twisted. Falsities are symbolized by those snakes in the following passages. In Isaiah:

> Iyim will answer in [Babylon's] palaces, and *snakes* in its pleasure palaces. (Isaiah 13:22)

In the same author:

> Thorns will climb into its palaces, thistle and briar into its strongholds, so that it becomes the *dwelling place of snakes,* a courtyard for daughters of the owl. (Isaiah 34:13)

In the same author:

> In the *dwelling place of snakes* is its lair; grass in place of reed and rush. (Isaiah 35:7)

In Jeremiah:

> I will make Jerusalem into heaps [of rubble], the *dwelling place of snakes.* (Jeremiah 9:11)

In Malachi:

> I have made the mountains of Esau a wasteland and given his inheritance to the *snakes in the wilderness.* (Malachi 1:3)

[5] In these passages the snakes stand for falsity that provides grounds for rationalizations. Dragons symbolize the same thing, except that they are rationalizations inspired by self-love and materialism and therefore by a craving for evil that perverts not only truth but also goodness. Rationalizations of this kind issue from people who deny religious truth and goodness at heart but champion it with their lips because of a craving for power and wealth. So they also issue from people who profane what is true and good. The latter and former kinds of people are meant by "the *dragon, the ancient snake,* which is called the Devil and Satan, which leads the whole inhabited world astray" (Revelation 12:9). They are also meant by the same creature—the dragon—that persecuted the woman who gave birth to a son snatched away to God and to his throne (Revelation 12:[3–]5) and that hurled water like a river from its mouth to swallow up the woman (Revelation 12:13, 15). [6] The son the woman gave birth to is the divine truth revealed at this day. The woman is the church. Its persecutors to come are the dragon-snake. The water like a river that the dragon hurled out is falsity springing from evil and consequent rationalizations that the persecutors will use to try to destroy the woman (the church). They will

accomplish nothing, though, which is depicted in the words "the earth helped the woman, and the earth opened its mouth and gulped down the river that the dragon had hurled out" (Revelation 12:16).

7294 *And Moses came to Pharaoh, as did Aaron, and they did so, as Jehovah had commanded* means that it was carried out, as can be seen without explanation.

7295 *And Aaron threw his staff down before Pharaoh and his servants, and it became a water snake* means that sheer illusion and consequent falsity took over in them. This is established by the symbolism of *throwing down a staff* as displaying power (noted just above at §7292), by the representation of *Pharaoh and his servants* as spirits who use falsity to inflict harassment, and by the symbolism of a *water snake* as illusions and consequent falsities (discussed just above at §7293).

[2] This portent symbolizes a first warning to the harassers to stop. Here is the situation with evil spirits who harass the upright in the other life: When they first arrive there from the world, they have good spirits and angels at their side, as they did when they were living as people in their bodies. (Even evil people have angels with them too, so that if they want, they can turn to heaven, accept its inflow, and reform.) That is why they at first associate with angels, since everything about a person's life follows that person. However, if their life in the world has made it impossible for them to accept the inflow of truth and goodness from heaven, angels and good spirits gradually withdraw from them. As angels and good spirits withdraw, these spirits become less and less rational, because being rational comes through heaven from the Lord. [3] The first step in the process by which the inflow of truth and goodness is removed and taken from them is what is depicted here by the transformation of Aaron's staff into a snake, symbolizing the predominance in them of sheer illusion and consequent falsity. The second step is depicted by the conversion of Egypt's waters into blood, symbolizing the distortion of genuine truth into falsity. The third step is the swarming of the frogs from the waters, symbolizing rationalizations based on pure falsity; and there are more steps to follow.

These same steps prevent the evil from understanding truth and goodness in the other life.

7296 *And Pharaoh too called sages and sorcerers* symbolizes misuse of the divine design, as the following shows: *Sages* symbolize people with knowledge of what is spiritual and of the correspondence between this and what is earthly. People who explored this subject and taught about it they called sages, because it was mystical knowledge. Since Egyptians were experts in this field, they called themselves the offspring of sages and of the monarchs of old, as is plain in Isaiah:

> How can you say to Pharaoh, "*I am the offspring of sages,* the offspring of the monarchs of old"? (Isaiah 19:11)

The Egyptians referred to knowledge of many kinds as a sage's wisdom, as did the Chaldeans (Jeremiah 50:35). And *sorcerers* symbolize people who pervert the divine design and therefore the laws of order. That is exactly what sorcerers and magicians are, as can be seen from sorcerers and magicians in the next life, where there are a lot of them. [2] You see, there are people who used deceit during their physical life and devised numerous methods for defrauding others, eventually being led by their success to credit everything to their own shrewdness. In the other world these people learn magic, which is actually a misuse of the divine design and especially of correspondence. It is in keeping with the divine plan that absolutely everything corresponds to something. Hands, arms, and shoulders, for example, correspond to power, so a staff does too. For that reason the spirits I am talking about form staffs for themselves and present images of shoulders, arms, and hands, with which they exercise their magical powers. The same holds true for thousands of other correspondences. The divine plan and correspondence are misused when features of that plan are used for evil rather than good purposes, such as controlling others or destroying them. The purpose of the design is to save people and therefore to do good to everyone. This then shows what is meant by a misuse of the divine design, as symbolized by the sorcerers.

And they did so too—the magicians of Egypt, with their spells means 7297
that by this misuse they seemed to do the same, twisting the purposes of the divine plan, as the following shows: *They did so too,* when said of the magicians of Egypt, means presenting an appearance that seems to be the same. Misuse does not change the consequences that result from the plan. No, those consequences look the same in outward form—though not in inward form, being opposed to the purposes of the plan. And *spells* symbolize the actual methods used for perverting the plan.

Where the Word mentions sorceries and spells, they symbolize the art of making falsity look like truth, and truth look like falsity, which is mainly accomplished through illusion. [2] That is what is symbolized by sorceries and spells in the following passages. In Isaiah:

> But these two things will come to you in an instant, on a single day: bereavement and widowhood. In their fullness they will come over you,

> *because of the abundance of your sorceries, on account of the* wide *scope of your spells.* Stand firm *in your spells* and *in the abundance of your sorceries* in which you have labored from your youth. (Isaiah 47:9, 12)

This is about Babylon and the Chaldeans. In the same author:

> Come up here, you *witch's children,* seed of an adulterer and [of her who] whored. (Isaiah 57:3)

In Nahum:

> Doom to the blood-soaked city because of the abundance of the whorings of a whore of good grace—the *mistress of sorceries,* selling out nations through her whorings, and clans *through her sorceries.* (Nahum 3:4)

The blood-soaked city stands for truth distorted; the whorings for goodness-from-truth distorted; and the sorceries for the art of presenting falsity as truth, and truth as falsity. [3] In Malachi:

> I will come close to you for judgment and will be a speedy witness *against sorcerers* and against adulterers and against those swearing falsely. (Malachi 3:5)

In John:

> *By your spell* were all the nations led astray. (Revelation 18:23)

This is about Babylon. In Micah:

> I will cut your horses off from your midst and destroy your chariots and cut off the cities of your land and demolish all your strongholds and *cut sorceries off from your hand.* (Micah 5:10, 11, 12)

This passage shows that sorceries symbolize the art of presenting truth as falsity, and falsity as truth. The horses that were to be cut off symbolize matters of the intellect (§§2761, 2762, 3217, 5321, 6125, 6534). The chariots to be destroyed symbolize teachings about truth (2762, 5321). The cities of the land that were also to be cut off symbolize truth known to the church (cities meaning truth, 2268, 2451, 2712, 2943, 4492, 4493; and the land meaning the church, 662, 1066, 1262, 1733, 1850, 2117, 2118, 3355, 4447, 4535, 5577). The strongholds symbolize truth in its role as defender of what is good. From all this you can now see the symbolism of the sorceries that were to be cut off from [Israel's] hand. They symbolize the art of presenting truth as falsity, and falsity as truth. This art in its various forms corresponds to the image-changing power used by the evil in the other life to make beauty look ugly and ugliness look pretty. These changes are a type of sorcery, because they too involve misusing the divine design and turning it upside down.

And they each threw their staff down, and these became water snakes **7298** symbolizes power derived from the divine design to make people's perception of truth grow dull. This can be seen from the symbolism of *throwing a staff down* as displaying power (mentioned at §7292) and from that of *water snakes* as falsity resulting from illusion (discussed at §7293) but in this case as dullness in perceiving truth. The more illusion interferes with the perception of truth, the more dullness creeps in.

In the other life too magicians induce this kind of obtuseness, which they do by exploiting and perverting the divine design. They know how to do away with the inflow from heaven, and once that happens, their victim's perception of truth becomes blunted. They know how to introduce illusions—presenting them in a light that resembles the light of truth—and simultaneously obscure the real truth. They know how to bring in dogma and in this way weaken a person's perception of truth. Not to mention other methods.

When dullness sets in, falsity appears true, and this true-seeming falsity is symbolized by sorceries and spells. From this you see how the magicians were able to produce [a miracle] that looked the same.

[2] Besides, it is in keeping with the laws of the divine plan that one ought not to accept the truth instantaneously; no one should be persuaded in a single moment that the truth has been proved beyond all doubt. This is an important piece of information. The problem with instant corroboration is that truth imprinted this way becomes dogmatic and lacks any reach or give. Such truth is represented in the other world as rigid and impervious to any good influence that would make it usable.

On that account, as soon as plain experience in the other world presents good spirits with any true idea, an opposing thought is presented right afterward to raise doubt. This allows them to think and ponder whether the idea is so, gather arguments, and thus use reason to introduce the truth into their mind. Doing so extends their range of spiritual vision on the subject all the way to its opposite. As a result, their intellect sees and perceives the entire nature of the particular truth, which enables them to let in heaven's inflow according to the current state of affairs. Truth takes various shapes, depending on the circumstances.

This is also why the magicians were permitted to do the same thing Aaron had done, because it cast the divinity of the miracle into doubt for the children of Israel. This gave them the opportunity to think and consider whether it was divine and finally to assure themselves it was.

7299 *And Aaron's staff swallowed up their staffs* means that this power was taken away from them. This can be seen from the symbolism of *swallowing up* as taking away and from that of a *staff* as power (dealt with above at §7292). Magicians in the other life are indeed deprived of their power to misuse the divine design and pervert its laws, by two methods. One is that angels use the Lord's divine power to neutralize the magic, which they do when the magicians practice it for the purpose of harming the upright. The power the Lord gives angels is strong enough to undo all the magic instantly. The other is that the magicians are stripped entirely of any magical power so that they can no longer bewitch anyone.

7300 *And Pharaoh's heart hardened* symbolizes obstinacy. This is established by the discussion in §7272 above of the symbolism of the *hardening* of a *heart* as obstinacy.

7301 *And he did not listen to them* means that spirits engaged in evil-from-falsity were unreceptive. This can be seen from comments above at §§7224, 7275. Pharaoh, who is being said not to have listened, represents people who subscribe to falsity and inflict persecution, and as long as they inflict persecution, they are engaged in evil-from-falsity. After all, the persecution is motivated by evil and uses falsity as its means.

7302 *As Jehovah had spoken* means as predicted, which is self-evident.

7303 Exodus 7:14–24. *And Jehovah said to Moses, "Pharaoh's heart has turned leaden; he has refused to send the people away. Go to Pharaoh in the morning (watch: he walks out to the water), and stand to meet him by the bank of the river, and take in your hand the staff that turned into a snake. And you shall say to him, 'Jehovah, God of the Hebrews, has sent me to you, saying, "Send my people away, and let them serve me in the wilderness," and here, you have not listened so far. This is what Jehovah said: "In this you will know that I am Jehovah: Here, I am striking with the staff that is in my hand on the waters that are in the river, and they will turn to blood. And the fish that are in the river will die, and the river will reek, and the Egyptians will labor to drink water from the river."'" And Jehovah said to Moses, "Say to Aaron, 'Take your staff and stretch your hand out over the waters of Egypt, over their streams, over their rivers, and over their pools, and over every gathering of their waters, and they will be blood. And there will be blood in all the land of Egypt and in containers of wood and in containers of stone.'" And Moses and*

Aaron did so, as Jehovah had commanded, and he lifted the staff and struck the waters that were in the river before the eyes of Pharaoh and before the eyes of his servants, and all the waters that were in the river turned to blood. And the fish that were in the river died, and the river reeked, and the Egyptians could not drink water from the river. And there was blood in the whole land of Egypt. And the magicians of Egypt did the same with their spells. And Pharaoh's heart hardened, and he did not listen to them, as Jehovah had spoken. And Pharaoh looked away and came to his house and did not take even this to heart. And all the Egyptians dug around the river [for] water to drink, because they could not drink from the waters of the river.

And Jehovah said to Moses symbolizes divine instruction. *Pharaoh's heart has turned leaden; he has refused to send the people away* means that they obstinately set themselves against leaving the people they were persecuting alone. *Go to Pharaoh in the morning* symbolizes being elevated to stronger confirmation. *Watch: he walks out to the water* means that the persecutors were then intent on falsities based on mistaken impressions. *And stand to meet him by the bank of the river* symbolizes an inflow adapted to their state. *And take in your hand the staff that turned into a snake* symbolizes power like the earlier kind. *And you shall say to him* symbolizes a command. *Jehovah, God of the Hebrews, has sent me to you, saying,* means from the Divine acknowledged by the church to those who were causing trouble. *Send my people away* means that they must leave. *And let them serve me in the wilderness* symbolizes worship in a dim state. *And here, you have not listened so far* symbolizes disobedience. *And Jehovah said, "In this you will know that I am Jehovah,"* means in order for them to be afraid of the Divine. *Here, I am striking with the staff that is in my hand on the waters that are in the river* symbolizes power over falsities that are based on mistaken impressions. *And they will turn to blood* means that [the persecutors] will render truth false. *The fish that are in the river will die* means that truth in the form of knowledge will be obliterated. *And the river will reek* symbolizes loathing for it. *And the Egyptians will labor to drink water from the river* means so that they hardly want to know anything at all about it. *And Jehovah said to Moses* symbolizes accomplishment. *Say to Aaron, "Take your staff and stretch your hand out over the waters of Egypt,"* symbolizes power against the falsity existing among the persecutors. *Over their streams, over their rivers* means against their doctrinal teachings. *And over their pools* means against concepts subservient to those teachings. *And over every gathering of waters* means where there is anything false. *And they will be blood* means that [the persecutors] will render truth false. *And there will be blood in all the land of Egypt* symbolizes total falsification. *And in containers of wood and in containers of stone* means of the goodness that comes from neighborly love and of the truth that leads to faith. *And Moses and Aaron did so, as Jehovah had commanded* means that it was carried out. *And he lifted the staff and struck the waters that were in the river* symbolizes strong power against falsity. *Before the eyes of Pharaoh and before the eyes of his servants* means in the awareness of all [those] inflicting harassment. *And all the waters that were in the river turned to blood* symbolizes the consequent falsification of all truth. *And the fish that were in the river died* means that truth in the form of knowledge was also obliterated. *And the river reeked* symbolizes loathing. *And the Egyptians could not drink water from the river* means that they hardly wanted to know anything at all about it. *And there was blood in the whole land of Egypt* symbolizes total falsification. *And the magicians of Egypt did the same with their spells* means that the falsifiers of truth misused the divine design to mimic the effect. *And Pharaoh's heart hardened* symbolizes obstinacy. *And he did not listen to them* symbolizes nonacceptance and disobedience. *As Jehovah had spoken* means as predicted. *And Pharaoh looked away and came to his house* symbolizes thoughts and reflections inspired by false notions. *And did not take this to heart* symbolizes willful refusal and consequent obstinacy. *And all the Egyptians dug around the river [for] water to drink* symbolizes a search for truth that they could apply to falsity. *Because they could not drink from the waters of the river* means that there was no application from pure falsity.

7304 *And Jehovah said to Moses* symbolizes divine instruction. This can be seen from the symbolism of *he said,* when a new command is given, as instruction, which is discussed in §§7186, 7267, 7288. Here it symbolizes divine instruction, because it was *Jehovah* who said it. The instruction was on how to proceed.

7305 *Pharaoh's heart has turned leaden; he has refused to send the people away* means that they obstinately set themselves against leaving the people they were persecuting alone, as the following shows: When a *heart* is said to *turn leaden,* or harden, it symbolizes obstinacy, as above in §§7272, 7300. And *refusing to send them away* means not leaving them alone. And *Pharaoh,* whom these words describe, represents the persecutors, as discussed before.

7306 *Go to Pharaoh in the morning* symbolizes being elevated to stronger confirmation, as the following shows: *Going to* (or approaching) *Pharaoh* symbolizes communication, as discussed at §6901. Here it symbolizes communication of information proving that it is the Divine who is warning them to stop causing trouble. And *morning* symbolizes a state of enlightenment and revelation, as discussed in §§3458, 3723, 5097, 5740. Here it symbolizes elevation, because it has to do with believers in falsity, who cannot be enlightened but whose awareness can be elevated.

Enlightenment is impossible for believers in falsity because falsity rejects and snuffs out all illuminating light. Only truth accepts such light.

Watch: he walks out to the water means that the persecutors were 7307
then intent on falsities based on mistaken impressions. This is evident from the representation of Pharaoh as persecutors (discussed before) and from the symbolism of *water*—here, the waters of Egypt—as falsity based on mistaken impressions. The reason this kind of falsity—falsity based on mistaken impressions—is being symbolized here is that the [water] snake that Pharaoh's staff turned into symbolizes such falsity (§7293). For the meaning of water as truth and in the opposite sense as falsity, see §§739, 790, 2702, 3058, 3424, 4976, 5668. For the meaning of Egypt's river as falsity, §6693.

And stand to meet him by the bank of the river symbolizes an inflow 7308
adapted to their state, as the following indicates: *Standing to meet* symbolizes an inflow. When divine law (represented by Moses) is said to have stood to meet believers in falsity who inflict persecution (represented by Pharaoh), standing to meet actually symbolizes an inflow, the reception of it, and a resulting awareness. And the *bank of the river* symbolizes the state of falsity that was being experienced by the persecutors. For the idea that Egypt's river means falsity, see §6693. Here it symbolizes falsity based on illusion (§7307). A riverbank—which is like a container, since it surrounds and holds a river—means the state of that falsity. Everything has its state, which provides a setting and a course for it.

And take in your hand the staff that turned into a snake symbolizes power 7309
like the earlier kind, as the following shows: A *staff* symbolizes power, as discussed in §§4013, 4015, 4876, 4936, 7026. Power like the earlier kind is symbolized by his taking the staff *that turned into a snake.* And a *hand* also symbolizes power, but spiritual power, from which comes the earthly power meant by the staff, as discussed in §§6947, 7011.

And you shall say to him symbolizes a command. This can be seen from 7310
the symbolism of *saying* as a command when divine law (represented by Moses) is addressing people immersed in falsity (represented by Pharaoh).

7311 *Jehovah, God of the Hebrews, has sent me to you, saying,* means from the Divine acknowledged by the church to those who were causing trouble, as the following shows: *Hebrews* symbolize something about the church, as discussed in §§5136, 6675, 6684, 6738. The Divine acknowledged by the church is *Jehovah, God* of the Hebrews, and Jehovah God is the Lord, Jehovah being the Lord's divine goodness, and God being his divine truth. And *has sent me to you* means to those who were causing trouble. The representation of Pharaoh (the person to whom Jehovah had sent Moses) as people who were causing trouble has been shown many times.

7312 *Send my people away* means that they must leave, as needs no explanation.

7313 *And let them serve me in the wilderness* symbolizes worship in a dim state. This can be seen from the symbolism of *serving* Jehovah as worship and from that of the *wilderness* as an uninhabited, untamed place (discussed in §§2708, 3900). In a spiritual sense a wilderness symbolizes dimness in respect to religious goodness and truth. The reason it means that kind of dimness here is that people in the spiritual church (represented by the children of Israel) are generally in the dark regarding religious truth (see §§2715, 2716, 2718, 2831, 2849, 2935, 2937, 3833, 4402, 6289, 6500, 6865, 6945, 7233). They are specifically in the dark when they emerge from a state of persecution and trial. People who are being persecuted are engulfed by falsity and sway like a reed in the wind, driven back and forth between doubt and assurance. When they have just recently climbed out of that state, then, their minds are dim; but light gradually pierces the dimness.

As this is the state experienced by victims of persecution, the children of Israel were led out into the wilderness to represent the state experienced by people of the spiritual church before the Lord's Coming. It also represents the state experienced by people of that church today who are being purged of falsity.

7314 *And here, you have not listened so far* symbolizes disobedience. This is plain from the symbolism of *listening* as obedience, as discussed in §§2542, 3869, 5017, 5471, 5475, 7216. *Not* listening, then, means disobedience.

7315 *And Jehovah said, "In this you will know that I am Jehovah,"* means in order for them to be afraid of the Divine. This is established by the discussion above at §7280, where similar words occur.

7316 *Here, I am striking with the staff that is in my hand on the waters that are in the river* symbolizes power over falsities that are based on mistaken impressions. This is established by the symbolism of a *staff* as power (mentioned above at §7309) and from that of the *waters that are in the river* as falsities based on mistaken impressions (also mentioned above, at §7307).

And they will turn to blood means that [the persecutors] will render truth false. This is established by the symbolism of *blood* as truth rendered false, as discussed in §§4735, 6978. In a positive sense, blood means truth radiating from the Lord and therefore the holy influence of faith. That is what the blood in the Holy Supper symbolizes. In a negative sense, though, blood means violence inflicted on divine truth. This violence is inflicted by falsification, so blood means the falsification of truth. 7317

These explanations and the remarks that follow show who it is specifically that Pharaoh represents, or who specifically is meant by these "persecutors." They are people in the church who declared its faith, persuaded themselves that faith saves, and yet lived a life contrary to faith's precepts. In short, they are people whose faith was dogmatic and whose life was evil.

[2] When these people arrive in the other world, they carry with them the assumption that they are to enter heaven because they were born in the church, were baptized, had the Word and its teachings, and declared their belief in those teachings. The main declaration for which they expect to be saved is that they believe in the Lord and in the idea that he suffered for their sins, thereby saving members of the church who proclaim their belief in him on the basis of doctrine. As new arrivals from the world into the next life, they do not want to know anything about a life of faith and neighborly love. Such a life they completely discount, saying that because they believed, everything evil they did in life has been erased and washed away by the blood of the Lamb. You can tell them that this goes against the Lord's words in Matthew, where we read:

> Many will say to me on that day, "Lord! Lord! Haven't we prophesied in your name and cast out demons in your name and exercised many powers in your name?" But then I will proclaim, "I do not know you. Leave me, you evildoers!" Everyone who hears my words and does them I compare to a prudent man. But everyone hearing my words and yet not doing them I compare to a stupid man. (Matthew 7:21, 22, 23, 24, 26)

And in Luke:

> Then you will start to stand outside and knock on the door, saying, "Lord! Lord! Open up to us!" But answering, he will say to them, "I do

> not know you, where you are from." Then you will start to say, "We ate in front of you, and drank, and in our streets you taught." But he will say, "I tell you I do not know you, where you are from. Leave me, all you evildoers!" (Luke 13:25, 26, 27)

But to this they answer that the only people meant here are those who believed they could work miracles, not those with the church's beliefs.

[3] After a while, though, the same spirits start to see that no one is let into heaven but those who lived a *life* of faith, meaning those who loved their neighbor. When they start to realize this, they begin to despise the teachings of their faith and even faith itself. Their faith was not true faith, merely a knowledge of religious concepts, and they adopted it not to guide their lives but in order to grow rich and rise up in the world. That is why they then despise what they had known as religious concepts, reject them, and soon throw themselves into falsities opposed to religious truth.

This is the change of state that comes over the lives of people who claimed to believe but who lived a life contrary to faith.

These are the inhabitants of the other world who use falsity to infest the upright and who are therefore meant specifically by Pharaoh.

7318 *The fish that are in the river will die* means that truth in the form of knowledge will be obliterated, as the following shows: *Fish* symbolize knowledge, as discussed in §§40, 991. Here they symbolize truth in the form of knowledge, since the text says they will die, swimming as they are in waters turned to blood, which means that this truth will be obliterated by falsification. And *dying* symbolizes being obliterated.

Here are some examples to illustrate what falsification of truth is: It is a falsification of truth to decide and say on the basis of twisted reasoning that since we cannot do good on our own, doing good contributes nothing to our salvation. It is also a falsification of truth to say that all the good we do is self-interested, that we do it for the reward, and that we therefore should not do any charitable deeds. It is a falsification of truth to say that since all goodness comes from the Lord, we should not do anything good but rather wait for inspiration. It is a falsification of truth to say that truth can exist in us without neighborly kindness, and accordingly that faith can exist without neighborly love. It is a falsification of truth to say that only the wretched and poor can go to heaven, or to say that only those can go who give all they own to the poor and reduce themselves to wretched circumstances. [2] It is a falsification of truth to say that anyone can be let into heaven out of pure mercy, no matter how that person had lived. It is an even worse falsification of truth to say that a human being has been given the authority to let anyone at all into heaven. It is a falsification of truth to say that sins are erased and washed away as dirt is washed away by water. It is an even worse falsification of truth to say that a human being has the authority to forgive sins and that the sins once forgiven have been eliminated entirely, leaving the sinner pure. It is a falsification of truth to say that the Lord took all our sins onto himself and bore them and that as a result we can be saved no matter what kind of life we have. It is a falsification of truth to say that only people in the church are saved. (The reasoning on which this falsification rests is that people in the church have been baptized, possess the Word, know about the Lord, resurrection, eternal life, heaven, and hell, and consequently know the faith through which they can be made righteous.)

There are countless falsifications like these, because not a single truth exists that cannot be rendered false and whose falsified form cannot be proved true by reasoning based on fallacies.

And the river will reek symbolizes loathing for it. This can be seen from **7319**
the symbolism of *reeking* as loathing (discussed at §7161) and from that of a *river*—here, the river of Egypt turned to blood—as falsified truth.

It needs to be known that nothing in the other world is more abhorrent and nothing therefore reeks worse than profaned truth. It is like the stench of a corpse, which results from the death of living flesh. You see, falsity does not smell bad unless it is juxtaposed with truth, nor evil unless it is juxtaposed with goodness. We never sense what a thing is like on its own, only by comparison with its opposite—which shows how badly profaned truth stinks. Profaned truth is falsity inextricably merged with truth, whereas falsified truth is falsity merely attached to truth (rather than merged with it) that lords it over truth.

And the Egyptians will labor to drink water from the river means so that **7320**
they hardly want to know anything at all about it, as the following shows: *Egyptians* symbolize people who render truth false. *Drinking* means being taught truth, as dealt with in §§3069, 3772, 4017, 4018, so *laboring to drink* means not wanting to be taught and therefore hardly wanting to know anything, at least about truth. And *river water* symbolizes falsity, as dealt with above at §7307. Here it symbolizes falsified truth.

This shows that *the Egyptians will labor to drink water from the river* means that spirits intent on falsity based on mistaken impressions would hardly want to know anything at all about truth and therefore would loathe it.

The reason for their loathing is that truth that has been twisted by falsity still fights back secretly and silently, laboring to shake the falsity off. So this type of truth is harsh. If the falsity and a belief in it are reduced just a little, this truth becomes actively condemnatory.

7321 *And Jehovah said to Moses* symbolizes accomplishment. This can be seen from what follows next, as it is included in what *Jehovah said.*

7322 *Say to Aaron, "Take your staff and stretch your hand out over the waters of Egypt,"* symbolizes power against the falsity existing among the persecutors, as the following shows: A *staff* symbolizes earthly power, and a *hand,* spiritual power, as treated of above at §7309. *Taking* a staff and *stretching out* a hand, then, mean exercising spiritual power through the earthly level. And the *waters of Egypt* symbolize falsities that cause persecution, as also treated of above, at §7307.

7323 *Over their streams, over their rivers* means against their false doctrinal teachings. This can be seen from the symbolism of *streams* and *rivers* as doctrinal teachings. Water means falsity; see above at §7307. So streams and rivers, which are masses of water, mean doctrinal teachings, and in this case, false ones. Rivers mean matters of intelligence and therefore matters of truth (see §§2702, 3051), so in the opposite sense they mean matters contrary to intelligence and accordingly matters of falsity.

7324 *And over their pools* means against concepts subservient to those teachings. This can be seen from the symbolism of *pools* as concepts subservient to the truth in a set of teachings, and in the opposite sense as concepts subservient to the falsities in a set of teachings.

Where the Word mentions pools, in a spiritual sense they mean an intelligent understanding based on concepts of goodness and truth, because pools in those passages are taken to mean gathered water, or lakes. Gathered water and lakes mean a whole range of concepts through which intelligence can be developed, as in Isaiah:

> Water will burst forth from the wilderness, and rivers in the wilderness plain, and *dry land will turn into a pool,* and the thirsty place into wellsprings of water. (Isaiah 35:6, 7)

[2] In the same author:

> I will open rivers on the slopes, and in the middle of *valleys* I will set springs; [I will make] the *desert into a pool of water,* and dry land into wellsprings of water. (Isaiah 41:18)

Making the desert into a pool of water stands for supplying concepts of goodness and truth and a resulting intelligence where none of these existed before. In the same author:

> I will devastate mountains and hills and wither all the grass and make rivers into islands and *drain the pools.* (Isaiah 42:15)

These pools stand for the same thing. Likewise in David:

> Jehovah makes rivers into a desert, and outlets of water into a dry gulch; *he makes the desert into a pool of water,* and a land of drought into outlets of water. (Psalms 107:33, 35)

In the same author:

> In view of the Lord you go into labor, earth; in view of the God of Jacob, *who turns the rock into a pool of water,* the flint into a spring of water. (Psalms 114:7, 8)

[3] In Isaiah:

> The *rivers of Egypt* will shrink and drain away, therefore the *fishers* will mourn, as will all who cast a hook into the river. So its foundations will be crushed. *Everyone is making a wage from pools of the soul.* (Isaiah 19:6, 8, 10)

Pools of the soul stand for matters of intelligence derived from religious concepts. Since the passage is talking about Egypt, though, pools of the soul are matters of intelligence derived from concepts known to the church—Egypt meaning these concepts. These kinds are religious concepts but on a lower level.

[4] In a negative sense pools of water mean evil growing out of falsity and consequent insanity. This is plain in Isaiah:

> I will cut off from Babel name and remainder and child and grandchild and will make it into an inheritance for the harrier and into *pools of water.* (Isaiah 14:22, 23)

Since pools in a negative sense mean evil growing out of falsity and consequent insanity, they also symbolize hell, where evil and insanity reign supreme. In that case, though, a pool is called a lake of fire or a lake burning with fire and sulfur, as in Revelation 19:20; 20:10, 14, 15; 21:8. Fire and sulfur stand for self-love with its obsessions, because these are nothing but fire. They are not physical fire but are rather blazes kindled by spiritual fire, spiritual fire being what gives a person life. Anyone who thinks about it can see plainly that love is the fire of life. Fires of this kind are what are meant by the sacred fires in the heavens and by the fires of hell. Physical flame does not exist there.

7325 *And over every gathering of waters* means where there is anything false. This can be seen from the symbolism of *waters* as falsity, as noted above at §7307. A *gathering* of waters, then, is a place where falsity collects.

7326 *And they will be blood* means that [the persecutors] will render truth false, which can be seen from the symbolism of *blood* as the falsification of truth, as discussed at §7317.

In a positive sense blood symbolizes holy love, so it symbolizes charity and faith, since these are love's holy attributes; consequently blood symbolizes sacred truth radiating from the Lord (§§1001, 4735, 6978). In a negative sense, though, blood symbolizes violence inflicted on charity and on faith and therefore on sacred truth radiating from the Lord. And since falsification inflicts violence, blood symbolizes falsification of truth. In a more serious degree blood symbolizes profanation of truth. Profanation was symbolized by the eating of blood, which is why the eating of blood was so strictly forbidden (§1003).

7327 *And there will be blood in all the land of Egypt* symbolizes total falsification. This can be seen from the symbolism of *blood* as falsification of truth (discussed directly above at §7326) and from that of *in all the land of Egypt* as everywhere and therefore as total.

Total falsification occurs when falsity starts to take control, because we then live by the evil we were born with and the evil we have acquired, and find pleasure in it. Since this behavior is banned by religious truth, we turn against such truth; and when we turn against truth, we dismiss it whenever we encounter it; and if we cannot dismiss it, we falsify it.

7328 *And in containers of wood and in containers of stone* means (total falsification) of the goodness that comes from neighborly love and of the truth that leads to faith. This is clear from the symbolism of *wood* as goodness that comes from neighborly love (discussed in §§2784, 2812, 3720) and from that of *stone* as truth that leads to faith (discussed in §§1298, 3720, 6426).

7329 *And Moses and Aaron did so, as Jehovah had commanded* means that it was carried out, as needs no explanation.

7330 *And he lifted the staff and struck the waters that were in the river* symbolizes strong power against falsity. This can be seen from the discussion above at §7316. "Strong power" is symbolized by his lifting the staff and striking from that position.

Before the eyes of Pharaoh and before the eyes of his servants means in the awareness of all those inflicting harassment. This can be seen from the symbolism of *eyes* as perception (discussed in §§4083, 4339) and from the representation of *Pharaoh* as people who use falsity to harass (discussed before). "All those" is symbolized when the text says *before the eyes of Pharaoh and before the eyes of his servants.* 7331

And all the waters that were in the river turned to blood symbolizes the consequent falsification of all truth. This is established by the symbolism of the *waters that were in the river* as falsity (mentioned above at §7307) and from that of *blood* as falsification of truth (also dealt with above, in §§7317, 7326). 7332

Why is it that people in the other world who subscribe to falsity and persecute others are allowed to render truth false? The purpose is to keep them from making simultaneous contact with heaven's inhabitants through truth in their faith and hell's inhabitants through evil in their life. The truth would then enable them to acquire some heavenly light and understanding, and they would force both to support evil in their life. After all, they would put their intelligence to work justifying their evil, meaning that they would subordinate the properties of heaven in them to the properties of hell. Another purpose is to prevent them from leading astray simple upright spirits, with whom truth puts them in contact.

Evil individuals in the other life in whom truth has not yet become false know how to use truth to gain control for themselves, because there is power in truth—power too strong to resist (§§3091, 6344, 6423, 6948). This is another way they would misuse truth.

Besides, truth does nothing to make the evil live better lives. No, they use truth only as a means of doing evil. When they cannot use truth that way, they laugh it to scorn. They are like wicked dignitaries of the church who would sneer at doctrinal truth if it did not serve them as a means of amassing wealth.

These are the reasons the evil are permitted to falsify truth in themselves.

And the fish that were in the river died means that truth in the form of knowledge was also obliterated. This can be seen from the remarks above at §7318, where the same words occur. 7333

And the river reeked symbolizes loathing. This can be seen from the remarks above at §7319. 7334

7335 *And the Egyptians could not drink water from the river* means that they hardly wanted to know anything at all about it. This can also be seen from remarks above, at §7320.

7336 *And there was blood in the whole land of Egypt* symbolizes total falsification. See above at §7327.

7337 *And the magicians of Egypt did the same with their spells* means that the falsifiers of truth misused the divine design to mimic the effect. This can be seen from the symbolism of *Egyptian magic* and *spells* as misuse of the divine plan, which is discussed in §§5223, 6052, 7296.

Regarding miracles, be aware that divine miracles are different from magical miracles—as different as heaven and hell. Divine miracles start with divine truth and proceed according to divine order, whose outward effects are miracles when it pleases the Lord to present them in that form. That is why all divine miracles represent states of the Lord's kingdom in the heavens and of the Lord's kingdom on the earth (that is, of the church). This is the inner framework of divine miracles. So it is with all the miracles in Egypt and with the rest of the miracles described in the Word. Moreover, all the miracles the Lord himself performed when he was in the world symbolized the future state of the church. For instance, the eyes of the blind and the ears of the deaf were opened, the tongues of the mute were loosened, the lame walked, and the maimed and leprous were healed. This meant that the kinds of people symbolized by the blind, deaf, mute, lame, maimed, and leprous would receive the gospel and be healed spiritually, through the Lord's coming into the world. That is what divine miracles are like inside.

[2] Magical miracles, on the other hand, have no inward content whatever. They are performed by the evil, for the purpose of gaining power over others, although on the outside they resemble divine miracles. The reason they look similar is that they result from divine order, which always looks the same on its lowest levels, where miracles are seen. For example, divine truth radiating from the Lord contains all power, which is why truth even on the lowest levels of divine order holds power. As a consequence, the evil can use truth to gain power and control others.

[3] For another example, the divine plan ordains that any notion of place and distance in the other world result from states of feeling and thought and that the more peoples' states diverge, the farther apart those people appear. This aspect of the plan is designed by the Divine to keep everyone in the universal human distinct from each other. Magicians in the other life misuse it by imposing changes of state on others, carrying spirits up high at one time, down low at another, and inserting spirits

into various communities to serve as their delegates. The same in countless other instances.

This evidence shows that although magical miracles look like divine miracles on the outside, they harbor a contrary goal within, which is to destroy religion. Within divine miracles is the goal of building religion up.

The two kinds of miracle are like two pretty women, one of whom is entirely rotten inside because she is a whore, while the other is entirely pure inside because she is chaste and genuinely loves marriage. Their outward forms are similar, but their inward forms are as different as heaven and hell.

And Pharaoh's heart hardened symbolizes obstinacy, as above in §§7272, 7300. 7338

And he did not listen to them symbolizes nonacceptance and disobedience, also as above, in §§7224, 7275, 7301. 7339

As Jehovah had spoken means as predicted, also as above, in §7302. 7340

And Pharaoh looked away and came to his house symbolizes thoughts and reflections inspired by false notions, as the following shows: *Looking away* symbolizes thought and reflection, because in a spiritual sense, looking away is not looking in some direction with one's eyes but looking with one's mind and therefore thinking and reflecting. And *Pharaoh's house* symbolizes falsity. As Pharaoh represents falsity, his house does too, which is why *coming* to his house symbolizes false notions. Since these words symbolize thoughts and reflections inspired by false notions, the next words are "he did not take this to heart." People whose thinking grows out of falsity do not take divine warnings to heart. 7341

And did not take this to heart symbolizes willful refusal and consequent obstinacy. This can be seen from the symbolism of *not taking something to heart* as not paying attention. Lack of attention to a divine message on the part of the evil is due to willful refusal, so the same words also symbolize this. And not taking it to heart has the same deeper meaning as hardening the heart, so obstinacy too is symbolized, as before in §§7272, 7300, 7338. 7342

To take up the subject of willful refusal, it needs to be known that our will is what governs us. Some believe the intellect is in control, but our intellect does not govern us unless our will goes along. The intellect actually favors the will, because regarded in itself the intellect is nothing but the will given form.

When I speak of the will, I mean desires that come from love. The human will is nothing else. These desires from love are what govern us, because they are our life. If our passion is for ourselves and for worldly advantages, that sums up our entire life. We cannot refuse such a passion, because to refuse it would be to refuse our very life. Principles embodying the truth make no difference. If the desires aroused by self-love and materialism dominate, they drag truth onto their side, making it false, and if truth does not fully indulge them, they reject it. That is why principles embodying religious truth accomplish nothing at all in us unless the Lord instills a passion aroused by spiritual love, or love for our neighbor. The more receptive we are to this passion, the more we accept religious truth. The desires from love for our neighbor are what creates a new will.

These remarks now show that we never take truth to heart if our will refuses it. That is why hellish people, whose desires or cravings are for evil, cannot accept religious truth and consequently cannot amend their ways. It is also why the evil render religious truth false so far as they can.

7343 *And all the Egyptians dug around the river [for] water to drink* symbolizes a search for truth that they could apply to falsity, as the following shows: *Digging* means searching, as discussed below. The *water around the river* symbolizes truth. The reason the water around the river means truth is that it was outside the river and had not turned to blood. For the meaning of water as truth, see §§739, 790, 2702, 3058, 3424, 4976, 5668. And *drinking* it symbolizes applying it to falsity. For the meaning of drinking as applying, see §5709; after all, when we drink something, we apply it to ourselves. It is important to realize, though, that truth is applied in accordance with the nature and state of the person applying it to himself or herself. People who yearn for truth apply truth in accordance with the state and nature of that yearning. People who yearn for falsity twist the truth and render it false when they apply it to themselves. This can be seen from the fact that divine truth flows into everyone but varies in each according to the state and nature of that individual's life. So the hellish turn divine truth into falsity, just as they turn divine goodness into evil, heavenly love into diabolical love, mercy into hatred and cruelty, and marriage love into adultery. In other words, they turn everything into its opposite, because the nature and state of their life are opposed to it. That is why *all the Egyptians dug around the river* symbolizes a search for truth that they could apply to falsity.

[2] That in people devoted to falsity and evil, truth turns into falsity, and goodness into evil—and the reverse—can be seen from the general rule that to the pure everything is pure, while to the impure, everything is impure [Titus 1:15].

It can also be illustrated by phenomena in nature, such as sunlight. The sun's light is white, but it changes with the objects into which it flows, producing colors. In beautiful objects it becomes beautiful, and in ugly objects it turns ugly.

The same thing can also be illustrated by the grafting of branches onto trees. A branch grafted onto a trunk bears its own kind of fruit, so as soon as the tree's sap enters the grafted branch it changes and becomes the branch's sap, capable of producing the branch's type of leaves and fruit.

The case is the same with the things that flow into a person.

[3] The reason *digging* means searching is that water, springs, and wells that are dug out symbolize truth, and truth requires not physical digging but searching. For that reason, when the same verb in the original language is applied to truth, it means to search. However, the prophetical books speak about water or a spring instead of truth, and about digging rather than searching. That is what prophetic language is like. This is clear where Moses talks about the spring at Beer, concerning which Israel sang this song:

> Gush up, you spring! Give answer concerning it! A *spring that the chieftains dug,* the nobles of the people *excavated,* by [the word of] the Lawgiver, with their staffs. (Numbers 21:16, 17, 18)

The spring here symbolizes a theology composed of divine truth. The digging symbolizes searching for that theology.

Because they could not drink from the waters of the river means that 7344
there was no application from pure falsity. This can be seen from the symbolism of *not being able to drink* as no application (for the meaning of drinking as applying, see directly above at §7343) and from that of the *waters of the river* as falsity (also dealt with above, at §7307). This explanation also follows from the inner meaning of the previous words. That is, not being able to drink from the waters of the river meaning that truth cannot be applied to pure falsity (that is, it cannot be rendered false by pure falsity) also follows from the fact that digging [for] drinking water around the river means searching for truth they could apply to falsity.

[2] Why is it that pure falsity does not work as a means of applying truth to falsity? The reason is that truth and falsity are diametrically opposed, and opposites cannot be brought into contact unless there are ways to connect them. The ways to connect them are illusions of the outer senses, and Scripture verses that speak according to appearances. For example, take the idea that nothing but goodness comes from the Lord and never anything evil. This true idea is rendered false by the illusion that the Lord in his omnipotence can do away with evil if he wants, and since he does not do away with it, he causes it, which makes him

the source of evil as well. As for Scripture verses that speak according to appearances, the same truth is rendered false by passages that say Jehovah (the Lord) is angry at us, punishes and condemns us, and throws us into hell. The reality is that we do this to ourselves when committed to evil. So we bring on the evils of our punishment, because the evil that punishes us and the evil we are guilty of are bound up together in the other life.

The same with countless other examples.

7345 Exodus 7:25, 26, 27, 28, 29 [= NRSV 7:25; 8:1, 2, 3, 4]. *And seven days were fulfilled after Jehovah's striking the river. And Jehovah said to Moses, "Come to Pharaoh, and you shall say to him, 'This is what Jehovah says: "Send my people away and let them serve me. And if you refuse to send them away, watch: I will afflict your whole border with frogs. And the river will cause frogs to creep out, and they will go up and come into your house and into your bedroom and onto your bed and into the house of your servants and of your people and into your ovens and into your kneading troughs. And onto you and onto your people and onto all your servants the frogs will come up."'"*

And seven days were fulfilled after Jehovah's striking the river means that this state ended after truth had been rendered false. *And Jehovah said to Moses* symbolizes new instruction. *Come to Pharaoh, and you shall say to him* symbolizes a command to the persecutors. *This is what Jehovah says: "Send my people away to serve me,"* means to leave people of the church alone to worship their God in freedom. *And if you refuse to send them away* means if they did not leave them alone. *Watch: I will afflict your whole border with frogs* symbolizes twisted reasoning based on pure falsity. *And the river will cause frogs to creep out* means that there would be twisted reasoning based on that falsity. *And they will go up and come into your house and into your bedroom* means that this reasoning will fill the mind all the way to its inner depths. *And onto your bed* means to its inmost core. *And into the house of your servants and of your people* symbolizes everything that exists on the earthly plane. *And into your ovens and into your kneading troughs* means into pleasures rising out of corrupt desires. *And onto you and onto your people and onto all your servants the frogs will come up* means that absolutely everything will be subject to reasoning based on falsity.

7346 *And seven days were fulfilled after Jehovah's striking the river* means that this state ended after truth had been rendered false, as the following shows: *Seven days* symbolizes a whole time span from beginning to end, so it symbolizes a complete state (§§728, 6508), just as a week does (§§2044, 3845). Seven days *fulfilled,* then, means the end of that span or state. And *after*

Jehovah's striking the river means after truth had been rendered false, because the striking of the river with Aaron's staff and the conversion of the water to blood means that truth was falsified; see §§7316, 7317, 7330, 7332.

And Jehovah said to Moses symbolizes new instruction. This can be seen from the symbolism of *Jehovah said*, when a new command is being given, as new instruction, as discussed in §§7186, 7267, 7304. 7347

Come to Pharaoh, and you shall say to him symbolizes a command to the persecutors. This can be seen from the symbolism of *coming to* (or approaching) *and saying*, when done on Jehovah's behalf, as a command, and from the representation of *Pharaoh* as spirits who use falsity to inflict persecution (mentioned in §§7107, 7110, 7126, 7142). 7348

This is what Jehovah says: "Send my people away to serve me," means to leave people of the church alone to worship their God in freedom. This can be seen from the symbolism of *sending away* as leaving alone, from the representation of the children of Israel—*my people*—as people of the spiritual church (discussed in §§6426, 6637, 6862, 6868, 7035, 7062, 7198, 7201, 7215, 7223), and from the symbolism of *serving me* as worshiping their God. Worship in freedom is meant because worship was impossible under an onslaught of falsity and because all worship that is true worship must be free (§§1947, 2875, 2876, 2880, 2881, 3145, 3146, 3158, 4031). 7349

And if you refuse to send them away means if they did not leave them alone. This is established by the symbolism of *sending away*, which means leaving alone, as directly above at §7349. *If you refuse* to send them away, then, means if they did not leave them alone. 7350

Watch: I will afflict your whole border with frogs symbolizes twisted reasoning based on pure falsity. This is clear from the symbolism of *frogs* as twisted reasoning. The source of this reasoning in pure falsity is symbolized by the fact that the frogs crept out of the river, as the next clause says (for the meaning of Egypt's river as falsity, see §§6693, 7307); and after all, the text says *the whole border would be afflicted.* 7351

These words also mean that the reasoning will be based on pure falsity rather than on falsified truth. This is because twisted reasoning based on falsified truth eventually turns into blasphemy against what is true and good. Besides, real truth refuses to be rendered false, because it cannot coexist with falsity. As long as the two coexist, truth fights falsity and finally detaches and separates itself from falsity. That is why we eventually deny truth altogether, once we have rendered it false. Otherwise falsity would tyrannize truth. For this reason, the evil in the other life who have been cast into hell are not allowed to argue from falsified truth, only from pure falsity.

[2] The meaning of frogs as twisted reasoning based on falsity can be seen in John:

> I saw three unclean spirits *like frogs* [coming] *from the mouth of the dragon* and *from the mouth of the beast* and *from the mouth of the false prophet.* For they are spirits of demons, working signs [of their intent] to go out to the monarchs of the earth and of the whole inhabited world, to gather them for the war on the great day of God Almighty. (Revelation 16:13, 14)

Individual details here reveal that frogs are forms of reasoning founded on false thinking that contradicts truth. The passage says the frogs came *from the mouth* of the dragon, *from the mouth* of the beast, and *from the mouth* of the false prophet. It also says that they went out to the monarchs of the earth, to gather them for war. The monarchs of the earth mean truth known to the church. (For the meaning of monarchs as truth and in the opposite sense as falsity, see §§1672, 1728, 2015, 2069, 3009, 3670, 4575, 4581, 4966, 5044, 5068, 6148; and for the meaning of the earth as the church, §§662, 1066, 1262, 1733, 1850, 2117, 2118, 3355, 4447, 4535, 5577.) War is spiritual combat (§2686) and therefore combat against religious truth and goodness. Clearly, then, frogs are forms of reasoning founded on false thinking that contradicts truth. [3] In David:

> He turned their waters to blood and killed their fish. *He made frogs creep out onto their land,* in the *rooms* of their *monarchs.* (Psalms 105:29, 30)

This says "in the rooms of their monarchs" because it means twisted reasoning attacking truth on the basis of falsity. The monarchs' rooms are inner truths and in the opposite sense inner falsity. (For monarchs as truth and in a negative sense as falsity, see just above.)

7352 *And the river will cause frogs to creep out* symbolizes [that there would be] twisted reasoning based on that falsity. This is evident from the symbolism of the *river* of Egypt as falsity (discussed in §§6693, 7307) and from that of *frogs* as twisted reasoning (discussed directly above at §7351). Frogs mean such reasoning because they live in the water, make incessant noise there with their croaking, and are among the unclean animals.

Some examples are needed to illustrate what twisted reasoning based on pure falsity is. People argue from pure falsity when they ascribe everything to the material world and hardly anything to the Divine, when in reality everything comes from the Divine and the material world is merely a tool in the hand of the Divine. People argue from pure falsity when they believe that we are like animals, only more perfect because we can think, and that we will therefore die the same as animals. People of this kind deny that faith with its thoughts and love with its desires unite us to the Divine, so they deny the resurrection and eternal life. As a result they speak from pure falsity. The same is true of people who believe there is no hell. It is also true of people who believe their only chance at pleasure comes during life in the world and who consequently think they have to enjoy it there, since when they die they will be utterly dead. People argue from pure falsity when they believe that everything comes of their own shrewdness or of luck, not of divine providence, except in the broadest sense. They do the same when they believe that religion is nothing but a way of keeping the masses in check. Most especially do people argue from pure falsity when they believe that the Word is not divine.

Briefly put, everyone who categorically denies divine truth argues from pure falsity.

And they will go up and come into your house and into your bedroom 7353
means that this reasoning will fill the mind all the way to its inner depths. This can be seen from the symbolism of a *house* as the human mind (discussed in §§3538, 4973, 5023) and from that of a *bedroom* as the mind's inner depths. The reason bedrooms have this symbolism is that they are located in a home's interior.

In the following passages, the private rooms symbolize inner depths, and bedrooms symbolize inner depths that are deeper still. In Isaiah:

> Go, people; *enter your private rooms* and shut the door after you. Hide yourself as for a little while, until the anger passes. (Isaiah 26:20)

In Ezekiel:

> He said to me, "Have you seen, son of humankind, what the elders of the children of Israel do in the dark, all of them *in the private rooms devoted to their idol?"* (Ezekiel 8:12)

In Moses:

> Outside, the sword will bereave, and *from the private rooms,* terror. (Deuteronomy 32:25)

In 2 Kings:

> Elisha the prophet, who is in Israel, tells Israel's king the words *that you speak in your bedroom.* (2 Kings 6:12)

The ancients compared the human mind to a house, and everything inside a person to the rooms. That is just what the human mind is like, too; its components are divided up in almost the same way a house is divided into rooms. The central part is the inmost core; the parts to the sides are the shallower levels, which they compared to the public rooms. Anything outside the mind that cohered with something within they compared to porticoes.

7354 *And onto your bed* means to its inmost core. This can be seen from the symbolism of a *bed* as the inmost part. Since a bedroom means the inner depths, the bed inside it means the inmost part.

7355 *And into the house of your servants and of your people* symbolizes everything that exists on the earthly plane, as the following shows: A *house* symbolizes the human mind, and since it is being associated with Egyptians and with Pharaoh's servants, it symbolizes the earthly mind. (For the meaning of a house as the mind, see just above at §7353.) And Pharaoh's *servants* and *people* symbolize everything that exists on the earthly plane. Earthly elements that serve to support falsity are called servants. The word *people* has to do with truth, and in a negative sense with falsity; see in §§1259, 1260, 3295, 3581, 4619, 6451, 6465. You can see, then, that *into the house of Pharaoh's servants and people* means into everything that exists on the earthly level.

7356 *And into your ovens and into your kneading troughs* means into pleasures rising out of corrupt desires, as the following shows: *Ovens* are for baking bread, so they symbolize an outer kind of goodness, and outer goodness is goodness on the earthly plane, which is usually called pleasure. You see, when the inner goodness associated with love and with love's desires flows into the earthly level, we sense it there as pleasure. This pleasure is symbolized by ovens in their positive sense. In a negative sense, though, like the sense here, ovens symbolize pleasure that rises out of twisted cravings, that is, pleasure rising out of the kinds of love belonging to hell, which are self-love and materialism. And *kneading troughs* likewise symbolize pleasure on the earthly level that rises out of cravings, but an even shallower type of pleasure, because kneading troughs are vessels for the preparation of bread dough.

When I say that twisted reasoning will incorporate itself into pleasures rising out of corrupt desires, I mean that people's central pleasure will be to use twisted reasoning based on falsity to deceive and misguide others. Some of the greatest pleasure the evil enjoy is to spread falsity, confirm its validity, mock the truth, and most of all, lead others astray.

[2] The meaning of an oven as the pleasure associated with positive desires rising out of neighborly love and faith, and in a negative sense as the pleasure associated with perverted desires rising out of self-love and materialism, is evident in Hosea:

> They are all committing adultery *like an oven fired up by the baker;* the stirrer ceases from kneading his dough. When their baker turns his mind *like an oven* to his ambush, he is sleeping the whole night; *in the morning he is burning* like a *fiery flame.* They all *heat up like an oven* and will consume their judges; all their monarchs fall. (Hosea 7:4, 6, 7)

The oven stands for the pleasure rising out of the corrupt cravings enjoyed by the evil. The burning, the heating up, and the fiery flame stand for the cravings themselves. (For the meaning of fire as a craving for evil, see §§1297, 1861, 2446, 5071, 5215, 6314, 6832, 7324 at the end.) "They [will] consume their judges; all their monarchs fall" means that goodness and truth perish. Anyone can see that without an inner meaning like this it is impossible to tell what is meant by "They are all committing adultery like an oven fired up by the baker," "They all heat up like an oven," "They [will] consume their judges," and "Their monarchs fall." [3] An oven is mentioned in a positive sense in Isaiah:

> . . . says Jehovah, who has a fireplace on Zion; and he has an *oven* in Jerusalem. (Isaiah 31:9)

Zion stands for a heavenly religion and accordingly for the loving goodness that characterizes such a religion. Jerusalem stands for a spiritual religion and accordingly for a goodness marked by spiritual love, or the goodness that comes from charity and the accompanying faith. The oven here stands for the inner pleasure connected with a desire for goodness and truth. It has this symbolism because the bread baked in it symbolizes goodness that comes of heavenly and spiritual love. (For this symbolism of bread, see §§276, 680, 2165, 2177, 3464, 3478, 3735, 3813, 4211, 4217, 4735, 4976, 5915.)

Since its use for bread determines the symbolism of an oven, the bread prepared for the sacrifices—called the minha—when baked in an oven was distinguished from the minha baked on a griddle and from the minha baked in a pot (Leviticus 2:4, 5, 7). Different varieties of goodness that comes of love were what these types of minha symbolized.

7357 *And onto you [and] onto your people and onto all your servants the frogs will come up* means that absolutely everything will be subject to reasoning based on falsity. This can be seen from the remarks above at §7355. Pharaoh, his *people,* and his *servants* mean absolutely everyone in the land of Egypt, so they symbolize falsity in absolutely every regard. The symbolism of Pharaoh and Egyptians as falsity has been demonstrated many times before.

It needs to be known that the inhabitants of hell, who are divested of the truth they knew in the world, cannot help saying what is false. So when spirits like this speak—which they do when they appear in the world of spirits—listeners immediately know that what they are saying is false. The upright in the other world recognize this from everyday experience.

The fact that they speak nothing but falsehood is also plain from the Lord's words in John:

> You are from your father, the Devil, and your father's desires you wish to do. He was a murderer from the start and did not stand on truth, because the truth is not in him. *When he tells a lie, he is talking on his own, because he is a liar and the father of [a lie].* (John 8:44)

After all, we each speak in accordance with what we desire and love; we cannot disparage what we love without stooping to pretense, hypocrisy, fraud, and deception. That is what the evil are accustomed to doing when they say something true, but the truth they speak in such a way is false in them. People committed to truth from a commitment to goodness, on the other hand, cannot speak anything *but* truth.

The Inhabitants and Spirits of Mars

7358 TO the minds of spirits and angels, Mars (like the rest of the wandering stars) always shows up in the same place. That place is a little way out in front, to the left, on a level with the chest. So it appears outside the environment of spirits from our own planet.

The spirits of one planet are separated from the spirits of another because the spirits of each planet relate to some particular area in the universal human and are therefore in very different states. The difference in state causes the spirits to appear separate from each other, off to the right or left, at a greater or shorter distance.

Spirits from Mars came to me and placed themselves at my left temple, where they breathed on me with a message; but I could not understand what they were saying. It was quite a gentle stream of words; as far as I remember, I had never perceived a gentler breath before. It was like the softest of breezes. At first it blew onto my left temple and the top of my left ear, from which it moved on to my left eye and slightly toward my right eye, then down (mainly from my left eye) to my lips. On reaching my lips it entered my mouth and passed through my mouth and Eustachian tube into my brain. At that point I finally understood the message and had the opportunity to speak with the spirits. 7359

While they were talking with me I observed that my lips moved, and my tongue too, a little. This was because of the correspondence between inner and outer speech. (Outer speech is speech involving articulated sounds that fall on the outer membrane of the ear and move from there to the brain by way of the tiny organs, the membranes, and the nerves of the inner ear.)

This experience taught me that the speech of Mars's inhabitants differed from speech of our planet's inhabitants, in that it was not audible but almost silent, wending its way to the inner ear and eye by a shortcut. Such being its character, it was more complete and perfect, more profuse with thoughts, and therefore more nearly like the speech of spirits and angels. Moreover, the actual feeling behind the words is expressed in their face, and the thought is expressed in their eyes, because for them, thought acts in unison with speech and feeling acts in unison with facial expression. They consider it atrocious to think one way and talk another, or to nurture one impulse and display another on their face. They do not know what hypocrisy is, or what pretense, deceit, and trickery are. 7360

The earliest people on our planet had the same kind of speech, as I was also allowed to learn by spending time with some of them. For a discussion of their speech, see §§607, 608. 7361

To shed further light on the matter, let me repeat what I had the privilege of learning from experience about the speech of this planet's earliest people. Here is the report:

> By means of a kind of inspiration I cannot describe, I was shown how the people of the earliest church had talked. To be specific, their speech was not articulated, as the verbal speech we use today is, but silent, produced not by external but by internal breathing. I also had the opportunity to sense what their internal breathing was like. It moved from the navel to the heart and then out through the lips without a sound when they were talking. It did not enter another person's ear from outside and vibrate on the part called the ear drum but followed an inner route and in fact a route through a passageway there that we now call the Eustachian tube.
>
> [2] I was shown that this kind of speech enabled them to express the thoughts of their heart and the ideas in their minds much more fully than articulated sounds or audible words ever could. Audible sounds too travel on the breath (external breath, though), because there is no word, nor even any element in a word, that can be conveyed without the use of breath. But the process was much more perfect with them, because it relied on internal breathing. Since internal breathing takes place on a deeper plane, it is more perfect and better adapted to the actual concepts of thought.
>
> In addition, they used subtle motions of the lips and corresponding facial changes. Since they were a heavenly kind of people, everything they thought shone out from their face and eyes, which altered to suit the thought—their face in its set and liveliness, and their eyes as to the glow in them. They were completely incapable of any facial expression that did not agree with their thinking. They considered pretense a heinous crime and deceit even worse. (§1118)

Because this was what their speech was like, and because they used internal breathing, they could keep company with angels.

7362 The breathing of spirits from Mars was also communicated to me ([like us,] spirits and angels have breathing; see §§3884–3894), and I perceived that it was internal breathing. The breath traveled from the area of my thorax toward my navel, rolling up from there through my chest, accompanied by an imperceptible movement of breath toward my mouth.

This evidence, along with the proof of other experiences, showed me that their bent of mind was heavenly, which meant that they were not unlike the people of the earliest church on this planet.

They talked with me about the life of the inhabitants on their planet. 7363
"We don't live under empires," they said. "Instead we divide up into larger and smaller communities in which people come together because of being like-minded. And this compatibility is something we can judge immediately by face and speech, which rarely deceive us. We then become instant friends. But we don't snub the rest. There is no rejection, let alone hatred.

"When we get together, it is a pleasure," they continued. "We talk with each other about what is going on in our communities, and especially events in heaven"—since many of them have open contact with angels in heaven.

Because they have this disposition and come together this way, it is easy to believe that all their communities taken together, throughout the planet, represent an all-encompassing angelic community. Every group there is different, but the Lord unites them all through the heavenly form so that they can be one. Unity rises out of variety arranged into a suitable form.

When a member of any of their communities starts to think what 7364
is wrong and consequently to want what is wrong, they break their ties with her or him. They leave such a person all alone to live a miserable life outside society, among the rocks or elsewhere, because they no longer concern themselves with an individual like that. Some communities try various means of forcing such people to come to their senses, but when the effort proves useless, they detach from them.

They take measures, then, to prevent the intrusion of a craving for control or for riches. That is, they work to prevent people from subjecting to their will the community in which they live (and then many other populations as well) out of a craving for control, or from seizing the goods of others out of a craving for riches. They each live content with their own goods and content with the status they have earned by a reputation for fairness and neighborly love. [2] This calm, pleasant state of mind would be destroyed if they did not eject people whose thoughts and intentions are malicious. It would be destroyed if they did not stand up shrewdly and strictly against self-love and love of worldly advantages when these first appear in a person. After all, these are the passions that have taken groups of people who associate voluntarily and turned them into empires and monarchies, which contain few citizens who do not wish to domineer and to take possession of everything belonging to others. That is because they contain few citizens who act justly and fairly at the call of justice and fairness, let alone citizens who do good at the call of neighborly love, or who act on truth at the call of faith. Rather, their citizens act on fear of the law, fear of suffering harm, fear for their life, and fear of losing wealth, position, and consequent prestige.

7365 More will be said about the inhabitants and spirits of Mars at the end of the next chapter [§§7475–7487].

Exodus 8

Teachings on Neighborly Love

I said above [§7255] that self-love and the love of worldly advantages in us make hell. Now I need to describe these kinds of love so that you can tell whether you exhibit them and consequently whether hell or heaven is in you; because we do have either hell or heaven within ourselves. The Lord teaches in Luke 17:21 that God's kingdom is within us, so that is also where hell is. 7366

Self-love reigns supreme in us—we exhibit self-love—when in our thoughts and deeds we focus not on our neighbor or the public at large, let alone the Lord, only on ourselves and those closest to us. We display self-love, then, when everything we do is for ourselves and our own, and if we do act to benefit our neighbor or the public at large, it is only with the intent of being seen. 7367

I am saying "for ourselves and our own" because we are inseparable from those closest to us, and they are inseparable from us. For instance, if a man does anything for his wife, children, grandchildren, sons-in-law, or daughters-in-law, he does it for himself because they are his. The same is true if we do anything for more distant relatives or for friends who bind themselves to us by catering to our self-love because through this bond they form a unit with us; they see themselves in us, and us in themselves. 7368

The more self-love we have, the more we remove ourselves from love for our neighbor, so the more self-love we have, the more we remove ourselves from heaven, since heaven is marked by love for one's neighbor. From this it also follows that the more self-love we have, the more we are in hell, because hell is marked by self-love. 7369

People engage in self-love when they despise their neighbor in comparison with themselves and consider their neighbor an enemy if he or she does not fawn on them and worship them. They engage even more deeply in self-love when they hate and persecute their neighbor on that 7370 account, and still more deeply when they burn with revenge against their neighbor on that account and desire their neighbor's ruin. In the end such people love to vent their rage on their neighbor, and if they are adulterers, they turn abusive.

7371 The pleasure this behavior yields them is the pleasure accompanying self-love, which, when it is present in a person, is the pleasure of hell. Any activity that harmonizes with the things a person loves is agreeable, so the delight is a clue to the nature of the love.

7372 The remarks above at §7370 indicate just who have devoted themselves to self-love. It does not matter how people appear on the outside, whether proud or humble, because the urges of self-love are located in the inner self. Most people today hide their inner self and train their outer self to put on a show of love for the public at large and for their neighbor, in direct opposition to the reality inside. This too is for the sake of themselves and their worldly advantages.

7373 As for love of worldly advantages, this reigns supreme in us—we exhibit this love—when in our thoughts and deeds we aim and strive only for financial gain, unconcerned whether we harm our neighbor or the public at large in achieving it.

7374 People engage in love of worldly advantages when they wish to divert the belongings of others to themselves by methods they have dreamed up, and especially when they wish to do so by trickery and deceit. People with this love envy others their property and covet it. If they do not fear the law, they also steal and even pillage.

7375 The more unbridled these two kinds of love are, and the more we are carried away by them, the more they increase. Finally they grow so excessive that they want to control not only everything in our own country but everything beyond its borders too, all the way to the ends of the earth. In fact, when these loves are given free rein, they climb all the way to the God of the universe—up so high that they try to climb onto God's throne and be worshiped as God himself. This is in keeping with the following words in Isaiah concerning Lucifer. (Lucifer stands for people immersed in self-love and materialism, who are called Babylon.)

> You have said in your heart, "I will scale the heavens; I will raise my throne above the stars of God and sit on the mountain of assembly, on the flanks of the north. I will climb above the loftiest parts of the cloud and become like the Highest One." But you were sent down to hell. (Isaiah 14:13, 14, 15)

This discussion now shows that these two kinds of love are the sources of all evil. After all, they are diametrically opposed to love for one's neighbor and to love for the Lord, so they are diametrically opposed to heaven, where love for the Lord and love for one's neighbor predominate. Consequently these two loves—self-love and love for worldly advantages—are what make hell in a person, because in hell they predominate. 7376

However, consider people who aspire to high position not for their own sake but for the sake of their country. Consider those who aspire to wealth not for its own sake but in order to provide the necessities of life for both themselves and their dependents, or for the sake of some good purpose that makes affluence delightful. People like this are not controlled by self-love and materialism. With them, position and wealth are a means of doing good. 7377

Exodus 8

1 [= NRSV 8:5]. And Jehovah said to Moses, "Say to Aaron, 'Stretch your hand with your staff over the streams, over the rivers, and over the pools. And bring frogs up over the land of Egypt.'"

2 [= 8:6]. And Aaron stretched his hand over the waters of Egypt, and the frogs came up and covered the land of Egypt.

3 [= 8:7]. And the magicians of Egypt did the same with their spells and brought frogs up over the land of Egypt.

4 [= 8:8]. And Pharaoh called Moses and Aaron and said, "Plead to Jehovah and have him remove the frogs from me and from my people. And let me send the people away, and they are to sacrifice to Jehovah."

5 [= 8:9]. And Moses said to Pharaoh, "Show respect for me: for what future time shall I plead on behalf of you and of your servants and of your people to have the frogs cut off from you and from your houses? Only in the river will they remain."

6 [= 8:10]. And he said, "Tomorrow." And [Moses] said, "[It will happen] according to your word so that you may know that there is no one like Jehovah our God.

7 [= 8:11]. And the frogs will be removed from you and from your houses and from your servants and from your people; only in the river will they remain."

8 [= 8:12]. And Moses and Aaron went out from Pharaoh, and Moses cried out to Jehovah over the matter of the frogs that [Jehovah] had laid on Pharaoh.

9 [= 8:13]. And Jehovah did according to Moses' word. And the frogs died out of the houses, out of the courtyards, and out of the fields.

10 [= 8:14]. And they gathered them in heaps and heaps. And the land reeked.

11 [= 8:15]. And Pharaoh saw that there was some breathing space, and he made his heart leaden and did not listen to them, as Jehovah had spoken.

12 [= 8:16]. And Jehovah said to Moses, "Say to Aaron, 'Stretch out your staff and strike the dust of the land, and it will become lice in all the land of Egypt.'"

13 [= 8:17]. And they did so, and Aaron stretched out his hand with his staff and struck the dust of the land, and there were lice on humans and on animals. All the dust of the land became lice in the whole land of Egypt.

14 [= 8:18]. And the magicians did the same with their spells, to bring forth lice. And they could not, and there were lice on humans and on animals.

15 [= 8:19]. And the magicians said to Pharaoh, "This is the finger of God." And Pharaoh's heart hardened, and he did not listen to them, as Jehovah had spoken.

16 [= 8:20]. And Jehovah said to Moses, "Get up early in the morning, and you are to stand before Pharaoh (watch: he walks out to the water) and say to him, 'This is what Jehovah says: "Send my people away and let them serve me.

17 [= 8:21]. Because if you fail to send my people away, then I myself am sending against you and against your servants and against your people and against your houses the winged pest. And the houses of the Egyptians will be filled with the winged pest, as will the land they are on.

18 [= 8:22]. And on that day I will set apart the land of Goshen, on which my people stands, so that the winged pest will not be there, in order that you may know that I, Jehovah, am in the midst of the land.

19 [= 8:23]. And I will put redemption [as a difference] between my people and your people. Tomorrow this sign will occur."'"

20 [= 8:24]. And Jehovah did so, and the winged pest came heavily to the house of Pharaoh and to the house of his servants and into all the land of Egypt. The land was destroyed in the path of the winged pest.

21 [= 8:25]. And Pharaoh called Moses and Aaron and said, "Go; sacrifice to your God in the land."

22 [= 8:26]. And Moses said, "It is not advisable to do so, because we would be sacrificing what the Egyptians abhor to Jehovah our God. Look, were we to sacrifice what the Egyptians find abhorrent in their eyes, would they not stone us?

23 [= 8:27]. A journey of three days we will go into the wilderness and sacrifice to Jehovah our God, as he said to us."

24 [= 8:28]. And Pharaoh said, "I myself will send you away, and you are to sacrifice to Jehovah your God in the wilderness, only you are certainly not to go far. Plead for me."

25 [= 8:29]. And Moses said, "Look, now, I am going out from you and will plead to Jehovah; and may he remove the winged pest from Pharaoh, from his servants, and from his people, tomorrow. Only Pharaoh is not to continue playing tricks by not sending the people away to sacrifice to Jehovah."

26 [= 8:30]. And Moses went out from Pharaoh and pleaded to Jehovah.

27 [= 8:31]. And Jehovah did according to Moses' word and removed the winged pest from Pharaoh, from his servants, and from his people. Not one was left.

28 [= 8:32]. And Pharaoh made his heart leaden this time too and did not send the people away.

Summary

THE inner meaning of the current chapter continues to discuss the devastation of spirits who are devoted to falsity and afflict the upright in the other life. The previous chapter depicted the first two steps in the process and part of the third step, which was that these spirits reasoned exclusively on the basis of pure falsity. Twisted reasoning based on pure falsity is symbolized by frogs. The frogs feature once again in the current chapter, which goes on to treat of the fourth and fifth steps in the devastation of believers in falsity who persecute the upright in the other life. The fourth step is that they were devoted to evil that would destroy everything good in them, including whatever earthly goodness they had. 7378

These details are symbolized by the lice created out of the dust of the land. The fifth step is that they were devoted to the falsities produced by that evil, which would destroy all truth. These details are symbolized by the winged pest.

Inner Meaning

7379 EXODUS 8:1–10 [= NRSV 8:5–14]. *And Jehovah said to Moses, "Say to Aaron, 'Stretch your hand with your staff over the streams, over the rivers, and over the pools. And bring frogs up over the land of Egypt.'" And Aaron stretched his hand over the waters of Egypt, and the frogs came up and covered the land of Egypt. And the magicians of Egypt did the same with their spells and brought frogs up over the land of Egypt. And Pharaoh called Moses and Aaron and said, "Plead to Jehovah and have him remove the frogs from me and from my people. And let me send the people away, and they are to sacrifice to Jehovah." And Moses said to Pharaoh, "Show respect for me: for what future time shall I plead on behalf of you and of your servants and of your people to have the frogs cut off from you and from your houses? Only in the river will they remain." And he said, "Tomorrow." And [Moses] said, "[It will happen] according to your word so that you may know that there is no one like Jehovah our God. And the frogs will be removed from you and from your houses and from your servants and from your people; only in the river will they remain." And Moses and Aaron went out from Pharaoh, and Moses cried out to Jehovah over the matter of the frogs that [Jehovah] had laid on Pharaoh. And Jehovah did according to Moses' word. And the frogs died out of the houses, out of the courtyards, and out of the fields. And they gathered them in heaps and heaps. And the land reeked.*

And Jehovah said to Moses symbolizes instruction. *Say to Aaron* symbolizes an inflow of inner law into outer law. *Stretch your hand with your staff* symbolizes the power inner truth has through outer truth. *Over the streams, over the rivers, and over the pools* means against falsity. *And bring frogs up over the land of Egypt* symbolizes twisted reasoning based on pure falsity. *And Aaron stretched his hand over the waters of Egypt* symbolizes the power inner truth has through outer truth, wielded against falsity. *And the frogs came up* symbolizes twisted reasoning based on pure falsity. *And covered the land of Egypt* means that the earthly mind took on this character. *And the magicians of Egypt did the same with their spells* symbolizes misuse of the divine design to create a similar appearance on the outside. *And brought frogs up over the land of Egypt* means so far as the reasoning of the earthly mind went. *And Pharaoh called Moses and Aaron* symbolizes the presence of divine law. *And said, "Plead to Jehovah,"* symbolizes humility born of fatigue. *And have him remove the frogs from me and from my people* means so as not to be forced to reason on the basis of pure falsity. *And let me send the people away, and they are to sacrifice to Jehovah* means that they would then leave people of the spiritual church alone to worship their God. *And Moses said to Pharaoh* symbolizes the answer. *Show respect for me* means that divine law is to be trusted. *For what future time shall I plead on behalf of you and of your servants and of your people?* symbolizes intervention on behalf of people who subscribe to falsity and inflict persecution. *To have the frogs cut off from you and from your houses* means to have all the twisted reasoning stop. *Only in the river will they remain* means that it would persist in the abode and company of falsity. *And he said, "Tomorrow,"* means permanently. *And [Moses] said, "[It will happen] according to your word,"* symbolizes confirmation of this. *So that you may know that there is no one like Jehovah our God* means that there is one God, and none besides him. *And the frogs will be removed from you and from your houses and from your servants and from your people* means that they would not be forced to reason on the basis of pure falsity. *Only in the river will they remain* means that the reasoning would persist in the abode and company of falsity. *And Moses and Aaron went out from Pharaoh* symbolizes being separated from people with twisted reasoning based on pure falsity. *And Moses cried out to Jehovah over the matter of the frogs that [Jehovah] had laid on Pharaoh* symbolizes intervention. *And Jehovah did according to Moses' word* means that it happened according to the Lord's word. *And the frogs died out of the houses, out of the courtyards, and out of the fields* means that reasoning based on pure falsity ceased to occur for them anywhere on their earthly plane. *And they gathered them in heaps and heaps* means that those false arguments were bundled together on the earthly plane. *And the land reeked* symbolizes the horrible, loathsome result.

And Jehovah said to Moses symbolizes instruction. This can be seen from 7380
the discussion in §§7186, 7304 of the symbolism of *saying* as instruction.

In Scripture narrative, the symbolism of *saying* is apparent from the speech that follows it, because it includes those words. The reason it symbolizes instruction here is that Jehovah says what should be done next. Besides, Moses represents divine law, through which Jehovah gives instruction.

7381 *Say to Aaron* symbolizes an inflow of inner law into outer law, as the following shows: Moses represents divine law (discussed in §§6723, 6752) and *Aaron* represents teachings about goodness and truth (discussed in §§6998, 7089). The teachings about goodness and truth that Aaron represents are the same thing as outer law arising from inner law, or rather arising from the Divine through inner law. And *saying* symbolizes an inflow, as at §§6152, 7291. The reason saying means an inflow here is that Moses is speaking to Aaron, and Moses is inner law, while Aaron is outer law. Inflow from the Divine takes place through the inner dimension into the outer.

Inner law is divine truth itself as it exists in heaven, and outer law is divine truth as it exists on earth. So inner law is truth adapted to angels, and outer law is truth adapted to people on earth.

[2] Since the inner law that Moses represents is truth adapted to angels, and the outer law that Aaron represents is truth adapted to people on earth, let me talk about them here. Truth adapted to angels is mostly incomprehensible to people on earth, and this is evident from the fact that what is seen and said in heaven is the type of thing that "eye had never seen nor ear had ever heard" [1 Corinthians 2:9]. That is because the conversation of angels is spiritual. What is spiritual is abstracted from the earthly realm and is therefore removed from the ideas expressed in human speech and from the words used to express them. [By the time we reach the spiritual world,] we have formed our thinking from the elements of nature, and in fact of nature at its coarsest. In other words, we have formed our thinking from what we could see and touch in the universe and on earth, all of which is made of matter. The ideas of our inner thinking lie above the material realm, but they still come to rest in that realm, and the place where they come to rest is the place where they seem to dwell. Their presence there enables us to tell what we are thinking. From these remarks you can see what the status and nature of religious truth is: it is accessible to human thought, is called the outer law, and is represented by Aaron.

[3] Let this example serve to illustrate: The idea of time and space is an inescapable part of our thinking; it clings to almost everything we think. If the ideas we derive from time and space were taken from us, we would not know what we were thinking and hardly even *whether* we were thinking. However, time and space do not even begin to enter into

angels' thinking but are replaced with states instead. This is because time and space are what distinguish the physical world from the spiritual world.

The reason time and space exist in the physical world but are replaced in the spiritual world by states is that in the physical world, the sun by its apparent cycles seems to create days and years. It seems to split the days into the four periods of night, morning, afternoon, and evening and to split the years into the four periods of winter, spring, summer, and fall. It achieves this by varying the light and shade, warmth and cold. That is where the idea of time in all its permutations comes from. The idea of space results from the use of time as a measurement, so where the one concept exists the other does too.

[4] In the spiritual world, on the other hand, the sun of heaven does not move or go through cycles that would create the impression of time and space. Heaven's sun radiates spiritual light and warmth, the light being divine truth and the warmth divine goodness, and these are what give rise to angels' idea of states. Their states of understanding and faith come from divine truth and their states of wisdom and love come from divine goodness. Changes of these states in angels are what correspond to the worldly states of light and shade and of warmth and cold connected with the physical sun, as it goes about marking time and measuring space.

This example to some extent clarifies the nature of inner truth, or truth adapted to angels, which is called inner law, and the nature of outer truth, or truth adapted to people on earth, which is termed outer law. It also shows why the things angels say to each other are incomprehensible and inexpressible to us.

Stretch your hand with your staff symbolizes the power inner truth has 7382
through outer truth. This is established by the symbolism of a *hand* as the spiritual power of inner truth and by the representation of a *staff* as the earthly power of outer truth, which are discussed in §§6947, 6948. For the idea that all power in the spiritual world belongs to truth, see §§3091, 3387, 4932, 6344, 6423, 6948.

To repeat, Moses represents inner law, which is the same as inner truth; Aaron represents outer law, which is the same as outer truth; and inner truth flows into outer truth, giving it power (§7381). So when Moses says to Aaron, "Stretch your hand with your staff," it symbolizes the power inner truth has through outer truth.

Over the streams, over the rivers, and over the pools means against falsity. 7383
This can be seen from the symbolism of Egypt's *streams* and *rivers* as false

doctrinal teachings (dealt with at §7323) and from that of *pools* as concepts subservient to those teachings (dealt with at §7324). Falsity is therefore what the streams, rivers, and pools symbolize.

7384 *And bring frogs up over the land of Egypt* symbolizes twisted reasoning based on pure falsity. This can be seen from the discussion in §§7351, 7352 of the symbolism of *frogs* as twisted reasoning based on pure falsity. That is also what frogs *correspond* to, because everything in the physical world, in whole and in part, corresponds with elements of the spiritual world. This is because the physical realm comes into being through the spiritual realm. The whole material world is consequently a theater representing the spiritual world (§§2758, 3483, 4939).

7385 *And Aaron stretched his hand over the waters of Egypt* symbolizes the power inner truth has through outer truth, wielded against falsity, as the following shows: *Aaron* represents teachings about truth and goodness, so he represents outer truth, as discussed in §§6998, 7009, 7089. A *hand* symbolizes power, as discussed in §§878, 4931–4937. In this case it symbolizes the power that inner truth wields through outer truth, as above at §7382. And the *waters of Egypt* symbolize falsity, as discussed in §§6693, 7307. The wielding of the power is symbolized by the fact that Aaron stretched out his hand and the frogs came up.

These remarks make it plain that *Aaron stretched his hand over the waters of Egypt* symbolizes the power inner truth has through outer truth, wielded against falsity.

7386 *And the frogs came up* symbolizes twisted reasoning based on pure falsity, as can be seen from the comments above at §7384.

7387 *And covered the land of Egypt* means that the earthly mind took on this character, as the following demonstrates: The word *cover* is being used of the earthly mind, so it means that this mind was filled with falsity and with reasoning based on falsity and therefore that it took on this character. And the *land of Egypt* symbolizes the earthly mind, as discussed in §§5276, 5278, 5280, 5288, 5301.

7388 *And the magicians of Egypt did the same with their spells* symbolizes misuse of the divine design to create a similar appearance on the outside. See §§7296, 7297, 7337, where similar words occur.

7389 *And brought frogs up over the land of Egypt* means so far as the reasoning of the earthly mind went. This can be seen from the symbolism of *frogs* as reasoning based on pure falsity (discussed in §§7351, 7352, 7384) and from that of the *land of Egypt* as the earthly mind (mentioned just above at §7387).

And Pharaoh called Moses and Aaron symbolizes the presence of divine law, as the following shows: *Calling* symbolizes presence, as noted at §6177. Calling symbolizes presence because calling someone means wanting to talk with that person and to communicate one's thoughts. In the other world, anyone we want to speak with and long to share our thoughts with appears in person, in keeping with a law of order. *Pharaoh* represents spirits intent on falsity who inflict harassment, as mentioned many times before. And *Moses* represents inner law, while *Aaron* represents outer law, as dealt with above at §7381. **7390**

And said, "Plead to Jehovah," symbolizes humility born of fatigue. This is clear from the symbolism of *pleading to Jehovah* as humility. Anyone who pleads is feeling humble, as is anyone who begs another to plead on her or his behalf. The reason pleading means humility is that angels pay attention not to the plea but to our humility when we are pleading. A plea devoid of humility is just an empty noise that does not reach an angel's ear or mind. **7391**

The next section will show that fatigue—growing tired of reasoning on the basis of mere falsity—is the cause of the humility.

And have him remove the frogs from me and from my people means so as not to be forced to reason on the basis of pure falsity, as the following shows: *Removing* means not being forced, because what prompted their plea was fatigue from having been forced to reason on the basis of pure falsity. And *frogs* symbolize reasoning based on pure falsity, as discussed in §§7351, 7352. And Pharaoh and the Egyptians represent persecutors devoted to falsity, as mentioned often. **7392**

[2] Regarding the fatigue that prompts the pleas or humility of harassing spirits, you need to know that they do not enjoy reasoning on the basis of pure falsity. It gives them no opportunity to hurt anyone, because pure falsity, which directly contradicts truth, earns ridicule from the upright—in this case from the people in the Lord's spiritual church whom they were harassing. In contrast, falsity based on illusions and appearances that render truth false (as symbolized by the blood to which the waters of Egypt turned, §§7317, 7326) did make it possible for the spirits to do harm, because illusions and appearances mislead people. They throw a shadow or veil over the truth, so to speak. Since arguing from pure falsity—from flat denial of the truth—does not enable them to do harm, it was irksome to them, and that is why they begged for mercy. Nothing delights the hellish but evildoing, whatever way that can be accomplished. Doing evil

is the central pleasure of their life—so much so that it *is* their life. When evildoing is not allowed, then, they grow weary. That is why Pharaoh pleaded for relief from the curse of the frogs but not from the curse of the blood described above [Exodus 7:14–23] or the curse of the lice described below [verses 12, 13, 14, 15 [= 8:16, 17, 18, 19]]. The curse of the frogs symbolizes an attack made through arguments based on pure falsity, which do not enable these spirits to do evil. The curse of the blood, though, symbolizes an attack made through falsity based on illusions and appearances. This kind of attack is a joy to them, because it does enable them to do evil. And the curse of the lice symbolizes evil, which is a joy to them because it *is* evil.

[3] The people who enjoy evildoing in the other life are all the ones who in the world help their neighbor not for their neighbor's sake, their country not for their country's sake, and the church not for the church's sake but for their own sake. So they are people who do what is true and good but not for the sake of truth and goodness.

The fact that they enjoy evildoing does not come to light in the world, because their outer self hides it. In the other life, though, when the outer layers are taken away and one is left to one's inner devices, that pleasure comes out and reveals itself. That is why such people are in hell. Everyone there loves to do evil, but everyone in heaven loves to do good.

7393 *And let me send the people away, and they are to sacrifice to Jehovah* means that they would then leave people of the spiritual church alone to worship their God. This can be seen from the symbolism of *sending away* as leaving alone (as in §§7312, 7349, 7350), from the representation of the children of Israel as people of the spiritual church (as in §§6426, 6637, 6862, 6868, 7035, 7062, 7198, 7201, 7215, 7223), and from the symbolism of *sacrificing to Jehovah* as worshiping their God. Sacrifices symbolized all worship in general (see §6905), so the sacrificing here means worshiping.

7394 *And Moses said to Pharaoh* symbolizes the answer. This is evident from the symbolism of *saying* as a response (as also at §7103), since the words are addressed to Pharaoh, who just finished speaking.

7395 *Show respect for me* means that divine truth is to be trusted. This can be seen from the symbolism of *showing respect* as trusting and from the representation of Moses as divine law (discussed in §§6723, 6752) and therefore as divine truth (discussed in §§6771, 7014, 7382).

7396 *For what future time shall I plead on behalf of you and of your servants and of your people?* symbolizes intervention on behalf of people who subscribe to falsity and inflict persecution. This can be seen from the symbolism of *pleading* as intervention (since the plea is on someone else's behalf) and from the representation of Pharaoh as people who subscribe to falsity and inflict persecution (mentioned in §§7107, 7110, 7126, 7142, 7317). Since these are the people Pharaoh represents, the addition of *his servants and his people* means every last one of them. *Servants* means lower-class assistants; *people* means every individual.

In heaven, an empire or country is represented as a person, and its communities are represented as the body parts, while the monarch is represented as the head.

This representation traces its cause to the fact that heaven as a whole presents the image of a single individual, and its communities represent the body parts, depending on the role they play. From this you can see how beautiful and appealing the representation of an [earthly] empire, country, or community would be in heaven if its citizens were likewise united to each other in charity and faith.

[2] What is more, wherever the Lord can, he unites communities this way, because the divine truth itself radiating from him introduces an orderly arrangement of this kind wherever it is welcomed. That is where the arrangement of heaven comes from. The same pattern exists on earth, but the communities that contribute to it are scattered throughout the globe, being made up of people motivated by love for the Lord and charity for their neighbor. These scattered communities are brought together by the Lord so that they too can present the image of a single individual, as the communities of heaven do. Such communities are located not just within the church but outside it as well. Taken together they are called the Lord's church scattered throughout the globe and gathered together from good people everywhere. Another name for it is a communion. This communion—this church—is the Lord's kingdom on earth united with his kingdom in the heavens and (consequently) with the Lord himself.

To have the frogs cut off from you and from your houses means to have all 7397
the twisted reasoning stop, as the following shows: *Frogs* symbolize twisted reasoning based on pure falsity, as discussed in §§7351, 7352, 7384. *Cutting off* means stopping. ("Cutting off" applies to [a plague of] frogs, while "stopping" applies to twisted reasoning.) Pharaoh, from whom the [plague of] frogs was to be cut off, represents believers in falsity who inflict persecution, as mentioned directly above at §7396. And *houses* symbolize the contents of the earthly mind. A house means the earthly mind (see §§4973, 5023, 7353), so houses in the plural mean its contents.

7398 *Only in the river will they remain* means that it would persist in the abode and company of falsity. This can be seen from the symbolism of a *river*—here, Egypt's river—as falsity (discussed in §§6693, 7307) and from that of *remaining* as persisting.

Here is the situation: Absolutely everything we take in stays with us, especially if we welcome it. People believe that what we take in is entirely erased and expunged when we cease to remember it, but it is not erased or expunged. No, it hangs on either in our inner memory or else in our outer memory among other impressions that have grown familiar. What becomes familiar seems inborn, which means that it comes into play spontaneously rather than being stirred up by conscious, deliberate recall. Take human speech, whose words flow in spontaneously from the thought behind them. Take our movements and actions, even our way of walking, and thought itself. We develop these traits and capacities gradually, from infancy, and in time they grow familiar, from which point on they operate spontaneously. These considerations and others like them show that everything we take in persists and that when we have developed something as a habit—when it has become familiar—we no longer sense its presence, even though it is there. The case is the same with the falsity and evil and with the truth and goodness we take in. They are what shape us and make us what we are. Everything we have seen, heard, thought, spoken, or done is imprinted on us; see §§2474, 2489.

[2] This discussion now shows how to understand the idea that the reasoning would persist in the abode and company of falsity. Once falsity has been set aside, it is allotted a place elsewhere on the earthly plane, and with it goes any energy or craving for twisted reasoning. It is just that these no longer occupy the center, directly under the mind's gaze.

That is why it happened (as a subsequent verse mentions) that the frogs were gathered in heaps and that the land reeked with them, meaning that those forms of false reasoning were bundled together on the earthly plane, where they had a horrible, loathsome result. See below at §§7408, 7409.

7399 *And he said, "Tomorrow,"* means permanently. This is evident from the symbolism of *tomorrow* as permanently and forever, as discussed in §3998.

7400 *And [Moses] said, "[It will happen] according to your word,"* symbolizes confirmation of this, as can be seen without explanation.

7401 *So that you may know that there is no one like Jehovah our God* means that there is one God, and none besides him, as the following consideration shows: When the text in its narrative sense says that there is no one like Jehovah God, in an inner sense it means that there is no God besides him and, since there is no God besides him, that there is one God. A number of times the Word says that there is no one like Jehovah God and that there is no God like him. The Word speaks this way because at the time, people in the land where the church existed worshiped many gods, just as they did in lands where the church did not exist, and they each promoted their god over the next person's. Names were what they used to differentiate the gods, the God of the people of Israel and Judah being called Jehovah. Even the people of Judah and Israel believed in the existence of many other gods, but they considered Jehovah greater than the rest because of the miracles he did. Whenever the miracles stopped, then, they immediately slipped into the worship of other gods, as Scripture narrative makes plain. They did say with their lips that there was one God and none besides him, but at heart they did not believe it. This then is why the Word says that Jehovah is greater than the other gods and that there is no one like him. In David, for instance:

> *Who is a great God like you?* You are the God working a miracle. (Psalms 77:13, 14)

In the same author:

> *Who is like Jehovah our God?* (Psalms 113:5)

In the same author:

> *A great God is Jehovah,* and a *great* monarch *over all gods.* (Psalms 95:3)

In the same author:

> Jehovah is great and highly praised; *he is to be feared over all gods.* (Psalms 96:4)

So Jehovah is also called *God of the gods* and Lord of the lords, in Psalms 136:2, 3; Daniel 2:47. Nonetheless the meaning in an inner sense is that God is one and that there is none besides him, as is plain in Isaiah:

> Remember former events from ages past, because I am God and there is *no God besides* and *none like me.* (Isaiah 46:9)

And the frogs will be removed from you and from your houses and from 7402
your servants and from your people means that they would not be forced to reason on the basis of pure falsity. This can be seen from the symbolism of

having the frogs removed as not being forced to reason on the basis of pure falsity (discussed above at §7392), from the representation of Pharaoh as harassers devoted to falsity (discussed before), from the symbolism of *houses* as the contents of the earthly mind (discussed at §7397), and from the symbolism of *his servants* and *people* as every one of the harassers who were devoted to falsity (also discussed above, at §7396).

7403 *Only in the river will they remain* means that the reasoning would persist in the abode and company of falsity, as can be seen from the discussion above at §7398, where the same words occur.

7404 *And Moses and Aaron went out from Pharaoh* symbolizes being separated from people with twisted reasoning based on pure falsity. This can be seen from the symbolism of *going out* as being separated; from the representation of *Moses and Aaron* as divine law, Moses being the inner law and Aaron the outer law (discussed at §7381); and from the representation of *Pharaoh* as harassers devoted to falsity (mentioned above at §7396). Here Pharaoh represents people who inflict harassment through twisted reasoning on the basis of pure falsity.

7405 *And Moses cried out to Jehovah over the matter of the frogs that [Jehovah] had laid on Pharaoh* symbolizes intervention. This can be seen from the discussion above [§7396] and therefore needs no further explanation.

7406 *And Jehovah did according to Moses' word* means that it happened according to the Lord's word. Moses' plea did come from his lips, but it was still from the Lord. Everything we think and consequently say, everything we intend and consequently do comes to us from elsewhere; we are merely an organ designed to receive the inflow (see §§6189–6215, 6307–6327, 6466–6495, 6598–6626). The same is true for the words and actions of Moses recorded here. *Jehovah did according to Moses' word,* then, means that it happened according to the Lord's word. (For the fact that Jehovah in the Word is the Lord, see §§1343, 1736, 2921, 3023, 3035, 5663, 6281, 6303, 6905.)

7407 *And the frogs died out of the houses, out of the courtyards, and out of the fields* means that reasoning based on pure falsity ceased to occur for them anywhere on their earthly plane, as the following shows: *Dying* means ceasing to occur. *Frogs* symbolize twisted reasoning based on pure falsity, as mentioned above [§§7351, 7352, 7384]. *Houses* symbolize the contents of the earthly mind, as dealt with above at §7397, and here they symbolize its inner parts. *Courtyards* symbolize the outer parts of the earthly mind. (For the idea that the earthly plane has an inner and an outer part, see §§3293, 3294, 4570, 5118, 5497, 5649.) And *fields* symbolize a more general type of content and therefore something still more external, since fields lie outside houses and courtyards.

The frogs died out of the houses, out of the courtyards, and out of the fields therefore means that reasoning based on pure falsity ceased to occur anywhere on their earthly plane.

And they gathered them in heaps and heaps means that those false argu- 7408
ments were bundled together on the earthly plane. This can be seen from the symbolism of *being gathered in heaps and heaps* as being bundled.

The reason that being gathered in heaps has this meaning is that everything in the human mind is arranged in series and bundles, so to speak, and in series within series, or bundles within bundles (see §§5339, 5530, 5881). The fact that it is all arranged this way is plain from the way everything is arranged in the body, where the nerves appear arranged in bundles and the glands in clusters, throughout the body. The pattern is still more perfect for the more refined elements invisible to the naked eye. The bundling I am describing is especially plain to see in the brain, in the two substances there, of which one is called cortical and the other medullary. It is no different at the more refined and even at the most refined levels, where the structures that receive those elements are the actual structures of life. [2] The fact that they are the structures or substances designed to receive life can be seen from all the visible evidence in living organisms. The same evidence makes it plain that the receiving structures or substances are arranged in the manner best adapted to the inflow of life. If life were not received by these substances or structures, nothing living would exist in the physical or in the spiritual world. The rudimentary filaments of life, which are extremely refined, come in series that resemble bundles and that make up these structures. Bundling also comes into play in the magnificent modifications of the components there. The modifications take as their template the structures or substances in which those components exist and from which they flow, because the substances or structures are the determining factors.

Scholars have conceived of the attributes of human life (such as thoughts and intentions) as being without substances or structures to receive them. The reason has been that they believe life (or the soul) to be a kind of flame or bit of ether and therefore something that dissolves upon death. From this comes the insane idea many of them have that there is no life after death.

This discussion shows how to understand the idea that false arguments were bundled together on the earthly plane.

7409 *And the land reeked* symbolizes the horrible, loathsome result. This is established by the symbolism of *reeking* as something horrible and loathsome (discussed in §§4516, 7161, 7319) and from that of the *land* (here, the land of Egypt) as the earthly mind (discussed in §§5276, 5278, 5280, 5288, 5301).

7410 Exodus 8:11, 12, 13, 14, 15 [= 8:15, 16, 17, 18, 19]. *And Pharaoh saw that there was some breathing space, and he made his heart leaden and did not listen to them, as Jehovah had spoken. And Jehovah said to Moses, "Say to Aaron, 'Stretch out your staff and strike the dust of the land, and it will become lice in all the land of Egypt.'" And they did so, and Aaron stretched out his hand with his staff and struck the dust of the land, and there were lice on humans and on animals. All the dust of the land became lice in the whole land of Egypt. And the magicians did the same with their spells, to bring forth lice. And they could not, and there were lice on humans and on animals. And the magicians said to Pharaoh, "This is the finger of God." And Pharaoh's heart hardened, and he did not listen to them, as Jehovah had spoken.*

And Pharaoh saw that there was some breathing space means that the fatigue ended. *And he made his heart leaden* symbolizes obstinacy. *And did not listen to them* symbolizes disobedience. *As Jehovah had spoken* means as predicted. *And Jehovah said to Moses* means being taught anew. *Say to Aaron* symbolizes an inflow of inner law into outer law. *Stretch out your staff* means for the purpose of displaying divine power. *And strike the dust of the land* means that it would dislodge damnable qualities on the earthly level. *And it will become lice* means that evil will rise out of it. *In all the land of Egypt* means throughout the earthly mind. *And they did so* means that it was carried out. *And Aaron stretched out his hand with his staff* symbolizes the power inner truth has through outer truth. *And struck the dust of the land* means that damnable qualities were dislodged. *And there were lice on humans and on animals* means that cravings for inner and outer evils resulted. *All the dust of the land became lice in the whole land of Egypt* means that damnable qualities produced this evil. *And the magicians did the same with their spells, to bring forth lice* symbolizes an attempt to twist the divine plan and mimic this effect too. *And they could not* means that it was in vain. *And there were lice on humans and on animals* symbolizes cravings for inner and outer evils. *And the magicians said to Pharaoh* symbolizes a perception and the communication of it to people intent on evil. *This is the finger of God* means that the power came from the Divine. *And Pharaoh's heart hardened* symbolizes obstinacy. *And he did not listen to them* symbolizes disobedience. *As Jehovah had spoken* means as predicted.

And Pharaoh saw that there was some breathing space means that the fatigue ended. This can be seen from the fact that the phrase *there was some breathing space* means that there was no longer any displeasure and therefore no longer any fatigue. For the fact that arguing from pure falsity was fatiguing and unpleasant to them, see above at §7392. Pleasure makes us breathe freely and easily; displeasure keeps us from breathing freely and easily. That is why *there was some breathing space* means that the displeasure or fatigue ended. 7411

And he made his heart leaden symbolizes obstinacy. This can be seen from the symbolism of a *heart* that *is made leaden,* or hardens, as obstinacy, as stated in §§7272, 7300, 7305. 7412

And did not listen to them symbolizes disobedience, as above in §§7224, 7275, 7301, 7339, where similar words occur. 7413

As Jehovah had spoken means as predicted, as above in §§7302, 7340. 7414

And Jehovah said to Moses means being taught anew, as above in §§7186, 7226, 7267, 7304, 7380. 7415

Say to Aaron symbolizes an inflow of inner law into outer law, as above at §7381. 7416

Stretch out your staff means for the purpose of displaying divine power. This can be seen from the symbolism of *stretching out* as exercising and displaying (as before [§7322]) and from that of a *staff* as power (discussed in §§4013, 4015, 4876, 4936, 6947, 7011, 7026). The power was divine, because there was no power in Aaron, let alone in his staff; rather, power was exercised *through* Aaron and his staff. It was exercised through his staff because any practice carried out in the church by divine command employed representative objects; this was the case before the Lord's Coming. So it employed the stretching out of a hand and staff, because the arm and hand correspond to power, and a staff consequently does too. 7417

The reason that any practice carried out in the church by divine command before the Lord's Coming employed representative objects was that everything represented the Lord, his kingdom in the heavens, and his kingdom on earth, or the church. The truth of this can also be seen in the Word, where the entirety of the highest sense is about the Lord, and the inner sense is about his kingdom and the church.

And strike the dust of the land means that it would dislodge damnable qualities on the earthly level. This is clear from the symbolism of *striking* as dislodging, from that of *dust* as something damnable (discussed below), and from that of the *land*—the land of Egypt—as the earthly mind (mentioned above at §7409). 7418

The reason *dust* means something damnable is that the places where evil spirits live, underfoot but off to the sides, look like a piece of land, and arid, uncultivated land at that. Under it lie certain hells. That land is what is called cursed ground, and its dust symbolizes something damnable. A number of times I have been allowed to see evil spirits there shake the dust off their feet when they wish to send someone to damnation. The place I have seen this happen is off to the right and slightly out in front, near the magicians' hell. That is where certain spirits are thrown down into their hell—spirits who knew all about religion when they lived in the world but lived a life of evil anyway.

This then is why dust symbolizes something damned, and shaking the dust off symbolizes damnation.

[2] It was because of this symbolism that the Lord ordered his disciples to shake off the dust of their feet where they were not welcomed. This is how Matthew describes it:

> If anyone does not welcome you or listen to your words, coming out of that house or city *shake off the dust of your feet.* Truly, I say to you: it will be more bearable for the land of Sodom and Gomorrah on judgment day than for that city. (Matthew 10:14, 15; Mark 6:11; Luke 9:5; 10:10, 11, 12)

The disciples here do not mean disciples but every aspect of the church and therefore every aspect of faith and neighborly love (§§2089, 2129 at the end, 2130 at the end, 3354, 3858, 3913, 6397). Not welcoming and not listening mean rejecting the truth taught by faith and the goodness urged by neighborly love. Shaking off the dust of one's feet symbolizes damnation. It was to be more bearable for Sodom and Gomorrah than for that city because Sodom and Gomorrah stand for people who live an evil life but know nothing about the Lord or the Word and therefore have not had the opportunity to accept them. This shows that the passage is not talking about a house or city that was not going to take the disciples in but about people in the church who do not live a life of religion. Anyone can see that an entire city could not be damned just because it did not welcome the disciples and instantly acknowledge the new theology they were preaching.

[3] The dust that people used to put on their head when they were mourning or repenting also symbolizes something damnable, as in Jeremiah:

> The elders of Zion's daughter are sitting on the *earth,* are keeping silent; *they have brought dust up on their head.* The young women of Jerusalem

> have wrapped themselves in sackcloth garments, have lowered their head *to the earth.* (Lamentations 2:10)

In Ezekiel:

> They will shout bitterly *and bring dust up on their heads.* They roll in ashes. (Ezekiel 27:30)

In Micah:

> Do not weep at all in the house of Aphrah; *roll in the dust!* (Micah 1:10)

In John:

> *They threw dust onto their heads* and cried out, weeping and mourning. (Revelation 18:19)

There are also scattered instances in the narrative books of the Word [Joshua 7:6; 2 Samuel 1:2; 15:32; Nehemiah 9:1]. Putting dust on one's head, dropping one's body or head to the ground, and rolling there in the dust represented humility, and when humility is real, it involves an acknowledgment and awareness that one is damned but has been rescued from damnation by the Lord. (See §§2327, 3994, 4347, 5420, 5957.)

[4] The dust produced by the crushing and grinding of the golden calf that the people made in the wilderness also symbolizes something damnable. Moses treats of it this way:

> Your sin that you committed, the *calf—I took it* and burned it with fire. *And I crushed it, grinding thoroughly, until it turned to fine dust,* and its *dust* I threw into the brook coming down from the mountain. (Deuteronomy 9:21)

Dust symbolizes something damnable in the following passages as well. In Genesis:

> Jehovah God said to the snake, "You will travel on your belly and *eat dust* all the days of your life." (Genesis 3:14)

In Micah:

> Pasture your people as in the days of old. The nations will see and will be ashamed of all their power; *they will lick dust like the snake.* (Micah 7:14, 16, 17)

In Isaiah:

> *The snake will have dust as its bread.* (Isaiah 65:25)

In the same author:

> Go down and *sit in the dust,* virgin daughter of Babylon. (Isaiah 47:1)

In David:

> *Our soul has bowed down to the dust;* our belly has clung to the *earth.* (Psalms 44:25)

In the same author:

> *My soul clings to the dust;* give me life. (Psalms 119:25)

Dust in the Word can also mean the grave, humility, or a large number.

7419 *And it will become lice* means that evil will rise out of it. This can be seen from the symbolism of *lice* as evil. What evil they symbolize and what the source of that evil is can be seen from the kind of evil that corresponds to such pests, which is mostly evil on the plane of the senses, a thoroughly external part of ourselves. The reason this is what corresponds to lice is that they are found on the outermost layer of skin, in dirty, scabby areas there.

That is what the sensory level is like in people who knew all about religion but lived an evil life. When their knowledge is taken from them—as happens to their kind in the other life—they are left dull-witted and stupid. The times they have been visible to me, they are hideous and loathsome.

Being plagued by evil is symbolized by the biting of lice.

This symbolism of lice cannot be proved from other Scripture passages, because the only other time they are mentioned is in David, in Psalms 105:31, which is about [the Israelites' exile in] Egypt.

7420 *In all the land of Egypt* means throughout the earthly mind. This can be seen from the symbolism of the *land of Egypt* as the earthly mind, as discussed in §§5276, 5278, 5280, 5288, 5301.

7421 *And they did so* means that it was carried out, as is self-evident.

7422 *And Aaron stretched out his hand with his staff* symbolizes the power inner truth has through outer truth. This can be seen from the discussion above at §7382, where similar words appear.

7423 *And struck the dust of the land* means that damnable qualities were dislodged. This can be seen from the remarks above at §7418.

7424 *And there were lice on humans and on animals* means that cravings for inner and outer evils resulted, as the following shows: *Lice* symbolize evil, as explained at §7419. A *human* symbolizes what is good, as discussed in §§4287, 5302, and therefore, in a negative sense, what is evil. And an *animal* symbolizes a desire for goodness, and in a negative sense a desire for evil, or a craving, as discussed in §§45, 46, 142, 143, 246, 714, 715, 719, 776, 2179, 2180, 3218, 3519, 5198. When the text says *humans and animals,* though, the human symbolizes inner goodness, and in a negative sense inner evil, while the animal symbolizes outer goodness, and in a negative sense outer evil.

The reason a human symbolizes inner goodness or evil is that our inner self and its character are what make us human, not our outer self. The outer self is not human without the inner self. In order to be likewise human, our outer self has to be totally subordinate to our inner self, to the point where it acts not on its own but under the power of our inner self.

The reason an animal symbolizes outer goodness, and in a negative sense outer evil, is that animals do not have the kind of inner dimension we have. The kind they have is immersed in their outer plane, and so thoroughly immersed as to be one with it. Together with the outer plane it looks down toward the ground without being lifted to anything inward.

[2] I describe these as cravings for evil because all evils come from desires and desires come from what we love.

Inner and outer evil are distinguished from each other by the fact that inner evil is evil in thought and will, while outer evil is evil in action. Evil is really an inner phenomenon, not an outer one, as is plain from the fact that a person can be evil and yet on the outside look like an honest man or even a man of faith and conscience. Some can even impersonate angels, when inwardly they are actually devils. That is how wide the gap can be between the inner appearance of the spirit and the outer appearance of the body.

All the dust of the land became lice in the whole land of Egypt means 7425
that damnable qualities produced this evil. This can be seen from the symbolism of the *dust of the land* as something damnable (discussed above at §7418), from that of *lice* as evil (discussed at §7419), and from that of the *land of Egypt* as the earthly mind (also mentioned above, at §7420).

And the magicians did the same with their spells, to bring forth lice sym- 7426
bolizes an attempt to twist the divine plan and mimic this effect too, as the following shows: *They did* symbolizes an attempt to do the same. (After all, the next phrase says they could not.) *Magicians* and *spells* stand for twisting the divine plan and outwardly appearing to mimic an effect,

as discussed in §§7296, 7297, 7337. And *bringing forth lice* means producing the evil symbolized by the lice, as discussed at §7419.

7427 *And they could not* means that it was in vain, as is self-evident.

7428 *And there were lice on humans and on animals* symbolizes [cravings for] inner and outer evils. This is established by the comments above at §7424, where the same words occur.

7429 *And the magicians said to Pharaoh* symbolizes a perception and the communication of it to people intent on evil, as the following shows: *Saying* symbolizes a perception (dealt with in §§1791, 1815, 1819, 1822, 1898, 1919, 2080, 2619, 2862, 3509, 5743) and also a communication of it (3060, 4131, 6228, 7291, 7381). *Magicians* symbolize people who twist the divine plan, outwardly appearing to mimic an effect, as dealt with just above at §7426. And *Pharaoh* represents people intent on falsity who inflict persecution, as dealt with in §§6651, 6679, 6683, 7107, 7110, 7126, 7142, 7317. Here he represents people intent on evil, because now that they have had their false reasoning taken from them, they are in a state of evil, as previous sections have made plain [7419, 7424, 7425].

7430 *This is the finger of God* means that the power came from the Divine. This can be seen from the symbolism of the *finger of God* as power coming from the Divine. A finger means power because fingers belong to the hands, and a hand symbolizes power (§§878, 4931–4937).

The following passages as well show that a finger means power:

> When I look at the heavens, the *work of your fingers,* the moon and the stars that you have prepared, . . . (Psalms 8:3)

In Luke:

> Jesus said, "If *by the finger of God* I cast out the demons, then surely the kingdom of God has reached you." (Luke 11:20)

When Jesus took a deaf man with speech difficulties aside, away from the people, and *inserted his finger into the man's ears* and, spitting, touched the man's tongue (Mark 7:32, 33), this too was an act representing divine power.

[2] The representation of a finger as power is also clear from the religious rituals of the Jews, in which blood was applied to the thumb, and the priest spattered blood with his finger. Here is how Moses describes it:

> You shall slaughter the ram and *put some of its blood on the thumb of the right hand of Aaron and his sons and on the big toe of his right foot.* (Exodus 29:20)

> The priest shall take some of the blood of the guilt [offering], and the priest shall put it on the tip of the right ear of the person to be cleansed of leprosy and *on the thumb of the person's right hand and on the big toe of the person's right foot.* Then the priest shall dip *his right finger* in some of the oil that is on *his left palm* and spatter some of the oil *with his finger* seven times before Jehovah. Some of the remaining oil that is on his palm the priest shall put on the tip of the right ear of the person to be cleansed and *on the thumb of the person's right hand and on the big toe of the person's right foot.* (Leviticus 14:14, 16, 17)

> You shall take some of the blood of the young ox and put it on the horns of the altar *with your finger.* (Exodus 29:12)

There are also instances in Leviticus 4:6; 9:9. [3] Clearly these details all symbolized secrets of heaven; clearly they all had a holy meaning. After all, the Word comes from the Divine and every tip of a letter in it was inspired (Luke 16:17), so the same must be true of these words. The inner meaning here makes it plain that thumbs and fingers mean the power that goodness wields through truth.

A finger symbolizes power in David too:

> A blessing on Jehovah, teaching *my hands* battle and *my fingers* war. (Psalms 144:1)

And in Isaiah:

> [Humankind] will not look to the altars, the *work of its hands,* and *what its fingers have made.* (Isaiah 17:8)

Altars stand for worship in general (§4541). The work of its hands and what its fingers have made stand for something self-generated and therefore something that results from a person's own power.

And he did not listen to them symbolizes disobedience, as above at 7431
§§7224, 7275, 7301, 7339.

As Jehovah had spoken means as predicted, as also above, at §§7302, 7432
7340, 7414.

Exodus 8:16, 17, 18, 19, 20 [= 8:20, 21, 22, 23, 24]. *And Jehovah said to* 7433
Moses, "Get up early in the morning, and you are to stand before Pharaoh (watch: he walks out to the water) and say to him, 'This is what Jehovah says: "Send my people away and let them serve me. Because if you fail to send my people away, then I myself am sending against you and against your servants and against your people and against your houses the winged pest. And the

houses of the Egyptians will be filled with the winged pest, as will the land they are on. And on that day I will set apart the land of Goshen, on which my people stands, so that the winged pest will not be there, in order that you may know that I, Jehovah, am in the midst of the land. And I will put redemption [as a difference] between my people and your people. Tomorrow this sign will occur."'" And Jehovah did so, and the winged pest came heavily to the house of Pharaoh and to the house of his servants and into all the land of Egypt. The land was destroyed in the path of the winged pest.

And Jehovah said to Moses symbolizes further instruction. *Get up early in the morning* means being elevated to [awareness of] a still greater sign of power. *And you are to stand before Pharaoh* symbolizes the manifestation of the Divine to spirits ruled by evil. *Watch: he walks out to the water* means that from that evil they think up a new round of falsities. *And say to him, "This is what Jehovah says,"* symbolizes a command. *Send my people away to serve me* means to leave people of the spiritual church alone to worship their God in freedom. *Because if you fail to send my people away* means if they did not leave them alone. *Then I myself am sending against you and against your servants and against your people and against your houses the winged pest* means that malevolent falsity would be theirs at every single turn. *And the houses of the Egyptians will be filled with the winged pest, as will the land they are on* means that malevolent falsity will occupy every corner of their earthly mind. *And on that day I will set apart the land of Goshen, on which my people stands, so that the winged pest will not be there* means that even though they will be located near people of the spiritual church, they will not be able to attack them with malevolent falsity. *In order that you may know that I, Jehovah, am in the midst of the land* symbolizes a resulting awareness that the Lord alone is the God of the church. *And I will put redemption [as a difference] between my people and your people* symbolizes deliverance of individuals in the spiritual church from spirits in the hells nearby. *And tomorrow this sign will occur* symbolizes a display of divine power from then on, forever. *And Jehovah did so* means that as it was said, so it was done. *And the winged pest came heavily to the house of Pharaoh and to the house of his servants and into all the land of Egypt* means that malevolent falsity erupted from them on every side. *And the land was destroyed in the path of the winged pest* means that [all] truth in the earthly mind was corrupted.

7434 *And Jehovah said to Moses* symbolizes further instruction. This can be seen from the symbolism of *saying,* when Jehovah is addressing Moses, as instruction, which is discussed in §§7186, 7226, 7267, 7304, 7380, 7415.

Here it symbolizes further instruction because Moses was being told what to do next.

Get up early in the morning means being elevated to [awareness of] a still greater sign of power. This can be seen from the symbolism of *getting up early* as being elevated. For the meaning of getting up as being elevated, see §§2401, 2785, 2912, 2927, 3171, 4103, and for that of early morning too as elevation, §7306. Strictly speaking, getting up early symbolizes a state of enlightenment (§§3458, 3723), but enlightenment, which comes from the Divine through an inflow of goodness and truth, is not possible for the evil people represented by Pharaoh and the Egyptians. Instead, they can be elevated to awareness, so getting up early in the morning in this case symbolizes such an elevation. That it is elevation to [awareness of] a still greater sign of power is evident from what follows, which treats of yet another new sign. 7435

And you are to stand before Pharaoh symbolizes the manifestation of the Divine to spirits ruled by evil, as the following shows: *Standing before someone* symbolizes presence, and in this case, the visible manifestation of the Divine, because the one standing was Moses, who is truth from the Divine. This truth is the means by which the Divine becomes visible. And *Pharaoh* represents spirits ruled by falsity, or in this case by evil, as above at §7429. 7436

Watch: he walks out to the water means that from that evil they think up a new round of falsities, as the following shows: *Walking out* symbolizes thoughts that move from evil to falsity. When the thoughts of people who are involved in evil move from that evil to falsity, they are said to walk out. Evil, you see, belongs to the will and therefore lies at the core. Falsity lies outside evil, because it belongs to the intellect and consequently to thought. Movement from one to the other is symbolized on a spiritual level by walking out. It also means going from ill will to evil, as in Mark 7:20, 21, 22, 23. And *water* symbolizes truth, and in a negative sense falsity, as discussed in §§739, 790, 2702, 3058, 3424, 4976, 5668. For the idea that falsity is meant by the water of Egypt's river (the water Pharaoh was walking out to), see §7307. 7437

[2] To expand on the subject of thoughts that progress from evil to falsity: It needs to be realized that people involved in evil cannot help proceeding from that evil to falsity in their thinking. Evil is what they will and therefore what they love, while falsity is what they think and therefore what they believe in. Whatever we will we love, and whatever we love we argue for and defend; and evil cannot be argued for or defended

except by false ideas. That is why the Word, when it compares evil to a city, compares falsity to the protective walls around the city.

The reason the thinking of people committed to evil turns toward falsity they can use in defense of evil is that evil is the highest pleasure of their life. In fact, it *is* their life. So when others give them to understand that it is after all evil, they try to mask it by dreaming up distortions that will prevent it from being viewed as evil. However, if evil does not dare let falsity render it visible, it hides deep within, refusing to show its face until its possessors cease to be afraid of the law and of losing the reputation they need in order to acquire wealth and compete for high office. Once they reach that point, their evil bursts out either in skillful ways or in open hostilities.

[3] From this discussion you can see that people devoted to evil cannot help turning the focus of their thoughts from evil to falsity. It is the same with people in a state of goodness; they cannot help turning the focus of their thoughts from goodness to truth. Goodness and truth unite, as do evil and falsity, and they unite so thoroughly that they provide clues to one another's existence. If you know that someone is governed by goodness, you can be sure that the person is governed by the truth accompanying that goodness. You can be sure that people governed by evil are governed by the falsity accompanying that evil. You can be sure that the better they are at twisted reasoning and at corrupting [the truth], and the more afraid they are of losing the reputation they need for the acquisition of wealth and position, and the more freedom they seek for evildoing, then the more dedicated to falsity they are. Surprisingly, after people like this have spent time using falsity to defend evil, they eventually persuade themselves that evil is good and that falsity is true.

7438 *And say to him, "[This is what Jehovah says,]"* symbolizes a command, as in §§7036, 7310.

7439 *Send my people away to serve me* means to leave people of the spiritual church alone to worship their God in freedom. This is established by the symbolism of *sending away* as leaving alone, by the representation of the children of Israel—*my people*—as members of the spiritual church (dealt with in §§6426, 6637, 6862, 6868, 7035, 7062, 7198, 7201, 7215, 7223), and by the symbolism of *serving* Jehovah as worshiping. The need for the worship to be free is evident from verses 21, 22, 23 [= 8:25, 26, 27] below and from the fact that all worship must be free if it is truly to be worship.

[2] The children of Israel were called Jehovah's people not because they were to be better than other nations but because they were to *represent*

Jehovah's people, meaning members of the Lord's spiritual kingdom. The way they lived in the wilderness makes it plain that they were not better than other nations, since they did not believe in Jehovah at all but rather believed at heart in the Egyptian gods. This can be seen from the golden calf they made for themselves, which they called "their gods that led them out of the land of Egypt" (Exodus 32:8). Their lack of superiority is also plain from the way they later lived in the land of Canaan, as described in the Word's narrative parts; from statements about them in the prophetic parts; and from the Lord's words.

That is why there are few of them in heaven, because the lot they received in the other world matched their life.

Do not believe, then, that they were chosen for heaven above others. [3] People who believe this do not believe that our life awaits each of us. Nor do they believe that we need to undergo preparation for heaven throughout our life in the world and that this preparation is what comes of the Lord's mercy. Instead they believe we are let into heaven out of mercy alone, no matter how we lived in the world. This view of heaven and of the Lord's mercy is brought on by the doctrine of faith alone and of salvation by faith alone without good deeds. People who subscribe to this doctrine do not care how a person lives. As a result, they also believe that evil can be washed away as simply as dirt by water, so that one can switch instantly to a life of goodness and consequently be let in to heaven. They do not realize that the evil would possess no life whatever if a life of evil were taken from them. They do not realize that if people who live a life of evil were accepted into heaven they would become aware of the hell in themselves, with increasing intensity the farther up into heaven they traveled.

[4] These considerations now make a couple of points evident: The people of Israel and Judah were by no means chosen, only accepted for the purpose of representing facets of heaven. And their representative role had to be played in the land of Canaan, because the Lord's church had existed there since earliest times, which meant that all the locations there came to represent heavenly and divine qualities. That made it possible to compose a Word in which the names symbolized attributes of the Lord and of his kingdom.

Because if you fail to send my people away means if they did not leave 7440
them alone. This can be seen from the symbolism of *sending away* as leaving alone and from that of Jehovah's *people* as members of the Lord's spiritual church, as directly above at §7439.

7441 *Then I myself am sending against you and against your servants and against your people and against your houses the winged pest* means that malevolent falsity would be theirs at every single turn, as the following shows: Pharaoh, his *servants,* and his *people* symbolize each and every element of the earthly mind, as discussed at §7396. When the text also adds *against your houses,* it means even in the inner parts of the earthly mind, as above at §7407. And the *winged pest* symbolizes falsity produced by the evil that the previous portent symbolized and therefore malevolent falsity. Just what kind of falsity it is that the winged pest symbolizes and what general category it belongs to becomes clear, then, from the evil that generates it. That evil was evil in the outermost part of the earthly mind and therefore evil on the sensory plane (see above at §7419). The falsity that rises out of it is of the same type. [2] It is also symbolized by the flies of Egypt mentioned in Isaiah:

> It will happen on that day that *Jehovah will whistle for the fly that is at the end of the rivers of Egypt* and for the bee that is in the land of Assyria, which will all come and rest in the rivers of the remote wilds and in the crevices of rocks. (Isaiah 7:18, 19)

The fly at the end of the rivers of Egypt means falsity in the outermost part of the earthly mind and therefore falsity on the sensory level closest to the body. It is being compared to such an insect because false notions on that level precisely resemble insects flying in the air, darkening and damaging the inner reaches [of the mind]. Most of the thinking on that level consists of imaginings and delusions, which lead to reasoning built, so to speak, on thin air.

This kind of winged pest is mentioned only in David, in Psalms 78:45; 105:31, which are also about Egypt.

[3] It is necessary to know that flying creatures in the Word all symbolize matters of the intellect, so they symbolize true ideas, and in a negative sense, false ideas (§§40, 745, 776, 778, 866, 988, 3219, 5149). However, flying creatures of the lowliest sort, which are insects, symbolize truth (and in a negative sense falsity) that is quite unimpressive and dim. One example is the kind of truth (or falsity) the senses can supply. Unless this is lit from within, it is completely dim and shadowy—because it lies closest to the body, right next to the material plane on which the heavenly plane rests—and is plunged into darkness.

7442 *And the houses of the Egyptians will be filled with the winged pest, as will the land they are on* means that malevolent falsity will occupy every corner of their earthly mind. This can be seen from the symbolism of *filling* as occupying, from that of a *house of the Egyptians* as the inner depths of the earthly mind (noted above at §7407), from that of the *winged pest* as malevolent falsity (dealt with directly above at §7441), and from that of the *land* of Egypt as the earthly mind in general (dealt with in §§5276, 5278, 5280, 5288, 5301).

[2] I need to explain briefly how it can be that even the inner depths of the earthly mind will be occupied by the vicious falsity inhabiting the outermost parts of that mind. What flows into us from the Lord through heaven flows into our inner reaches and then continues on to our lowest, outermost reaches, where we can actually feel it. So it flows all the way down to our senses and through our senses into our physical body. If our sensory level is full of illusions based on fallacies and appearances—and especially on outright falsity—then inflowing truth also turns into illusion there. This is because it is received there in whatever shape is imposed on it; see §7343. In addition, the more we turn truth into falsity, the more the inner levels it passes through close off. Eventually they remain open just far enough to let through the bare minimum needed for endowing us with the ability to reason and to justify evil by the use of falsity.

[3] Since this is how matters stand with us, it is necessary when we are being reborn for our earthly plane to be reborn all the way down to the level of the senses. Unless this is reborn, we receive no truth or goodness, because as mentioned above, inflowing truth is perverted there, which closes off our inner reaches. When our outer reaches have been reborn, then, we are reborn through and through. That is the meaning of the Lord's words to Peter when washing Peter's feet, as recorded in John:

> Simon Peter said, "Lord, do not wash my feet only but also my hands and head!" Jesus said to him, "Those who have bathed have no need except to have their feet washed and [then] are all clean." (John 13:9, 10)

Feet symbolize earthly elements (§§2162, 3761, 3986, 4280, 4938–4952). Washing means purifying (§§3147, 5954 at the end). Hands symbolize the inner parts of the earthly plane, and the head symbolizes spiritual elements. It is therefore clear what the text means in saying that those who have bathed have no need except to have their feet washed and [then] are all clean. It means that not until even the outer parts of our earthly plane have been reborn have we ourselves been reborn. So once even our earthly dimension has been reborn, all its contents become subordinate to inner values. When those inner values flow into the earthly dimension, it is as if they are flowing into their general containers, through which they make themselves tangible to us. If this is the situation in which we find ourselves, we then feel a desire for the truth taught by faith and for the goodness urged by neighborly love.

[4] However, the actual plane of the senses, which is the outermost level of the earthly dimension, is barely capable of being reborn, because it is completely full of matter-based thinking that relies on earthly, body-oriented, and worldly evidence. Consequently, people who are being reborn (especially now) are not reborn in regard to their sensory level, only in regard to the part of the earthly level that lies just above the senses. The Lord raises them up to this level from the sensory level when they think about religious truth and goodness. The ability to be lifted above the senses is a gift they receive when the Lord is regenerating them.

Concerning the nature of the sensory plane and elevation of one's thought above that plane, see §§5084, 5089, 5094, 5125, 5128, 5767, 6183, 6201, 6310, 6311, 6313, 6315, 6316, 6318, 6564, 6598, 6612, 6614, 6622, 6624, 6844, 6845, 6948, 6949.

7443 *And on that day I will set apart the land of Goshen, on which my people stands, so that the winged pest will not be there* means that even though they [will be] located near people of the spiritual church, they will not be able to attack them with malevolent falsity, as the following shows: *Setting something apart* means separating it to cut off communication. A *day* symbolizes a state, as discussed in §§23, 487, 488, 493, 893, 2788, 3462, 3785, 4850. Setting it apart on that day, then, means separating it in that state. The *land of Goshen* symbolizes the central, inmost part of the earthly level, as discussed in §§5910, 6028, 6031, 6068, and since the children of Israel were in Goshen, it also symbolizes the church (§6649). The children of Israel—Jehovah's *people*—represent members of the spiritual church, as discussed above at §7439. And the *winged pest* symbolizes malevolent falsity, as discussed above at §7441. *So that the winged pest will not be there* consequently means that they will not be able to flow in, so it means that they will not be able to attack with that kind of falsity.

The reason they would not be able to attack with that falsity is that it rises out of evil in the outermost part of the earthly mind—in other words, out of evil on the level of the senses. People with goodness and truth can be lifted above the sensory level and its false thinking (in keeping with the remarks above at §7442), and when they are lifted up they are also separated from anyone who embraces the false thinking there.

In order that you may know that I, Jehovah, am in the midst of the land symbolizes a [resulting] awareness that the Lord alone is the God of the church. This can be seen from the symbolism of *knowing* as an awareness and from that of the *midst of the land* as the home of the truth and goodness that people in the Lord's church possess. Truth that comes of goodness lies at the inmost point (§§3436, 6068, 6084, 6103), so the middle of the land symbolizes the church, just as the land of Goshen does (as discussed directly above at §7443). *I, Jehovah,* means that he alone is the *I Am* and therefore that he alone is God. (For Jehovah in the Word being the Lord, see §§1343, 1736, 2921, 3023, 3035, 5663, 6303, 6905, 6945, 6956.) 7444

Clearly, then, *that you may know that I, Jehovah, am in the midst of the land* symbolizes an awareness that the Lord alone is the God of the church.

And I will put redemption [as a difference] between my people and your people symbolizes deliverance of individuals in the spiritual church from spirits in the hells nearby, as the following shows: *Redemption* symbolizes being brought out of hell (as discussed at §7205) and is used specifically of people being delivered from devastation (§2959). The children of Israel—*my people*—represent members of the spiritual church, as discussed above at §7439. And the Egyptians—*your people*—represent spirits in the hells nearby who inflict persecution, as mentioned at §7090. 7445

Clearly, then, *I will put redemption [as a difference] between my people and your people* symbolizes deliverance of individuals in the spiritual church from spirits in the hells.

And tomorrow this sign will occur symbolizes a display of divine power from then on, forever, as the following shows: *Tomorrow* means forever, as discussed at §3998. And a *sign* symbolizes proof and therefore recognition that a thing is true, as mentioned at §6870, so it symbolizes a display of divine power. Once upon a time the truth was revealed by signs, and so was divine power. 7446

And Jehovah did so means that as it was said, so it was done, as is self-evident. 7447

And the winged pest came heavily to the house of Pharaoh and to the house of his servants and into all the land of Egypt means that malevolent falsity erupted from them on every side, as the following shows: The *winged pest* symbolizes malevolent falsity, as discussed above at §7441. And the *house of Pharaoh,* the *house of his servants,* and *all the land* symbolize each and every part of the earthly level, as discussed at §§7396, 7441, 7442. Here 7448 they mean *from* each and every part, or on every side, because the meaning is that such falsity erupted.

The most direct meaning of the coming of the winged pest to the house is that falsity entered the abode of evil and united with it. When it unites with evil, though, it brings about an eruption of evil. That is why *the winged pest came to the house of Pharaoh and to the house of his servants and into all the land of Egypt* means that malevolent falsity erupted, and erupted on every side.

7449 *And the land was destroyed in the path of the winged pest* means that all truth in the earthly mind was corrupted. This is evident from the symbolism of *being destroyed* as being corrupted, from that of the *land* of Egypt as the earthly mind (discussed at §§5276, 5278, 5280, 5288, 5301), and from that of the *winged pest* as malevolent falsity (discussed at §7441). I mention that all truth was corrupted because malevolence working through falsity totally corrupts truth.

7450 Exodus 8:21–28 [= 8:25–32]. *And Pharaoh called Moses and Aaron and said, "Go; sacrifice to your God in the land." And Moses said, "It is not advisable to do so, because we would be sacrificing what the Egyptians abhor to Jehovah our God. Look, were we to sacrifice what the Egyptians find abhorrent in their eyes, would they not stone us? A journey of three days we will go into the wilderness and sacrifice to Jehovah our God, as he said to us." And Pharaoh said, "I myself will send you away, and you are to sacrifice to Jehovah your God in the wilderness, only you are certainly not to go far. Plead for me." And Moses said, "Look, now, I am going out from you and will plead to Jehovah; and may he remove the winged pest from Pharaoh, from his servants, and from his people, tomorrow. Only Pharaoh is not to continue playing tricks by not sending the people away to sacrifice to Jehovah." And Moses went out from Pharaoh and pleaded to Jehovah. And Jehovah did according to Moses' word and removed the winged pest from Pharaoh, from his servants, and from his people. Not one was left. And Pharaoh made his heart leaden this time too and did not send the people away.*

And Pharaoh called Moses and Aaron symbolizes the presence of divine law. *And said, "Go; sacrifice to your God in the land,"* means that they would not block them from worshiping their God, but it would have to be nearby. *And Moses said,* symbolizes the answer. *It is not advisable to do so, because we would be sacrificing what the Egyptians abhor to Jehovah our God* means that what was hellishly hideous and disgusting would flow in. *Look, were we to sacrifice what the Egyptians find abhorrent in their eyes* means that if they worshiped God in the presence of such spirits, those spirits would disturb the worship. *Would they not stone us?* means that the religious truth embodied in their worship would be wiped out. *A journey of three days we will go into the wilderness* means that they would distance themselves entirely in order to be free. *And sacrifice to Jehovah our God* means that this would enable them to worship. *As he said to us* means as he had commanded. *And Pharaoh said, "I myself will send you away, and you are to sacrifice to Jehovah your God in the wilderness,"* means that they would leave them alone and not harass them so that they could worship their God freely. *Only you are certainly not to go far* means although they should be nearby. *Plead for me* means that [Moses and Aaron] should intervene. *And Moses said, "Look, now, I am going out from you,"* symbolizes removal of apparent divine truth among them. *And will plead to Jehovah* symbolizes intervention. *And may he remove the winged pest from Pharaoh, from his servants, [and] from his people* means for bringing an end to the state marked by malevolent falsity. *Tomorrow* means permanently. *Only Pharaoh is not to continue playing tricks by not sending the people away to sacrifice to Jehovah* means as long as he does not fool them by lying and fail to leave them alone to worship their God freely. *And Moses went out from Pharaoh* symbolizes removal of apparent divine truth among spirits intent on malevolent falsity. *And pleaded to Jehovah* symbolizes intervention. *And Jehovah did according to Moses' word* means that it happened according to the Lord's word. *And removed the winged pest from Pharaoh, from his servants, and from his people* symbolizes the end of the state marked by this kind of falsity. *Not one was left* symbolizes complete removal. *And Pharaoh made his heart leaden this time too* symbolizes obstinacy yet again. *And did not send the people away* means that they did not leave individuals in the spiritual church alone.

And Pharaoh called Moses and Aaron symbolizes the presence of divine law. This is established by the symbolism of *calling* as presence (discussed in §§6177, 7390) and by the representation of *Moses and Aaron* as divine law, Moses representing the inner law and Aaron the outer law (discussed in §§7381, 7390). 7451

And said, "Go; sacrifice to your God in the land," means that they would not block them from worshiping their God, but it would have to be nearby, as the following shows: *He said, "Go,"* means that they would not block it. *Sacrificing* symbolizes worshiping, as mentioned above at §7393. And *in the land*—the land of Egypt—means nearby. The fact that "in the land" means nearby is plain from Moses' answer and Pharaoh's reply (verses 22, 23, 24 [= 8:26, 27, 28]). Moses said that it was not advisable to do so, 7452 because they would be sacrificing what the Egyptians found abhorrent in their eyes. Rather, he said, they would go a journey of three days into the wilderness and sacrifice to Jehovah their God. Pharaoh replied that they were certainly not to go far. So in an inner sense the land means the home of spirits who believe in falsity and inflict harassment. To learn how close by these spirits were, see §7090.

7453 *And Moses said,* symbolizes the answer, as before, in §§7103, 7394.

7454 *It is not advisable to do so, because we would be sacrificing what the Egyptians abhor to Jehovah our God* means that what was hellishly offensive and disgusting would flow in, as the following shows: *Not advisable to do so* means not capable of happening. *What is abhorrent* symbolizes what is hellishly offensive and disgusting. And *sacrificing to Jehovah God* means worshiping their God, as mentioned above at §7452. Sacrificing what the Egyptians abhor to Jehovah God, then, means that they worshiped God with a type of worship that believers in falsity abhorred because of their hellish opposition to such worship, which would disturb that worship.

[2] Evidence from the other world also shows what the situation is in all this. Every spirit (and especially every community) is enveloped in an aura given off by his or her beliefs and life, and this aura is a spiritual one. It enables spirits (and especially communities) to be recognized for what they are, because it is detected by perceptive individuals. Sometimes it is perceived from fairly far away, even if the spirit is hidden and is not communicating by thought or by word.

This spiritual aura can be compared to the physical aura that surrounds a human body in the world. A physical aura is composed of particles pouring off a person, and keen-scented animals can smell it. (Concerning the spiritual auras that surround spirits, see §§1048, 1053, 1316, 1504–1519, 2401, 2489, 4464, 5179, 6206 at the end.)

[3] You can see, then, that if hellish spirits were in the vicinity of people worshiping God, their aura would disturb the worshipers, because it would produce a hideous, loathsome sensation in them.

These remarks show how to understand the idea that what was hellishly offensive and disgusting would flow in if they worshiped God near those spirits.

This discussion of spiritual auras—or the aura of beliefs and life given off by every spirit and especially by a group of spirits—also makes it plain that absolutely nothing is hidden. Whatever a person had thought, said, or done in the world lies out in the open, because that is what makes up the aura.

The same kind of aura also pours off the spirit of a person still occupying a body in the world. It too enables the person's nature to be recognized.

In case you believe that what you think in secret or do in secret is secret, it is as plain to see in heaven as objects seen in noonday light. As the Lord says in Luke:

> Nothing is concealed that will not be revealed, or hidden that will not be known. So whatever you said in the dark will be heard in the light. And what you spoke in the ear in your private rooms will be proclaimed on the roofs. (Luke 12:2, 3)

Look, were we to sacrifice what the Egyptians find abhorrent in their eyes 7455
means that if they worshiped God in the presence of such spirits, those spirits would disturb the worship. This can be seen from the explanation directly above at §7454.

Would they not stone us? means that the religious truth embodied in 7456
their worship would be wiped out. This can be seen from the symbolism of *stoning* as erasing and wiping out falsity, but in a negative sense, when done by the evil, as erasing and wiping out religious truth.

If the hellishly offensive and disgusting inflows described above at §7454 were to affect people who were worshiping reverently, the reverence of their worship would be obliterated. That is because sincere worshipers are held back from such hellishness, and people who believe in goodness and live good lives are lifted above the level of the senses, where hellish qualities reside. When such qualities flow in, though, they stir up the filth on the sensory level that (as just mentioned) sincere worshipers are held back from and people who believe and live well are lifted above. This extinguishes the holiness of the worship. The same thing can be seen from experience, because when we are worshiping God, then as long as some obscene object is placed in front of our eyes and is not removed, our worship is destroyed and annihilated. That is what is meant by the assertion that if spirits devoted to the falsity that comes of evil were in the neighborhood, they would wipe out the religious truth embodied in the worship.

[2] Regarding the symbolism of *stoning,* be aware that the people of Israel and Judah (among whom the representation of a church had been established) had two death penalties. One was stoning, the other was being hanged on wood. Stoning was for people who wanted to destroy truth in the form of requirements for worship, while hanging was for people who wanted to destroy the goodness in a person's life. People who

wanted to destroy the truth governing worship were stoned because a stone symbolized truth and in a negative sense falsity (§§643, 1298, 3720, 6426). People who wanted to destroy the goodness in a person's life were hanged on wood because wood symbolized goodness and in a negative sense cravings for evil (§§643, 2784, 2812, 3720).

[3] The use of stoning as the penalty for anyone who destroyed the truth governing worship is evident from the following passages. In Ezekiel:

> At last they will raise a mob against you and *stone you with stone* and cut you up with their swords. (Ezekiel 16:40)

This is about Jerusalem after it was corrupted and about the destruction of religious truth through falsity. That is why it says that they will stone it with stone and also that they will cut it up with swords. A sword symbolizes truth that fights against and destroys falsity, and in a negative sense, falsity that fights against and destroys truth (§§2799, 4499, 6353, 7102). [4] Likewise in another place in the same author:

> Raise a mob against them *so that the mob can stone them with stone* and cut them up with their swords. (Ezekiel 23:[46,] 47)

This is about Jerusalem and Samaria, which symbolize the church. Jerusalem symbolizes a heavenly-spiritual church; Samaria, a spiritual church. The chapter depicts the way religious goodness and truth were destroyed in both. [5] In Moses:

> Whenever an ox strikes a man or a woman with its horn, so that the person dies, *the ox shall surely be stoned.* (Exodus 21:28)

Striking a man or a woman with its horn symbolizes falsity fighting against and destroying truth and goodness. A horn means falsity engaged in battle and also the power of falsity (§2832). In the Word, a man and a woman symbolize truth and goodness. This makes plain the inner meaning of that command and the reason the ox was to be stoned. [6] In the same author:

> One who blasphemes the name of Jehovah shall surely be killed; *the whole congregation shall surely stone that person.* (Leviticus 24:16)

Blaspheming the name of Jehovah means using ill-intentioned falsity to inflict violence on the truth and goodness embodied in worship. The name of Jehovah is every means of worshiping Jehovah, collectively (see §§2724, 3006), so it is everything that goes to make up faith and neighborly love

(§6674). That is why an Israelite woman's son who blasphemed the name of Jehovah was *taken outside the camp and stoned* (Leviticus 24:11, 14, 23). It was also ordered that *people who served other gods should be stoned* (Deuteronomy 17:3, 5), and the same for those who incited people *to serve other gods* (Deuteronomy 13:6–10). Serving other gods symbolizes profane worship, which blots out true worship.

[7] If [tokens of] virginity were not found with a girl when she got married, she was to be *stoned* because she had done folly in Israel, *whoring* in her father's house (Deuteronomy 22:20, 21). This was because whoredom symbolized the falsification and therefore destruction of truth (§§2466, 4865). In the city, if a man lay with a girl who was a virgin betrothed to a man, they were *both to be stoned* (Deuteronomy 22:23, 24). This was for the same reason, whoredom, since spiritual whoredom is turning truth into falsity.

In Luke:

> They argued to each other that if they said that John's baptism was from heaven, [Jesus] would say, "Why did you not believe him?" But if they said, "From human beings," *all the people would stone them.* (Luke 20:5, 6)

This passage too mentions stoning because of the attack on truth. The Jews wanted to *stone* Jesus for saying that before Abraham existed, he was (John 8:58, 59), and this was because that nation considered the claim false. For the same reason, they wanted to *stone* him for saying that he and his Father were one (John 10:30, 31, 32, 33), since they considered it blasphemy, as the passage in fact says.

This discussion now shows what stoning means and why it was commanded. It is also clear that stoning as a punishment dating from ancient times existed in Egypt and therefore that it was derived from the representative practices of the ancient church.

A journey of three days we will go into the wilderness means that they 7457
would distance themselves entirely in order to be free. This is clear from the symbolism of *going a journey of three days into the wilderness* as distancing oneself entirely. This symbolism follows from the contents of the inner meaning above. That meaning was that they could not worship God in the vicinity or presence of spirits from hell (as discussed above at §§7452, 7454, 7455, 7456) and consequently that they would distance themselves in order to be free.

7458 *And sacrifice to Jehovah our God* means that this would enable them to worship. This can be seen from the symbolism of *sacrificing to Jehovah* as worship (mentioned above in §§7393, 7452) and from the fact that worship happens when people are in freedom (§7349).

7459 *As he said to us* means as he had commanded, which is self-evident.

7460 *And Pharaoh said, "I myself will send you away, and you are to sacrifice to Jehovah your God in the wilderness,"* means that they would leave them alone and not harass them so that they could worship their God freely. This can be seen from the symbolism of *sending away* as leaving alone and therefore as not harassing, and from the symbolism of *sacrificing to Jehovah God* as worshiping their God (mentioned above at §7458). The idea that they would do it freely follows, because it says that they would sacrifice in the wilderness, meaning not nearby, as demanded earlier. To be nearby was to be unfree; see §§7454, 7456.

7461 *Only you are certainly not to go far* means although they should be nearby. This can be seen from the symbolism of *not going far* as not being remote, not being distant from the land of Egypt.

7462 *Plead for me* means that [Moses and Aaron] should intervene. This can be seen from the symbolism of *pleading for one,* when requested of Moses by Pharaoh, as intervention, as above at §7396.

7463 *And Moses said, "Look, now, I am going out from you,"* symbolizes removal of apparent divine truth among them. This can be seen from the representation of *Moses* as divine law (treated of in §§6723, 6752) and therefore as divine truth too (7014, 7382), and from the symbolism of *going out* as removal (as above at §7404). After all, Pharaoh's calling of Moses and Aaron symbolizes the presence of divine truth (7451), so their going out from him here symbolizes its removal.

To discuss the presence and removal of divine truth among the evil: You need to know that truth imparted by the Divine sometimes appears to them, through the presence of an angel near them. However, truth from the Divine does not flow into them through their inner levels, as it does with good people, because their inner levels are closed off. Instead it affects only their outer levels. When it does, they feel afraid and therefore humble, because the presence of truth from the Divine leaves them shaken and strikes them with a fear like the fear of death. When truth from the Divine is removed, though, they return to their old state and lose their fear. That is what is meant by the presence of apparent divine truth and its removal.

The same thing was represented by Pharaoh's humbling himself as long as Moses was present, and promising to send the people away to sacrifice to Jehovah, but making his heart leaden when Moses went out from him (verse 28 [= 8:32] below). This was because Moses represented divine law, or divine truth, as shown above.

[2] Divine law is the same as divine truth because "divine law" means the Word and accordingly divine truth.

The symbolism of the law as the Word and accordingly as divine truth is clear in the following passages. In John:

> Jesus said, "*Is it not written in your law,* 'I have said, "You are gods"'? If he called those people gods to whom the Word came (and the Scripture cannot be done away with), . . ." (John 10:34, 35)

"Written in [your] law" means written in the Word, since the phrase in question was written in David [Psalms 82:6]. In the same author:

> The crowd said, "*We have heard from the law* that Christ remains forever." (John 12:34)

This too was written in David [Psalms 89:29; 110:4]. In the same author:

> Jesus said, "[This happened] *so that there would be a fulfillment of the word written in the law,* 'they hated me without a reason.'" (John 15:25)

Again this was written in David [Psalms 35:19]. In Luke:

> . . . (*it has been written in the Law of the Lord* that every male opening the womb was to be called sacred to the Lord) and in order to offer a sacrifice *according to what has been written in the Law of the Lord:* a pair of turtledoves or two pigeon chicks. (Luke 2:23, 24, 39)

This was written in Moses [Exodus 13:12; 34:19–20; Leviticus 12:6–8]. In the same author:

> A lawyer testing Jesus said, "What should I do to inherit eternal life?" Jesus said to him, "*What has been written in the Law?* How do you read it?" (Luke 10:25, 26)

[3] In the same author:

> The *Law and the Prophets* lasted till John; from then on the good news of God's kingdom is being spread. It is easier for heaven and earth to pass away *than for one tip of a letter in the law to fail.* (Luke 16:16, 17)

There are other passages too where the Word is called the *Law and the Prophets,* such as Matthew 5:18; 7:12; 11:13; 22:40. In Isaiah:

> Tie up the testimony, *seal the law* for my trainees. (Isaiah 8:16)

The law stands for the Word. In the same author:

> Deceptive offspring, offspring [who] did not want to hear the *law of Jehovah.* (Isaiah 30:9)

In the same author:

> He will establish judgment on the earth; *in his law* the islands will hope. (Isaiah 42:4)

This is about the Lord. "His law" stands for the Word. In the same author:

> Jehovah will enlarge *his law.* (Isaiah 42:21)

In Jeremiah:

> This is what Jehovah has said: "If you do not obey me—*to walk in my law* that I have set before you—or listen to the *word of my servants the prophets, . . .*" (Jeremiah 26:4, 5)

The law stands for the Word. Not to mention many other passages. Plainly, then, the law means the Word, and since it means the Word it means divine truth, as in Jeremiah:

> "This is the pact that I will strike with the house of Israel after these days," says Jehovah. "*I will put the law in the midst of them,* and *upon their heart I will write it.*" (Jeremiah 31:33)

Jehovah's law here stands for divine truth.

[4] The law in a broad sense means the whole Word, in a less broad sense the narrative part of the Word, in a still less broad sense the part of the Word written through Moses, and in a narrow sense the Ten Commandments; see §6752.

All this now explains the reason for saying that Moses represents both divine law and divine truth.

7464 *And will plead to Jehovah* symbolizes intervention, as in §§7396, 7462.

7465 *And may he remove the winged pest from Pharaoh, from his servants, and from his people* means for bringing an end to the state marked by malevolent falsity. This can be seen from the symbolism of the *winged pest* as malevolent falsity (discussed at §7441), from the representation of *Pharaoh* as people devoted to vicious falsity who inflict persecution (discussed before), and from the symbolism of *his servants and his people* as each and every one of them (discussed in §§7396, 7441). To remove that malevolent falsity from each and every persecutor is to put an end to the state.

Be advised that every miracle performed in Egypt symbolizes some distinct state experienced by those people in the other life who believe in falsity and inflict harassment. There are ten states they come into one after the other before they are completely stripped of all truth and therefore before they are thrown into hell. You see, people who possess religious knowledge but live an evil life do not go to hell immediately after death, they go gradually. First they have to be convinced they are ruled by evil, then their religious knowledge is taken from them, and finally they are left to the evilness of the life they lived. Many consecutive stages are needed to accomplish this, and those stages are the ones depicted by the miracles performed in Egypt and consequently by the evils that befell the Egyptians before they drowned in the Suph Sea.

These secrets cannot be known without revelation. To angels they are quite familiar.

Tomorrow means permanently. See §§3998, 7399. 7466

Only Pharaoh is not to continue playing tricks by not sending the people 7467
away to sacrifice to Jehovah means as long as he does not fool them by lying and fail to leave them alone to worship their God freely, as the following shows: *Pharaoh* represents people committed to vicious falsity who inflict harassment. *Playing tricks* means fooling someone by lying. *Sending away* means leaving alone. The children of Israel represent people of the spiritual church. And *sacrificing to Jehovah* means worshiping their God, as mentioned in §§7393, 7452, 7458. For the idea that worship must be free, see §§7454, 7456. This makes it plain that *only Pharaoh is not to continue playing tricks by not sending the people away to sacrifice to Jehovah* means as long as he does not fool them by lying and fail to leave the people of the spiritual church alone to worship their God freely.

And Moses went out from Pharaoh symbolizes removal of apparent divine 7468
truth among spirits intent on malevolent falsity. This can be seen from the comments above at §7463.

And pleaded to Jehovah symbolizes intervention, as above at §§7396, 7469
7462.

7470 *And Jehovah did according to Moses' word* means that it happened according to the Lord's word. This can be seen from the explanation above at §7406.

7471 *And removed the winged pest from Pharaoh, from his servants, and from his people* symbolizes the end of the state marked by this kind of falsity. This can be seen from the comments above at §7465, where similar words occur.

7472 *Not one was left* symbolizes complete removal, as can be seen without explanation.

7473 *And Pharaoh made his heart leaden [this time too]* symbolizes obstinacy yet again. This can be seen from the symbolism of hardening one's heart, or making it leaden, as obstinacy, as noted in §§7272, 7300, 7305.

7474 *And did not send the people away* means that they did not leave individuals in the spiritual church alone. This can be seen from the symbolism of *sending away* as leaving alone and from the representation of the children of Israel—the *people*—as individuals in the spiritual church, as discussed in §§6426, 6637, 6862, 6868, 7035, 7062, 7198, 7201, 7215, 7223.

[2] Regarding the spiritual church represented here by the children of Israel: keep in mind that it has an inner part and an outer part. People with a goodness born of neighborly love are in the inner part of the church, while people with a goodness born of faith are in the outer part. People who view the truth that leads to faith from a standpoint of charity for their neighbor are the ones with a goodness born of neighborly love. People with a goodness born of faith, on the other hand, are those who view neighborly love from the standpoint of faith and therefore who do good not under the prompting of such love but out of obedience to faith. In other words, they do good because it has been commanded. The latter are properly the ones represented here by the children of Israel, because they are the ones persecuted in the other life by spirits devoted to falsity. People motivated by neighborly love cannot be persecuted in the same way, because spirits immersed in falsity and evil cannot go near anyone who practices neighborly kindness, the Lord being present in such kindness. If people like this *are* attacked, the target of the attack is merely illusions and appearances that led them to consider something untrue as true. Or else the target is concepts their church's doctrine teaches as true even though they are untrue. In the other life such people willingly reject falsity and accept truth, because charitable goodness is open to truth, which it loves and desires.

[3] Since I have mentioned this persecution so many times, I ought to identify and describe it. Persecution is accomplished by the introduction of falsity that contradicts truth. This falsity is refuted by an inflow from heaven—or rather from the Lord through heaven—into the people being persecuted. Such is the state in which people being purged of falsity are held until they have been instilled with the truth belonging to faith and gradually with inner kinds of truth as well. The more they have absorbed these kinds of truth, the more they are freed from persecution.

This persecution is not the same as times of trial. Trials are accompanied by pangs of conscience, because people undergoing them are kept in a state of damnation, which causes them anguish and grief.

[4] This reveals the nature of the purging that takes place in the other world, as experienced by people with a goodness born of faith. What is purged in this case is falsity. However, with people who dedicated themselves not to the goodness promoted by faith but to the supposed truth taught by a knowledge-based faith—yet lived an evil life—what is purged is truth. People who are being purged of falsity absorb more and more of the truth and goodness embraced by faith and neighborly love, but people who are being purged of truth shed more and more truth and wrap themselves in the evil they committed during their life.

This shows what the Word means by times of devastation and desolation.

The Spirits and Inhabitants of Mars (Continued)

TO themselves the spirits of Mars look like people, as they had in the world, so they look like people to others too. In the next life we always look the same to others as we do to ourselves, since perceptions are shared. 7475

When I expressed surprise at this, they said they could not help looking like that, for two reasons. For one thing, when they lived in the world, they knew they were spirits clothed with a body; and for another, they did not think much about their body there, only about the life of their spirit within the body. As a consequence, when they arrive in the other life they are barely conscious of a change in the state of their life, and since they continue to think about the life of their spirit, as they did in the world, they continue to look like themselves.

It is true that all spirits have a human form, but not as obviously as the spirits of Mars, because these keep the concept of themselves they had in the world.

Besides, even while people are alive in the world, if they know and believe they will have a human form in the next life, that thought increases as their body diminishes. When they shed the body that had served their purposes in the world, they continue to look like themselves because of the image imprinted on their mind.

7476 The spirits of Mars are among the best of all the spirits from this solar system. For the most part they are heavenly individuals, you see, not unlike the people of the earliest church on this planet (described in §§1114–1125 and elsewhere).

When their nature is being represented, they are shown with their face in heaven and their body in the world of spirits. Those who are angels are represented with their face toward the Lord and their body in heaven.

7477 Our Lord they acknowledge and revere more than other spirits do. They say that he is the only God, that he rules both heaven and the universe, and that everything good comes from him. They frequently said that the Lord is the one who leads them and that he often appears to them on their planet.

The fact that the Lord rules both heaven and the universe is also known to Christians on our planet from the Lord's words in Matthew:

> All power in heaven and on earth has been given to me. (Matthew 28:18)

But Christians do not believe it the way people from Mars do.

7478 Once when the Lord's name came up, I saw those spirits humbling themselves so deeply and profoundly that it cannot be described. In their humility they had the thought that on their own they were in hell and were therefore entirely unworthy to look at the Lord, who is holiness itself. The thought went so deep with them (because of their belief in it) that they were almost beside themselves. On their knees in that thought they remained waiting for the Lord to lift them up and essentially rescue them from hell. When they come out of a humble state like this, they are full of goodness and love and consequently of heartfelt joy.

When humbling themselves like this, they turn their face away from the Lord, not toward him, because they do not dare face him then.

The spirits around me kept saying they had never seen such humility.

I talked with some from that planet about the beliefs they had there. 7479
They consistently said people there believe that they exhibit nothing but filth and hellishness and that everything good is the Lord's. In fact, they went so far as to say that on their own they are devils and that the Lord rescues them and constantly withholds them from hell.

They were surprised that there were so many evil spirits around me and that these even talked with me. I was allowed to answer that this was permitted to the evil spirits so that I could learn what they are like and why they are in hell—the reason being that hell suits the way they lived their life. I was also able to say that many of them were people I had known while they were alive in the world, when they had been settled in positions of high rank, caring about nothing but worldly advantages. I added, though, that there was never any spirit, not even the most hellish, who could harm me, because I was under the Lord's constant protection.

I was taught that the spirits of Mars relate to something deep inside a 7480
person, midway between the intellect and the will, and therefore to thought marked by emotion. The best of them relate to the emotion behind the thought. It is because they relate to these qualities that their face moves as one with their thoughts and that they cannot put on an act for anyone (a situation mentioned earlier, in a discussion of them at §§7360, 7361).

And because they relate to that part of the universal human, the middle 7481
area between the cerebrum and the cerebellum corresponds to them. When the spiritual operation of the cerebrum and cerebellum unites in people, their face acts in unison with their thoughts. From their face gleams the actual emotion behind the thought, and from the emotion—along with certain clues given off by the eyes—gleams the general idea of the thought.

As a result, whenever they were near me I could actually feel the front part of my head being pulled toward the back, or the cerebrum toward the cerebellum.

Once when some spirits from Mars were with me, occupying my men- 7482
tal space, spirits from our own planet came and wanted to flood the same space. The spirits of our planet then went sort of crazy, however. This was because the two are completely incompatible. Spirits from our planet focus on themselves and the world, so their thoughts are turned in on themselves. Spirits from Mars, on the other hand, focus on heaven and therefore on the Lord and their neighbor, so their thoughts are turned away from

themselves. This is the source of the conflict. At that point, though, some *angelic* spirits from Mars arrived, and their arrival cut off all contact, so the spirits from our planet withdrew.

7483 I was shown an inhabitant of that planet. The face was like the face of our planet's inhabitants, but the lower part was black, not from a beard (which the inhabitants do not have) but from a blackness there instead. This too is a result of correspondence.

The blackness reached right from the ears down both sides. The upper part of the face looked tanned, like the faces of inhabitants of our planet that are not pale.

7484 They said they eat fruit—especially a certain round fruit that grows out of the ground there—and vegetables too.

7485 They wear clothes made of fiber manufactured from the bark of certain trees. This fiber has the right consistency for being woven, and they can also glue it together with a kind of resin they have.

7486 In addition to everything else, they said they know how to make liquid fire there, which gives them light in the evening and night.

7487 I will continue with the inhabitants and spirits of Mars at the end of the next chapter [§§7620–7622].

[Continued in Volume II]

Biographical Note

EMANUEL SWEDENBORG (1688–1772) was born Emanuel Swedberg (or Svedberg) in Stockholm, Sweden, on January 29, 1688 (Julian calendar). He was the third of the nine children of Jesper Swedberg (1653–1735) and Sara Behm (1666–1696). At the age of eight he lost his mother. After the death of his only older brother ten days later, he became the oldest living son. In 1697 his father married Sara Bergia (1666–1720), who developed great affection for Emanuel and left him a significant inheritance. His father, a Lutheran clergyman, later became a celebrated and controversial bishop, whose diocese included the Swedish churches in Pennsylvania and in London, England.

After studying at the University of Uppsala (1699–1709), Emanuel journeyed to England, the Netherlands, France, and Germany (1710–1715) to study and work with leading scientists in western Europe. Upon his return he apprenticed as an engineer under the brilliant Swedish inventor Christopher Polhem (1661–1751). He gained favor with Sweden's King Charles XII (1682–1718), who gave him a salaried position as an overseer of Sweden's mining industry (1716–1747). Although Emanuel was engaged, he never married.

After the death of Charles XII, Emanuel was ennobled by Queen Ulrika Eleonora (1688–1741), and his last name was changed to Swedenborg (or Svedenborg). This change in status gave him a seat in the Swedish House of Nobles, where he remained an active participant in the Swedish government throughout his life.

A member of the Royal Swedish Academy of Sciences, he devoted himself to studies that culminated in a number of publications, most notably a comprehensive three-volume work on natural philosophy and metallurgy (1734) that brought him recognition across Europe as a scientist. After 1734 he redirected his research and publishing to a study of anatomy in search of the interface between the soul and body, making several significant discoveries in physiology.

From 1743 to 1745 he entered a transitional phase that resulted in a shift of his main focus from science to theology. Throughout the rest of his life he maintained that this shift was brought about by Jesus Christ, who appeared to him, called him to a new mission, and opened his perception to a permanent dual consciousness of this life and the life after death.

He devoted the last decades of his life to studying Scripture and publishing eighteen theological titles that draw on the Bible, reasoning, and his own spiritual experiences. These works present a Christian theology with unique perspectives on the nature of God, the spiritual world, the Bible, the human mind, and the path to salvation.

Swedenborg died in London on March 29, 1772 (Gregorian calendar), at the age of eighty-four.